SELECTED WORKS
OF ABBOT SUGER OF
SAINT-DENIS

SELECTED WORKS OF ABBOT SUGER OF SAINT-DENIS

Translated with introduction
and notes by

Richard Cusimano and
Eric Whitmore

The Catholic University of America Press
Washington, D.C.

Copyright © 2018
The Catholic University of America Press
All rights reserved

Library of Congress Cataloging-in-Publication Data
Names: Suger, Abbot of Saint Denis, 1081–1151, author. |
Cusimano, Richard, 1939– translator.
Title: Selected works of Abbot Suger of Saint-Denis /
translated with introduction and notes by Richard Cusimano
and Eric Whitmore.
Description: Washington, D.C. : Catholic University of America
Press, 2018. | Includes bibliographical references and index.
Identifiers: LCCN 2017033723 | ISBN 9780813237084
(pbk)
Subjects: LCSH: Suger, Abbot of Saint Denis, 1081–1151. |
Abbaye de Saint-Denis (Saint-Denis, France) | France—Church
history—987–1515. | France—History—Louis VI, 1108–1137. |
France—History—Louis VII, 1137–1180.
Classification: LCC BX4705.S8737 A25 2018 |
DDC 282.092—dc23
LC record available at https://lccn.loc.gov/2017033723

Contents

List of Illustrations	vii
Preface	ix
List of Abbreviations	xiii

Introduction: Suger's Contributions   1

SELECTED WORKS OF ABBOT SUGER OF SAINT-DENIS

1. The Book on the Consecration of the Church of Saint-Denis   33

2. The Book of Abbot Suger of Saint-Denis: His Accomplishments during His Administration   66

3. The Illustrious King Louis [VII], Son of Louis [VI]   127

4. The Life of Suger   184
   The Circular Letter of the Monastery of Saint-Denis Concerning the Death of Abbot Suger   207

APPENDIXES

A. Legends and Myths of Saint Denis in the Early Literary and Historical Records   217

B. The Early Royal Banners of France: The *Oriflamme* and the *Vexillum*   223

CONTENTS

   C. French Kings and Queens Buried in the   227
      Abbey of Saint-Denis

   D. Terms of Measurement and Money in Suger   243

Glossary of Medieval Words in the Selected Works   245
of Abbot Suger of Saint-Denis

Glossary of Medieval Latin Words in the Selected   259
Works of Abbot Suger of Saint-Denis

Selected Bibliography   275

Index   283

Illustrations

Suger's Additions to the Basilica of Saint-Denis	39
Chapels and Altars in Saint-Denis	47
The Church of Saint-Denis in 1144	53
Félibien's Sketch Map of Saint-Denis (1702)	59
The Possessions of the Abbey of Saint-Denis in the Twelfth Century	70
The Second Crusade	139
Normandy in the Twelfth Century	142
Royal Tombs in the Abbey Church of Saint-Denis and Its Crypt	233

Preface

Suger, the twelfth-century abbot of Saint-Denis, has not received the respect and attention that he deserves for his contributions to history. Bernard of Clairvaux and Peter the Venerable have garnered more attention, and students of medieval history know their names well. Yet Suger has earned due praise for his architectural innovations, for the Church of Saint-Denis is truly one of the most beautiful churches in Europe. It soars into the sky with its elevated walls and rows of multistoried stained glass windows. Its interior is light-filled and spacious. Churches that adhere to the Romanesque style of architecture are dark and bulky in comparison. Tourists who journey to Paris flock to the cathedral of Notre Dame, whereas most do not even know that Saint-Denis exists. Those who do visit it are amazed by its aesthetic loveliness. Its architect, Suger, would be most pleased. Like the later Thomas More, the abbot of Saint-Denis was indeed a man for all seasons.

Suger's writings provide a wealth of information about the events of his era, but their translators wish that his Latin syntax were less convoluted in structure and meaning. He abandoned the straightforward approach that most medieval chroniclers used to convey events, but he continued their habit of not providing the antecedents of pronouns, thus leaving his readers searching for clarity. Suger also used the pronouns "I" and "we" in reference to himself in the same sentence or paragraph. It is no wonder that few attempts have been made to render his writings into English.

As a writer, Suger attempted to return to the classical style of the ancient Roman authors. His main models were Cicero, Seneca, and especially Lucan, whose work had poetic qualities. Some of Suger's poems seem as if a Lucan emulator of lesser ability had composed them. The clear and straightforward style of the anonymous monk of Saint-Germain-des-Prés, who completed Suger's biography of Louis VII, stands in sharp contrast to that of the writer who began it.

The notes to our translations are divided into footnotes and endnotes. Detailed information and numerous additional sources are in the endnotes, which supply background information and put events mentioned in the text into their historical context. The endnotes come at the conclusion of each translated section rather than at the end of the volume, and they are indicated in the text by Roman numerals. The footnotes at the bottom of each page are denoted using Arabic numerals, and identify places and persons, as well as giving parenthetical comments. All biblical passages are cited from the Latin Vulgate edition.

Translating Latin personal and place names into English presents another problem. A clear English equivalent is used if possible; if none was available, the name is left in its Latin form (e.g., Odo, Herveus, and Pagan). In this translation, first names are rarely given in their French form, but place names remain in French. This approach seemed the most natural.

Two glossaries have also been placed at the end of this volume. The first contains the meanings of medieval terminology that may be unfamiliar to the reader, while the second defines the Latin words that Suger commonly used in his writings.

As the title of this work states, only select works of Suger have been chosen for translation. They are presented here in chronological order of compositon. We chose the texts that seemed likely to be of greatest interest for students at both the undergraduate and graduate levels for medieval history, art, and architecture courses. Art and architecture students will be more interested in *The Consecration*, whereas history students will be attracted to all the translations. The general history reader may be interested in them as well. Scholars of the Middle Ages are not the primary audience, as they will consult the Latin texts. Translations of Suger's letters and charters would work best as a separate volume—Françoise Gasparri separated the texts in this way when she translated Suger's works into French. Additionally, it should be noted that the Catholic University of America Press has published a translation of another of Suger's writings, *The Deeds of Louis the Fat*.

Albert Lecoy de la Marche's edition of Suger's writings was used for the translations of *The Book on the Consecration of the Church of Saint-Denis*, *The Book of Abbot Suger of Saint-Denis: His Accomplishments during His Administration*, and *The Life of Suger*. Auguste Molinier's edition was used for the translation of *The Illustrious King Louis [VII], Son of Louis [VI]*. The translators followed the numeric divisions used in these editions. Françoise Gasparri's Latin edition of Suger's writings was useful as well. Erwin Panofsky's and Sumner McKnight Crosby's works on Abbot Suger and the abbey of Saint-Denis were indispensable sources of information for the footnotes and endnotes in these translations. Panofsky's translation, however, is not complete, for only Suger's renovations to the abbey church were of interest to him. His English also seems a little outdated to the modern ear. There are also numerous primary sources now available on the Internet and in print that were not available to Panofsky.

For the sake of clarity, a large number of commas that are not in Lecoy's and Molinier's editions of Suger's writings have been added to this text in order to set off subordinate clauses, prepositional phrases, and further identifications. Periods have replaced semicolons, long paragraphs have been divided into shorter ones, and antecedents for pronouns have been introduced to help the modern reader understand the text.

Several people assisted in the production of this translation of Suger's writings. Thetis Cusimano helped with proofreading, while Joel Whitmore contributed the maps, illustrations, and technical support for all formatting problems. Elizabeth Bolgiano assisted with the index. Sue Sullivan, Margaret Coady, and Angie Champagne provided much-needed moral encouragement during the years required for these translations.

Abbreviations

ANS	*Anglo-Norman Studies*
EMS	English Monarchs Series
MGH	Monumenta Germaniae Historica
NMT	Nelson's Medieval Texts
OMT	Oxford Medieval Texts
PL	Patrologia Latina (ed. Migne)
RHF	Recueil des Historiens des Gaules et de la France (ed. Bouquet and Delisle)
RS	Rolls Series
SRM	Scriptores rerum merovingicarum

Introduction

Suger's Contributions

Suger is famous today mainly as the skilled renovator and architect of his spectacular abbey church, still standing, not far from a Metro stop, in Paris. The church itself, which King Dagobert founded in the seventh century, had become the burial site of Frankish and French kings, queens, and magnates, beginning with Dagobert himself in 639 and ending with the burial of the last Bourbon king, Louis XVIII, in 1824. Martyred in the third century in Paris, Saint Denis had become a special patron saint of France soon after his death. As they went into battle, the later Capetian kings shouted the war cry, *Montjoie! Saint Denis!* The abbey had indeed risen to be the most prestigious in medieval France.

Given by his father as a child to the abbey of Saint-Denis, Suger ascended from the status of an oblate to become an intimate friend of and counselor to Kings Louis VI and Louis VII, as well as acting as regent for Louis VII when the king left France on the Second Crusade. At the young age of twenty-three, Suger could be found at the royal court during the reign of King Philip I in 1104, when he overheard the king advising Suger's friend, the future Louis VI, to safeguard the castle of Montlhéry, strategically located on the main road between Paris and Orléans. Except for brief periods, Suger's presence at the royal councils of the next two kings was almost universal.

Never shy, Suger gives his readers a large amount of biographical material in his writings. He seems almost obsessed that his works and deeds not be forgotten. He acquired numerous properties and estates for his abbey, and also improved the ones it already possessed. In this way, he doubled and tripled the abbey's annual revenues from both its old and its new resources. He built new buildings, barns, walls for villages, and increased the return of grain from all the abbey's lands. Suger's most noteworthy accomplishment, however, was at the abbey of Saint-Denis itself. He enlarged, decorated, improved, and redesigned the church there. Without exaggeration, it is safe to say that Suger became the foremost church architect of twelfth-century France. He set the tone for the building of churches for the rest of the Middle Ages. His innovations and changes at Saint-Denis led to the development of the medieval Gothic style found in so many medieval European churches.[1]

Suger's other contributions to the growth and strengthening of medieval France, however, go far beyond his church. He was the foremost diplomat of his period. The kings of France whom he served sent him on missions throughout Europe. He represented them at imperial and princely courts, and traveled into Italy numerous times to attend papal audiences on their behalf. He was present at the more important church councils held during his time. Kings, princes, popes, bishops, and his fellow abbots all held him in high esteem. All consulted him on matters of state.

Contrary to church law, warrior bishops and abbots could be found in the eleventh and earlier centuries, especially in Germany, but the tradition of the clergy actually fighting in battles had become more rare in Suger's time. Although the abbot of Saint-Denis did not take up sword or mace in hand, he should not be overlooked as a military tactician and engineer. He reinforced the defenses of his abbey's estates, especially Toury, and he was present with King Louis VI in the royal expeditions against the robber baron, Hugh III of Le Puiset.[2] Suger accompanied the soldiers that his abbey sent to support the king's forces when needed, such as the planned imperial

---

1. For a full discussion of this topic, see Lindy Grant, *Abbot Suger of St-Denis: Church and State in Early Twelfth-Century France* (London: Longman, 1998), 28–31.
2. Suger, *The Deeds of Louis the Fat*, trans. Richard Cusimano and John Moorhead (Washington, D.C.: The Catholic University of America Press, 1992), 87–89.

invasion into France that failed to occur in 1124.[3] In this instance, Suger assisted in drawing up the plans of battle. He was also present when Louis VII brought up his forces to put down the revolt against him by the burghers of Poitiers in 1138, where he counseled the king not to take severe reprisals against them.[4] Suger traveled to the Atlantic coast with Louis to retake the castle of Talmont-by-the-Sea from the rebellious Count William VIII of Lezay.[5] There Suger advised the king in vain against sending an advance party of soldiers into the castle without first securing its tower. Suger's precise knowledge of the many military excursions taken by both Kings Louis VI and VII also indicates his presence on them.

Suger's administrative skills were also second to none. His predecessor, Abbot Adam, put him in charge of Saint-Denis's estate at Berneval in 1107, when he was about twenty-six years old. He moved from there to become the provost of Toury in 1109. After Suger became abbot of Saint-Denis in 1122, he immediately began improving the abbey's numerous estates and acquiring others as well. He used the additional revenues to improve the life of the monks there, renovate the abbey church, and increase its artistic and liturgical treasures. His administrative skills were so excellent that he was unanimously selected to guide the kingdom when King Louis VII departed on the Second Crusade.[6]

Suger's Early Years

In medieval times, the day and year that a person died was known with greater certainty than the date of his birth. For a pious person like Abbot Suger of Saint-Denis, the day of his death would be when he entered heaven to live forever in the presence of God. For this reason, the monk William of Saint-Denis, who wrote the biography of Suger translated in this volume, related: "Then this beloved father and eminent pastor died while reciting the Lord's Prayer and the Apostle's Creed on the Ides of January, in the seventieth year of

3. Ibid., 127.
4. See below, *The Life of Louis VII*, 133–34.
5. Ibid., 134–37.
6. For Suger's regency, see below, *Life of Suger*, Bk. III, 12–13, 197–202.

his life, nearly sixty years after receiving the monastic habit, and in the twenty-ninth year of his abbacy."[7] William emphasized the abbot's date of death and other significant dates in his religious life; he omitted the dates of other important events in his life, verified from numerous other primary sources. The quotation above informed William's readers that Abbot Suger was born in roughly 1081 and died on January 13, 1151.

Suger and his biographer, William, often referred to the abbot's small physical stature and humble birth. He indeed had a small body but by no means a humble origin. Recent research indicates that he was born into a family of minor nobility who held property in the area of Chenneviéres-les-Louvres, a village located about eleven miles northeast of Saint-Denis.[8] Suger's father was named Helinand, but his mother has remained unknown. The abbot had two brothers named Ralph and Peter, and a cousin also named Suger who became an oblate at Saint-Denis in 1111. In addition, Abbot Suger had several other cousins who held important positions in both church and state.

Suger's father offered him as an oblate at the great altar in the abbey church of Saint-Denis in 1091, when he was ten years old. Later in life Suger was so proud of this event, as he told in his writings, that he enriched the same great altar, as well as added many other treasures to the church itself. The young Suger spent most of his next ten years as a schoolboy at the nearby priory of Saint-Denis-de-L'Estrée, where he met a fellow student, the future King Louis VI. Thus began a friendship that helped raise Suger to high secular and clerical offices.[9] Suger seems also to have studied a few years in the school of the abbey of Saint-Benoît-sur-Loire, which he referred to in a letter addressed to Pope Eugenius III.[10]

---

7. See below, *Circular Letter*, 210.

8. See John F. Benton, "Introduction: Suger's Life and Personality," in *Abbot Suger and Saint-Denis: A Symposium*, ed. Paula Lieber Gerson (New York: Metropolitan Museum of Art, 1986), 3–15, for recent information on Suger's birth, ancestry, and life.

9. Françoise Gasparri, ed. *Suger: Oeuvres* (Paris: Les Belle Lettres, 2008), 1:viii.

10. See Suger to Pope Eugenius III in the former's *Oeuvres Complétes de Suger*, ed. A. Lecoy de la Marche (Paris: Jules Renouard, 1868), no. 14 (263–64).

Administrator to Abbots, Popes, and King Louis VI

By the early 1100s, the young Suger had already gained the trust of Abbot Adam of Saint-Denis (r. 1099–1122), whose secretary he became in 1106. In that same year Suger attended the Council of Poitiers, where Prince Bohemond of Antioch and a papal legate pleaded for a crusade to the Holy Sepulcher.[11] In 1107 Pope Paschal II came to France to seek support against Emperor Henry V during the Investiture Controversy.[12] While in France, Paschal dedicated the monastic Church of La-Charité-sur-Loire with Suger in attendance.[13] Suger met the pope there to plead his abbey's case against Bishop Galo of Paris, who was harassing the Church of Saint-Denis with many complaints.[14]

In 1107 Suger received his first administrative position as provost of the village of Berneval, a possession of Saint-Denis located on the Norman coast near Dieppe.[15] While there he had to plead this estate's case at the court of the English King Henry I against the royal tax collectors. He made many further appearances at this monarch's court during his lengthy reign and gained the king's friendship. At Berneval, Suger began his long career as an effective administrator, increasing the abbey's possessions and revenues there.

Suger left Berneval in 1109 and went to Toury, a special and important village of Saint-Denis, where he again served as provost.[16] This estate had long suffered the attacks and harassments of the lords of the nearby castle of Le Puiset that had been built in the eleventh century by Queen Constance, the wife of King Robert II, to protect Toury.[17] Ironically, however, the castle's lords, especially Hugh III, often used it for the opposite purpose of pillaging and plundering this region of Beauce. To fend off Hugh's depredation,

---

11. Suger, *The Deeds*, 45.
12. Grant, *Abbot Suger*, 88.
13. Suger, *The Deeds*, 47. See also Recueil des Historiens des Gaules et de la France, ed. M. Bouquet and L. Delisle (Paris, 1869–1904), 14:120–21 [hereafter "RHF"].
14. Suger, *The Deeds*, 47.
15. See below, *The Administration*, XXIII, 93–94.
16. Ibid., XII, 81–84, and Suger, *The Deeds*, 87.
17. Suger, *The Deeds*, 84–85.

Suger fortified, strengthened, and garrisoned Toury with a large number of troops.[18] In March 1111, Suger was included among an impressive number of prelates who met at Melun to seek further help from King Louis VI against Hugh. The king then sent forces that successfully destroyed the castle of Le Puiset.[19] Suger's first visit to Rome occurred in March 1112, when he accompanied Abbot Adam to the Lateran Synod, where Pope Paschal II repudiated the concessions concerning investiture that he had made to Emperor Henry V at Châlons-sur-Marne.

Suger apparently left his post at Toury and returned to Saint-Denis in 1113, but the actual date of his return is not known with certainty.[20] He disappeared from the records until 1118, when he went to meet Pope Gelasius II at Maguelonne, an island in the Mediterranean Sea about seven miles south of Montpellier, to arrange a meeting between the king and the pope.[21] However, the pope died at Cluny on January 29, 1119, before they could meet. The representatives of the Roman church who attended Gelasius's funeral at Cluny then elected Archbishop Guy of Vienne as Pope Calixtus II. The pope visited Paris in October of that year and also came to Saint-Denis, but Suger nowhere discusses this visit.[22]

The New Abbot of Saint-Denis

Suger traveled to Italy again on a mission for King Louis VI and met Pope Calixtus II at Bitonto in Apulia in January 1122.[23] On his return journey into France, Suger learned that Abbot Adam had died and that the monks of Saint-Denis had elected him to replace Adam.

---

18. Ibid., 95–103.
19. Ibid., 86–90. This castle was destroyed and rebuilt on several occasions. The first two instances were in 1111 and 1112. The third destruction occurred in 1118, when its walls were torn down.
20. Grant, *Abbot Suger*, 96.
21. Suger, *The Deeds*, 119–20.
22. *Louis VI le Gros: Annales de sa vie et de son règne (1081–1137)*, ed. Achille Luchaire (Geneva: Mégaritis Reprints, 1979), no. 265 (126).
23. Suger, *The Deeds*, 119–23.

After returning to his abbey, he was ordained a priest on March 11 and consecrated as abbot on March 12.[24] In 1123 he again returned to Rome, remaining there for six months. During that time he attended the Lateran Council in March, which was convened to bring the quarrel over lay investiture to a peaceful conclusion after the Concordat of Wörms.[25]

In 1124 King Louis VI rushed to Reims to defend the kingdom against the planned invasion of France by Roman Emperor Henry V, who had been invited to invade by his father-in-law, King Henry I of England.[26] Louis's relationship with the king of England had seriously deteriorated during 1124 into open conflict over the Vexin. Suger wrote that Emperor Henry intended to attack Reims because Pope Calixtus II had anathematized the emperor in that city in 1119.[27] In his account the abbot appears jubilant over his own role in gathering the French forces and developing the battle plan. The emperor, however, decided to withdraw on August 14, and Suger proudly proclaimed the retreat as a victory although no battle had taken place. Louis returned to Saint-Denis to give thanks to its patron saints for protecting the kingdom.

Suger attended the Diet of Mainz in September 1125, and witnessed the election of Lothar III of Supplinburg (1075–1137) as king of Germany.[28] Suger also accompanied King Louis on his second expedition into Auvergne in 1126 to protect its bishop, Aimery of Clermont (r. 1111–50), from harassment by Count William VI (1096–1136).[29] The abbot took great delight in the king's victory there, although Duke William X of Aquitaine came to the count's rescue by pledging to the king that he would take charge of the count, who was his vassal, and settle matters with the king later at Orléans.

Stephen of Senlis (d. 1141) was consecrated bishop of Paris in

---

24. Ibid., 122–23.
25. Ibid., 125–26, and Grant, *Abbot Suger*, 110. This was the first of four Lateran Councils held between 1123 and 1215.
26. Emperor Henry V had married King Henry I's daughter, Matilda, in 1114.
27. Suger, *The Deeds*, 127–32.
28. See below, *Life of Louis VII*, II, 128–29. See also Michel Bur, *Suger: Abbé de Saint-Denis, Régent de France* (Paris: Perrin, 1991), 122–23.
29. Suger, *The Deeds*, 135–37.

1123. A few years later, a dispute arose between him and his cathedral chapter whose principal archdeacon was Stephen of Garlande (ca. 1070–1148). A commission, headed by Suger and Abbot Gilduin of Saint-Victor in Paris (r. 1113–55), was appointed in 1126 to arbitrate the dispute. As a result, the bishop received control over the cathedral school, but the archdeacons and canons attached to the cathedral maintained control over their properties.[30]

At this time Suger and Stephen of Garlande were both intimate counselors of King Louis VI. They were also prominent members of the king's court, where Stephen's influence waxed and waned as he lost his offices of chancellor and seneschal in 1127, but regained the chancellorship in 1132. Stephen never recovered the office of seneschal. Suger's own power at court wavered at times, but remained intact throughout the reigns of Kings Louis VI and VII.

A schism arose in the Roman church in 1130 when rival cardinals elected two popes: Gregorio Papareschi, who took the name Innocent II, and Peter Leo, who chose to be called Anacletus II. The party of Anacletus won control of Rome, so Innocent sought refuge in France. King Louis VI convened a council of important clergymen at Étampes to decide which pope to support, and the council selected Innocent as the legally elected pontiff.[31] The king approved the choice and sent Suger to bring Innocent the news and welcome him at Cluny, where he had arrived in late October. The pope spent Easter 1131 (March 22) at Saint-Denis.

Recovered Importance for the Abbey Saint-Denis

A terrible misfortune befell the kingdom on October 13, 1131, when the king-designate, Prince Philip, died while racing his horse through the streets of Paris. The horse stumbled over a pig that had jumped in

---

30. See Grant, *Abbot Suger*, 126.
31. Suger, *The Deeds*, 145–51; *A Translation of the Chronicle of Morigny, France, c. 1100–1150*, trans. Richard Cusimano (Lewiston, N.Y.: Edwin Mellen Press, 2003), 96; and Orderic Vitalis, *The Ecclesiastical History of Orderic Vitalis*, ed. and trans. Marjorie Chibnall (Oxford: Oxford University Press, 2002), 6:418–20.

front of it and threw its rider headlong, causing injuries from which the young prince soon died.³² He was buried "in accordance with royal custom," as Suger tells us, in the tomb of the kings at Saint-Denis. The abbot here reasserted the right of his church to be the official burial place of French kings, a custom that had begun with Dagobert in 639.³³ To the great dismay of Suger, King Louis VI's father, Philip I, had chosen the abbey of Saint-Benoît-sur-Loire for his burial in 1108. Upon the death of Prince Philip, the abbot quickly counseled the king to journey to Reims to have his second son, Louis, anointed as king-designate by Pope Innocent II, who had opened a council there on October 18.³⁴ The coronation ceremony took place on October 25. Suger did not write that he was present at Reims, and his somewhat brief description of these events suggests that he was not there.

Duke William X of Aquitaine died on Good Friday, April 9, 1137, while on a pilgrimage to the tomb of Saint James at Compostela in northern Spain.³⁵ Before the duke died, however, he offered his daughter Eleanor in marriage to Prince Louis, a proposal that King Louis happily accepted. The king put together a large expedition of distinguished persons, which included Suger, to accompany his son to Bordeaux for the marriage ceremony. While on the return journey, the abbot learned that King Louis had died in Paris on August 1 from an illness that had plagued him for almost two years.³⁶ King Louis VI was quickly buried in the abbey Church of Saint-Denis with the prior, Herveus, making the funeral arrangements during Suger's absence.

At some point in 1135–37, Suger began his renovation of the ab-

---

32. Suger, *The Deeds*, 149–51; *Morigny* (ed. Cusimano), 104–6; and *Orderic Vitalis* (ed. Chibnall), 6:420–22.

33. Suger inserts a clause in an 1129 charter reiterating Saint-Denis's role as the burial site for French kings. See *Receuil des Actes de Louis VI, roi de France (1108–1137)*, ed. J. Dufour (Paris: Academie des Inscriptions et Belles-Lettres, 1992–94), II, no. 281 (100–106), and Suger, *The Deeds*, 150.

34. Luchaire, *Louis VI*, no. 476 (220), no. 478 (221–22).

35. *Orderic Vitalis* (ed. Chibnall), 6:480–82; Suger, *The Deeds*, 156–59; and *Morigny* (ed. Cusimano), 124–28.

36. For the length of the illness and date of the death of King Louis VI, see Luchaire, *Louis VI*, no. 559 (254) and no. 595 (270). See also *Orderic Vitalis* (ed. Chibnall), 6:490n4, and Suger, *The Deeds*, 158.

bey church. He started with the western façade and narthex, and consecrated this part of the church on June 9, 1140.[37] He began his renovations of the eastern end and choir on July 13, 1140, and consecrated them on June 14, 1144. He heightened the walls and allowed a flood of light to enter the church through its brilliant stained glass windows. He added rich tapestries, an abundance of gold, and jewel-encrusted treasures to the building. He gloried in all these accomplishments in his writings translated in this work.

Suger and King Louis VII

It is difficult to determine the nature of the relationship between Suger and the young king, Louis VII. The abbot was a generation older and had been an intimate friend and counselor of his father. However, Suger and Louis VII never became alienated, and during the early years of his kingship, the young king continued to take the advice of the older man.

A prominent example occurred in 1138, when Poitiers revolted against the authority of the king by forming a commune.[38] At first Louis ordered Theobald, count of Blois and Champagne, to suppress the rebellion; but when he delayed, the king sent Suger, unsuccessfully, to stir Theobald into action. So Louis himself gathered his forces and marched into Poitiers, where he forced the Poitevins into a bloodless surrender. He dissolved the commune, extracted an oath of loyalty from the citizens, and seized some of their children, planning to disperse them throughout the realm as hostages to ensure the future loyalty of their parents. The citizens gathered before the palace and tearfully pleaded with Louis to rescind his order. Showing his inexperience, the king seemed unable to decide on a course of action. So he consulted Suger as to what he should do. The abbot advised the king to show clemency, rescind his order, and thus win the allegiance of the entire Aquitaine, which is what happened.

---

37. S. Crosby, *The Royal Abbey of Saint-Denis: From Its Beginnings to the Death of Suger, 475–1151*, ed. Pamela Z. Blum (New Haven, Conn.: Yale University Press, 1987), 105 and 117.

38. For an account of this rebellion, see below, *Life of Louis VII*, VI, 132–34.

Having suppressed the rebellion in Poitou, the king then rushed to the Atlantic coast to put down the revolt of Count William VIII of Lezay, who had unlawfully seized the castle of Talmont-by-the-Sea.[39] Abbot Suger accompanied the king, along with Bishop Jocelin of Soissons, whose subsequent advice went contrary to that of Suger. Count William had invited the king's advance party to enter the castle walls to make their preparations for the king's arrival, and Jocelin advised them to do so against the counsel of Suger, who warned of the danger of this action without first securing the castle's tower. The king's advance party did go forward, and was soon taken captive by the treacherous count, forcing the king to take prompt military action to rescue his men. He seized the castle and burned everything inside it up to the precinct of the tower. Suger's incomplete account of the *Life of Louis VII* ends abruptly in describing these events.

The archbishop of Bourges, Alberic of Reims (r. 1136–41), died in May 1141, and the canons of the cathedral chapter there elected Peter of La Châtre as his successor. Suger supported Peter, contrary to the wishes of King Louis, who wanted his own chancellor, Cadurc, to succeed the archbishop.[40] Facing royal opposition, Peter fled to the protection of Count Theobald in Champagne, whose relationship with the king was stormy at best. Ultimately the king invaded Champagne where he burned the city of Vitry in 1143, including a church there with about 1,300 people who had taken refuge inside. During the peace negotiated between the king and the count following this invasion and massacre, Suger and Bishop Jocelin of Soissons represented the royal interests. As a result, the king's forces withdrew from Champagne in return for concessions from Count Theobald. A treaty between the king and the count was not finalized until two years later, when it was signed at Saint-Denis on October 9, 1144.[41]

---

39. For a full account of this rebellion, see below, *Life of Louis VII*, VII, 134–37.
40. La Châtre, Indre, Centre-Val de Loire is located about 197 miles south of Saint-Denis. See also Grant, *Abbot Suger*, 149–52.
41. Ibid., 152.

Co-Regent during the Second Crusade

On December 25, 1145, at Bourges, guilt over the burning of Vitry led Louis VII to pledge that he would go on a crusade to bring aid to the Christians in the Holy Land.[42] The king convened an assembly on Easter (March 31, 1146) at Vézelay, where both he and Abbot Bernard of Clairvaux made speeches that stirred the members of the assembly to take up their crosses and journey to the East with him.[43] Suger was apparently not present at Vézelay. His primary role on this crusade was to raise money to support the expedition. The king then convened a council that gathered on February 16, 1147, at Étampes to provide for the welfare of the kingdom during his absence.[44] At the recommendation of Bernard of Clairvaux, the council selected Abbot Suger of Saint-Denis as regent of the king to represent the clergy and Count William II of Nevers (1098–1148) to represent the nobility. However, Count William declined the appointment in order to become a monk at Chartreuse. So the council chose Count Ralph I of Vermandois (r. 1117–52), the first cousin of the king's father, to replace Count William.[45]

King Louis, along with Pope Eugenius III (r. 1145–53), who had sought refuge in France at this time, celebrated Easter Sunday, April 20, 1147, at Saint-Denis with Suger and the monks.[46] The king and the pope also attended the Lendit Fair of Saint-Denis on June 11 of that year, accompanied by the king's wife, Eleanor of Aquitaine, and his mother Adelaide of Maurienne. There in the abbey church the king venerated the relics of the Holy Martyrs, and before the high altar received from Suger the *vexillum* or *oriflamme*, the standard of the county of Vexin that the kings of France were to carry into battle, a custom having originated with Suger and King Louis VI in 1124.[47]

---

42. Odo of Deuil, *De profectione Ludovici VII in orientem*, ed. and trans. Virginia Gingerick Berry (New York: W. W. Norton and Company, 1948), 8.
43. *Morigny* (ed. Cusimano), 156–58, and Odo, *De profectione*, 8.
44. For the details of the Council of Étampes, see Odo, *De profectione*, 12–14.
45. *Morigny* (ed. Cusimano), 158–60, and Odo, *De profectione*, 20.
46. Odo, *De profectione*, 14–18; Suger, *The Deeds*, 128; and Grant, *Abbot Suger*, 157–59.
47. For the *vexillum* or *oriflamme*, see below, appendix B, 223–26.

This ceremony marked the official beginning of the Second Crusade.

Suger spent his co-regency primarily concerned with garnering support from his fellow French prelates for his office. He also worked to finance the needs of the crusading king, put down rebellions and conflicts at home, and maintained a working relationship with his co-regent, Count Ralph of Vermandois, all of which he did with varying degrees of success. Suger wrote a letter to the king in early 1149, urging him to return to France as soon as possible because many of the magnates who had journeyed to the East with him had already returned and were causing numerous troubles,[48] including a disturbance in the kingdom from Louis's own brother, Count Robert I of Dreux (ca. 1123–88). In that letter Suger summarized the successes of his regency when he informed the absent king that he has kept the king's land and vassals at good peace, administered justice, maintained revenues, gathered foodstuffs in anticipation of the king's return, and preserved the royal residences and palaces intact. King Louis and his wife, Eleanor, returned to France in November 1149, which allowed the aged Suger to retire to his abbey where he died shortly thereafter on January 13, 1151, surrounded by his friends and intimates. Thus passed from this world one of the greatest churchmen of twelfth-century France.

Recognition of Suger's Contributions by His Contemporaries

Attending his burial on January 15, 1151, were six bishops, many abbots, and other monks, along with King Louis VII, who wept bitterly during the funeral service.[49] The Master of the Temple in Jerusalem, Evrard of Barres, was also present with a large contingent of his knights. The body of Suger was laid to rest in the church that he had spent so much of his abbey's revenues to enlarge and beautify. William of Saint-Denis, Suger's biographer, unfortunately

---

48. Suger to King Louis, in *Oeuvres* (ed. Lecoy), no. 11 (258–60), and Grant, *Abbot Suger*, 177–78.
49. For Suger's funeral rites, see below, *Circular Letter*, 207–16.

did not give the exact site of his burial. Suger seems to have been originally buried in the floor of the church at the entrance leading from the cloister into the south transept. Subsequently, a tomb for his remains was constructed in 1259 near this same location. A later source, written in 1795, confirmed that his tomb had been in this same position.[50] On October 22, 1793, during the French Revolution, Suger's tomb was destroyed and his remains thrown into a common pit in the cemetery on the north side of the church.[51]

The writings of Suger translated in this volume give testament to his numerous skills. The translators agree with his biographer, William of Saint-Denis, when he said:

Good Jesus, how much energy and spirit he had! When he approached, tyrants fled, *the sons of darkness hid themselves, and the sons of light and the day rushed to him.*[52] When the kingdom fell into disorder; and, as often happens, wars break out, he was the foremost proponent of harmony and the most vigorous restorer of peace. He was Caesar in spirit, Cicero in speech, a suppressor of rebellions, and a vanquisher of seditions.[53]

Suger's Writings

Historical Writing at Saint-Denis

In the early twelfth century, a great tradition of chronicle writing on the history of France and its kings began at the abbey of Saint-Denis.[54] Although Suger did not initiate the practice, he is perhaps the most influential and famous of all those who wrote there. At the beginning of the century, an anonymous monk penned a universal chronicle, *Gesta Gentis Francorum*, which began with the birth of Christ and ended with the death of King Philip I in 1108. The information contained in it is not reliable. Several other monks

---

50. Anonymous, *A History and Description of the Royale Abbaye of Saint Denis With an Account of the Tombs of the Kings and Queens of France and Other Distinguished Persons Interred There* (Ann Arbor: University of Michigan Library, 2009), 83.
51. See below, appendix C, 241niv.
52. Similar to the ideas expressed in 1 Thes 5:5.
53. For this quotation, see below, *Life of Suger*, Bk. II, 193.
54. See Gabrielle M. Spiegel, *The Chronicle Tradition of Saint-Denis: A Survey* (Brookline, Mass.: Classical Folia Editions, 1978).

of Saint-Denis continued to chronicle events in France and set the pattern that subsequent histories followed. Suger continued the tradition with his accounts of the deeds of Kings Louis VI and VII. The best known of the subsequent chroniclers are Odo of Deuil, Rigord, and William the Breton. However, Suger did not limit himself to biographical writing. He also left for posterity his book on the consecration of the church and an account of his administration of the abbey and its possessions.

The Book on the Consecration of the Church of Saint-Denis

Abbot Suger wrote this short book on the reconstruction and consecration of the abbey church shortly after the formal dedication of the completed choir on June 11, 1144. He appears to have finished the book quickly, for he referred to *The Consecration* in his next writing, *The Administration*, which he began writing in 1145.[55] He apparently wrote *The Consecration* to circulate among his fellow churchmen, especially the archbishops and bishops who participated in the consecration ceremony of the church and its numerous altars.

Suger began *The Consecration* with an elaborate prologue that contained themes taken from the work of Pseudo-Dionysus. He emphasized the incompatibility of divine and human natures, and explained the anagogical method that allows humans to get a glimpse of the divine by contemplating the beauty of the physical world. These were not new ideas but ones that Suger used in his life's work, explaining his reason for beautifying the Church of Saint-Denis and for collecting the precious works of craftsmanship that he added there.

Suger then digressed to the founding of the church by King Dagobert in the seventh century before giving his reason for enlarging the church. It was desperately overcrowded when people flocked to it on the major feast days. Never one to shy away from the recitation of a miracle, Suger reported several that took place during the reconstruction, but the most memorable one occurred during a thunderstorm, when the arm of the aged Saint Simeon prevented the roof from col-

---

55. See below, *The Administration*, XXVIII, 98.

lapsing and ruining the work that had already been accomplished.⁵⁶

Suger then proceeded to the consecration of the church, naming the prestigious archbishops and bishops whom he had invited to participate in the ceremonies. He followed with a long description of the relocation of the relics of the Holy Martyrs, Saint Denis and his companions, Saints Rusticus and Eleutherius. After the consecration itself, which King Louis VII, his wife Queen Eleanor of Aquitaine, his mother the dowager Queen Adelaide of Maurienne, and many magnates of the kingdom attended, Suger finally concluded his small book with all the dignitaries revering the newly relocated shrine of the Holy Martyrs.

The earliest extant manuscript of this work comes from around 1200, and was probably written at Saint-Denis; a later copy was produced at the abbey of Saint-Victor in Paris.⁵⁷ François Duchesne produced the first published edition of *The Consecration* in 1641 from the Vatican Regina manuscript that had previously been in the collection of Claude Alexandre Petau.⁵⁸ In writing *The Consecration*, Suger was apparently inspired by the work of Leo of Ostia, who wrote a tract on the rebuilding and papal consecration of the great abbey of Monte Cassino that Suger had visited in 1123.⁵⁹ Both Suger and Abbot Desiderius of Monte Cassino wished to bring marble columns from Rome to install in their churches, and both gathered artists

---

56. See below, *The Consecration*, V, 50–51.

57. They can be found in the Vatican Regina (ms. 571, f. 119r–129v) and the Paris Arsenal (ms. 1030, f. 81r–82v and 137r–143v), respectively. Grant, *Abbot Suger*, 33 and n3.

58. *Oeuvres* (ed. Gasparri), 1:lix. The final two pages of Suger's text were missing, but Jean Mabillon restored them in his *Vetera Analecta* (Paris, 1675–85), using the Saint-Victor manuscript. Michel-Jean-Joseph Brial published a partial edition of *The Consecration* in his *Rerum Gallicarum Scriptores*, vol. XIV, 312–18, at Paris in 1806. Jacques-Paul Migne produced another edition in his Patrologia Latina (vol. 186, col. 1239–54) at Paris in 1854 [hereafter "PL"]. Albert Lecoy de la Marche published his edition of *The Consecration* in his *Oeuvres Complètes de Suger* at Paris in 1867. A few decades later, Erwin Panofsky completed his edition and English translation of *The Consecration* in his *Abbot Suger: On the Abbey Church of Saint-Denis and Its Art Treasures* (Princeton, N.J.: Princeton University Press, 1946); and finally Françoise Gasparri published her edition and French translation of *The Consecration* in her *Suger: Oeuvres*, 1:3–53, at Paris in 2008.

59. Grant, *Abbot Suger*, 33.

from all parts of Europe to beautify their church renovations. This trip to Italy was one of the many that he made on behalf of his abbey to settle church affairs and do the business of the kingdom.

The Book of Abbot Suger of Saint-Denis: His Accomplishments during His Administration

Suger himself told the reader in the opening chapter that he began writing *The Administration* in 1145 at the request of his fellow monks to prevent the memory of his accomplishment from being lost to posterity.[60] He wished to leave behind a record of the new properties acquired, the recovery of lost ones, and the improvement of those the abbey already possessed in order to forestall their loss to the abbey through fraud or the wicked behavior of his successors as abbot. As Suger continued his prologue, it becomes obvious that he wanted to increase the revenues of his abbey in order to reconstruct, enlarge, and add precious objects to the abbey church.

The author resumed his narration with a somewhat long, but by no means complete, list of the properties that he acquired or improved. Suger did not follow their chronological order of purchase or repair, but the region where they were located. He started with the fortified burg of Saint-Denis and the area around it, and then discussed the Lendit Fair on the road to Paris and the Île-de-France itself, a district centered on the capital city. The forest of Yvelines received great attention in this part of the narration. Suger next proceeded to Beauce, the rich agricultural region between Paris and Orléans where Saint-Denis possessed some of its most productive properties. He continued to the southwest and discussed the abbey's possessions in Gâtinais, where Orléans was the principal city. He then went east to Essonnes and its main city of Corbeil on the Seine River just south of the Val-de-Marne. He finished his list of properties with those located in Upper Normandy to the northwest of Paris. In a sense, Suger had literally come a full geographical circle in his narration.

The second part of *The Administration* returned to the reconstruc-

---

60. See below, *The Administration*, 66.

tion and consecration of the abbey church and its oratories. Suger considered his alterations of the church as the high point of his life's work, and so he reiterated the themes of his prior book, *The Consecration*. He started with the repairs to the church walls, which he had painted in blue and other rich colors, and moved next to the enlargement of the church, repeating its overcrowded condition on major feast days as his reason for doing so. He next inserted a brief interlude describing the dedication of several oratories by select bishops, including their subsequent procession out of and back into the church.

Suger continued *The Administration* with the rebuilding of the west entrance and towers, adding new entrances and gilded bronze doors with appropriate inscriptions on them. One of the inscriptions gave 1140 as the year of the consecration. The enlargement of the upper part of the church on its eastern end followed. Suger raised the area behind the main altar where he built a new altar and tabernacle to house the relocated relics of the Holy Martyrs. He gilded this altar's frontal, added numerous jewels to it, and then moved the relics there. He then imported Lotharingian goldsmiths to fashion the golden crucifix, one of the most famous ornaments Suger placed in the church. The goldsmiths gilded and adorned this crucifix with precious gems and pearls purchased by Suger for its construction.

Since the main altar and the compartment containing its prestigious relics had fallen into disrepair, Suger refurbished it with golden panels all the way around, fixed expensive gems to them, and turned his attention to the relics' compartment. He had an overwhelming desire to view the sacred relics and attest to their authenticity. Therefore, Suger invited a goodly number of archbishops and bishops to the viewing ceremony to prevent any charge of fraud as to the relics' authentication. All turned out as he hoped after everyone saw the inscriptions contained with the relics. Suger continued to refurbish everything in the church that had become dilapidated, and he never stopped adding precious ornaments to increase the prestige of his abbey and its church.

Suger left a record of these extraordinary accomplishments in *The Administration*, which he completed in 1148 or shortly thereafter, as he mentioned the death of Evrard III of Breteuil who expired during that same year while on the Second Crusade.[61] However, Suger seems never to have revised the text, as he omitted some of his property acquisitions recorded in his charters. In addition, Suger's list of the bishops in *The Administration* as taking part in the consecration of the church differs from those bishops designated in *The Consecration* as participating in that same event.

The Administration does not initiate a genre of writing unique for its time period, but it belongs to a type that records the deeds of significant churchmen.[62] Other examples in this genre are the *Liber Pontificalis*, the *Chronica Casinensis* that gives an account of the accomplishment of Abbot Desiderius, and a fragmentary narrative of the deeds of Henry of Blois, the bishop of Winchester and abbot of Glastonbury.[63] Both Suger and Henry were unusual in that they wrote about their accomplishments themselves. Both asked their readers to remember them in their prayers. They wished to protect their abbeys' possessions from future loss and wrote for the memory of future generations. Only one manuscript of *The Administration* has survived. It dates from sometime between 1160 and 1180, and can be found in the Bibliothèque Nationale (lat. 13835) in Paris.[64] Copyists from the fifteenth and sixteenth centuries entitled it *Gesta Sugerii abbatis* (*The Deeds of Abbot Suger*), a title much more suited to the content of the text. It is unfortunate that the title did not survive in later editions.[65]

---

61. *The Administration*, 84. See also Grant, *Abbot Suger*, 34.

62. The information in this paragraph comes from Grant, *Abbot Suger*, 35.

63. Desiderius was abbot of Monte Cassino in 1058–86; he was elected pope as Victor III in 1086 and ruled the church until his death in 1087. Henry of Blois was abbot of Glastonbury from 1126 and bishop of Winchester from 1129 until his death in 1171. He was a grandson of William the Conqueror and brother of King Stephen of England (r. 1135–54).

64. The information in this paragraph comes from *Oeuvres* (ed. Gasparri), 1:lx–lxii.

65. Dom Jacques Doublet was the first to analyze the text in his *Histoire de l'Abbaye Royale de S. Denys en France* (Paris: 1625). Using the surviving manuscript, André Duchesne produced the first published edition of *The Administration* in 1641 (reprinted in 1648) under a new title, *Sugerii abbatis liber de rebus in administratione sua gestis*. In 1706 Michel Félibien reproduced Duchesne's edition with an analysis of Suger's text under the title *Histoire de l'abbaye royale de Saint-Denys en France*. Members of the Congregation of Saint-Maur continued the work of Dom Martin Bouquet, a renowned

The Illustrious King Louis [VII], Son of Louis [VI]

At the beginning of the Second Crusade in 1147–48, Suger was still writing an account of the deeds of Louis VII similar to the one he had already written on the king's father, Louis VI.[66] However, illness and death brought an end to his life and work in 1151. Suger had covered only the first year or two of Louis VII's reign before he himself died, but the graphic depiction of the events indicates that he had been making notes about them shortly after they took place.[67]

In this writing, Suger described only the actions and affairs of Louis VII that he himself witnessed and where he played a major role. The young king was in Aquitaine when he learned of his father's death. He had journeyed there, along with Suger, for his marriage to Eleanor in Bordeaux. Shortly thereafter, Louis traveled northward to suppress a rebellion at Orléans, as the city had formed a commune without royal authority. He quickly put an end to the commune. Suger then strayed from his narration to point out how fortunate France was to have a male heir to succeed to the throne and so avoid the strife and warfare that the Roman Empire and England endured for not having a male successor.[68] He realized that he had digressed, as he indicated he would return to the subject matter at hand.

---

historian and fellow member of the Congregation, and added the second part, which concerned the reconstruction of the abbey church, to Suger's *The Administration* in their *Recueil des Historiens des Gaules* (1781), vol. XII, 96–102. In the nineteenth century, using the Duchesne edition, Jacques-Paul Migne included *The Administration* as PL 186:1211–40, in 1854. Albert Lecoy de la Marche reproduced the manuscript in his *Oeuvres completes de Suger* (29:151–209). Along with an English translation and an excellent commentary, Erwin Panofsky included part of Lecoy's edition of the Latin text of *The Administration* in his *Abbot Suger on the Abbey Church of St.-Denis and its Art Treasures*, as only the second part where Suger discussed his reconstruction of the abbey church held interest for him as an art historian. The most recent edition of *The Administration*, along with a French translation, is found in vol. 1 of *Oeuvres* (ed. Gasparri).

66. Odo of Deuil, Suger's successor as abbot of Saint-Denis, tells us in his *De profectione* that he himself was making notes of the journey to the Holy Land for the work Suger was writing about Louis VII. See Odo, *De profectione*, 2–4.

67. Grant, *Abbot Suger*, 37.

68. The king's father, Louis VI, and his mother, Adelaide of Maurienne, had produced six sons and one daughter.

As Suger resumed his narrative, Louis, his wife, Eleanor, and his mother, Adelaide, were all living unhappily together in the royal palace. Adelaide seems to have been the cause of the trouble, for, as Suger claimed, she had a tendency to nag and frequently criticized her son for his lack of assertiveness. Adelaide and Count Ralph of Vermandois, the king's seneschal and first cousin of his father, felt that Louis was spending entirely too much money on Eleanor and wanted him to restrain himself.[69] They felt that he would not be able to meet the needs of royal generosity as well as have enough funds to administer the kingdom. As a result of the quarrel, Adelaide retired to her dower lands at Compiègne and Count Ralph departed from the court, leaving the office of seneschal vacant for a while. Suger next ensured the loyalty of the leading men of the kingdom to the young, inexperienced Louis. He began with the counts and castellans in the region around Paris and then traveled to Burgundy where the king received the homage and fealty of Count Theobald and the entire territory.[70]

In 1138 Louis put down the revolt of another commune, this time in Poitiers. The king summoned Count Theobald to assist him, but the count repeatedly procrastinated. Louis then sent Suger to Theobald for money and soldiers for the expedition against the city, but the count continued to do nothing. Louis finally assembled an elite force and moved against Poitiers where the city surrendered without a fight. Louis resolved to take the sons and daughters of the leading citizens of Poitiers as hostages to ensure the city's future loyalty, but such a terrible scene of weeping and wailing of their parents ensued that the king went to Suger for counsel as to what he should do. Suger advised him to release the hostages with a stern warning to the citizens that worse action would occur if the city revolted again.

At the same time as the revolt in Poitiers, Baron William of Lezay unlawfully seized the castle of Talmont-by-the-Sea, located on the

---

69. The seneschal was an official in a noble household that made all domestic arrangements, supervised the servants, and sometimes administered justice.
70. Theobald (ca. 1090–1152) became count of Blois and Chartres as Theobald IV in 1102 and then count of Champagne as Theobald II in 1125. He helped his brother Stephen of Blois become king of England in 1135.

Atlantic coast in central western France.[71] King Louis ordered William to appear before him, but the baron apparently failed to do so because the king dispatched Suger and Bishop Jocelin of Soissons to negotiate with William.[72] The negotiations failed, and Louis moved against William in force. The king took the castle except its tower. Suger's last line of the text broke off in mid-sentence with the conspirators taking refuge in the tower. Illness and death had overtaken him.

An anonymous monk of the abbey of Saint-Germain-des-Prés continued Suger's work on Louis VII and started where Suger had left off. Auguste Molinier edited the monk's writing under the title *The History of King Louis VII* and attached it to his edition of Suger's *Life of Louis the Fat*, which he published in Paris in 1887. Unfortunately, the monk never affixed his name to his continuation. The work itself, however, indicates that he was perhaps Burgundian in origin.[73] He had probably been a monk at the abbey of Vézelay before moving to Saint-Germain-des-Prés in Paris.[74] As if he had been an eyewitness, the monk described in graphic detail the atrocities the burghers of Vézelay committed against Abbot William of Mello and his monks in 1166. He also detailed the persecutions and slaughter that Count William II of Chalon unleashed on the monks of the abbey of Cluny and the burghers of the town. The dates for some of the events mentioned in the text indicate that he wrote it at some point in 1171–73.

The continuation begins with a brief mention of the marriage of Louis to Eleanor of Aquitaine in 1137. After a short account of the king's destruction of the castle of Montjay, the monk discusses at length the Council of Vézelay in 1146 where the king and his wife pledged to go on the Second Crusade. He also provides a long

71. William of Lezay had earlier been castellan there.
72. Jocelin of Vierzy, bishop of Soissons (r. 1126–52), known as "the Red," was a close friend of Suger.
73. The information in this paragraph comes from *Vie de Louis le Gros par Suger suivie de L'Histoire du Roi Louis VII*, ed. Auguste Molinier (Paris: Alphonse Picard, 1887), xxxi–xl.
74. The monk became a friend of Abbot Theobald of Saint-Germain-des-Prés, who had also previously been a monk at Vézelay. These two abbeys enjoyed a close relationship during the twelfth century.

list of the leading men of the kingdom who agreed to accompany them. The monk then briefly reports the murder of Abbot Herbert of Saint-Pierre-le-Vif of Sens by the burghers of that town and the punishment the king inflicted on them for their actions.

There follows an account of King Louis's expedition into Normandy to help Count Geoffrey of Anjou and his son Henry, the future king of England, take control of a region that they and Louis considered to be rightfully theirs. In return for the royal assistance, they rendered the Norman Vexin to Louis's control. The young Henry, however, soon violated the liege homage that he had recently pledged to Louis in Normandy, and the king moved against him. In the end, the king forgave Henry for his rebellion and restored several castles to him. The narrator of these events, which occurred in 1148–52, pointed out King Louis's naiveté in doing so.

The monk next describes the divorce proceedings between Louis and Eleanor. Louis's relatives and kindred revealed to him that he and his wife were related within the degrees of consanguinity that, according to Catholic law, prohibited marriage. An impressive number of archbishops and bishops, along with numerous magnates and barons of the kingdom, gathered at Beaugency where Archbishop Hugh of Sens dissolved the marriage in 1152. Louis then married Constance of Castile, who bore him a daughter, Margaret.

After quickly recounting Louis's settlement of the dispute over the castle of Gien, the monk briefly announced the tragic death of Queen Constance as she gave birth to a second daughter in 1160. Five weeks later in that same year, Louis took the advice of several important churchmen and barons, and married Adela of Champagne, as he desperately needed a male heir.

Not long after his marriage, Louis invested and seized the castle of Mouchy in northern France to return half of its holding to its rightful possessor. He then described the schism that occurred in the Roman church over the disputed papal election of 1159 between the supporters of Alexander III and those of Victor IV. Alexander later journeyed to France in 1162 to win the support of Louis and the French clergy for his papacy, which he immediately received. Other emperors and kings soon followed Louis's example and also recognized Alexander as pope. The one exception was Emperor Frederick I Barbarossa of Germany, who, according to the narrator, suffered terrible consequences for not doing so.

Louis then took action against the count of Clermont and his allies, and ended their harassment of the churches in Auvergne. In the next section of the text, the monk describes the atrocities the count of Chalon committed against the abbot and monks of Cluny. The author then recounts the details of a slaughter similar to the one the burghers of Vézelay inflicted on the monks and abbot of that town's abbey. Louis ended this uprising against the abbot through negotiations without shedding blood. The monk ends his account of the actions and events in the life of King Louis VII with the birth of the king's long-desired male heir in 1165, when Queen Adela delivered the future King Philip II Augustus (r. 1180–1223). The narrator concluded that God had finally rewarded the king for his defense of the churches of the kingdom. A number of manuscripts have survived for *The History of King Louis VII*.[75]

The Life of Suger

William, a monk of Saint-Denis, who was a protégé and intimate friend of Abbot Suger, began writing his abbot's biography in 1152

---

75. Both *Vie de Louis* (ed. Molinier), xxxi–xl, and *Oeuvres* (ed. Gasparri), lxii–lxiii, give a good explanation of them. The information in this paragraph comes from these two sources. All relevant manuscripts are in the Bibliothèque Nationale in Paris in its lat. collection and are listed and dated as follows, using the capital letters of Molinier: A: lat. 12711, folios 174–76 (end of the twelfth century); D: lat. 12710, folios 51v–52 (end of twelfth century, ancient Saint-Germain); C: lat. 17657, folios 122–122v (dated 1332, College of Navarre); G: lat. 6265, folios 51–52 (dated 1515, from a volume of Saint-Magloire); H: 12712, folios 192v–193 (sixteenth century); J: lat. 15046, folios 315–16v (first half of thirteenth century, Saint-Victor); and K: lat. 5925A, folios 194–194v (third quarter of fifteenth century, belonging to Nicolas Lefèvre). Molinier used the A and D manuscripts as the basis for his *Vie de Louis*. Molinier's edition was employed for this English translation of Louis's history. Using manuscript G, André Duchesne published the first edition of *The History of King Louis VII* in Paris in his *Historiae Francorum Scriptores*, vol. IV (1641). Employing the same manuscript, members of the Congregation of Saint-Maur published the next edition as they continued the work of Dom Martin Bouquet in their *Recueil des Historiens des Gaules*, vol. XII (1781). Molinier published his edition in Paris in 1887. Along with a French translation, Françoise Gasparri has published the final edition of Suger's incomplete fragment, sections I–VII, in writing *The History of King Louis VII* in vol. 1 of her translation of *Oeuvres*.

and finished it in 1154. The dates of composition have been determined from its content.[76] The author had to write in exile, for William had been a member of the faction that opposed the election of Odo of Deuil as Suger's successor, and the new abbot sent him south to Saint-Denis-en-Vaux, a priory of the mother abbey in Poitou. While there, William decided to write an encomium on the life of Suger as a veiled but negative comparison to Odo's abbacy. William also wished to counter the harsh criticism of Suger being leveled against his former abbot at the time.[77]

William began his work with a prologue, typical of medieval authors, in which he complained about his lack of knowledge of the subject matter, and indicated that he would follow no definite order in his narration, indicting his own writing ability. He addressed and dedicated his work to Geoffrey, a fellow monk of Saint-Denis, who had requested that William write Suger's biography. With tongue in cheek, so to speak, William told Geoffrey that he should be writing the biography because he knew more about Suger than William did.

According to William, Suger seemed divinely ordained to lead the abbey and be involved in the affairs of the kingdom. The abbot's spirit, although housed in a small body that could barely contain it, was too beautiful, too great, and too virtuous for him to be an obscure person. With remarkable self-control, Suger presided over both the monastery and the royal court. The kings of France sought his wise counsel and treated him with deference and respect, as did bishops and prelates. However, Suger's rivals demeaned him for his humble origins.

Suger shouldered the heavy burden of managing the affairs of the kingdom, as William writes, but those duties never kept him from divine services and private prayer.[78] He was no stranger to the liberal arts, and could discuss books on logic and rhetoric in great detail. He continually studied theology, even as he grew old, and

---

76. See Grant, *Abbot Suger*, 44n39.
77. Ibid., 44.
78. In this paragraph, William is addressing the criticism that Suger immersed himself in worldly affairs to the detriment of his own spiritual health. William asserts that, although he loved the pagan poets, he never neglected his studies in theology and scripture.

became so well versed in scripture that he could explain any biblical passage when asked. He read the pagan poets as well, and his retentive memory allowed him to recite up to thirty lines of Horace by heart, if they contained a worthy lesson. Suger became a well-known orator in his times and had eloquence in both his native tongue and Latin. His knowledge of history was superb, for he could recount the deeds of any French king or prince that a person happened to name. Suger had been an intimate counselor of Kings Louis VI and VII, and attended so many of the royal councils that the palace seemed empty when he was not there.

To answer the accusation against the deceased abbot that he played favorites at the abbey, William asserts that Suger never rushed to judgment when one of the monks was accused of wrongdoing. The abbot first considered the motives of the accuser, then conducted a thorough investigation, and disciplined the accused only if Suger was certain of his guilt. The abbot would act not to punish the sinner but to prevent him from sinning again. Ignorant and jealous men were impugning Suger's character, for they considered him too harsh and rigid, William says, but Suger's close friends did not consider him so. They thought him amiable, kind, and fun-loving; and like a good parent, he would admonish, scold, and threaten with the rod only to ensure good behavior.

Kings admired his high ideals, sought his conversation, and were guided by his counsel. Among those who did so were King Roger II of Sicily, King David I of Scotland, King Henry I of England, and King Louis VII of France, according to William. Suger especially enjoyed a close friendship with the English king, who chose him to negotiate a peace settlement with King Louis VI over the Vexin. Counts admired Suger as well. Theobald of Blois and Champagne selected him as his advocate with the kings of France, and Geoffrey V Plantagenet of Anjou sent him flattering letters of petition and honored him in every way. Thus William concludes the First Book of his text.

At the beginning of the Second Book, William pauses to reflect that Suger's rivals became ill when they read what he was writing about the abbot, but he would continue nonetheless. Whenever Suger was absent from the monastery on the business of the kingdom, he always appointed a competent administrator to take care of monastic affairs.[79] Whenever the abbot traveled, churchmen from other communities flocked to him, seeking his charity and assistance. He was merciful to the sick and the poor. When wars broke out, he was a proponent of peace. His wisdom and passion would have allowed him to govern the whole world, William boasted. Suger never ate or drank to excess; he diluted his wine with water, nibbled at his food, and sent out the rest to the poor. He never grew fat as other abbots often did. William continued to praise Suger's devotion and devout heart in all his religious functions and in his superb care of the monks at Saint-Denis.

In addition, some of Suger's detractors claimed that he had spent too much of the abbey's resources on the reconstruction of the abbey church and the expensive ornaments that he decorated it with, totally forgetting how he had increased the abbey's revenues significantly during his administration. To counter this criticism, William describes how Suger had transformed a dark church into a light-filled one, adding to it precious fabrics, chalices, and other vessels used in the celebration of the Mass. William also praises the newly renovated shrine of the Holy Martyrs, and then concluded this section of his text by mentioning a letter of praise for Suger that Bernard of Clairvaux wrote to Pope Eugenius III.[80] William also counters another letter that Bernard had written to Suger, in which Bernard criticized Suger's ostentatious lifestyle, especially in the way he traveled.[81] William describes Abbot Peter of Cluny's visit to Saint-Denis and his praise for Suger's abstemious manner of living as well.

William begins the Third Book with the departure of King Louis VII on the Second Crusade in June 1147. A Council had already met at Étampes in February to select regents to administer the kingdom in Louis's absence, and Suger reluctantly agreed to be one of them

---

79. It is not hard to read between the lines and see what criticisms of Suger that William was countering in this paragraph.

80. For this letter to Pope Eugenius III (r. 1145–53), see Letter of Saint Bernard to the Pope, *Oeuvres* (ed. Lecoy), no. 4 (419).

81. See Bernard of Clairvaux, *The Letters of St. Bernard of Clairvaux*, trans. Bruno Scott James (Chicago: Henry Regnery, 1953), no. 80 (110–18).

after Pope Eugenius persuaded him to do so. Suger did not approve of this crusade and had advised Louis to attend to the affairs of state instead of journeying to the East. Brigands and outlaws soon took advantage of the king's absence, and attacked churches and robbed whomever they could. Suger successfully suppressed this violence, kept the kingdom intact, and earned the allegiance of all, even from the districts south of the Loire River. His efforts were costly to his own private revenues as well as to those of the crown. At the same time, Suger had to provide resources to the crusading king and preserve enough money for the administration of the realm upon the king's return. In addition, Pope Eugenius had put Suger in charge of the French clergy and churches. Suger removed individuals from ecclesiastical office, saw to the consecration of bishops and abbots when vacancies occurred, and found approval in Rome for whatever he did.

According to William, the king's brother, Count Robert I of Dreux, who had accompanied Louis on crusade, returned to France before him and immediately stirred up trouble. Robert attempted to assume royal power with the support of certain disenchanted men, both clerical and lay, who were not satisfied with the affairs of state. With help from men loyal to Louis, Suger checked all of Robert's schemes and preserved the kingship for Louis, but evil detractors and outright liars began sending messages to Louis, confusing his naïve mind about what Suger was doing.

By this time Louis had landed in southern Italy on his return journey. Pope Eugenius went to meet him in order to convince him that the rumors the king was hearing about Suger were the fabrications of jealous men who resented the abbot's achievements. According to William, Louis esteemed and admired Suger from this point forward. Suger was extremely disappointed over the outcome of the Second Crusade, and began planning for another one at the urging of Pope Eugenius. Suger sent money from the abbey's coffers to the East to support this undertaking, and so gave his enemies another opportunity to criticize him. William again came to his abbot's defense by reminding the critics of the substantial increase in the abbey's revenues resulting from Suger's efforts.

By now Suger had aged and was approaching his last days. William's last task was to describe Suger's meritorious death and well-attended funeral. During autumn 1150, Suger fell ill with a fever that wracked his small, weakened body with so much pain that he had to be held up by the arms of others while he said Mass. Suger realized he would not be able to fulfill his sworn vow of a new crusade, so he had one of the renowned, warlike magnates of France pledge to do it, using the money that Suger had already sent to the East to enlist soldiers. With no regrets, Suger joyfully waited for his final hour. As the Nativity approached, he begged the Lord to put off the day of his death until after Christmas so that the monks of Saint-Denis could enjoy the festivities. The Lord answered his prayer, for he died on January 13, 1151.

The Circular Letter of the Monastery of Saint-Denis Concerning the Death of Abbot Suger

Shortly after Suger died, William, the same monk of Saint-Denis who wrote *The Life of Suger*, sent out a circular letter to other churches and monasteries, announcing the death of his beloved abbot and intimate friend. Typical of such letters, William asked for condolences and compassion from his fellow churchmen to help the monks of Saint-Denis bear their overwhelming sorrow over the death of their abbot. Geoffrey, a fellow monk at the abbey to whom William had dedicated *The Life*, also requested that William write and distribute *The Circular Letter*. Essentially, it is a eulogy on the life and accomplishments of Suger.

William repeats much of the information that he gave in his biography of the abbot. He adds that Suger summoned Bishops Jocelin of Soissons, Baldwin of Noyon, and Peter of Senlis to his deathbed to hear the final confession of his sins, noting that they continued to administer the sacraments to him for nearly fifteen days, until he died while saying the Lord's Prayer and the Apostles' Creed. Six bishops, many abbots, and other monks attended his burial and solemn funeral rites, as did King Louis VII, many magnates of the realm, and the Preceptor of the Templars, Evrard of Barres. William ends *The Circular Letter* with a poem honoring Suger's virtues.

William's *Life of Suger* and *The Circular Letter* have been preserved as the second group of letters in the Bibliothèque Nationale in Paris in only one manuscript, ms. lat. 14192, which dates to the middle of the twelfth century.[82]

82. The information in this footnote comes from *Oeuvres* (ed. Lecoy), xvi, and *Oeuvres* (ed. Gasparri), 1:xlii. Charles de Combault, baron of Auteuil, published the first edition of the manuscript in his *Histoire des ministres d'Etat* (Paris, 1642). A few years later, François Duchesne, the son of André Duchesne, published a second edition in his *Sugerii Vita* (Paris, 1648). Michel Félibien published a third edition in his *Histoire de l'abbaye royale de Saint-Denys en France*, cxciv–cciii (Paris, 1706). William's two writings next appeared in RHF, vol. XII (1781), compiled by members of the Congregation of Saint-Maur as they continued the work of Dom Martin Bouquet. Albert Lecoy de la Marche published his edition at Paris in 1867 in his *Oeuvres*, 375–411, and Françoise Gasparri published the most recent edition, with a French translation, in her *Oeuvres*, 2:292–373.

SELECTED WORKS OF ABBOT SUGER OF SAINT-DENIS

And in a time of violence, he provided reconciliation
—Sirach 44:17, as quoted by William of Saint-Denis in his *Life of Suger*, I, 191

[1]

The Book on the Consecration of the Church of Saint-Denis[1]

I

The remarkable power of a unique, single, and supreme reason makes the divine and human natures equal by lessening the disparity between them; and although inferiority of origin and opposition of nature cause the divine and the human natures to appear to be incompatible, a pleasant conformity alone joins them into a single, superior, and measured harmony.[i] Those who in fact strive to become glorious by participating in the supreme and eternal reason often sit on the throne of an acute mind as if they were on a tribunal, arguing endlessly over the similar and the dissimilar in order to discover and determine opposites. With charity's help they take a healthy drink from reason's fountain of everlasting wisdom in order to withstand the war and division within themselves. They prefer the spiritual to the corporeal and the eternal to the transitory, and put aside the anxieties and powerful vexations of bodily pleasure from the external senses. They elevate themselves above that oppression and focus their undivided attention on the expectation of an eternal reward as they zealously pursue eternity alone. They for-

---

1. Suger began this work in 1144 and completed it somewhat quickly.

get carnal desires by admiring and looking at other things. By using supreme reason and being in the community of eternal blessedness, they deservedly rejoice to be united with glorious consciousness according to the promise of the only-begotten Son of God: *in patience you will possess your souls*.[2]

However, since human nature, burdened and seriously wounded by the corruption of its original state, embraces the present more than anticipates the future, it would in no way endure if the abundant help of supreme and divine love did not mercifully furnish human reason and rational intelligence the ability to accomplish this union. Thus it is written: *His mercy is above all of his works*.[3] For this reason we boldly and truthfully profess with others that the more mercy alone saves us through baptismal regeneration and renewal by the Holy Spirit, the more we should strive humbly and devoutly with our total will and power to offer Him our moral integrity as the most pleasing burnt offering of a purified spirit in the same amount that He Himself has given to us. Thus, He who can as God, Who should as Creator, equalizes that dangerous disparity in us if we do not resist. Using the inexpressible love by which He inexpressibly and indivisibly united His divinity to our captive humanity, He abolishes the hostilities of opposites inside us that we incurred by the loss of His friendship through original sin. With the severe torment of the flesh put to sleep and the turmoil from vices stilled, and with the dwelling place made peaceful He pacifies the incompatibilities within us. Thus, we become unimpeded in mind and body and offer pleasing service to Him, and can then reply and proclaim the fullness of His tremendous benefits towards the noble church that he allowed us to lead and us. We shall not remain silent in his praise, lest we incur the loss of his favors and hear that dreadful voice: *no one has been found who would return and give glory to God*.[4]

Therefore, *justified by faith from our inner peace*, as the Apostle says, *we have peace with God*, making known publicly this one special fa-

---

2. Lk 21:19.

3. Ps 144 (145):9. The chapter in the parentheses indicates the modern numbering of the Psalms.

4. Lk 17:18.

vor of the divine bounty among many others.⁵ Like those who out of gratitude voluntarily return to their donors the gifts imparted to them, we have labored with our pen to bring to the attention of our successors the glorious and worthy consecration of this holy church and the sacred translation of our most precious lords and apostles Denis, Rusticus, and Eleutherius and other saints on whose ready protection we rely. For this reason, we have recorded the order of things, the solemnity, and even the persons involved so that we may return as best we can worthy acts of gratitude to the divine mercy for so great a gift, and may obtain the favorable intercession of our holy protectors with God for our earnest care given to such a great work and for recording such a great solemnity.⁶

II

The glorious and famous King Dagobert of the Franks was a man well known for his royal generosity in the administration of the kingdom while still remaining devoted to the Church of God. When he had fled to the village of Catulliacum to avoid the unbearable wrath of his father Clothar, King Dagobert discovered that the venerable images of the Holy Martyrs resting there seemed similar to handsome men clothed in snowy white garments who required his service, for which they promised him their unwavering help in words and deeds.⁷ With remarkable enthusiasm the king ordered that a basilica dedicated to the saints be built as a royal charitable bequest. He constructed it with

---

5. Similar to Rom 5:1.
6. The "protectors" are the Holy Martyrs: Saints Denis, Rusticus, and Eleutherius.
7. Dagobert I was the king of Austrasia from 623 to 629 and ruler of the Franks from 629 to 639. He was the last Merovingian king to exercise actual political power, as after him the dynasty fell under the influence of the mayors of the palace. He founded the abbey of Saint-Denis and was the first Frankish king to be buried in its church. Catulliacum was a small Gallo-Roman settlement that grew up along the main road leading from Paris to northern France. For more detail on the village of Catulliacum, see Sumner McKnight Crosby, *The Abbey of Saint Denis, 475–1122* (New Haven, Conn.: Yale University Press, 1942), 1:37–38. Clothar II was king of Neustria from his infancy in 584 and king of the Franks from 613 until his death in 629. For "service," the Latin word *servitium* is used here, which meant the service owed to a master by his dependent. See further, appendix A, 221.

an amazing variety of marble columns and enriched it beyond measure with abundant treasures of the purest gold and silver. He made sure that tapestries, which were woven with gold and generously adorned with an assortment of pearls, hung from its walls, columns, and arches; and the church seemed to surpass all other churches in ornamentation. Blossoming in every way with unrivaled charm and arrayed in incomparable splendor, it began to shine with every earthly beauty.[ii] The king, however, made only one mistake when he did not allow as much space as was needed; but he did not err in his devotion or good will. Perhaps he thought that there was no other edifice larger or equal to it in size in the early church at that time, or that a smaller church would reflect more acutely and delectably to the eye the splendor of the shining gold and gems by their nearness, or that its treasures would sparkle more radiantly than they would if the church were built larger.

The basilica usually encountered great problems because of the charming feature of its extraordinarily small size when the multitudes of the faithful increased in number as they frequently congregated there to seek the intercession of the saints. Thus, on feast days the church often filled to capacity and the overflow of the crowds rushing into it poured back out through all its doors, and the outward push of those already inside did not allow those entering to enter and forced out those who had just entered. You could sometimes see a strange sight. The pressure of the tightly packed crowd pushed against those struggling to come inside to venerate and kiss the holy relics of the Nail and Crown of the Lord, and so no one among the countless thousands of people could move a foot from being so pressed together.[iii] Everyone from that thick mass of people could do nothing but stand there, frozen like a marble statue. The only thing one could do was to scream. The distress of the women, however, was huge and unbearable; trapped between powerful men they felt like a wine press was crushing them. Blood rushed from their faces as if they stared death in the eyes; they cried out in pain as if they were giving birth, and many of them were shamefully knocked down. With merciful support from the men they were raised above the heads of the crowd, hanging there as if they were walking on the floor. Many women were also gasping for their last breath, breathing heavily to the despair of all in the cloister of the brothers.[8] While displaying the relics of the Passion of the Lord for those arriving to see them, the brothers were overcome by the crowd shoving and squabbling and were forced to escape on many occasions through the windows with the relics because they had no other way out. I heard about this problem at school as a boy from the brothers who taught me, and when as a young man I moved away I grieved over it, and as a grown man I committed myself to correct it.[iv] *But when it seemed good to God who singled me out while I was in my mother's womb and called me by his grace*, He put my insignificant self in charge of the administration of this very important holy church even though my merits did not deserve it.[9] Driven only by the inexpressible mercy of Almighty God and help from our lords the Holy Martyrs, we intended with total dedication and passion to correct the basilica's problem mentioned above and rush the enlargement of this place. We would never have presumed to attempt or even consider this project unless the reason that demanded it had been very great, necessary, useful, and honorable.

In the front of the church, on the western end, at the main entrance of the great doors, the narrow portico was tightly enclosed on both sides by twin towers that were short, in poor condition, and threatening to collapse.[10] So, with God's help we quickly began to work initially on that part and laid a solid material foundation for a straight nave and twin towers,[v] but also a very solid spiritual one about which is said: *no one can lay down any other foundation than the one that has already been laid, namely Jesus Christ*.[11] We trusted in His invaluable counsel and constant assistance and made progress in this huge, expensive undertaking. At first we spent little and needed many things, then we spent lavishly and needed nothing at all; we

---

8. See also *Oeuvres* (ed. Lecoy), Charter X, 357–58, and below, *The Administration*, XXV, 95.

9. Gal 1:15.

10. The renovation of the western façade and narthex began at some point in 1135–37 and was consecrated on June 9, 1140. For a discussion of this term *ab aquilone*, see *Abbot Suger* (ed. Panofsky), 209–12, and *Oeuvres* (ed. Gasparri), 1:181–82n19.

11. 1 Cor 3:11.

truly had an abundance of everything and acknowledge that: *God provided us with everything needed.*[12] By a gift of God, a new quarry of very solid stone of a quality and amount never before found in these regions was uncovered. A large number of skilled masons, stonecutters, sculptors, and other craftsmen arrived here; so the Divinity freed us from our anxieties by this and other signs, and showed His approval by strengthening us and supplying unexpected resources. I compared the least thing to the greatest, and the riches of Solomon could not have been any more plentiful for his temple than our resources for this work, for the same Author of the same kind of work gave abundantly to his servants. The same Author for the same type of work provided more than enough to the worker.

In a project of this sort I was primarily concerned about the harmony and coherence of the old and new work,[13] and so we thought about, explored, and searched through different regions of remote districts to find marble columns or ones of equal quality. One thought alone remained in our mind and spirit amid our worries when we could not find any, namely there were marvelous columns at Rome in the palace of Diocletian and other baths that we had often seen. We could transport them from the city safely by ship across the Mediterranean Sea at great expense to our friends and also by paying passage-money to our enemies, the nearby Saracens. From there we could bring them across the English Sea and then up the winding bends of the Seine River.[14] We suffered great anxiety many times over a number of years while thinking about and searching for columns. Then suddenly the bountiful generosity of the Almighty contributed to our efforts something we could not imagine or believe, and to the amazement of everyone, revealed by the merits of the Holy Martyrs suitable and very high quality columns. Thus, against all hope and anyone's expectation, the divine pity saw fit to grant us a most pleasant site in good condition;

---

12. 2 Cor 3:5.
13. See also *Oeuvres* (ed. Lecoy), Charter X, 356–57, and *Oeuvres* (ed. Gasparri), 1:182n24.
14. For theories on the transportation of these columns, see *Abbot Suger* (ed. Panofsky), 213–14, and *Oeuvres* (ed. Gasparri), 1:183n25.

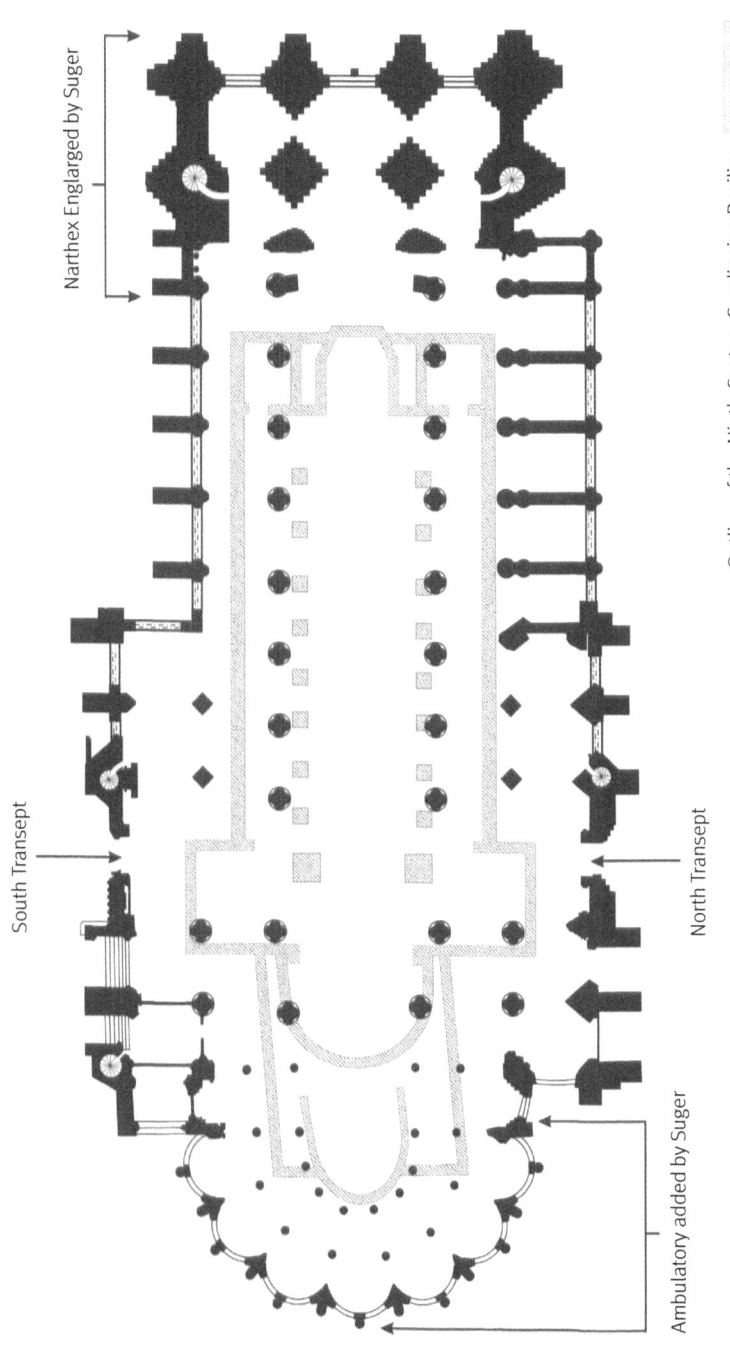

Suger's Additions to the Basilica of Saint-Denis

therefore we thought we should return to Him tremendous acts of appreciation for relieving us from our burdensome efforts. There was a wonderful quarry located near the fortified town of Pontoise at the border of our lands; it adjoined a deep hollow that had been dug, not by nature but hard work, and it had furnished a livelihood to stonecutters from ancient times.[15] So far the quarry had yielded nothing of exceptional quality but saved, as we believe, the beginning of its great service for a grand, divine building, as if it brought forth its first fruits for God and the Holy Martyrs. Our men and the devout neighbors of the site, both noble and non-noble, used ropes to drag the columns up from the bottom of the slope and pulled them out like draft animals with the other end of the ropes wrapped around their forearms, chests, and upper arms. Various craftsmen laid down the tools of their trade all along the middle slope of the town and went out to meet them in order to lend their strong backs for the difficult route, thereby paying homage to God and the Holy Martyrs as much as they could by their service.[16] An incredible miracle worth telling occurred that we heard about from those who witnessed it, and so we have decided to put it down in writing for the praise of Almighty God and His saints.

III

One day when a dark cover of clouds hid the stormy sky in a downpour of rain, the men who normally assisted with the project took a break because of the violent force of the rain as some wagons approached the quarry. The ox-drivers complained and shouted out loudly that they had been left stranded because the laborers were standing around wasting time. They continued their uproar and so some weak and feeble men, along with some boys, a total of seventeen if I remember the number correctly, as well as a priest rushed to

---

15. Pontoise, Val-d'Oise, Île-de-France is a commune located about fifteen miles northwest of Saint-Denis. The castle there was demolished in 1740.

16. For an account concerning the "cults of the carts" in France and this acquisition of columns from a quarry near Pontoise, see *Abbot Suger* (ed. Panofsky), 214–15, and *Oeuvres* (ed. Gasparri), 1:183–84n28.

the quarry. They picked up one of the ropes, tied it to a column, and left another one lying on the ground because there was no one who would even try to drag it. But invigorated by religious zeal the little flock said, "Saint Denis, take this idle column as your own and, if it pleases you, help us. No one can blame us if we cannot move it." Then they fell to the task forcefully, dragged the column out, and delivered it in a wagon to be used in the construction of the church. This column was the size that normally one hundred and forty or at least one hundred men could scarcely drag from the bottom of the pit. They could not have done this impossible feat by themselves but only by the will of God and the intercession of the saints whom they had invoked. Thus it became publicly known throughout the whole of the nearby region that this work completely pleased Almighty God, since He chose to assist the workers to the praise and glory of His name through these and similar miracles.

There happened next another amazing deed worth remembering that makes a good story, and it should be told by a credible source. With a great part of the work done and the flooring of the ancient and new buildings joined, we no longer felt the great fear we had harbored for a long time over the wide cracks in the ancient walls; and so we were ready to repair the damage in the great capitals and bases supporting the columns. We consulted our carpenters and some men from Paris about finding beams, and they honestly felt that hardly any could be found in these regions because of a lack of forests and that we would have to transport them from the district of Auxerre.[17] Since everyone agreed about this, we worried about the huge amount of labor and the length of time the work would be delayed. But one night after returning from celebrating Matins, the thought came to me while lying in bed that I myself should go through all the forests of these regions and search everywhere to prevent those delays and hardships by finding the beams here.[18]

---

17. Auxerre, Yonne, Burgundy is a city located about 112 miles southeast of Saint-Denis.
18. The night Office of Matins was the first and longest of the eight canonical hours, usually celebrated between midnight and 3 a.m., depending upon the season. It was sometimes expanded into an all-night service, called a *pervigilium*, on special occasions such as the eve of great feasts.

Putting aside other tasks, we headed out early in the morning and rushed to the forest called Yvelines with the carpenters and the measurements for the beams. Having passed through our possessions in the valley of Chevreuse, we summoned our sergeant wardens and those experienced with other forests, and asked them under sworn oath whether we could find there beams of those sizes no matter how hard we had to look.[19] They smiled, but really wanted to laugh at us, if they had had the nerve. They were surprised that we were totally unaware that nothing of the kind could be found in the entire land. For our dependent, Milo, castellan of Chevreuse,[vi] who held from us half the forest with another fief, had left no timber of that size intact and untouched, so that he could build three-story towers[20] as well as ramparts because he had to endure lengthy wars against our Lord King and Amalric of Montfort.[vii] But we ignored what they said.

Bolstered by our faith, we started combing through the forest, and within one hour we found a timber of sufficient size. What else can I say? Searching thoroughly through the thickets, through the dark forests, and through the thorn brambles, we marked out by the ninth hour or sooner twelve timbers (for that was the necessary number) to the astonishment of all, especially to those accompanying us. Then after the timbers had been carried to the sacred basilica, we joyfully had them set into the roofing of the new addition to the praise and glory of the Lord Jesus, Who had protected the beams from the hands of thieves and had saved them for Himself and the Holy Martyrs as was His purpose. Since we could find only the exact number of timbers needed, the divine bounty was not too excessive or too conservative in this matter, *providing everything according to exact weight and measure.*[21]

---

19. Chevreuse, Yvelines, Île-de-France is a commune located about twenty-eight miles southwest of Saint-Denis. For the rights of Saint-Denis in the forest of Yvelines, see below, *The Administration*, X, 76–79, and *Oeuvres* (ed. Gasparri), 1:184n30.

20. Suger uses the word *tristega* here, meaning a three-story mobile tower made of wood, built to surmount walls and ramparts during sieges in warfare.

21. Similar to Wis 11:21. According to *Abbot Suger* (ed. Panofsky), 217–18, the beams were needed as tie-beams for the roof of the central nave.

IV

These important and obvious signs of significant events continually motivated us, and we eagerly rushed to complete the building while deciding the manner, the degree of solemnity, and the individuals who would consecrate the church to Almighty God.[22] Having invited the honorable and worthy Archbishop Hugh of Rouen and other venerable bishops, Odo of Beauvais and Peter of Senlis,[viii] to perform the ceremony, we chanted various modes of praise amid a large crowd of diverse church dignitaries and a huge gathering of clergy and people. First, the three bishops stood together in the middle of the new addition and blessed the water in the font placed there. They then went forth with the procession through the oratory of Saint Eustace[ix] and through the square called from ancient times "Pantera" because all things for buying and selling there are used goods.[23] They returned through the other bronze door that opens onto the sacred cemetery; and by anointment with the most holy Chrism and the eternal benediction, and by displaying the true body and blood of the Supreme Pontiff Jesus Christ, they devoutly accomplished everything that befit such a great and sacred structure.

The bishops dedicated the very beautiful upper oratory, an abode worthy of angels, in honor of the holy and always Virgin Mary Mother of God, as well as Saint Michael the Archangel, all the angels, Saint Romanus who lies buried in the same place, and many other saints whose names are inscribed there.[24] They dedicated the lower oratory on the right side in honor of Saint Bartholomew and many other saints; but on the left side where Saint Hippolytus[25] is

---

22. The consecration of the church took place on June 9, 1140; see *Oeuvres* (ed. Lecoy), Charter X, 358.

23. See also below, *The Administration*, I, 68. The Pantera square was located in front of the main entrance of the church. Stalls were erected there to sell a variety of merchandise. For a discussion on the etymology of the word *Pantera*, see *Abbot Suger* (ed. Panofsky), 218–19, and *Oeuvres* (ed. Gasparri), 1:185n39.

24. Saint Hilary of Arles ordained Saint Romanus (d. 463) a priest at Besançon in roughly 444; his feast day is February 28.

25. For the location of this chapel and the relics of Saint Hippolytus, see *Abbot Suger* (ed. Panofsky), 155–56, and *Oeuvres* (ed. Gasparri), 1:206n172.

said to rest, they dedicated an oratory in honor of him and of Saints Lawrence, Sixtus, Felicissimus, Agapitus, and many others, to the praise and glory of Almighty God.[x] In addition, we fervently desired to become sharers through the gift of God of so great a blessing as reward for our considerable labor; and so in order that the oratories might have a perpetual annuity, we granted them a property bordering the cemetery near the Church of Saint-Michel[26] as an endowment to pay for the expenses of the lighting as was customary.[xi] We had bought it for eighty pounds from William of Cornillon.[27] The actual date of the consecration, lest it be forgotten, can be read in gold letters above the gilded doors that we had done in honor of God and the saints:

> The year one thousand one hundred and forty was
> The year of the Word when the church was consecrated.

After the consecration of the oratory of Saint Romanus and those of the other saints, which was celebrated with the help of the highest majesty in the front part of the church, our success had so renewed our enthusiasm that we turned our intention to the narrow confines[xii] that for a long time had unbearably restricted the area below the Holy of Holies.[xiii] Freed from the previous work, we delayed the completion of the upper part of the towers and dedicated all possible labor and expense to enlarge the mother church as fittingly and gloriously as we reasonably could, for we were grateful that divine favor had reserved such a great work for so small a successor of such great and noble kings and abbots. We then sought the advice of our most devout brothers whose *hearts were on fire for Jesus while he talked to them on the road;*[28] and after serious consideration we chose under God's inspiration to respect the blessing that divine action conferred through the extension of His own hand at the con-

---

26. For a discussion of this property and church, see *Oeuvres* (ed. Gasparri), 1:186n43.

27. William of Cornillon and his son, William, were friends of Abbot Suger. For William of Cornillon, see below, *The Administration*, I, 68; *Oeuvres* (ed. Lecoy), Charter X, 357; and *Oeuvres* (ed. Gasparri), 1:186n43.

28. Similar to Lk 24:32, which used the singular in this instance, but we changed it to the plural in reference to the brothers.

secration of the ancient church, as the venerable writings confirm.[29] We would honor those sacred stones as if they were relics and would strive to make the greatly needed new part illustrious in the beauty of its length and width.

We prudently decided to remove the vault that was not level with the higher one, which covered over the apse containing the bodies of our lords the saints, all the way to the upper side of the crypt, to which it was joined.[xiv] The crypt then provided its roof as a floor for those coming up by either stairway and presented the visitors a more elevated place to gaze upon the reliquaries adorned with gold and precious gems. Geometrical and arithmetical instruments supplied the accurate calculations to ensure that the middle of the old nave of the church was aligned to the middle of the new enlargement with its upper columns and middle arches placed over the lower ones built in the crypt. Then, the size of the old side aisles, likewise, had to conform to the dimensions of the new ones, except in that elegant and superb addition with its circuit of oratories that allowed the entire church to radiate with magnificent, uninterrupted light pouring through the sacred stained-glass windows that illuminated its interior beauty.[30]

The wise counsel suggested by the Holy Spirit, whose anointing instructs us in all things, made clear in splendid succession the action we should take. We assembled a group of distinguished men, both bishops and abbots, and invited our lord and most serene King Louis of the French to attend; then on the Sunday, the day before the Ides of July, we organized a solemn procession of beautifully attired persons.[31] In its front part the bishops and abbots carried in their hands the insignia of the Lord's Passion, the nail and Crown of the Lord,[xv] as well as the arm of the aged Saint Simeon[xvi] and

29. For the consecration of the ancient church supposedly by the hands of Christ himself, see below, *The Administration*, XXV, 95, and *Oeuvres* (ed. Gasparri), 1:203–4n162.

30. For more on the new nave and the construction of the ambulatory and chapels, see *Abbot Suger* (ed. Panofsky), 222–23; *Oeuvres* (ed. Gasparri), 1:187–88nn51–52. See also below, *The Administration*, XXIX, 100.

31. King Louis VII (r. 1137–80). The procession took place on July 14, 1140. See above (43) and *Oeuvres* (ed. Gasparri), 1:188–89n59.

other holy relics with their protective powers; and we humbly and devoutly descended into the excavations prepared for laying the foundations. Having called upon the help of the Holy Spirit the Paraclete[xvii] to insure that a good beginning of the house of God conclude with a good ending, the bishops prepared the mortar with their own hands using the holy water from the dedication ceremony that had occurred on the fifth day before the Ides of June.[32] They then laid the first stones while reciting a hymn to God and solemnly singing the psalm *His Foundations* all the way to its end.[33]

The most serene king also descendèd into the excavations and laid his stone with his own hands; and followed by many others, both abbots and religious, we laid our own stones. Other people laid gems out of love and reverence for Jesus Christ while they chanted *All Your Walls are Precious Stones*.[34] We rejoiced at such an important and festive laying down of the holy foundation, but we were still very apprehensive about the tasks ahead, the changing times, the alienation of people, and my own failings. Following the unanimous advice of the brothers, the encouragement of those present, and with the consent of the Lord King, we allocated an annual revenue of one hundred fifty pounds from the treasury[xviii] to complete these works; to be specific, we used the offerings at the altar and at the relics, one hundred from the Lendit Fair, and fifty from the feast of Saint Denis.[35] For the same reason, we also dedicated fifty pounds from our estate in Beauce, named Villaine, that previously lay uncultivated; but, with the help of God and our labor, we improved it enough to yield eighty to one hundred pounds each year.[36] If by some misfortune this estate should fail to render these amounts, our other estate in Beauce would make up the difference, since we had doubled and tripled its revenues.[xix] We also committed two hundred pounds for the continuation of these same works, in addition to the money brought to the treasury from the devotion of the faithful, or

---

32. June 9, 1140.
33. Ps 86 (87).
34. Similar to Is 54:12.
35. October 9.
36. Villaine, Eure-et-Loir, Centre is today an isolated farmstead to the west of Rouvray-Saint-Denis. See below, *The Administration*, XI, 81.

Chapels in the Ambulatory 1144

1. Chapel of Saint Innocent
2. Chapel of Saint Osmanna
3. Chapel of Saint Eustace
4. Chapel of Saint Peregrinus
5. Altar of the Virgin
6. Chapel of Saint Cucuphas
7. Chapel of Saint Eugenius
8. Chapel of Saint Hillary
9. Chapel of Saints John the Baptist and John the Evangelist

Chapels in the Crypt 1144

1. Chapel of Saint Benedict
2. Chapel of Saint Edmund
3. Chapel of Saint Stephen
4. Chapel of Saint Christopher
5. Altar of the Virgin
6. Chapel of Saints Sixtus, Felicissimus, and Agapitus
7. Chapel of Saints George and Walburga
8. Chapel of Saint Barnabas
9. Chapel of Saint Luke

Chapels in the Ambulatory in Félibien's Drawing of 1702

1. Chapel of Saint Firmin, Evangelist and Martyr
2. Chapel of Saint Osmanna, Virgin
3. Chapel of Saint Maurice, Martyr
4. Chapel of Saint Peregrinus, Evangelist and Martyr
5. Altar of the Virgin
6. Chapel of Saint Cucuphas, Martyr
7. Chapel of Saint Eugenius, Martyr
8. Chapel of Saint Hillary, Evangelist
9. Chapel of Romanus, Confessor

Chapels and Altars in Saint-Denis

any other contribution made to both works. We would do this until we were absolutely certain that the front and upper structures along with their towers would be totally and honorably finished.

V

We assembled a multitude of workers to complete the task and pressed on for three years through summer and winter at great expense, lest God should justly complain about us: *your eyes have seen my imperfection*.[37] With His helping hand we made satisfactory progress; and in imitation of things divine the foundation was laid, *for the rejoicing of the whole world, Mount Zion, on the north flank, the city of the great King*,[38] in the middle of which God will not be moved.[xx] But stirred by the petitions of sinners, He will not scorn being placated and propitiated by the fragrant burnt offerings of penitents. Indeed, twelve columns representing the number of the twelve Apostles, and likewise in the aisles just as many columns, signifying the same number of Prophets, suddenly lifted up the middle of the edifice to a lofty height. This plan followed the example of the Apostle who built a spiritual edifice: *Now you are no longer strangers and foreigners*, he says, *but fellow citizens with the saints and members of God's household; you have been built up upon the foundation of the Apostles and the Prophets, with Jesus Christ Himself as the main cornerstone; He joins together every wall and in Him every edifice, whether spiritual or material, rises up into a holy temple in the Lord*.[39] The more we strive to build materially in a more lofty and suitable way in Him, the more *we learn to construct ourselves spiritually into a dwelling place of God in the Holy Spirit*.[40]

For now, we were primarily concerned about the translation of our lords, the most Holy Martyrs, and other saints who were scattered throughout the church and venerated in separate chapels. We

---

37. Similar to Ps 138 (139):16.
38. Similar to Ps 47 (48):2–3.
39. Similar to Eph 2:19–22. For changes that Suger made to this biblical passage, see *Abbot Suger* (ed. Panofsky), 223–24, and *Oeuvres* (ed. Gasparri), 1:189–90n68.
40. Similar to Eph 2:22.

were also devoutly motivated to beautify their most sacred reliquaries, particularly those of the lords. So we selected a site and moved them where those approaching might gaze upon them in a more impressive and visible way, and we strove with the help of God to produce a splendid resting place by employing the elegant craftsmanship of goldsmiths and an abundance of gold and precious gems. We made the exterior outstanding by adorning it with these and similar materials; but for security, we made plans to fortify the very impressive interior all around with a wall of the strongest stones. We decorated their outside with gilded panels of cast copper to prevent the rough texture of the stones from degrading the tomb's appearance, but the work was not as elegant as it should be.[41] The respect that we, as well as everyone else, felt for these worthy fathers demanded that we miserable men who experience and need their protection should make the effort to cover their most sacred ashes. Since their venerable spirits, shining like the sun, stand before Almighty God, we covered them as best we could with very costly pure gold and a large quantity of hyacinths, emeralds, and other precious gems.

However, there is another work that we also chose to do in an outstanding way. We erected an altar to make offerings to God in a place before the bodies of the Saints where one had never previously stood. Supreme Pontiffs and people of authority could appropriately offer propitiatory and acceptable hosts to God there as they called upon the intercession of these Saints who gave themselves up to God as fragrant burnt offerings. I also began to doubt myself and wanted to erect a modest golden altar frontal, but the Holy Martyrs delivered to us an unforeseen abundance of gold and precious gems, which kings themselves scarcely possess. They seemed to be telling us from their own mouths: "Whether or not you want it, we want it to be the very best," and so we did not dare nor could we finish it other than with splendid and very costly material and craftsmanship. For when they were here, even Pontiffs themselves who had received pontifical rings as an honor of the dignity of their office did not refuse to place on the altar frontal these rings that were

41. For the construction of the new tomb of Saints Denis, Rusticus, and Eleutherius, see below, *The Administration*, XXXI, 101–2. See also *Abbot Suger* (ed. Panofsky), 169.

adorned with a wonderful variety of precious stones. Even those who were not here were inspired by their love of the Holy Martyrs and voluntarily sent over their rings from lands across the sea. The renowned king also willingly offered brilliant emeralds enhanced by their inclusions while Count Theobald gave hyacinths and rubies, and the magnates and princes contributed precious pearls of various colors and qualities; and they motivated us to complete the work in a splendid style.[xxi] Indeed, so many gems for sale were brought to us from almost all parts of the world and the resources to buy them were given to us, by the gift of God, that we could not let them slip away without great disgrace and affront to the saints. As so often is the case, experience has taught us that if a work has a good intention, with God's help it will have a good completion. Thus, should anyone rashly attempt to steal or knowingly defile this adorned frontal that such great men devoutly gave to these great protectors, let him incur the wrath of the lord Denis and be pierced by the *sword of the Holy Spirit*.[42]

We also feel there is something else worth mentioning. The work on the new addition with its capitals and upper arches had already reached the highest point of the structure, but the principal arches that were vaulted independently were not yet connected to the mass of the vaults. Then suddenly there arose a frightful and almost unbearable storm with ominous dark clouds, torrential rain, and extremely violent gusts of winds. It became so strong that it severely shook sturdy houses, the stone towers, and the wooden bell scaffolding. The storm happened on the anniversary of the glorious King Dagobert[xxii] when the venerable Bishop Geoffrey of Chartres was solemnly celebrating at the main altar a community Mass of thanksgiving for the king's soul.[43] Then powerful crosswind gusts struck the arches that had no supports or braces to resist them, and the arches started vibrating menacingly as they swayed back and forth,

---

42. For the sword of the Holy Spirit, see a similar passage in Eph 6:17.

43. Geoffrey II of Lèves, bishop of Chartres in 1116–49. Chartres, Eure-et-Loir, Centre-Val de Loire is a commune located about sixty-four miles southwest of Saint-Denis. For a discussion of the community Mass (*in conventu*), see *Abbot Suger* (ed. Panofsky), 226, and *Oeuvres*, (ed. Gasparri), 1:191n81.

threatening to collapse at any moment with disastrous results. Terrified by the pressure on the arches and the roofing, the bishop repeatedly extended his hand in that direction and gave a blessing by quickly stretching out the arm of the aged Saint Simeon and making the sign of the cross with it.[44] Therefore, it clearly seemed that the mercy of God and the merit of the Saints, rather than the sturdiness of the structure, prevented it from crashing down. This storm inflicted heavy damage everywhere on buildings believed to be very solid, but it lacked the force, when repelled by divine power, to damage our new unsupported arches as they swayed high overhead.

Another incident worth remembering occurred next; it did not happen by chance, as some who hold the following belief say about this sort of thing:

> Fortune swings back and forth randomly,
> It rises and falls, and
> Chance governs the affairs of men.[45]

But the divine bounty gives abundantly in things great and small to those trusting in it, and provides what it knows to be profitable for them. One day we met with our friends, officials, and stewards to discuss the preparations for the assembly of the court to be held during the upcoming consecration, for we expected it to be well attended. By the month of June the price of nearly all foodstuffs had become expensive; but despite the hard times, we had provided well enough for just about everything; but one preparation alone gravely concerned us. We had to acquire mutton in the district of Orléans and towards Burgundy, because a disease had killed many sheep that year.[46] Since the men going to those places to buy the mutton had started out late, I reluctantly instructed that they be given a thousand *solidi*, or whatever amount was needed, to allow them to return here on time.[47] The next morning in my usual rush from

---

44. For Saint Simeon, see above, *The Consecration*, IV (45nxvi) and *Oeuvres* (ed. Lecoy), Charter X, 355–56.

45. Lucan, *Pharsalia*, Bk. II, vv. 12–15.

46. Orléans, Loiret, Centre-Val de Loire is a city located about eighty-nine miles south of Saint-Denis. Burgundy is an administrative region of east-central France.

47. Derived from the Roman coin first issued by Emperor Constantine, the medi-

my small cell to the celebration of the holy sacrifice of the Mass, a monk of the white brothers suddenly pulled me back into my cell, despite my protests.[48] I was somewhat annoyed with him because he was preventing me from such an important act of worship. Then after I had spoken to him rather rudely, he said, "Lord Father, we have heard that you need mutton for the approaching ceremony of your consecration, and thus my brothers have sent me to bring to your Paternity a large flock of rams so that you may select the ones you want and send us back those you do not want." After hearing this message, we instructed him to wait for us until after Mass, and when the Mass ended we brought him to our brothers and told them about his offer. They attributed this gift to divine generosity because it had unexpectedly assigned to these monastic brothers the task to bring here the only thing we lacked, thus saving us from an exhausting search for it.

VI

The completion of the difficult project that our deferred wish had long desired now demanded that we proceed with the consecration of the new church.[49] We sincerely endeavored to make the consecration and the translation of the saints, our lords, become a very solemn ceremony, as an act of gratitude and as the most satisfying fruit of our labor. So after his royal majesty, the most serene King Louis of the French, who ardently desired to look upon his protectors the Holy Martyrs, graciously consented, we consulted together and selected the second Sunday of June for the day of the ceremony, which is the third day before the Ides and the feast day of the Apostle Barnabas.[50]

---

eval *solidus* was a monetary unit equal in value to one-twentieth of a pound (*livre*). It later became the English shilling and the French *sous*.

48. This monk of the white brothers almost certainly belonged to the Order of Cistercians. Named after their original foundation at Cîteaux (Côte-d'Or, Burgundy) in 1098, they were known as White Monks because of the white choir robe they wore over their habit. The Cistercians seem always to have had large numbers of sheep.

49. Construction on the eastern end of the church had begun on July 13, 1140.

50. Sunday, June 11, 1144.

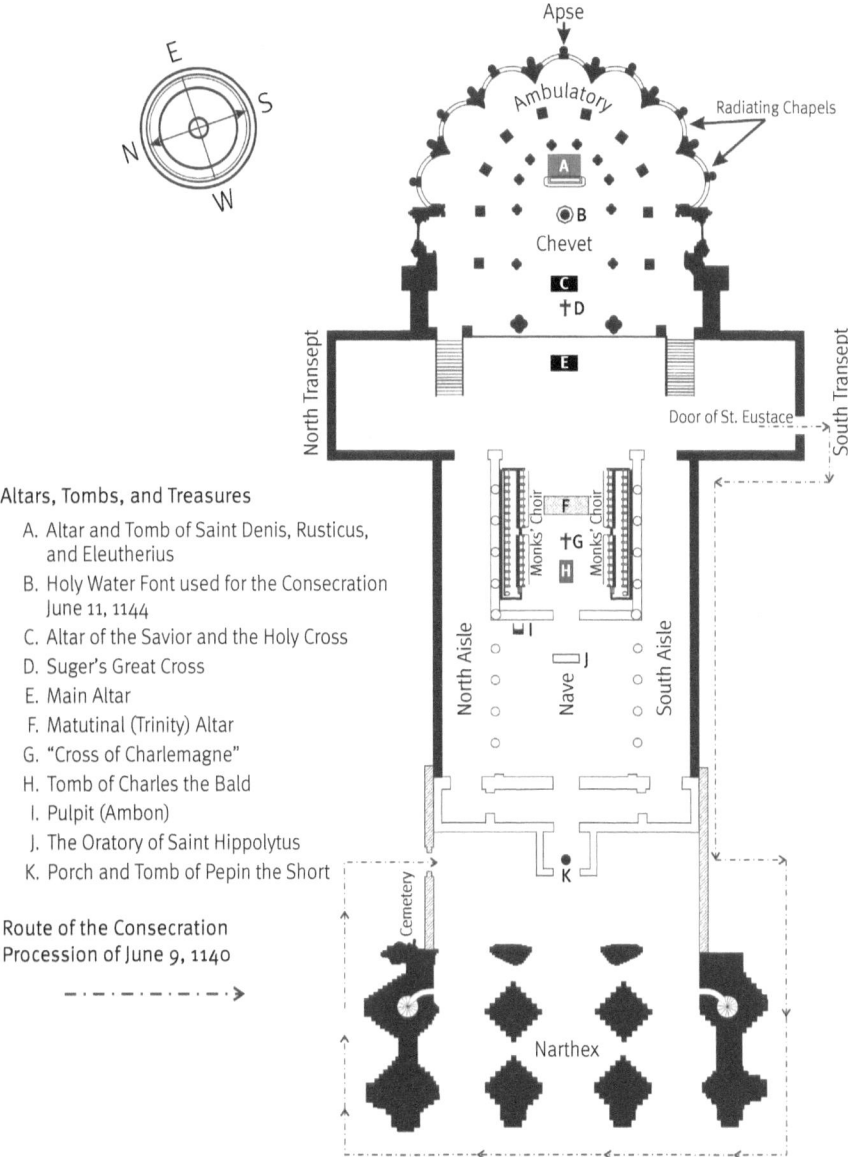

The Church of Saint-Denis in 1144

We sent out a large number of invitations by messengers, couriers, and heralds who carried them throughout nearly all the regions of Gaul, and ardently encouraged their archbishops and bishops to attend this great solemnity out of a sense of duty to the saints and their apostolate. We happily welcomed to this celebration many of them from different places and would have happily welcomed all of them if they could have attended. The Lord King Louis, his wife, Queen Eleanor, his mother, and the magnates of the kingdom arrived two days later.[51] A countless number of magnates, nobles, bands of knights, and troops of foot soldiers also came here from various regions and realms. The following are the names of the archbishops and bishops who participated: Archbishop Samson of Reims, Archbishop Hugh of Rouen, Archbishop Guy of Sens, Archbishop Theobald of Canterbury, Archbishop Geoffrey of Bordeaux, Bishop Geoffrey of Chartres, Bishop Jocelin of Soissons, Bishop Simon of Noyon, Bishop Elias of Orléans, Bishop Odo of Beauvais, Bishop Hugh of Auxerre, Bishop Alvise of Arras, Bishop Guy of Châlons, Bishop Algare of Coutances, Bishop Rotrou of Évreux, Bishop Milo of Thérouanne, Bishop Manasses of Meaux, and Bishop Peter of Senlis.[xxiii] Since they had all come to this important, noble, and grand event as the highest dignitaries of their churches, their reverence and outward attire indicated their inward devotion of mind and heart. We, however, were not concerned with outward acts, for we had instructed that these be performed in abundance, with nothing held back. On the Saturday before the ceremony, we took the bodies of the Saints from their chapels; and following custom, placed them most fittingly in draped tents at the exit of the choir. As we devoutly awaited such a very joyous event, we prepared the sacramental instruments of the consecration and planned how

---

51. Eleanor of Aquitaine (1122–1204) became the heiress of Aquitaine in 1137 and married the future king, Louis VII, three months later. Aquitaine is a region is southwestern France that borders the Atlantic Ocean on the west and the Pyrenees Mountains on the south. During the Middle Ages, Aquitaine was both a kingdom and a duchy, and its borders fluctuated many times. See also Suger, *The Deeds*, 156–57. Adelaide of Maurienne married King Louis VI the Fat in 1115, and after his death she married Matthew I of Montmorency (1100–1160). She died in the convent of Montmartre in 1154. See Suger, *The Deeds*, 120, 147, 150, and below, *Life of Louis VII*, IV, 131nxviii.

this lengthy and holy procession of such important persons could easily wind its way through the inside and outside of the church. So we humbly asked the glorious and most humble King Louis of the French to have his magnates and nobles keep the crowd back from the procession, and he answered even more humbly that he himself would be happy to do it along with his own retainers.

We spent the whole night from Vespers to the Holy Office of Matins in praise of the Divinity, devoutly imploring Our Lord Jesus Christ to make propitiation for our sins and mercifully visit this holy place for His own honor and out of love for His Saints.[52] We also asked that He deem it worthy to be present at these sacred rites in His power and person. Then, very early in the morning, the archbishops and bishops came to the church from their individual lodgings, along with the archdeacons, abbots, and other honorable persons. They arranged themselves by episcopal rank and stood with great solemnity and reverence in the upper part of the choir, between the tombs of the Holy Martyrs and the altar of the Holy Savior, near the font of holy water to be used for the consecration.[xxiv]

What a sight! Those in attendance saw with great devotion a large, beautiful choir of eminent Pontiffs in white garments, fully adorned with pontifical miters and precious orphreys worn over their ecclesiastical vestments. Holding their pastoral crosiers in their hands, they walked around the font, and called upon the name of the Lord to bless the water. These glorious and admirable men were so piously celebrating the wedding of the eternal Bridegroom that it seemed to the king, as well as to the nobility standing nearby, that they were seeing a choir more celestial than terrestrial, a ceremony more divine than human. Outside the church, the physical push from the unbearable size of the crowd agitated all the people stuck in it; and while the choir was vigorously throwing and sprinkling the blessed water onto the exterior walls of the building with the aspergillum,[53] the king himself and his officials checked the turbu-

---

52. Vespers, the sixth of the eight canonical hours, is the sunset or evening prayer said between 4 and 6 p.m., depending on the season of the year.

53. The aspergillum is a small, perforated container with a handle, which is used to sprinkle holy water in church services.

lent onrush of people with staffs and rods, and protected the choir members who were returning to the doors.

VII

After the mysteries of the sacred consecration were performed in proper order, the time had come for putting the holy relics in their new place; so we approached the ancient and venerable tombs of the saints, our lords, who up to this time had never been moved from their places.[xxv] The bishops, the Lord King, and all of us prostrated ourselves as best we could in the narrow place; then after the entrance had been opened, everyone present looked into the venerable shrines built by King Dagobert that contained the most holy and beloved-to-God bodies of the Saints.[54] All chanted and wept with infinite joy, and then calling upon the devout and humble king they said, "Go quickly and help bring here with your own hands our lord, apostle and protector, so that we may venerate his most sacred ashes, embrace the most sacred urns, and rejoice for the rest of our lives to have received them and held them. For these are holy men who gave up their bodies as witnesses to God, who for our salvation burned with the fire of charity, who left behind their land and relatives, who by their apostolic authority instructed all Gaul in the faith of Jesus Christ, who fought courageously for Him, who while nude remained steadfast against rods and while tied up confronted wild and hungry beasts, who endured stretching upon the rack and the flame of the furnace unharmed, and then finally suffered blessed decapitation with dull axes. Let us go forward, Christian king, let us receive our blessed helper Denis, humbly beseeching him to pray for us to Him who faithfully fulfills His promises; the love and kindness that you, Denis, possess will always have the prayers answered for whomever you shall ask." Without hesitation muscles were stretched; arms reached out, and so many and so esteemed were the hands thrust forward that not even the seventh

---

54. It was said that Saint Eligius (ca. 588–660), who served as a goldsmith and treasurer for King Dagobert, had made these shrines. For Saint Eligius, see *Abbot Suger* (ed. Panofsky), 158–59.

hand itself could reach the sacred shrines.[55] Thus, the Lord King wedged himself into the middle of them, took the silver reliquary of our special patron from the hands of the bishops, that is from the hands of the Archbishops of Reims, Sens, Chartres and others, and went forth devoutly and nobly leading the way.[56] What a sight to behold! Never had anyone seen such a procession, except the one seen during the old consecration by the heavenly host, when the bodies of the Holy Martyrs and confessors were taken from the draped tents on the shoulders and necks of bishops, counts, and barons to meet the most holy Denis and his companions at the ivory door.[xxvi] They then proceeded with candelabra, crosses, and other festive ornaments through the cloister singing many songs of praise; and they carried back their lords affectionately while shedding tears of joy. No greater joy in anything could have possibly made them feel more sublime.

The procession then returned to the church and ascended the stairs to the upper altar that had been chosen as the resting place of the saints. The relics of the saints were placed back on top of the old altar, while the new main altar in front of their new tomb was being prepared for its consecration. We entrusted that consecration to the Lord Archbishop Sampson of Reims. Twenty other altars[57] were also being prepared for their splendid and solemn consecrations.[xxvii] To the Lord Archbishop Theobald of Canterbury, we entrusted the consecration of the altar in the center that was dedicated to our Savior, the choir of Holy Angels, and the Holy Cross. We assigned the altar dedicated to the Blessed and ever Virgin Mary, Mother of God, to Lord Archbishop Hugh of Rouen; the altar to Saint Peregrinus to Lord Bishop Hugh of Auxerre; the altar to Saint Eustace to Lord Bishop Guy of Châlons; the altar to Saint Osmanna to Lord Bishop Peter of Senlis; the altar to Saint Innocent to Lord Bishop Simon of

---

55. For an explanation of the phrase *septima manus*, see *Abbot Suger* (ed. Panofsky), 229, and Philippe Verdier, "Some New Readings of Suger's Writings," in *Abbot Suger and Saint-Denis* (ed. Gerson), 159–62.

56. For "reliquary," see Madeline Pelner Cosner, *Medieval Wordbook* (New York: Facts on File, 1996), 49.

57. For the location of these chapels and altars, see below, "Chapels and Altars in Saint-Denis," 47.

Noyon; the altar to Saint Cucuphas to Lord Bishop Alvise of Arras; the altar to Saint Eugenius to Lord Bishop Algare of Coutances; the altar to Saint Hilary to Lord Bishop Rotrou of Evreux; and the altar to Saint John the Baptist and Saint John the Evangelist to Lord Bishop Nicholas of Cambrai. We assigned the consecration of the main altar dedicated to the Virgin Mary, Holy Mother of God, in the crypt below to Lord Archbishop Geoffrey of Bordeaux; on the right side, the altar of Saint Christopher the Martyr to Lord Bishop Elias of Orléans; the altar to Saint Stephen the Protomartyr to Lord Bishop Geoffrey of Chartres; the altar to Saint Edmund the King to Lord Archbishop Guy of Sens;[58] and the altar to Saint Benedict to Lord Bishop Jocelin of Soissons. On the left side we entrusted the consecration of the altar to Saints Sixtus, Felicissimus, and Agapitus to Lord Bishop Milo of Thérouanne; the altar to the Apostle Barnabas to Lord Bishop Manasses of Meaux and also the altar to Saint George the Martyr and Saint Walburga the Virgin to the same bishop; and the altar to Saint Luke the Evangelist to Lord Bishop Odo of Beauvais.

All the bishops performed these consecrations and solemnly celebrated Masses in the upper and lower levels so festively, so solemnly, so uniquely, so harmoniously, so near each other, and so joyfully that from its very concord and unified harmony their lovely melody was deemed an angelic concert, rather than a human one; and all voices shouted from the heart: *Blessed be the glory of the Lord in His dwelling place;*[59] *blessed, praised, and exalted above all be Your name,*[60] Lord Jesus Christ, whom God the Father anointed Supreme Pontiff with the oil of exaltation in front of Your communicants. With the sacramental anointing of the most holy Chrism and the reception of the most holy Eucharist, You uniformly join the material world with the immaterial, the corporeal with the spiritual, the human with the divine. You sacramentally return the purified to their original condition; and by these and similar visible blessings, You invis-

---

58. This should be Hugh of Toucy, archbishop of Sens (1142–68), and not Guy. See below, endnote xxiii.
59. Ezek 3:12.
60. Similar to Dn 3:52.

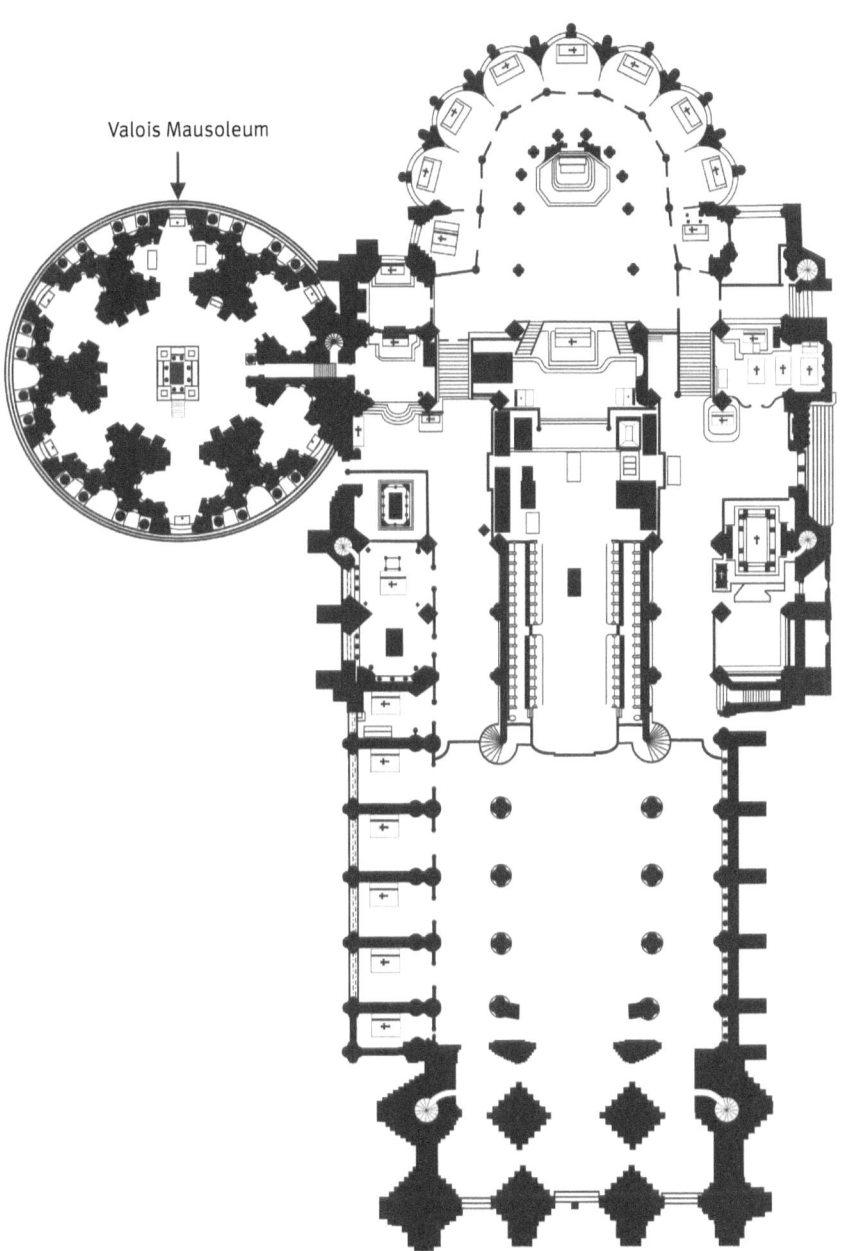

Félibien's Sketch Map of Saint-Denis (1702)

ibly restore and miraculously transform the present church into a heavenly kingdom. So *when you have given over the kingdom to God the Father,*[61] may You mightily and mercifully fashion us, the angelic creation as well as heaven and earth into one principality; and may You live and reign, being God, forever and ever. Amen."

ENDNOTES

i. For the inspiration behind these concepts, see Pseudo-Dionysius the Areopagite, *The Celestial and Ecclesiastical Hierarchy of Dionysius the Areopagite,* trans. John Parker (London: Skeffington and Son, 1894), 20. For the Neo-Platonic influence on Suger, see *Abbot Suger* (ed. Panofsky), 18–24, and *Oeuvres* (ed. Gasparri), 1:179n1. Suger believed that Dionysius the Areopagite, the disciple of Saint Paul, was the same person as the third century martyr, Saint Denis, as well as the sixth century Syrian Neo-Platonist Pseudo-Dionysius. On this confusion, see below, appendix A, 217.

ii. This description of the old Carolingian church is taken word for word from the *Gesta Dagoberti I,* except for the part about the marble columns. See Hincmar, *Gesta Dagoberti I regis Francorum,* ed. B. Krusch, Monumenta Germaniae Historica [hereafter "MGH"], Scriptores rerum merovingicarum 2 [hereafter "SRM"] (Hanover: Impensis Bibliopolii Hahniani, 1888), 406–7, and *Abbot Suger* (ed. Panofsky), 207–8. See also *Oeuvres* (ed. Gasparri), 1:180nn9–10.

iii. For the relics from the passion of Christ, see W. Martin Conway, "The Abbey of Saint-Denis and Its Ancient Treasures," *Archaeologia or Miscellaneous Tracts Relating to Antiquity* 66 (February 1915): 103–58, here 130–31. See also *Oeuvres* (ed. Gasparri), 1:180–81n12. For a discussion of the windows, see *Abbot Suger* (ed. Panofsky), 208.

iv. Suger was away from the abbey as a *juvenis* studying in Burgundy from 1104 to about 1106, either at Fontevraud or the abbey of Saint-Benoît-sur-Loire. From 1107 to 1112, he was first provost of Berneval-le-Grand and then Toury; see *Abbot Suger* (ed. Panofsky), 208, and Oeuvres (ed. Gasparri), 1:181n16.

v. For a discussion of the problem mentioned here, see *Abbot Suger* (ed. Panofsky), 212–13. A spire 282 feet (86 meters) tall was constructed on top of the north tower in the thirteenth century, but it was struck by lightning in 1837 and collapsed. The spire was repaired, but lightning struck it once again in 1840; and as a result, the structure was in danger of collapsing under its own weight. Therefore, the architect Viollet-Le-Duc tore down the entire north tower in 1845. Today, only the original south tower remains.

vi. Milo II (b. about 1055 at Montlhéry, d. 1118) was lord of Montlhéry, castellan of Bray-sur-Seine, and viscount of Troyes. He was the son of Milo I "the Great," lord

61. 1 Cor 15:24.

THE CONSECRATION OF THE CHURCH   61

of Montlhéry, and his wife Lithuise, viscountess of Troyes. His brother was Guy Trousseau. See further Suger, *The Deeds*, and *Morigny* (ed. Cusimano), 46–50.

vii. King Louis VI, born in 1081, reigned from 1108 until his death in 1137; see Suger, *The Deeds*. Amalric III (d. 1137) was lord of Montfort (ca. 1101–37), as well as count of Evreux and uncle of King Louis VI. Montfort-l'Amaury, Yvelines, Île-de-France is about thirty-five miles southwest of Saint-Denis. See Suger, *The Deeds*, 81–82, 132, 136, 144–45, and *Oeuvres* (ed. Gasparri), 1:184–85n33.

viii. Hugh IV of Amiens was archbishop of Rouen in 1130–64; Odo II was bishop of Beauvais in 1133–44; and Peter was bishop of Senlis in 1134–51. Rouen, Seine-Maritime, Haute-Normandie, is a city located about eighty-two miles northwest of Saint-Denis. Beauvais, Oise, Picardy, is a city located about forty-two miles northwest of Saint-Denis. See also below, *The Administration*, XXVI, 96, where Manasses of Meaux is placed at the ceremony in the place of Odo of Beauvais. *Oeuvres* (ed. Lecoy), Charter X, 356–57, and *Oeuvres* (ed. Gasparri), 1:185n36.

ix. In *The Administration*, XXVI, 96, the procession exited from the door of Saint Eustace in the south transept. For a discussion of this door, see *Abbot Suger* (ed. Panofsky), 156–59. The oratory of Saint Eustace was in the ambulatory and had no door. For the route of this procession, see "The Church of Saint-Denis in 1144," figure, 53.

x. The saints mentioned here are as follows:
1. Saint Bartholomew the Apostle was one of the twelve apostles of Jesus and is sometimes identified as Nathanael (Jn 1:45–51, 21:1–2). Eusebius of Caesarea wrote that Bartholomew went on a mission to India where he left a copy of the Gospel of Matthew; see Eusebius, *The History of the Church*, trans. G. A. Williamson, ed. Andrew Louth (London: Folio Society, 2011), 142. In India, Bartholomew converted King Ptolemius and his family, but this conversion angered the king's brother, Astarges, who had Bartholomew arrested and martyred sometime in the first century. One account said Bartholomew was beheaded, and another said he was flayed alive and crucified. His feast day is August 24.
2. Saint Hippolytus of Rome (170–235) was a controversial person who was involved in a doctrinal dispute with Pope Calixtus I (r. 217–22). Known as the Martyr of Rome, Hippolytus was killed in 232 in Sardinia where he had been exiled for being elected antipope, the first antipope in the history of the church. His feast day is August 22.
3. Saint Lawrence of Rome was one of the seven deacons of Rome under Pope Sixtus II (r. 257–58). Lawrence was arrested when he refused to turn over the riches of the church to the prefect of Rome, and then was martyred in Rome in 258 by being roasted on a gridiron. His feast day is August 10.
4. Pope Sixtus II (r. 257–58) was beheaded during the persecutions of the Emperor Valerian in 258, along with six of his deacons: Januarius, Vincentius,

Magnus, Stephanus, Felicissimus, and Agapitus. The seventh deacon, Lawrence of Rome, was martyred a few days later. The Tridentine calendar commemorated the feast day of Sixtus II, Felicissimus, and Agapitus on the feast of the transfiguration of the Lord on August 6, and their feast day remained on that date until 1969 when it was moved to August 7, the day after they died.

xi. *Abbot Suger* (ed. Panofsky), 219, indicates that no ecclesiastical edifice should be consecrated until an adequate endowment, a *dos ecclesiae* or "church dowry," was provided for its upkeep. *Oeuvres* (ed. Lecoy), Charter X, 357, refers to this endowment for lighting the chapels as a *dos catholica* or "general dowry."

xii. After finishing the western narthex in 1140, Suger began the reconstruction of the eastern end of the church known as the chevet, which included the apse and ambulatory with its radiating chapels. He completed this work in 1144. Suger's reconstruction of the church introduced new architectural elements to the old Romanesque church, such as pointed arches, ribbed vaults extending in different directions and supported by clustered columns, and large stained glass windows in the clerestory that flooded the interior with light.

xiii. The "Holy of Holies" refers to the tabernacle atop the main altar that was separated from the congregation by the monks' choir. The name is the same one used for the portable tent that God commanded the Israelites to construct and carry with them (Ex 26:34). The tabernacle stored the consecrated hosts dispensed to the congregation during Communion.

xiv. The meaning of this sentence is unclear. For an explanation of what it might mean, see Crosby, *The Royal Abbey of Saint-Denis, 475–1151*, 89; *Abbot Suger* (ed. Panofsky), 169 and 220–21; and *Oeuvres* (ed. Gasparri), 1:186n49.

xv. The passion relics were a part of the crown of thorns and a nail from the holy cross. According to legend, Emperor Constantine VII received Charlemagne in Constantinople on his journey to the Holy Land. Constantine gave the relics to Charlemagne, who took them back to the Palatine Chapel in Aachen. His son, Charles the Bald, then gave them to the abbey of Saint-Denis in the ninth century. The passion relics may have led to the institution of the Lendit Fair during the feast of the relics of the passion. The fair drew so many pilgrims and had such success that a second fair, the "outer Lendit," was established on the plain of Saint Denis near Paris in honor of the passion relics of Notre-Dame. Suger acquired the rights to this second fair and its revenues from King Louis VI. See *Oeuvres* (ed. Gasparri), 1:188n55.

xvi. The Gospel of Luke described Simeon the Prophet or Righteous as a "just and devout" man of Jerusalem (Lk 2:25–35). Simeon met Mary, Joseph, and Jesus as they entered the Temple to fulfill the Jewish Law, which required them to present Jesus forty days after his birth. The Holy Spirit had visited Simeon and told him he would not die until he had seen the Lord's Christ. Simeon took Jesus into his arms and uttered a prayer, which in the Latin mass is known as the *nunc dimittis*, and then alluded to the crucifixion. He died soon afterward. His feast day is celebrated on February 2. Charles the Bald gave to Saint-Denis the arm of Saint Simeon, which was housed in a beautiful reliquary overlaid with gold and inlaid with precious gems. For Saint Simeon, see above (15) and *Oeuvres* (ed. Lecoy), Charter X, 356. For the relics of the arms of the apostle Saint James, Stephen the Protomartyr, and Saint Vincent, see below, *The Administration*, XXXIII, 108. For a description of all the holy relics located at Saint-Denis, see Conway, "Abbey of Saint-Denis."

xvii. The Greek word "paraclete" literally means "a counselor at one's side." John used this word in the New Testament when he described the Holy Spirit as another "Paraclete," who teaches (Jn 14:16), reminds the disciples of what Jesus taught (Jn 14:26), witnesses for Jesus (Jn 15:26), and instructs about sin (Jn 16:7-8).

xviii. The term *gazofilacium* used in the Latin text is derived from the Greek γαζα, "treasure," and φυλακειον, "guard-house," and probably refers to a money chest or collection box that was attached to the main altar. See *Abbot Suger* (ed. Panofsky), 223; *Oeuvres* (ed. Gasparri), 1:189nn60 and 63; and Crosby, *The Abbey of Saint-Denis, 475–1122*, 1:104 and 184.

xix. Suger does not identify the precise estate belonging to Saint-Denis in Beauce. The others, besides Villaine, were Guillerval, Monnerville, Rouvray-Saint-Denis, Toury, Poinville, and Fains/Vergonville.

xx. Ps 45:6 (Vulgate). *Abbot Suger* (ed. Panofsky), 223, maintains that Suger uses a play upon the words *medium* and *commovere*. Verse 6 says that God "will not be moved" in the "middle" of the real Zion; however, the new choir of Saint-Denis, a symbol of Zion, located in the "middle" of the central nave with its central altar, "will move" God to be merciful.

xxi. Theobald (1090–1152) was the count of Blois and Chartres (IV) from 1102, and count of Champagne (II) from 1125. Inclusions are foreign bodies contained within the mass of a gem or mineral.

xxii. This anniversary occurred on January 19, 1143, because the foundations of the chevet were laid on July 14, 1140 (see below, *The Administration*, XXVIII, 99, which says that the rebuilding of the church lasted "three years and three months"). See also *Abbot Suger* (ed. Panofsky), 226.

xxiii. Those attending the consecration of the Church of Saint-Denis were:
1. Samson of Mauvoisin, archbishop of Reims (r. 1140–61).
2. Hugh of Amiens, archbishop of Rouen (r. 1130–64).
3. Hugh (not Guy) of Toucy, archbishop of Sens (r. 1142–68).
4. Geoffrey III of Loroux, archbishop of Bordeaux (r. 1136–58).
5. Theobald of Bec, archbishop of Canterbury (r. 1139–61).
6. Geoffrey II of Lèves, bishop of Chartres (r. 1116–49).

7. Jocelin, bishop of Soissons (r. 1126–52).
8. Simon of Vermandois, bishop of Noyon (r. 1123–48).
9. Elias, bishop of Orléans (r. 1137–46).
10. Odo, bishop of Beauvais (r. 1133–44).
11. Hugh of Mâcon, bishop of Auxerre (r. 1137–51).
12. Alvise, bishop of Arras (r. 1131–48).
13. Guy II of Montaigu, bishop of Châlons-sur-Marne (r. 1144–47).
14. Algare, bishop of Coutances (r. 1132–50/51).
15. Rotrou of Beaumont-le-Roger, bishop of Evreux (r. 1139–65).
16. Milon I, bishop of Thérouanne (r. 1131–58).
17. Manasses II, bishop of Meaux (r. 1134–58).
18. Peter, bishop of Senlis (r. 1134–51).
19. Finally, another bishop was present at this ceremony but was left out of this list: Nicholas I of Chièvres, bishop of Cambrai (r. ca. 1137/38–67), who consecrated the altar of Saint John the Baptist and Saint John the Evangelist. See *Oeuvres* (ed. Gasparri), 1:191–92nn88–89.

Bishop Theobald of Paris (r. 1144–59) was absent probably because he was not elected in time for the consecration ceremony.

xxiv. *Abbot Suger* (ed. Panofsky), 228, proposes that the altar of the Savior and the holy cross was near the western end of the chevet in the new upper choir close to Suger's great cross. See above, "The Church of Saint-Denis in 1144," figure, 53.

xxv. *Abbot Suger* (ed. Panofsky), 228–29, argues that the phrase *neque enim adhuc ad loco suo mota erant* does not literally mean that the holy relics had never been "moved." What the phrase implies is that the holy relics had never been transferred to a new burial place until June 11, 1144. Suger had temporarily displayed the relics on the main altar of the church in 1124 when Louis VI assembled his armies in anticipation of an invasion by Emperor Henry V (see Suger, *The Deeds*, 131). It was during this event that Louis VI adopted the use of the *oriflamme* of the abbey of Saint-Denis that Dagobert is said to have given to the abbey. For more on the *oriflamme*, see below, appendix B (223–26).

xxvi. *Abbot Suger* (ed. Panofsky), 229–30, states that Louis VII and his retinue carried the shrines of the patron saints, Denis, Rusticus, and Eleutherius, from their original burial place up into the crossing, the junction of the four arms of a cross-shaped church. All of the other relics that were to be transferred to the new chevet had been placed in "draped tents" near the exit of the monks' choir. Lesser dignitaries then picked up these "draped" relics and walked to meet the procession carrying the relics of the patron saints at the "ivory door." It is not clear whether this "ivory door" was a Carolingian door that led into the cloister, or a door from the original burial place of the saints into the crossing. The two separate processions met inside of the church and formed a unified procession that walked into the cloister, with Louis VII leading the way carrying the relics of the patron saints, while the lesser dignitaries followed behind carrying the other relics.

xxvii. The phrase *aliis ... aris viginti* is somewhat confusing. There are not twenty new altars in addition to the one in front of the new tomb of the patron saints; see also *Abbot Suger* (ed. Panofsky), 230–31. There were chapels and altars in the ambulatory of the chevet and in the crypt directly below the upper altars. Suger counted the radiating chapels from the chapel of the Virgin in both the ambulatory and crypt, but we have labeled them from lower left to lower right on the sketch map ("Félibien's Sketch Map"), 59. The altars and chapels are arranged in the following order:
1. The altar of Saint Benedict sits below that of Saint Innocent.
2. The altar of Saint Edmund sits below that of Saint Osmanna.
3. The altar of Saint Stephen sits below that of Saint Eustace.
4. The altar of Saint Christopher sits below that of Saint Peregrinus.
5. The altar of the Virgin sits below its counterpart (altar of the Virgin) in the ambulatory.
6. The altar of Saints Sixtus, Felicissimus, and Agapitus sits below that of Saint Cucuphas.
7. The altar of Saint Barnabas sits below that of Saint Eugenius.
8. The altar of Saints George and Walburga sits below that of Saint Hilary.
9. The altar of Saint Luke sits below that of Saints John the Baptist and John the Evangelist.

[2]

The Book of Abbot Suger of Saint-Denis

His Accomplishments during His Administration

I

During the twenty-third year of my administration I was sitting one day in general chapter with our brothers discussing our dependents as well as private affairs when these beloved brothers and sons, out of love, began begging me not to allow the memory of all our labors to be lost.[1] They wanted me to write down for the future a record of those additions that the generous bounty of Almighty God had bestowed upon this church during the time of my prelacy. We had purchased new properties and recovered lost ones; we had improved and increased the number of our possessions, and we had constructed buildings and accumulated gold, silver, precious gems, and fine textiles. The brothers promised me two results from this one task. First, this writing would gain for me the continual prayers of all future brothers for the salvation of my soul, and second it would

---

1. Abbot Suger did not give a title to this work. The titles given above are from later copies of the text. The first sentence of the text indicates that the abbot began this work in 1144/45. He completed it in 1146/47.

deeply enkindle their zealous care for the divine services of the Church of God. I ardently agreed with their heartfelt and reasonable request, but I did not do so from any desire for empty glory or to seek human praise or any transitory reward. I wanted to prevent our church from losing revenues after my death from any type of fraud, and I desired that no wicked successors of mine lose the sizable increases that the generous bounty of God brought during the time of my administration through my failure to write this record.

I will begin with the reconstruction of the nave of the church of the blessed martyrs Denis, Rusticus, and Eleutherius[i] that nurtured me lovingly from my youth to old age, and then continue this narrative with the construction of buildings and the increase of treasures as each event happened. For current and future readers I will also include a complete and accurate account of the abbey's fortified town that is its principal seat, as well as the abbey's surrounding region and the increase of its revenues.

There was a public agency inside the fortified town commonly known as a toll and exchange that consistently collected sixty *solidi* every week.[2] However, Ursellus, a Jew of Montmorency, held ten of these *solidi* in pawn, along with the manor called Montlignon for eighty marks of silver and another large amount of money.[3] However, we redeemed them at great expense, both the manor valued at twenty pounds or more and the ten *solidi*. We did so by paying three thousand *solidi* to Matthew of Montmorency who was happy to take possession of the manor on his Jew's behalf and by paying ten pounds and ten *modii* of grain to the wife of the Jew; and we increased the return from the toll and exchange by another ten *solidi* to be used for the improvement of the manor without having to im-

2. Derived from the Roman coin first issued by Emperor Constantine, the medieval *solidus* was a monetary unit equal in value to one-twentieth of a pound. It later became the English shilling and the French *sous*.

3. Montmorency is located in the Val d'Oise, Île-de-France, about seven miles northwest of Saint-Denis. It is today an affluent suburb of Paris. In medieval times, it was a fief of the Montmorency family. For the location of the possessions of Saint-Denis, see below, "The Possessions of the Abbey of Saint-Denis in the Twelfth Century," figure, 70. Montlignon is located in the Val d'Oise, Île-de-France, about eight miles northwest of Saint-Denis. Of Scandinavian origin, the mark was equivalent to eight ounces of silver, about two-thirds of the English pound.

pose further exactions.⁴ Therefore, when the ten *solidi* of the Jew and the ten *solidi* of the new increase from the toll and exchange became fixed for every week of the year, this increase of twenty *solidi* amounted to fifty-two pounds annually, with another twenty pounds coming from the manor. The tax on the manor that used to bring in twelve pounds on the octave of Saint Denis now brings in twenty pounds or more.⁵ So, we allocated eight pounds of this increase for the care of the infirm brothers and another eight pounds as well from a house erected in the meat market, after we purchased an additional house there for the butchers' use. So, we now had ninety pounds. The toll used to yield twenty pounds whereas it had even at one time yielded forty pounds. However, we frequently collected seventy pounds from it, and we could have easily collected more each year if we had not banned plundering and anathematized those who do it.

From the revenues of the Lendit Fair[ii] that the Lord Louis's father gave to Saint-Denis, we quietly and peacefully allocated three hundred *solidi* for the refreshment of the brothers on the feast of the blessed Apostles Peter and Paul.⁶ For the same purpose we dedicated another thirty-five from the tax on the bakers' stalls in the Pantera as well as ten *solidi* from my nephew Girard, with five of his ten coming from his household and another five coming from the toll on his madder.⁷ We gained another tax of fifteen *solidi* from three dwellings located in the courtyards of the house of William of Cornillon that I acquired for eighty pounds; two other dwellings located there were still vacant.⁸ We collected an additional seventy *solidi*

---

4. Matthew (1100–1160) was the lord of Montmorency where the Jew, his tenant and subject, resided. Derived from a Roman unit, a *modius* was a dry measure roughly equivalent to a peck, which was eight dry quarts.

5. October 9. The octave is the eighth day after a feast, counting all the days inclusively. It thus always falls on the same day of the week as the feast.

6. June 29. For the donation of the proceeds of the Lendit Fair outside on the highway given by King Louis VI to Saint-Denis in 1124, see Suger, *The Deeds*, 131.

7. Madder is an herb used to produce a red dye. Pantera square was located in front of the main entrance of the Church of Saint-Denis. Stalls were erected there to sell a variety of merchandise. See above, *The Consecration*, IV, 43.

8. Cornillon, Seine-et-Marne, Île-de-France is located about fifty miles southwest of Saint-Denis. William of Cornillon and his son William were friends of Abbot Suger.

from the tax on the new tenants in the vacant area of the small courtyard of the brothers. There was a courtyard outside the village where no tenant had ever resided, but sergeants protected it at their own expense.ⁱⁱⁱ We realized an increase of twenty pounds annually from this courtyard and another new one adjacent to it after eighty or more new tenants moved into them. In addition, we planted and cultivated there at Saint-Lucien an expensive enclosed vineyard estimated to be nearly eighty arpents because our church greatly needed it.[9] We granted to it those twenty pounds from the courtyards in order to cultivate it properly and thus greatly benefit our church. A lack of wine had often caused us to deliberately pawn out all kinds of things, including crosses, chalices, and liturgical vestments, at many places as well as at Lagny.[10]

The increase from the mills at the abbey's fortified town never failed to yield eight *mines* of grain daily for the refectory of the brothers when previously they had usually yielded only five every day.[11] After an accurate tabulation, the increase each week amounted to thirty-nine and one-half *modii*. The monetary increase came to one hundred forty-six pounds and ten *solidi*. We acquired a house just outside the gate of Paris towards Saint-Merri for one thousand *solidi* because we were frequently involved in the affairs of the kingdom and deemed it a suitable and respectable lodging for our horses and us, as well as for our successors.[12] This gate of Paris that used to return twelve pounds now pays us fifty, which represents an increase of thirty-eight pounds.

The abbot used the rent from these houses to illuminate three chapels in the renovated abbey church; see *Oeuvres* (ed. Lecoy), Charter X, 357. William of Cornillon is also mentioned in *The Consecration*, IV, 44. See also Grant, "Abbot Suger," 223; *Abbot Suger* (ed. Panofsky), 219–20; and *Oeuvres* (ed. Gasparri), 1:186n43.

9. Saint-Lucien, Eure-et-Loir, Centre is located about fifty-one miles southwest of Saint-Denis. Eighty arpents is about sixty-eight acres.

10. Lagny-sur-Marne, Seine-et-Marne, Île-de-France is located about twelve miles southeast of Saint-Denis.

11. Twenty-four *mines* equal one *modius*; see *Oeuvres* (ed. Gasparri), 1:61n20.

12. Saint-Merri is today a small church on the Right Bank of the Seine located about eight miles south of Saint-Denis. It is dedicated to Saint Medericus who came to Paris on a pilgrimage and died there in 700 A.D.; he is today the patron saint of the Right Bank.

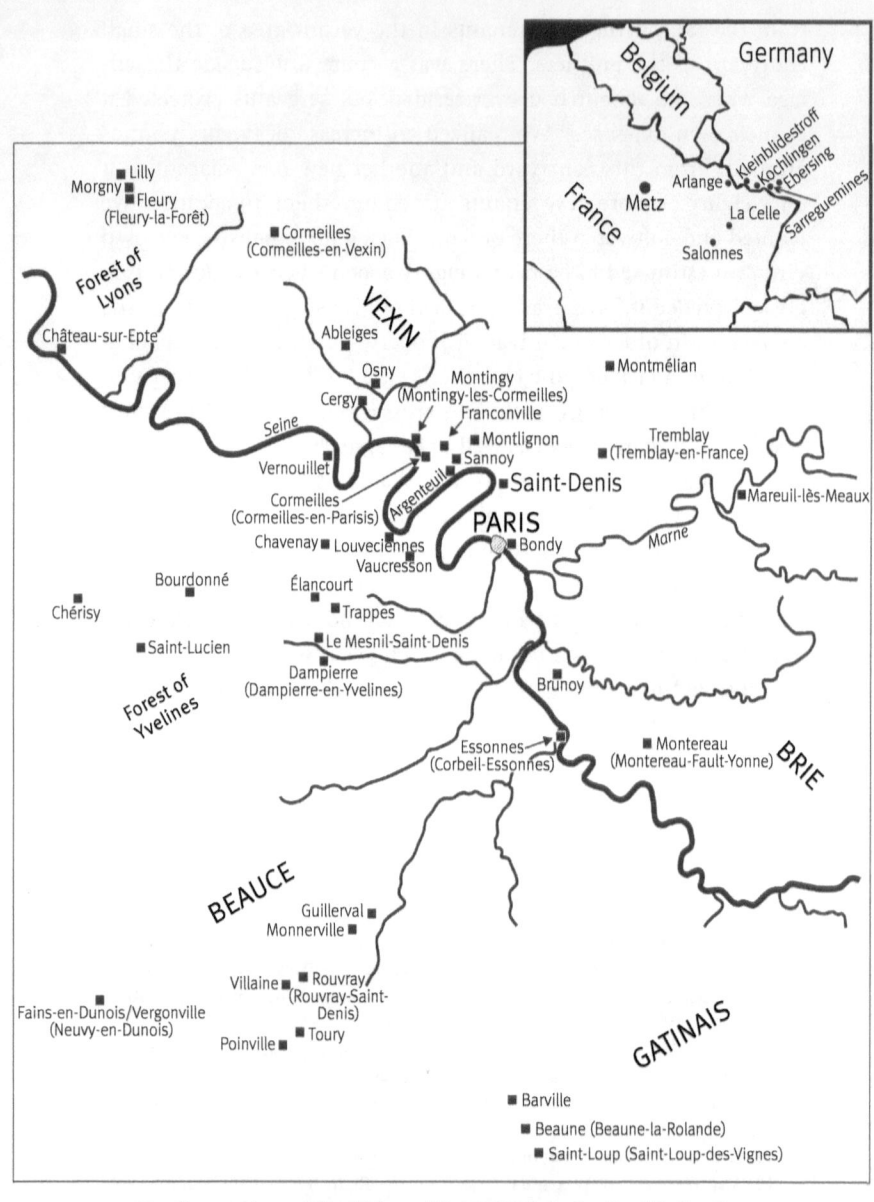

The Possessions of the Abbey of Saint-Denis in the Twelfth Century

II

Tremblay. The count of Dammartin was harassing the manor of Tremblay by exacting many services, one of which was a tallage[iv] of five *modii* of grain that I had granted him in return for peace.[13] He had the habit of collecting a tallage whenever he wished; for example he demanded rams and his right of hospitality in the manor's village many times every year at the expense of the villeins. So we reached an accord with the count that would eliminate all these burdens and thus allow the entire manor to be left in peace for us without any exaction or customary duty, and in return for his homage[v] we would give him ten pounds annually from our purse on the octave of Saint Denis.[14] We then eagerly built additions to that village, erecting a new courtyard with a new granary at its entrance to store our shares of the crop from every villein and the grain from four *carrucates* of our land.[vi] We stored the grain from the tithes on the tenement lands in the other granary inside the village wall, and we reserved the straw in each granary for our own use. But hardly ever were we able to collect ninety *modii* of grain from that manor; so we had no alternative but to have our steward pay us one hundred ninety *modii* in addition to what the villeins produced. The villeins also furnished anything the ploughmen and oxen required, and supplied the oxen and everything needed for the wheeled ploughs. In return they kept the revenue from the oven.

We, however, kept our tax, the *tensamentum*, the *mortmain*, the forfeitures, and a tallage whenever we wanted.[vii] The increase of grain here amounted to ninety *modii*. We surrounded the old courtyard with a wall and erected there an easily defended house that was connected to the church. With this fortification our successors will be able to defend their dependents and their possessions against every enemy if they so deemed.

---

13. Dammartin-en-Goële, Seine-et-Marne, Île-de-France is located about twenty-two miles northeast of Saint-Denis. The count mentioned here is Alberic I (ca. 1100–ca. 1181/83). Tremblay-en-France, Seine-Saint-Denis, Île-de-France is located about twelve miles to the northeast of Saint-Denis. Part of the Charles de Gaulle airport is located there today.

14. October 16.

III

The repossession of the abbey of Argenteuil.[viii] I used to read the ancient charters of possessions in the archives during my studies while growing up, and I became well acquainted with the registers of immunities because of the dishonest acts of numerous defrauders.[ix] The convent of Argenteuil's charter of foundation by Hermenricus and his wife Numma came frequently into my hands, and it stated that the convent belonged to Saint-Denis from the time of King Pepin.[x] But our abbey lost it because of an unfortunate contract during the reign of his son Charlemagne. This emperor had acquired Argenteuil from our abbot and brothers in order to put one of his daughters, who refused an earthly marriage, as abbess over the nuns there; but the contract stipulated that after her death Argenteuil would return to our church.[xi] However, the upheaval of the kingdom and the dispute among his grandsons, the sons of Louis the Pious, which has lasted until this day, did not allow the contract to be fulfilled.[xii]

My predecessors had often tried to resolve this matter but had little success. So, having consulted with my brothers for advice, I sent messengers to carry to Pope Honorius of good memory at Rome the old foundation and donation charters regarding Argenteuil as well as the confirmation of our privileges.[15] We asked the pope to investigate our jurisdiction at Argenteuil according to canon law and, after interrogation, to restore the convent to us. The pope, who was a man of good judgment and a defender of justice, restored that place to us with its dependencies because of our just claims and the irregular conduct of the nuns who were living there in sin. He wanted to reform religious life in that convent. King Louis, son of Philip and our dearest lord and friend, confirmed that restitution to us, and using the authority of his royal majesty he affirmed with a

---

15. Honorius II was pope from December 21, 1124, to February 13, 1130. Foundation charters recorded the actual foundation of a property, and donation charters recorded gifts to it. A privilege was an exemption to law or custom. For further information concerning this dispute over the priory, see Thomas G. Waldmann, "Abbot Suger and the Nuns of Argenteuil," *Traditio* 41 (1985): 239–72.

charter whatever royal temporalities he had there.[16] Anyone who wishes to learn the exact contents of this restitution can find it in greater detail in the charters of the kings and the papal privileges. The prelates who will competently handle these affairs in the future will be able to know what a great increase of revenue our abbey derived from the convent of Argenteuil and its dependencies. Those dependent properties are Trappes, Élancourt, Chavenay, Bourdonné, Chérisy, and the manors of Montmélian, Bondy, and Montereau near Melun, among others.[xiii]

The old tax of Argenteuil, which had not belonged to the abbey, increased by twenty pounds, for we would have had only twenty pounds from it in the past, but it now returns forty. Previously we would have had six *modii* of grain, but we now receive fifteen.

IV

The Vexin. According to the privileges of immunity of the church, the renowned county of Vexin that lies between the Oise and Epte Rivers was held by Saint-Denis in fief.[17] When King Louis of the French, son of Philip, rushed against the Roman emperor,[xiv] who was invading the French kingdom, King Louis asserted before the full chapter of Saint-Denis that he held the Vexin from the saint and, if he were not king, he would perform homage to him as his lawful standard-bearer.[xv] We endeavored with the help of God to enlarge this domain with the following extensions. We obtained the church of Cergy and the franchise of its court from King Louis.[18] From his son Louis during the dedication of that church, we received jurisdiction as agent over the village and all its returns, except wine and oats.[19] The younger Louis gave us all this from his royal generosity, for the salvation of his soul, and for the protection

16. Philip I, king of France (r. 1060–1108). For this charter of April 14, 1129, see *Louis VI* (ed. Luchaire), no. 431 (199–200) and no. 433 (200–201).
17. A privilege of immunity is a special right or exemption granted to a person or entity to free the grantee from certain obligations or liabilities.
18. Cergy, Val-d'Oise, Île-de-France is located about eighteen miles northwest of Saint-Denis.
19. Louis VII, king of France (r. 1137–80).

of his person and the kingdom. King Louis also devoutly gave to the Holy Martyrs his possessions at Cormeilles and Osny, and everything he held at Trappes,[20] except his right of lodging.[xvi]

However, we laid out large sums of money on these and many other acquisitions, especially for the continual care and maintenance of our half of the plough-land. We had to cultivate the land and vineyards; we had to check the greed of mayors and sergeants, and to repel ruthless attacks from dishonest advocates, which cost us huge expenses equipping our soldiers[xvii] during the early days of our abbacy.[21] Our brothers had been content to receive five *solidi* each day to operate the kitchen during the administration of my predecessors; but with the help of God, I used the abundant increase of revenues to give them without fail an additional five *solidi* daily, as well as another fourteen *solidi* for their refreshment on Thursdays and Saturdays. Up to now the surplus from our increase normally exceeds one hundred *modii* of grain. So we decided to distribute this surplus for our own needs, those of the churches, the poor after Easter and at other useful times, for example during the last months of the year when the higher price of grain usually brings hardship to ill-prepared communities. Every year the increase of revenue amounted to one hundred fourteen pounds and twelve *solidi*.

V

Cormeilles-en-Parisis.[22] The increase of the tax from Cormeilles in the countryside of Paris was eight pounds; in the past we collected twelve pounds, but now we collect twenty. We used to have ten or twelve *modii* of grain from there, but now we have eighteen. We received four pounds from the increase of the new tax at Sannois and

20. Cormeilles-en-Vexin, Val-d'Oise, Île-de-France is located about twenty-three miles northwest of Saint-Denis. Osny, Val-d'Oise, Île-de-France is located about twenty-one miles northwest of Saint-Denis. Trappes, Yvelines, Île-de-France is located about twenty-five miles southwest of Saint-Denis.

21. Sergeants were warriors beneath the rank of knights who fought either mounted or on foot. Advocates were lords who acted as patrons. They vowed to protect a monastery or church from its secular enemies.

22. Cormeilles-en-Parisis, Val-d'Oise, Île-de-France is located about thirteen miles northwest of Saint-Denis.

one hundred *solidi* from the old one.²³ We collected forty *solidi* from the new increase of the tax at Franconville and forty from the old one, in addition to acquiring the fief.²⁴ We gave the tithe from our fief that we had bought from Pagan of Gisors to the clerical churchwardens out of love for God, but we kept for ourselves the tithe of our enclosure.²⁵

VI

*Montigny.*²⁶ We collected fifty *solidi* from the new tax at Montigny and seventy from the old one.

VII

*Cergy.*²⁷ We acquired forty *solidi* from the tax on the woodland at Cergy and received the homage of the knight Theobald of Puiseux, and forty donkeys to pack goods.²⁸

VIII

*Louveciennes.*²⁹ As did our predecessors, we customarily leased in return for fifteen pounds whatever we collected at Louveciennes every year, including the tax, as well as the grain and the wine. We

---

23. Sannois, Val-d'Oise, Île-de-France is located about eight miles northwest of Saint-Denis.
24. Franconville, Val-d'Oise, Île-de-France is located about nine miles northwest of Saint-Denis.
25. Gisors, Eure, Upper Normandy is located about forty-two miles northwest of Saint-Denis. It is on the Norman side of the Epte River, which functioned as the boundary between the Norman and French Vexin. On Pagan (1075–1125), see further Suger, *The Deeds*, 26 and 71. The churchwardens were poor clerics who provided upkeep for the church at Cormeilles.
26. Montigny-les-Cormeilles, Val-d'Oise, Île-de-France is located about twelve miles northwest of Saint-Denis.
27. Cergy, Val d'Oise, Île-de-France is located about eighteen miles northwest of Saint-Denis.
28. Puiseux-Pontoise, Val-d'Oise, Île-de-France is located about twenty-one miles northwest of Saint-Denis.
29. Louveciennes, Yvelines, Île-de-France is located about fifteen miles southwest of Saint-Denis.

reached some agreements dealing with ancient manors that stopped the villeins who cultivated the vineyards from keeping the revenues, and thus acquired nearly one hundred *modii* of wine in addition to the annual tax in coin and grain.

IX

Vernouillet.[30] We redeemed Vernouillet that had been held in pawn for forty years, and now collect ten pounds from it when we would not have collected more than sixty *solidi* in the past.[xviii] We allocated the total revenues that we received from this place for the care of our sick brothers.

X

Vaucresson.[31] We built a village at Vaucresson, erected a church and a residence, and had the uncultivated land plowed. The men who worked hard to build the manor realize well how worthwhile the place is because there are now about sixty tenants living on it, and many others would willingly come there if someone would provide for it. More than two miles of abandoned land surrounded the manor, and so the location made a perfect den for thieves.[xix] Although totally useless for our church, it was just right for robbers and their henchmen because of the nearby woods. That is the reason we settled our brothers there to serve God, so that the lairs where dragons used to live would sprout forth the green shoots of the reed and the rush.[32]

Saint-Denis had a domain, consisting of the manors of Le Mesnil-Saint-Denis, Dampierre, and others in the valley of the castle called Chevreuse, that had had three tallages levied against it many times in the past, one by the lord of the castle of Chevreuse, another by the lord of the castle of Neauphle, and the third by Simon of Viltain.[33]

30. Vernouillet, Yvelines, Île-de-France is located about twenty-four miles west of Saint-Denis.

31. Vaucresson, Hauts-de-Seine, Île-de-France is located about fifteen miles southwest of Saint-Denis.

32. Is 35:7.

33. Le Mesnil-Saint-Denis, Yvelines, Île-de-France is located about twenty-nine

The greed of these men had nearly ruined the domain, but we freed it from this sort of oppressive exaction at great expense, granting to these men only what belonged to their right of advocacy. In the same way we recovered our hunting rights in Yvelines within the boundaries of the land that they had many times unlawfully usurped from Saint-Denis.[34] We assembled our true friends and vassals, namely Count Amalric of Evreux and Montfort,[xx] Simon of Neauphle, Evrard of Villepreux, and many others to prevent this recovery from being lost to memory forever, and we went to Yvelines and stayed there in tents for an entire week.[35] Each day during that week we had a large number of deer taken to Saint-Denis, not for any slight reason but to recover this right of our church. We had the deer distributed among the infirm brothers, the visitors in the guesthouse, and the knights in the village also to prevent this right from being lost to memory forever. We gave the office of advocate for our land, one-half of the forest, and one hundred *solidi* every year to the lord of Chevreuse, our vassal, so to speak, to prevent him from restoring a tallage or oppressing the land; but we kept the ancient domain for ourselves.[36] We can collect those one hundred *solidi* from that land whenever we wish, without any objection.

We have made the effort to write about the following possession

---

miles southwest of Saint-Denis. Dampierre-en-Yvelines, Yvelines, Île-de-France is located about twenty-three miles southwest of Saint-Denis. Chevreuse, Yvelines, Île-de-France is located about twenty-one miles southwest of Saint-Denis. Construction of the castle there began in 1020 under the direction of Guy I of Montlhéry (d. 1095). The castle, called La Madeleine, still stands as modified in later centuries. The exact descendent of Guy collecting this tallage mentioned here is uncertain. Neauphle-le-Château, Yvelines, Île-de-France is located about thirty miles southwest of Saint-Denis. The lord mentioned here was Simon III of Neauphle who died about 1150. Viltain is today La Ferme de Viltain, Yvelines, Île-de-France, which is located about twenty-one miles south of Saint-Denis.

34. Yvelines was a forested area located just to the southwest of Paris. It is today a French department. For further information on the Yvelines, see *The Consecration,* III, 42n19.

35. Simon III of Neauphle and his wife, Eve, founded the Cistercian abbey of Vaux-de-Cernay in the valley of Chevreuse. He also rebuilt the castle of Neauphle after King Louis VI destroyed it in 1125. Simon died in about 1150. Villepreux, Yvelines, Île-de-France is located about twenty miles southwest of Saint-Denis. Evrard of Villepreux, lord of La Ferté (d. 1169), was a knight and friend of Suger.

36. Milo III (ca. 1075–ca. 1147).

in Beauce to prevent the result of our labor from being totally lost to memory, for we worked hard to enlarge it with the help of God.[37] Saint-Denis's first manor was Guillerval near Saclas, and the list of King Dagobert[xxi] shows that he gave both places to our abbey.[38] The manor had been disorganized for a long time or perhaps always was, for it did not have a house where the abbot might rest his head, a granary, or any demesne land on the entire estate.[xxii] Every year the inhabitants paid a small tax for their houses and only twenty-five *modioli* of grain, an amount that did not equal four of our *modii*, as the tax on the lands they cultivated.[39] So, we agreed to improve this manor out of love for our lords, the Holy Martyrs, and purchased for the church three *carucates* of land on that estate.[40] A great war between John of Étampes, the son of Pagan who was a noble and valiant man, and a knight of Pithiviers had disrupted this manor for over forty years.[41] So, we paid each of these men a large amount of money and purchased the manor for our church so that neither of them would possess what each of them was fighting over. We kept it for ourselves and so put an end to the war; and with the consent of these men's relatives and friends, namely Baldwin of Corbeil and many others, we had our rights to the manor confirmed by a charter.[42]

We were delighted by the charm of this new land, especially the middle part of the village, and were pleased with the refreshing springs and rushing streams nearby. We enclosed the beautiful

37. Beauce, one of France's best agricultural regions, with wheat as its principal crop, is in northern France between Paris and Orléans. Chartres is its principal city.

38. Guillerval and Saclas are in the Essonne department, Île-de-France and are located about forty-eight miles south of Saint-Denis.

39. A *modiolus* is a short measure of a *modius*, and both are dry measures of grain. Suger indicates here that twenty-five of them did not equal four *modii* as his abbey measured them.

40. See endnote vi below.

41. Étampes, Essonne, Île-de-France is located about forty-two miles south of Saint-Denis. John of Étampes was the son of Isembard (called Pagan) of Étampes and Aelis of Corbeil. His wife was Eustachie of Châtillon. Pithiviers, Loiret, Centre is located about sixty miles south of Saint-Denis.

42. Corbeil-Essonnes, Essonnes, Île-de-France is located about thirty-two miles south of Saint-Denis.

courtyard with a wall, built a strong and defensible house in it, and constructed granaries and everything necessary for the manor, all at tremendous cost. We traveled around nearly the whole circuit of upper Beauce filling every fishpond with a great supply of fish to relieve the effects of a drought. We placed two wheeled ploughs on that manor, one for the new land and the other for the old; and we improved a manor that had been worth hardly anything, to make it able to yield fifty or more *modii* of grain every year. Then we ceased collecting the small tax the inhabitants were previously paying on their houses and kept for ourselves a share of the crop from the entire estate, except from the plow-land held by the steward. In return, the steward pledged to totally resolve any complaints from the villeins or problems that arose from the change of customs.

XI

Monnerville.[43] The manor of Monnerville, close to Guillerval, also belonged to Saint-Denis; and it was in the worst condition of them all. Tyranny from the castle of Méréville had reduced it to beggary and had beaten it down just as if Saracens had sacked it.[44] The lord of the castle abused his right of lodging in the village by taking it whenever he wished and bringing with him whomever he pleased.[45] He greedily devoured the goods of the villeins and carried away his exaction of grain at harvest time as if it were customary practice. He gathered his stacks of wood two or three times a year to the loss of the manor's demesne land and exacted all kinds of unbearable burdens by taking tallages on pigs, lambs, geese, and chickens as if this were also customary practice. After this severe and lengthy oppression had nearly reduced the village to a wilderness, we decided to boldly resist him and not stop until we had rid this holy inheritance from his harassments.[xxiii] When we took him to court, he claimed

---

43. Monnerville, Essonnes, Île-de-France is located about forty-nine miles south of Saint-Denis.
44. Méréville, Essonnes, Île-de-France is located about fifty-two miles south of Saint-Denis.
45. Hugh of Méréville (d. ca. 1186). He was the son of Guy I of Méréville, viscount of Étampes. On the right of lodging, see below, endnote xvi.

that he had inherited these customary rights from his father, grandfather, and great-grandfather. However, we settled the issue in the following way, with the help of God and some advice from our vassals and friends. After his wife, sons, and the Lord King Louis, from whom he said he held the manor, consented to the settlement, the lord of the castle, Hugh, acknowledged his injustice and under sworn oath totally ceded, remitted, and renounced forever all these customary rights in favor of Saint-Denis, as a charter of the Lord King Louis shows in great detail.[xxiv] We, however, wanted to retain his homage to our church; so we granted him two *modii* of grain by the measure used at Étampes, one of wheat and the other of oats that he could pick up in our courtyard from one of our monks or servants. Once freed from torment, this manor, which had barely rendered us ten or fifteen pounds, now usually renders from our stewards one hundred *modii* of grain each year by the measure used at Étampes, which is often worth one hundred pounds, depending on the price of grain.

In the same way we strove to improve the manor called Rouvray that was rendered completely destitute from the burden of services it rendered to the castle of Le Puiset.[46] One day after the destruction of the castle, Lord Hugh of Le Puiset met with us and suggested that we cultivate and share equally with him the produce of the uncultivated land that had been reduced to a wilderness by oppression from the castle.[xxv] We refused his offer although some felt it would be to our advantage, and we strove to accomplish by ourselves for the profit of the church the task that we declined to do with him. We could not bring ourselves to restore the land with a partner who, we deeply felt, destroyed it just as his ancestors had done. Hugh and his ancestors had forcefully exacted from that land the very customs that we listed at Monnerville, for example the tallage on grain, pigs, sheep, lambs, geese, hens, chickens, and wood; and thus he had left the land totally infertile and worthless for both him and us. However, we built a walled homestead on that barren land, erected a

---

46. Rouvray-Saint-Denis, Eure-et-Loir, Centre is located about fifty-six miles south of Saint-Denis, and Le Puiset, Eure-et-Loir, Centre is located about sixty-eight miles south.

tower over the gate to ward off robbers, and set aside three *carucates* there to alleviate the misery of the land and the loss to our church.

We restored the manor named Villaine, returned the disordered land to order, and so improved it that it returned to us one hundred pounds per year, and on many occasions one hundred twenty pounds, when previously it barely rendered twenty.[47] We justly attributed these great benefits to the Holy Martyrs; and, with a sealed charter, we allocated from the fruit of our labor eighty pounds every year to the construction of their church until it was completed. We also eliminated the bad custom of the straw tax that was held by the viscount of Étampes.[48]

XII

Toury.[49] Toury, a well-known manor belonging to Saint-Denis, was the principal one among others and a unique and special estate of Saint-Denis, which provided nourishing food to pilgrims, merchants, and other travelers on the public highway. It was also a relaxing place for the weary. While still a young man, I had undertaken as provost to provide for that estate during the time of our predecessor, Abbot Adam of good memory.[xxvi] It was at that time so pitifully run down by the crushing exactions imposed by the lords of the castle of Le Puiset that it languished, almost completely deserted by its villeins, and lay wide open to extortions from the men of Le Puiset, like meat served to the people of Ethiopia.[50] This important farmstead of Saint-Denis could never adequately protect itself to prevent Lord Hugh from crushing it through his minions. With no regard for sacrilege he carried off whatever he found and threw the neighboring villages into chaos by frequently taking his right of food and lodging.[51] He imposed tallages in grain, one for himself, another for his sen-

47. Villaine, Eure-et-Loir, Centre is today an isolated farmstead located to the west of Rouvray-Saint-Denis.
48. Suger uses the word *palagium* here that seems to be the same as *paleagium*, which is the straw tribute. The viscount was Guy I of Méréville.
49. Toury, Seine-et-Loir, Centre is located about sixty-one miles south of Saint-Denis.
50. Ps 73:14. Some Ethiopians were thought to be cannibalistic.
51. See below, endnote xvi.

eschal and another for his provost, and had them carried to his castle by imposing transport duties on the villeins.⁵² Those who lived there could barely survive under the weight of such despotic tyranny.

After I lived there for nearly two years, these and other evil acts wore me down, as also did the misery people suffered and the losses our church incurred. We were not the only ones, for all the churches that held land in this region were burdened in the same way. For this reason we met; and, after considerable deliberation, decided how we could avoid the unbearable yoke and tyranny of this wicked castle. Our efforts helped influence the venerable Bishop Ivo of Chartres, the chapter of Notre-Dame, the abbot of Saint-Père, the Church of Saint-Jean-en-Vallée, the bishop of Orléans, the Church of Saint-Aignan, the abbot of Saint-Benoît, and the archbishop of Sens.[xxvii] We went before the glorious King Louis, each one of us on his own behalf, and tearfully informed him about the plundering of the churches, the despair of the poor and orphans, and the loss of alms that he and his predecessors had given to the churches. The king was a man of remarkable zeal, who was totally devoted to duty, and a distinguished defender of churches. So he promised to help us and pledged, on oath, that he would absolutely not allow this evil man to destroy churches and church properties. The reader can find in the deeds of this king the details of his splendid actions, the effort and revenues he expended, and the gravity of what he accomplished.⁵³

The castle of Le Puiset was completely destroyed in just retribution for its crimes; and our land of the Saints, as well as other lands, regained their earlier freedom; and lands laid barren by war once again flourished in peace. No longer fallow, the land returned to fertile cultivation. After the death of our predecessor of good memory, Abbot Adam, I was elevated to the office of abbot of this sacred ministry, although I was unworthy and not present.⁵⁴ However, I did not

---

52. A seneschal was an official in a noble household that made all domestic arrangements and supervised the servants. He sometimes administered justice as well.

53. See Suger, *The Deeds*, 95.

54. Abbot Adam of Saint-Denis, 1099–1122, died on February 19. When Suger was elected as his successor, he was on a mission on behalf of King Louis VI to Pope Calixtus II, 1119–24; see further Suger, *The Deeds*, 122.

forget my former zeal and efforts, and firmly undertook to enlarge Toury, because I had resided there for a long time as provost. In the courtyard that I strengthened with a palisade of stakes and interlaced branches, I erected a walled castle and had a fortified tower built over the main gate. I constructed suitably equipped fortified houses and preserved intact the freedom of the village and the entire land.

One day when I was hurrying to Orléans with a band of knights to catch up with the Lord King, I discovered that the provost of Le Puiset had reverted to the earlier evil deeds; so I shamed him by taking him captive and transported him, chained and disgraced, to Saint-Denis.[55] The property of churches should grow, and prelates should carefully maintain them during a time of peace. Thus after retaining the tithes, we set the rents that the villeins who lived there had to pay for the tillable lands that we held in demesne at Toury; and we ordered that these rents be written down so that they will never be forgotten. To show how much the proceeds of Toury increased through our efforts, we now receive eighty pounds every year from the provost of this estate that used to return not more than twenty pounds. The customary duties improved every day, which easily explain this increase of profit.[xxviii]

The ancient advocacy of this land belonged from antiquity to La Ferté-Baudouin that cruelly oppressed it for a long time.[56] When there appeared no other way to refute this advocacy, it just so happened that a young woman, the granddaughter of Adam of Pithiviers, received it by hereditary right. Having learned this, we took the advice of our friends and sought at great expense to give her in marriage in the way we wished. We arranged that the young woman and the advocacies be given to a young man from our household, to end the turmoil in the land and prevent the usual troubles from the native people from distressing her. As stipulated in the contract,

---

55. This provost was an official of Hugh III of Le Puiset.
56. The modern La Ferté-Alais, Essonne, Île-de-France is located about forty-five miles south of Saint-Denis on the Essonne River. Suger covers in detail King Louis's siege of this castle, then held by Hugh of Crécy, in Suger, *The Deeds*, 64–68. Advocates were lords who acted as patrons. They vowed to protect a monastery or church from its secular enemies. They were supposed to protect church properties, not abuse them.

we paid one hundred pounds from the funds of Saint-Denis to the husband as well as to the father and mother of the young woman, with the approval of the Lord King Louis who held this advocacy in fief. In exchange for this and another thirty pounds that the Lord King would thereafter receive, they, as well as their successors, would forever perform for us and our successors homage, service, and justice whenever we demanded it of them.[xxix] If they fail to do this, we can fully retain the entire fief of the advocacy, as if it were our own, until they give us satisfaction, as they and their parents conceded and the Lord King approved. We have listed below the fiefs that we purchased with our own revenues to provide garrison services for two months every year in the castle of Toury.

XIII

Poinville.[57] For this reason we acquired Poinville that Geoffrey the Red held from his kinsman, Berard of Ensonville, so that Berard might hold it in fief as our vassal.[58]

XIV

Fains and Vergonville.[59] Likewise, we purchased another possession called Fains and Vergonville along with other dependent villages from Galeran of Breteuil,[xxx] his wife Judith, and his son Evrard, a valiant man who died on the military expedition to Jerusalem, at the great cost of nearly one hundred fifty marks of silver.[60] One might say we recovered it because it had belonged to Saint-Denis as a gift from Hubert of Saint-Gaury since ancient times. We granted it to the almonry of Saint-Denis, trusting in the mercy of God that those alms distributed to the poor will mercifully obtain for us the

---

57. Poinville, Eure-et-Loir, Centre is located about seventy miles southwest of Saint-Denis.
58. Ensonville, Eure-et-Loir, Centre is located about forty-nine miles southwest of Saint-Denis in the heart of Beauce.
59. Fains and Vergonville are today called Neuvy-en-Dunois, Eure-et-Loir, Centre, which is located about eighty-two miles southwest of Saint-Denis.
60. See Odo, *De profectione*, 52 and n37.

gift of divine reward from Almighty God, for it is said that alms extinguish sin like water extinguishes fire.[61] We had this donation confirmed by a charter of King Louis; and then placed it in the public archives, so that the alms may firmly serve the needs of the poor forever.

XV

Beaune.[62] Beaune in the district of Gâtinais is known as one of the better possessions of Saint-Denis, among all the others there. It spreads out for nearly four leagues, produces an abundance of grain and wine, and is ideal for growing every kind of fruit. It also abounds with all kinds of goods, if it is not abused by the Lord King's sergeants or our own.[63] It lacked inhabitants and remained uncultivated because of the negligence of its stewards, and had fallen into such poverty that it could not even pay the expenses of the shoe-making shop of this church. The estate fell into the hands of our abbot through forfeiture of a debt, and he leased all of it to the sergeants of the district for thirty pounds a year. At the beginning of our prelacy we found Beaune destroyed and nearly reduced to a wilderness. So we informed our most dear Lord King Louis of the French, whose honor we strove to serve devotedly and faithfully, about this great loss to our church. The king had imposed oppressive and nearly destructive services in that district, which included the provision of lodging three times per year, one from a levy on the villeins that was enough for himself and his officials, and two from the revenues owed him by Saint-Denis. This burden totally exhausted the district. The king was a man of exceptional generosity; so he took pity on this great loss to the church and the sufferings of the poor, and released this dependency of the church and us forever from these services out of gratitude for our

---

61. Sir 3:33. The almonry was the place or room in an abbey, church, or other church building where alms (i.e., money, food, clothing, or other things of value) were distributed.

62. Beaune-la-Rolande, Loiret, Centre is located about seventy-one miles south of Saint-Denis.

63. Sergeants were warriors beneath the rank of knights, who fought either mounted or on foot.

love and service to him.[64] However, he confirmed to us, by a charter from his royal majesty, the levy of eight pounds per year that he had from the villeins. Rejoicing at his gift, we reclaimed the lands that the mayor and others had usurped and alienated from us, returning them to the plows after twenty years, and replanted the vineyards at Saint-Loup.[65] We restored other vineyards near Beaune that were almost destroyed, and purchased additional ones from one of our vassals for twenty pounds minted at Orléans. We repopulated villages that were totally depopulated by plunder.

XVI

The tithe of Barville.[66] Despite some losses, we recovered the tithe of Barville as best we could, along with some others, for the benefit of the Church. Certain knights asserted that this tithe, which produces twenty or thirty *modii* of grain for us each year, had been their right to collect for a hundred years, in return for paying a tax of two *solidi*. The houses of the demesne were dilapidated and had fallen to total ruin, but one event above all else persuaded us to have them rebuilt as elegantly and defensibly as they are now. After I had decided to establish our rights over that residence, one day when I was elsewhere, as God willed, a house collapsed catastrophically and completely crushed even the bed on which I would have been lying had I been there. The floor of the upper room and the casks and containers of wine in the storeroom were also destroyed. After seeing such great ruin, everyone firmly believed that the mercy of God had spared me. We built a very good granary there and dug two ponds that, if well maintained, will adequately provide, for a long time, a large supply of fish for those arriving there. The number of improvements to the land and the amount of misery alleviated, with God's help, is very evident; for it now often returns more than two hundred pounds, when previously, it had returned only thirty.

---

64. See *Louis VI* (ed. Luchaire), no. 111 (135–36).
65. Saint-Loup-des-Vignes, Loiret, Centre is located about seventy-three miles south of Saint-Denis.
66. Barville, Loiret, Centre is located about seventy miles south of Saint-Denis.

XVII

The burg of Essonnes that is now Corbeil.[67] The burg of Essonnes, which is located on the Essonne River, belonged to Saint-Denis. It had been given to the Holy Martyrs by the ancient generosity of the kings, as is written in their ancient charters. However, the brutality of a certain tyrant transferred it to the castle of Corbeil; and thus he strove to disinherit the Holy Martyrs on earth, and himself from a place in heaven.

XVIII

La Celle was built in the place called Champs. After many years, nearly two hundred or more, since the mother Church of Essonnes that is now the parish of Corbeil was, like some kind of statue, the only thing left standing in that place, the bishops of Paris removed it from Saint-Denis out of jealousy of the liberty the monastery always enjoyed;[xxxi] and to brazenly support their action, they gave it to Cluny[xxxii] and its daughter-houses—Saint-Martin-des-Champs[xxxiii] and the church of Gournay.[68] But those tyrants of the castle of Corbeil were hardened in their wickedness, and so shamefully appropriated everything for themselves that they hardly left anything behind except a barren land; and with blatant sacrilege they confiscated everything for their own use, as if they were the rightful owners. A partially ruined chapel dedicated to the Blessed Mary, as people report, was still standing there in the place called Champs.[69] It was the smallest one I have ever seen. There was an ancient, abandoned altar in the chapel, upon which sheep and goats often munch the thick grass growing on its top. Many people have sworn that they have often seen candles burning there on Saturdays, which is a sign of the sanctity of the place. The chapel inspired native inhabitants

---

67. Corbeil-Essonnes, Essonne, Île-de-France is located about thirty-three miles south of Saint-Denis.
68. Gournay-sur-Marne, Seine-Saint-Denis, Île-de-France is located about thirteen miles southeast of Saint-Denis.
69. Notre-Dame-des-Champs, Corbeil-Essonnes, Île-de-France is a few miles south of Corbeil-Essonnes and is located about thirty-two miles south of Saint-Denis.

who were sick, and afterwards even many people born elsewhere, to rush to it, seeking to be healed; and they were healed. But as God willed, when the place became overcrowded with many people from near and far, our venerable brothers, prior Herveus,[xxxiv] and Odo of Torcy, men of good memory, were sent there to serve our Lord and His Blessed Mother.[70] Their mission was to renovate and make that small place suitable for divine worship. To the amazement of all, a large number of miracles soon occurred there in a short period of time; thus everyone cherished and praised the site, and it grew rich from their gifts. A multitude of the sick, those troubled by unclean spirits, the blind, the lame, and the dispirited were cured there. The countless number of miracles the Blessed Mother of God has performed has honored this renowned place, and to add to its honor we have included below two recent miracles that we have seen or heard about.

XIX

The miracle of the mute person. The mother of one of our monks, the venerable Abbot Robert of Corbie, was a noble matron, widowed for many years, who routinely visited the shrines of saints for the salvation of her soul.[xxxv] She arrived at the chapel with a twelve-year-old girl, who had never been able to speak, and spent one Saturday night with the mute girl in that little church while she beseeched the divine ears relentlessly for herself and her own people. Then, when the brothers began the *Te Deum Laudamus*,[xxxvi] it was reported that a glorious queen as beautiful as the moon and as brilliant as the sun appeared to the girl, who was enrapt in ecstasy.[71] The queen was dressed in a royal gown and wore a crown of gold and precious gems as she crossed in front of the girl, moving from the left to the right side of the altar. When she lovingly called the girl by her very own name *"Lancendis,"* the matron and many others heard the girl answer "My Lady" in a clear voice and with unusual elo-

---

70. Odo was a monk at Saint-Denis. He came from Torcy, Seine-et-Marne, Île-de-France, which is located about twenty-four miles southeast of Saint-Denis.
71. Song 6:9.

quence. From then on she knew how to speak and could do so as if she had spoken her entire life. Those present glorified this astonishing miracle with the highest praise, and retold the story throughout the neighboring regions. We knew that the girl had been mute for five years before this event, and then we knew her for the next five years as being able to speak. Therefore, we should rightfully praise and esteem this holy place.

XX

The woman with dropsy. As we promised, we deem it worthwhile to relate the second miracle. A woman with dropsy, who was swollen as if she were pregnant, was constantly shouting out in pain like an insane person because she was suffering unbearable pressure from watery fluid; and so she was carried by the hands of friends to the Blessed Mary at the chapel. She lay in wait for many days before the holy altar, but the stench from her putrid and decayed body repelled many of the people arriving there. When there seemed to be no hope for her recovery because the swelling and the bloody fluid had already combined to make her face hideous, many of the healthy people as well as the sick ones started to complain and to respectfully demand that she be removed from the chapel. However, our venerable brothers preferred to mercifully tolerate her unwelcome presence rather than unmercifully take her away. One Sunday night when the divine hand is especially at work on such cases, the woman with dropsy happened to fall asleep, which was unusual for her. Then suddenly the glorious empress, the Virgin Mary, covertly drained the excessive fluid out through her womb and swiftly restored her to a slender and healthy state. What a sight! Our brothers and many others who were present saw such a large volume of fluid and mucus flowing onto the ground that they had to quickly carry it away with bowls, buckets, and pots. The people there were so amazed by the magnitude of this event that they praised Almighty God and His Mother with even greater devotion. They tearfully sang the *Te Deum Laudamus*, and humbly begged Almighty God to continue, as He had begun, to honor His Mother in that chapel.

Following these events and other miraculous and amazing signs, we chose to honor and glorify this extraordinary place, as God willed, out of love for the Mother of God and immediately began construction on the site. We appointed twelve brothers with a prior so that a community of brothers might serve God there, and constructed a cloister, a refectory, a dormitory, and other monastic buildings. We supplied the church with appropriate adornments, priestly vestments, altar coverings, and hooded cloaks. We had two books brought there from our mother church—an ancient daily office and the Gradual of Emperor Charlemagne. We sent over a fine three-volume set of Scriptures, and were just as concerned about providing food for the brothers; so we assigned them two demesne fields from our own land near the place.[xxxvii] We planted for them a very productive enclosed vineyard that was suitable for a large abbey, and acquired numerous vines for it by various means. At no cost to the place, we built and gave the brothers full ownership of four wine presses capable of producing nearly eighty *modii* of wine each, and even to this day the presses have provided such large volumes that they can generally enjoy anywhere from two hundred fifty to three hundred *modii* of wine.[72] We also had the meadows on our own pieces of land there dug up in places, and prepared gardens for the planting of vegetable seeds. Saint-Denis had another possession that yielded very little because it had been neglected for a long time. It lacked a steward but perhaps had been administered by an outside one from a neighboring village. Since it usually produced only a *modius* or less of grain and two or three *sextarii* of nuts, we placed three wheeled-plows in the new courtyard and built a new granary for the brothers.[73] The abundant pastures and improved lands allowed us to place sheep and cows there as well as feed for their nourishment. From our own holdings we pledged to them another possession of Saint-Denis near Brunoy from which they frequently receive ten *modii* of grain and nearly ten

---

72. A *modius*, in liquid measure, was about nine quarts.
73. A *sextarius* was roughly equivalent to a pint (liquid and dry); in dry measure the *sextarius* was about one-sixteenth of a *modius* (a *modius* is roughly a peck or eight dry quarts).

of wine, as well as hay for the draft animals.[74] We gave the brothers the proceeds we began to recover from a mill that had been inoperable for nearly sixty years, but on the condition that they pay twenty *solidi* to the refectory of Saint-Denis on the day after the feast day of Saint Denis.[75] The brothers also receive one hundred *solidi* from the taxes and tallages from that same village. They collect from the district around Corbeil seventeen pounds from taxes, in addition to the other revenues received from sales, fairs, miscellaneous customary duties, mills, and ovens as well as eight *modii* of oats, together with some chickens and an entire prebend from Saint-Spire.[76]

XXI

Mareuil.[77] The village of Mareuil in the district of Meaux suffered tremendous harassment from its seigneurial agent, Ansold of Cornillon, whose jurisdiction extended almost up to the houses themselves.[78] The peasants, as well as anyone else, did not dare risk leaving the village, for Ansold's sergeants would use all kinds of pretexts under his jurisdiction as agent to capture and lead them away to Ansold's court where they had to buy back the livestock straying away from the village. Therefore, for the peace of the village, we gave him a thousand *solidi* so that that he would surrender his seigneurial agency to us when he set out on the expedition to Jerusalem. We had this agency confirmed to us by the hand of Bishop Manasses of Meaux and his church, as well as by the seal of Count Theobald,[xxxviii] with the consent of his wife and his son, so that the

---

74. Brunoy, Essonnes, Île-de-France is located about twenty-five miles south of Saint-Denis.

75. October 10. The medieval French *solidus* (*sous*) was a monetary unit equivalent to one-twentieth of a *librum* (*livre*) and could be divided into twelve *denarii* (*derniers*).

76. A prebend is a stipend given to a cleric from the revenues of the church. Saint-Spire is a church in the town of Corbeil-Essonnes.

77. Mareuil-lès-Meaux, Seine-et-Marne, Île-de-France is located about thirty-two miles east of Saint-Denis.

78. Meaux, Seine-et-Marne, Île-de-France is on the Marne River and is located about twenty-eight miles east of Saint-Denis. Cornillon, Seine-et-Marne, Île-de-France is also situated on the Marne, just downriver from Meaux.

agency might from then on remain with Saint-Denis.[79] For Ansold confessed that he had held that agency unlawfully.

We also desired to make our successors aware of the terms of a certain exchange contract. Therefore, we took the trouble to record it so that the contract might be altered in the future, with the help of God, to our greater advantage. Ever since the noble kingdom of the French developed into a monarchy, the church of Saint-Denis flourished from the generosity of the kings, who gave it both numerous and great possessions as the royal power spread throughout the tetrarchy of the kingdom: Italy, Lotharingia, France, and Aquitaine.[xxxix] But division among their sons caused everything that unity held together to break apart into small pieces. For this reason, Saint-Denis lost Arlange, Ebersing, Salonnes[xl] and many other possessions as well as towns in the district of Metz—the burg of Guemines, Blidestroff, and Cochelingen.[xli] We frequently asserted our right to these possessions in the presence of the pope in order to recover them, citing the injustice and unsavory nature of the persons who were maliciously stealing those properties and dying unrepentant, without confessing their sins. The place called La Celle, with its dependencies named in the charters of the Emperor Louis, was given to Saint-Denis in full liberty in an exchange contract, and we placed our brothers there to serve God with the hope that it would grow and make a steady recovery.[80]

---

79. Manasses II was the bishop of Meaux (r. 1134–58). For this confirmation, see *Oeuvres* (ed. Lecoy), 371 (a charter of about 1140).

80. *Oeuvres* (ed. Lecoy), 183n2, identifies La Celle as a priory in the diocese of Metz that Emperor Louis the German (ca. 810–76) originally gave to Saint-Denis. See also ibid., 367, for the accord of 1125 between Suger and Mainard, count of Mosbach, involving a priory in Le Pays Messin (Moselle, Lorraine), a territorial entity in the neighborhood of Metz.

XXII

Chaumont.[81] We also strove to acquire from Archbishop Hugh of Rouen[82] and the Lord King Louis of the French the church of Saint-Pierre, located near the castle of Chaumont, as well as its abbey and the prebends of the canons after they died.[xlii] We also solemnly installed twelve brothers there and a thirteenth, the prior, to glorify this church and spread the divine worship; and we had that reverend archbishop consecrate this church and bless the cemetery in front of it, with God's approval. This new church was joined, like a noble member to its head, to the church of Saint-Denis; and it provided a suitable and ideal lodging for our successors as they traveled from the Vexin to Normandy, as well as for those staying in that district for the upkeep of our other possessions there. We will also make every effort to enrich it from our own resources or acquisitions and nourish it like a new seedling. We also confirmed to the brothers, who serve God there, twenty *modii* of wine every year from the tithes that the Lord King Louis gave us at Cergy, because they have no vineyards; and we also confirmed to them half of the tithe that we collected at Ableiges.[83]

XXIII

Berneval.[84] I received from my predecessor[85] my first administrative position as provost on the holding called Berneval on the coast of the Norman sea; and although I was still quite young, I freed it from the oppression of royal tax collectors, who are called *graffiones*, after much effort and many pleas at court during the time of the

---

81. Chaumont-en-Vexin, Oise, Picardy is located about thirty-nine miles northwest of Saint-Denis.

82. Hugh of Amiens, a monk of Cluny, was archbishop of Rouen (r. 1130–64).

83. Ableiges, Val-d'Oise, Île-de-France is located about twenty-four miles northwest of Saint-Denis.

84. Berneval-le-Grand, Seine-Maritime, Upper Normandy is located on the cliff-lined coast of the English Channel about five miles northeast of Dieppe and roughly 128 miles northwest of Saint-Denis. Suger became provost there in about 1107.

85. Suger's predecessor was Adam, abbot of Saint-Denis (1099–1122).

most valiant King Henry.[xliii] At the beginning of our authority there we returned the parish churches, which the priest Roger and his brother Geoffrey claimed by hereditary right, to the holdings of the church; and we gave these parish churches and their revenues to the treasury in perpetuity, in order to restore and increase the number of textiles in this church. Since there were almost no revenues for this purpose, we attached to the church another village named Carrières, which had been recently built in those districts.[86] But if the financial situation does not improve, the village will have to pay four marks and the churches seven pounds. We have increased the other customary revenues from the village of Berneval including the taxes and other income, we believe, to almost fifteen pounds. For the refreshment of the brothers on the celebration of the anniversary of the most pious King Dagobert,[xliv] we allocated the customary right, commonly called *aquaria*, that we helped wrest away from our provost who had held it during the time of our predecessor of good memory.[87]

We strove to have the villages of Morgny, Lilly, and Fleury contribute no less than twenty-five to thirty pounds, when they usually returned no more than seven to ten. We did the same for Château-sur-Epte.[88]

XXIV

The decoration of the church. After we had allocated these revenue increases, we returned our focus to the remarkable construction of buildings, so that our successors and we might give thanks to Almighty God by this work. We also wanted our good example to motivate them to continue this task, and if necessary, to finish it. For, no one should fear severe poverty or hindrance from any sort of

---

86. Carrières was located in Normandy near Berneval.
87. This was the local term for fishing rights.
88. Morgny, Eure, Upper Normandy is located about fifty-six miles northwest of Saint-Denis. Lilly, Eure, Upper Normandy is located about fifty-seven miles northwest of Saint-Denis. Fleury-la-Forêt, Eure, Upper Normandy is located about fifty-eight miles northwest of Saint-Denis. Château-sur-Epte, Eure, Upper Normandy is located about forty miles northwest of Saint-Denis.

authority if one cheerfully contributed from his own resources to this work out of love for the Holy Martyrs. Under God's inspiration, we began the first work on this church because the ancient walls were so old that they were threatening to collapse in some places. Therefore, we assembled the best painters we could find from various regions, had them make urgent repairs, and then paint those walls in beautiful gold and other rich colors. I gladly made these repairs because while studying there in the schools, I wanted to do it if I ever had the chance.[89]

XXV

The first addition to the church.[xlv] While the work on the walls was being completed at great cost, we frequently witnessed and experienced the overcrowded conditions in the church on feast days, especially on the feast of Saint Denis, the Lendit Fair, and many other festivals. The narrow confines of the place made it necessary for the women to be passed quickly over the heads of the men to get to the altar, just as if they were moving across the floor, all amid great distress, clamor, and confusion.[90] The advice of wise men and the pleas of many monks encouraged me to enlarge and extend the noble abbey church that the divine hand had consecrated lest I displease God and the Holy Martyrs; so, under the inspiration of the divine will, I decided to begin that task.[91] I begged the divine mercy, in our chapter assembly and in our church, that He who is the beginning and the end, the Alpha and the Omega, might join a good end to a good beginning with a sound middle.[92] I begged that He not prevent a man stained with blood from building a temple, someone who wholeheartedly preferred to do this more than acquiring all the treasures of Constantinople.[93] So, we started our work with the

---

89. Suger also mentions his boyhood intention to renovate the church in *The Consecration*, II, 37.

90. Suger also describes this problem above in *The Consecration*, II, 36–37, as well as in *Oeuvres* (ed. Lecoy), Charter X, 357–58.

91. For the consecration of Dagobert's church in 636 by the hand of Christ, see Crosby, *The Abbey of Saint-Denis, 475–1122*, 1:43–44.

92. Rv 1:8, 21:6, 22:13.

93. See also below, *The Administration*, XXXIII, 106. On "a man stained with

doors at the former entrance, tearing down an addition that Charlemagne reportedly built for an important occasion; for his father, the Emperor Pepin, requested that he be buried outside, at the entrance of the doors, lying face down instead of on his back, to atone for the sins of his father, Charles Martel.[xlvi] We set to work there, and it is obvious that we pushed ourselves unceasingly to enlarge the body of the church, to triple the number of entrances and doors, and to erect tall, graceful towers.

XXVI

The dedication. We had a very venerable person, Archbishop Hugh of Rouen, and many other bishops dedicate the chapel of Saint Romanus to serve God and His Holy Angels.[94] Those who serve God there realized how secluded, how holy, and how ideal this place was for divine services; for while celebrating Mass in that chapel, they felt like they were already dwelling in heaven. At the same ceremony, the venerable persons, Bishops Manasses of Meaux and Peter of Senlis,[95] dedicated two chapels in the lower nave of the church, one to Saint Hippolytus and his companions on one side, and on the other side, one to Saint Nicholas.[96] These three bishops exited the church through the door of Saint Eustace in a single, glorious procession that passed in front of the main doors, accompanied by a large number of clergy singing and a multitude of people rejoicing.[97] The bishops led the procession and proceeded to the holy consecration, entering through the single cemetery door that had

---

blood," see 2 Sm 16:7–8. For Suger's comparison of himself to King David, see *Abbot Suger* (ed. Panofsky), 149.

94. Saint Romanus (d. ca. 640) was, like Hugh of Amiens, also bishop of Rouen where he was venerated. Romanus was a Frank who was raised at the court of King Clotaire II and was said to have worked many miracles. His chapel was located on the south side of the church in the ambulatory behind the main altar.

95. Peter was bishop of Senlis (r. 1134–51). *The Consecration*, IV, 43, above has Bishop Odo of Beauvais in place of Manasses of Meaux assisting Hugh of Rouen and Peter of Senlis.

96. For detailed discussions of these two chapels, see *Abbot Suger* (ed. Panofsky), 155, and *Oeuvres* (ed. Gasparri), 1:206n172.

97. The Saint Eustace door leads out from the south transept.

been moved from the old building to the new one. The jubilant ceremony was finished to the honor of Almighty God, and while we were girding ourselves for the difficult work on the upper part of the church, the bishops lifted our depressed spirit, and pleasantly inspired us to cheer up and not worry about the work ahead or any shortage of funds.[98]

XXVII

The gilded cast-bronze doors. We summoned metal casters, chose sculptors, and erected the main doors that displayed scenes of the Passion, the Resurrection, and the Ascension of the Savior, and had them gilded at considerable expense and great cost, as befits this remarkable portico. We also erected other doors, new ones on the right side, and the antique ones on the left, beneath the mosaic, where we worked hard to have something innovative, contrary to custom, made and placed in the arch above the door. We decided to modify the towers and the upper crenellation of the façade, both for the beauty of the church and, if circumstances required, for practical purposes. We also instructed that the year of the consecration of this part be inscribed in gilded copper letters as follows, so that it will never be forgotten:

> For the glory of the church that nourished and raised him,
> Suger labored with zeal to make that church beautiful.
> He shares with you what is yours, O martyred Denis
> He prays that you win for him a place in Paradise.
> The year one thousand one hundred and forty, was
> The year of the Word when this church was consecrated.

These verses are also inscribed on the doors:

> All you who seek to extol the fame of these doors,
> Admire neither the gold nor the expense, but their craftsmanship.
> The work shines brightly; but the work that brightly shines
> Should brighten minds, so that they pass through true lights
> Towards the true light, where Christ is the true door.

---

98. For this procession and ceremony, see above *The Consecration,* IV, 43.

> The golden doors reveal the material inherent in them.
> A dull mind rises towards truth through material things;
> And once seeing this light, it rises above being immersed in them.

And on the lintel:

> Receive, O stern judge, the prayers of your Suger,
> Mercifully include me among your very own sheep.[99]

XXVIII

The enlargement of the upper part of the church.[100] In the same year, elated by this holy and happy task, we hurried to begin work on the chamber of divine propitiation in the upper part of the church, where the host of our redemption would be sacrificed perpetually and repeatedly in solitude, away from the confusion of the crowds. One reads in the text about the consecration of this upper section[101] that our brothers, fellow servants, and we were mercifully considered deserving to bring this holy, glorious, and celebrated work to an excellent conclusion, with the help of God, who brought success to our undertakings and us. We were extremely indebted to God and the Holy Martyrs because, by its lengthy postponement, He reserved this task for our lifetime and labor. For who am I, or what is my Father's house, that I should even presume to start, or hope to finish this glorious and delightful building without relying on the aid of divine mercy and the Holy Martyrs, or without complete devotion of my mind and body to this work?[102] He who gave me the will also gave me the ability, and because the work was done with a good intention, it now stands upright, in a state of perfection, with God's help. The divine hand certainly played a role in these endeav-

---

99. For the biblical influences and those from *The Celestial Hierarchy* of the writer Pseudo-Dionysius in these poems of Suger, see *Oeuvres* (ed. Gasparri), 1:209n180.

100. The upper part (*pars superior*) of the church includes the areas where the eastern end of the church begins to be elevated at the end of the nave; the lower part (*pars inferior*) refers to the crypt, and the front part (*pars anterior*) to the western end of the church. Suger began renovations on the new choir and chevet in 1140 and completed them about 1144.

101. See above, *The Consecration*, IV, 44–45.

102. 1 Sm 18:18.

ors and protected this glorious building, because the entire magnificent structure, from the crypt below to the lofty vaults above, with its remarkable and wide variety of arches and columns, as well as its roof, was completely finished in three years and three months.[103]

We added only one word in the inscription of the earlier consecration[104] to include the year of the church's completion:

> The year one thousand one hundred and forty
> Fourth of the Word was when it was consecrated.

We also decided to add these words to the verses of that inscription:

> Once the new rear part was joined to the front,
> The church gleamed, light-filled in its middle.
> For it shone brightly, once coupled with bright light,
> And the new light flooded it. Bright was the
> Noble work that was enlarged in our lifetime.
> I, Suger, under my leadership, it was done.

I was now ready to follow up my successes because I preferred nothing more under heaven than to continue to honor my mother church that had nurtured a boy with maternal affection, supported a misguided youth, adeptly strengthened a mature adult, and solemnly placed him among the princes of the church and kingdom. So we pushed ourselves to complete the work, and strove to elevate and enlarge the transept wings of the church to the configuration of the old and new construction that would join them.

XXIX

The continuation of both works. After this was done, certain people persuaded us to focus our efforts on the construction of the front towers, where one tower had already been completed. However, we

---

103. Construction on the eastern end of the church began on July 13, 1140, and was consecrated on June 14, 1144. Suger here shortens the actual length of time in order to employ a Trinitarian symbol. The actual interval from the laying of the foundation stone to this point was about three years and eleven months; see further *Abbot Suger* (ed. Panofsky), 166.

104. See above *The Consecration*, IV, 44.

were convinced that the divine will redirected us to another task; so we began to renovate the middle area of the church called the nave, and to harmonize and align it with each of the renovated parts. We left intact as much of the ancient walls as possible, upon which, according to the testimony of the ancient writers, the Supreme Pontiff, the Lord Jesus Christ, had laid His hand. We did this to maintain respect for the ancient consecration, as well as appropriate coherence to the modern work according to the plan already initiated.[105] We had one overriding reason for redirecting our work. If we turned our focus away from renovating the nave of the church to work on the towers, the nave would have taken too long to complete as planned. It might not have been finished in our lifetime, that of our successors, or possibly ever at all, should some misfortune occur. For what threatened to discredit the builders, more than anything else, was the possibility of a long delay in joining the new and old work. But since the extension of the side aisles had already begun, either we ourselves, or those of us whom the Lord chooses, will finish this construction with His help. For to remember the past is to display the future. The most generous Lord, who will not allow us to lack any resources to complete the project, furnished to the craftsmen a rich supply of sapphire-colored glass for the stunning windows, as well as other expensive objects, and a sum of money of about seven hundred pounds or more. For, He is the beginning and the end.[106]

XXX

The ornaments of the church. To prevent oblivion, the rival of truth, from sneaking up and stealing away a worthy endeavor, we will also describe the church's ornaments, by which the divine hand, in the time of our administration, decorated His church that is considered His bride. We acknowledge and declare that our lord, the three times blessed Denis, is generous and benevolent, and we believe that he has won many great favors from God and achieved many things. Thus, we could have accomplished a hundred times more

---

105. See above *The Consecration,* IV, 44–45.
106. Rv 1:8 and 21:6.

than we have done for his church if human frailty, changing times, and shifting customs had not prevented it. However, the ornaments that we have collected for him by the gift of God are as follows.

XXXI

The golden altar frontal in the upper part of the church. We estimate that we have placed in the altar frontal that stood before the most holy body of Denis about forty-two marks of gold and a large quantity of precious gems, hyacinths, rubies, sapphires, emeralds, topazes, and a variety of distinctive pearls, more than we ever expected to find. Kings, princes, and many other eminent men followed our example and removed the rings from their fingers, and ordered that the gold, gems, and precious pearls from these rings be set into the altar frontal out of love for the Holy Martyrs. What a sight! Likewise, archbishops and bishops placed their investiture rings there for safekeeping, and offered them devoutly to God and His saints. A multitude of gem sellers converged on us from various kingdoms and regions, and they rushed to sell us more than we wished to buy with the contributions we received from everyone.[107] These are the verses on the altar frontal:

> Exalted Denis, open the portals of Paradise,
> And keep Suger safe under your sacred defenses.
> You who built a new dwelling for yourself through us,
> Render us to be received into the dwelling of heaven,
> To eat our fill at the heavenly table, instead of the present one.
> Things symbolized are more pleasing than that which symbolizes.

It was only proper to place the most holy bodies of our lords as honorably as possible in the upper vault, but because one of the side panels of their most holy sarcophagus had been torn off at some unknown time, we set aside fifteen marks of gold and had its back panel, its side ones, as well as its top and bottom, gilded with about forty ounces of gold.[108] In addition, we had the receptacles containing

---

107. See above *The Consecration,* V, 49–50.
108. See above *The Consecration,* V, 49. For a detailed description of the tomb, see

the most holy bodies enclosed with gilded panels of cast copper, and we set polished stones near the inner stone vaults. We also erected a series of gates to keep away any disturbances from people, but in a way that allowed venerable persons to properly view the receptacles containing the holy bodies with great devotion and an outpouring of tears. These are the verses inscribed on those holy tombs:

> Where the heavenly ranks stand guard, people beseech and mourn
> The ashes of the Saints, while the clergy sing in ten-part harmony.
> The petitions of the devout are directed to the spirits of the Saints.
> If they are acceptable to them, their sins are forgiven.
> The bodies of the Saints lie buried here peacefully.
> May they take with them us, who plead with constant prayer.
> Here is a marvelous sanctuary for those who come to it.
> Here the accused have a safe refuge. The avenger is helpless against them [the Saints].

XXXII

The golden crucifix.[109] If possible, we should strive, with total devotion, to have people adore the life-giving Cross, the healing standard of our Savior's eternal victory, about which the Apostle says, *Let me find no glory except in the Cross of Our Lord Jesus Christ.*[110] We should adorn it very gloriously, making it glorious, not only to men but also to the angels, for it is the sign of the Son of man appearing in the heavens in the last days.[111] We should greet it perpetually like the Apostle Andrew, "Hail, O Cross, you are consecrated with the body of Christ and adorned with His limbs like pearls."[112] But since we could not do what we wished, we wished to do the best we could, and strove, with the help of God, to accomplish our task. So, we ourselves searched everywhere, along with our agents, for

---

Abbot Suger (ed. Panofsky), 168–76, and *Oeuvres* (ed. Gasparri), 1:215n206. The upper vault (*volta superior*) here designates the apse.

109. For this cross, see Conway, "Abbey of Saint-Denis," 139–40.

110. Gal 6:14.

111. Mt 24:30–31.

112. *The Passion of Andrew* (dating to beginning of the sixth century); see *Abbot Suger* (ed. Panofsky), 56n16.

a supply of precious pearls and gems, and provided as much precious material in gold and gems as we could find for this marvelous ornament, and assembled skilled craftsmen from various regions. They worked with painstaking precision and elevated the venerable Cross, so that the gems on its backside could be admired; and on its front side, in plain sight of the priest celebrating Mass, they displayed for adoration the figure of our Lord Savior, as if He were still suffering on the Cross in order to recall His Passion. In fact, Saint Denis had rested in that very place for five hundred years or more, from the time of Dagobert up to the present. We also wish to mention one amusing but notable miracle that the Lord performed for us during our efforts. I had to interrupt the project because we did not have enough gems, and could no longer provide a sufficient supply of them, for their scarcity made them expensive. Then, monks of two religious orders from three abbeys, that is Cîteaux, another abbey of that same order, and Fontevraud, unexpectedly entered our small chamber connected to the church and offered to sell us a supply of gems—hyacinths, sapphires, rubies, emeralds, and topazes—more than we would have ever hoped to find in ten years.[113] They had acquired them as alms from Count Theobald, who had received them from his brother, Stephen, the English king.[114] Stephen had obtained them from the treasures of his deceased uncle, King Henry, who had collected them throughout his life in marvelous cups.[115] We, however, relieved from the burden of finding gems, rendered thanks to God and paid four hundred pounds for them, even though they were worth much more.

We added these gems, a great number of other precious ones, and large pearls to make this holy ornament perfect. We remember, if I am not mistaken, that we had applied to it about eighty marks of

113. The abbey of Cîteaux, Côte-d'Or, Burgundy was founded in 1098 by a group of monks from Molesme abbey. Saint Robert of Molesme was its first abbot. Duke William IX of Aquitaine founded Fontevraud abbey, Maine-et-Loire, Pays de la Loire in 1100 and placed it under the leadership of Robert of Arbrissel.

114. Stephen of Blois (ca. 1097–1154) was the grandson of William the Conqueror by his daughter Adela and ruled England (1135–54).

115. Henry I (b. 1068) was the third son of William the Conqueror and ruled England (1100–1135). His sister Adela was Stephen's mother.

fine gold. The four Evangelists adorned the pedestal of the Cross, and the sacred image rested upon a pillar that was enameled with very delicate craftsmanship depicting the history of the Savior, and with testimonies from the allegories of the ancient law.[116] The magnificent capital up above on the pillar displayed images that depicted the death of the Lord. We were able to finish the cross in about two years by using a number of Lotharingian goldsmiths, sometimes five to seven at a time. The mercy of our Savior hastened even more to honor and exalt the prestige of this magnificent and holy instrument when He sent to us our Lord Pope Eugenius to celebrate Holy Easter.[xlvii] It was the custom of the Roman Pontiffs residing temporarily in Gaul to honor the sacred apostleship of Saint Denis on that day, as we have seen his predecessors Calixtus[xlviii] and Innocent[xlix] do. Pope Eugenius solemnly consecrated this crucifix on Easter Sunday, and allotted a share of the revenue from his own chapel for the inscription from the true Cross of the Lord, which surpasses each and every pearl. In the presence of everyone Pope Eugenius publicly anathematized, with the sharp blade of the blessed Peter and the sword of the Holy Spirit, whoever should steal anything from this place, or recklessly raise his hand against that crucifix. We had this sentence of anathema inscribed at the foot of the Cross.

XXXIII

We rushed to decorate the main altar of Saint-Denis that had only a beautiful and expensive frontal panel given to it by the third emperor, Charles the Bald.[l] It was at this altar that we had been offered to the monastic community, and so we had it encased with golden panels on each side, including a more costly fourth one that gave the altar a golden appearance all the way around.[117] We placed the candelabra of King Louis, son of Philip, which were worth twen-

---

116. For a further description of the cross, see *Oeuvres* (ed. Gasparri), 1:217–18nn216–17.

117. Suger was offered to Saint-Denis as a child oblate in 1091 at the age of ten. On the improvements that Suger made to this altar, see *Abbot Suger* (ed. Panofsky), 185–86, and *Oeuvres* (ed. Gasparri), 1:220n224.

ty marks of gold, on each side of the altar to prevent any opportunity of their being stolen.[118] We placed hyacinths, emeralds, and all kinds of valuable gems on the panels, and launched a thorough search for other ones to be added. These are the verses inscribed on the panels. On the right side:

> Abbot Suger had these altar panels erected,
> Except the one that King Charles already gave,
> Make the unworthy worthy by your favor, Virgin Mary.
> May the fountain of mercy wash away the sins of king and abbot.

On the left side:

> If a wicked man should plunder this splendid altar,
> Let him perish and be justly damned, just like Judas.

Since foreign craftsmen had a more extravagant style than our native ones, we had the back panel embellished by them, with amazing artistry, at tremendous expense, with a bas-relief that was marvelous in its shape and material, so that those viewing it could then say, "The quality of the craftsmanship surpassed that of the material."[119] We fastened to the main altar many of our purchases and a larger number of ornaments of the church that we were afraid of losing, such as the golden chalice with a mutilated foot and some other objects. Since the diversity of materials, like the gold, gems, and pearls, cannot be easily recognized by only looking at them without a description, we wrote down an explanation that only learned men can understand, for it shines brilliantly with the glaring rays of cheerful allegories. We also included verses on the panels to make the meaning of the allegories clear:

> With a loud voice the people cry out to Christ: Hosanna![120]
>
> The true host shared at the supper bore the burden of all.[121]

---

118. These candelabra are also mentioned by Suger in *The Deeds*, 154, where he says they were made of 160 ounces of gold. Louis VI's father was King Philip I (r. 1060–1108).
119. Ovid, *Metamorphoses*, 2.2.5.
120. The triumphal entry of Christ into Jerusalem.
121. The Last Supper.

The Savior of all on the Cross hurries to bear the Cross.[122]

Christ's flesh sealed what Abraham atoned for with his son.[123]

Melchizedek pours a libation, for Abraham vanquishes the enemy.[124]

Seekers of Christ with a Cross carry a cluster of grapes on a staff.[125]

The admiration we felt for our mother church often led us to reflect upon the different ornaments, the new as well as the old. We would stand transfixed, gazing at that marvelous Cross of Saint Eligius,[li] along with the smaller crosses, and at that incomparable ornament, commonly called "the Crest," which were placed upon the golden altar.[126] Then we would utter a deep heartfelt sigh and say, "Every precious stone is your covering, the sardonyx, topaz, jasper, chrysolite, onyx, beryl, sapphire, carbuncle, and the emerald."[lii] Those who know the properties of gems are greatly surprised to see that none of them are in short supply here except the carbuncle, but that all the others are present in large numbers. Delight for the beautiful house of God and the splendor of the many colored gems sometimes made me forget about my worldly cares; and devout meditation moved me to reflect on the differences among the holy virtues by directing my attention away from material to immaterial things. I seemed to see myself as if I were dwelling in some strange region of the earth, partly in the filth of the earth, and partly in the purity of heaven, and that I was capable of being transferred, by the gift of God, from this lower realm to a higher one by the anagogical method.[127] I used to talk to people from Jerusalem who had seen the treasures of Constantinople and the ornaments of Hagia Sophia and would happily ask them whether our treasures were comparable in quality to those over there. When they indicated that ours were more valuable, we realized that those marvelous treasures that

---

122. The carrying of the cross by Christ and the crucifixion.
123. The aborted sacrifice of Isaac by Abraham (Gn 22:1–14).
124. Melchizedek's offering of bread and wine to Abraham (Gn 14:18).
125. The return of the spies with the cluster of grapes (Nm 13:24).
126. This "Crest" was commonly called *Escrin de Charlemagne*. For a full description of it, see *Abbot Suger* (ed. Panofsky), 183, and *Oeuvres* (ed. Gasparri), 1:223n229.
127. These thoughts reflect the influence on Suger of *The Celestial Hierarchy* of Pseudo-Dionysius.

we had formerly heard about had been safely hidden away, out of fear of the Franks, to prevent the rapacious greed of some fools from suddenly turning the close relationship gained between the Greeks and the Latins into sedition and the ravages of wars. The Greeks are well known for their cleverness.[128] Thus, our treasures safely displayed here could perhaps be of greater value than the ones displayed unsafely over there amid turmoil. We have heard from many reliable men, including Bishop Hugh of Laon, about the amazing and nearly unbelievable superiority of Hagia Sophia's and other churches' ornaments used in the celebration of the Mass.[129] If this is true, and we have no reason to doubt what these people have said, then those priceless and unrivaled treasures should be displayed for all to decide for themselves. Let everyone make up his own mind.[130] I confess that what pleases me the most is when rather expensive, or even very expensive, treasures are preferred for dispensing the most holy Eucharist. The word of God, or command of the prophet, has decreed that golden vessels, golden vials, and small golden mortars be used to catch the blood of goats, bulls, and the red heifer; so, there are even greater reasons to display, for perpetual service and total devotion, the golden vessels, precious stones, and very expensive created things that receive the blood of Jesus Christ.[131] However, our treasures and we are not worthy enough for these purposes. If a new creation were to transform our substance into that of the holy cherubim and seraphim, we would still be inadequate and unworthy to serve for this great, ineffable sacrifice, even after our sins have been mercifully forgiven. Our critics also insist that a pious mind, a pure spirit, and a sincere intention are all that is needed for this function, and we readily, personally, and particularly agree that these characteristics are important.[liii]

We also acknowledge that we should serve God with all internal purity and all outward majesty in external ornaments of sacred ves-

---

128. For the cleverness and nefarious nature of the Greeks, see Odo, *De profectione*.
129. Hugh I was bishop of Laon from August 1112 to March 1113, a decade before Suger became abbot of Saint-Denis. Suger might be referring here to Barthélemy de Jur, bishop of Laon in 1113–51, whom he knew well.
130. Rom 14:5.
131. Heb 9:13–14.

sels, although there is absolutely nothing that is worthy enough for the service of the holy sacrifice. We should fittingly serve our Redeemer in every way possible, He who did not refuse to provide us with everything we needed without exception. He has united our nature to His, to make a single remarkable person, and setting us on His right-hand side, He has promised that we would truly possess His kingdom,[132] our Lord who lives and reigns forever and ever.[133]

In addition, we endeavored to renovate the altar out of reverence for the sacred relics, which, according to the testimony of the ancients, is called "the holy altar."[134] The glorious King Louis, son of Philip, used to say that he had heard it called this name by the elders of the community as a child growing up here. The altar did not appear in good condition because of its old age, a lack of diligent care, and from the constant activity while being set up with marvelous decorations that were arranged differently for specific feast days, with the finest ones used for the most important feasts. The sacred porphyry stone on top of the altar was suitable in the quality of its color as well as in its large size. The stone was encased in a hollow wooden frame overlaid with gold, but the frame was nearly splintered into pieces over the course of many years. An arm of the Apostle Saint James was believed to have been elegantly set into the front part of this hollow frame, with a document of its authenticity inside that could be viewed through a transparent window of very clear crystal.[135] An interior inscription in the same kind of visible document also attested that the arm of the protomartyr Stephen lay hidden in the right side of the frame, and in the left side, the arm of Saint Vincent the Levite and martyr.[136] For a long time I was over-

132. Mt 25:33–34.
133. Tb 9:11 and Rv 1:18, 5:13, 11:15, 15:7.
134. This altar was established by Abbot Hilduin (r. 814–41) and originally dedicated to the Trinity. On its location in the church, see *Abbot Suger* (ed. Panofsky), 186–87, and *Oeuvres* (ed. Gasparri), 1:226n240.
135. Suger indicates in *Oeuvres* (ed. Lecoy), Charter X, 354, that this arm was that of James the Lesser, the brother of the Lord. Suger also mentions in this charter that he wished to be buried next to the relics of the saints mentioned in this passage so that he might receive their perpetual protection.
136. Saint Vincent the Levite, probably a deacon, was martyred at Agen in Gascony in about 300 A.D. for disrupting a Druid ceremony. Acts 6–7 states that Saint

come with joy by the desire to see these relics and kiss them because I wanted to be strengthened by the protection of these important holy relics, but I feared to offend God if I were to do so. Then, our faith emboldened us to examine the holy relics while maintaining respect for their ancient authenticity; so we chose the manner and the day for examining them, selecting the most holy day of the martyrdom of our lords, the blessed martyrs, which is the eighth day before the Ides of October.[137] Archbishops and bishops of the various provinces attended the ceremony out of a sense of indebtedness to their apostolate of the Gauls, and willingly came to offer their devout prayers at the celebration of a great solemnity. Those who attended were the archbishops of Lyon, Reims, Tours, and Rouen as well as the bishops of Soissons, Beauvais, Senlis, Meaux, Rennes, Saint-Malo, and Vannes, along with an assembly of abbots, monks, clerics, magnates, and a countless crowd of people of both sexes.[liv] After the office of Terce had been chanted on the day of the solemnity, a solemn procession was organized in the sight of everyone in attendance on that momentous day.[138] Based solely on the testimony and inscription of our fathers, we had great trust in the authenticity of the relics, just as if we had already examined all of them. We gathered together the archbishops, bishops, abbots, and reliable persons to help lift up the altar, and explained to them that we wished to open the altar and see this treasure of very holy relics. After deliberation, a few of our intimate friends suggested that our personal reputation and that of the church would be better protected if we were to examine the relics in private, in order to verify what the documents claimed. Stirred by the ardor of my faith I instantly answered them that I would prefer to find out in front of all the witnesses whether what the documents claimed is true rather than to examine them in private and have those, who did not witness anything, cast doubt on the authenticity of the relics. There-

---

Stephen, who was stoned to death, became the first Christian martyr, thus the title "protomartyr."

137. October 9. Suger also discusses this event in *Oeuvres* (ed. Lecoy), Charter X, 354–55.

138. Terce, one of the canonical hours, was the third hour after dawn and was recited at 9 a.m.

fore, we carried the altar down into our midst and summoned goldsmiths, who carefully opened those small compartments containing the most sacred arms, and, sitting on top of the compartments, were the crystals showing the inscriptions. In full view of all, we found, as God granted, everything exactly as we hoped.

We also discovered the reason for putting the relics in those small compartments. The Emperor Charles the Third lay gloriously buried before that very altar, and he had ordained by imperial decree that they be removed from an imperial reliquary on his behalf and placed near him to protect his soul and body.[139] Much to the delight of everyone, we also found there the decree sealed with the imprint of Charles's ring as proof of this. Seven lamps in silver vessels, which we restored from their broken pieces, were to burn perpetually day and night forever before that holy altar, as the emperor had decreed for a good reason, for he believed that the highest hope for his body and soul lay in storing the holy relics there. He pledged, with his golden seals, his manor called Rueil,[140] together with its appendages to cover the expenses of these relics, as well as the ceremonies on the anniversary of his death and a meal for his own men.[lv] That is also why six large magnificent candles, which were rarely or never set up anywhere else in the church, were lit around this altar on nearly sixty different solemn festivals. This is also why this altar is adorned with splendid decorations, as often as the altar of the blessed Denis.

We also erected a cross of amazing size, and placed it between the altar and the tomb of Charles.[lvi] According to tradition, a very beautiful necklace of Queen Nanthilde, the wife of King Dagobert, who founded this church, was attached to the middle of it, while another necklace was fastened to the brow of Saint Denis; and although this latter one was smaller, the most skilled craftsmen attest that no other necklace equals it.[141] We put it there mainly out of

139. Charles the Bald (r. 875–77).

140. It is today called Rueil-Malmaison, Hauts-de-Seine, Île-de-France and is located about twelve miles southwest of Saint-Denis in the western suburbs of Paris. See also *Oeuvres* (ed. Lecoy), Charter X, 353.

141. Nanthilde (ca. 610–42) married Dagobert in 629 and was the third of his many consorts. Her son, Clovis II, inherited Neustria and Burgundy from his father.

reverence for the iron collar that was clasped around the neck of the blessed Denis in the prison of Glaucinus, and it deserved our, and everyone else's, worship and veneration.[142]

The venerable Abbot Robert of Corbie of good memory had likewise erected in that same part of the church a beautifully embellished silver panel, in recognition of having taken his vows here, and to give thanks for the many benefices he had received from this church. He was a professed monk of this holy church and had been raised here from childhood, and, as God ordained, we supported him to preside as abbot over the monastery of Corbie.[143]

XXXIV

We also renovated the choir of the brothers into its present form out of sympathy for their hardships, for they persistently performed church services there while they suffered greatly, and sometimes became sick from the coldness of the marble and copper; and we strove to enlarge the choir, with God's help, because our community had grown larger.

After we re-covered its ivory panels that had been disfigured from being stored too long in and even under treasure chests, we restored our magnificent old pulpit whose delicate sculpture on those panels, which by now were ruined, had depicted ancient historical scenes that made it priceless.[144] We restored the copper animals on its right side to prevent this rich, marvelous material from perishing, and then raised the pulpit to a higher level for the reading of the Holy Gospel. In the early days of our abbacy we had removed an obstructive, dark wall that cut across the middle of the church, in order to prevent any large barriers from dimming the beauty of the church's huge interior.

She is buried in Saint-Denis. On these necklaces and their placement on the two relics, see *Abbot Suger* (ed. Panofsky), 190–91.

142. For this prison, see Crosby, *The Abbey of Saint-Denis, 475–1122*, 1:25 and 47.

143. With Suger's support Robert became abbot of Corbie in 1127; he died in January 1142. Bathilde (ca. 626–80), wife of Clovis II, founded the abbey in about 660. Corbie, Somme, Picardy is located about eighty-four miles north of Saint-Denis.

144. The Huguenots destroyed this pulpit in the mid-1500s.

We also restored the ancient and renowned, but dilapidated throne of the glorious King Dagobert because of the eminence of its official use and the value of the throne itself.[145] For, as ancient times attest, after the kings of the Franks had assumed royal authority over the kingdom, they customarily sat on that throne to receive the homage of their magnates for the first time. We also had the eagle in the middle of the choir regilded because its gilded veneer had been rubbed away by the constant touch of admirers.[146]

In addition, we employed the hands of many masters from diverse lands to paint a splendid variety of new glass windows in the upper and lower levels, beginning with the first window that starts with the Tree of Jesse in the apse[lvii] of the church, all the way to the window above the main door at the church's entrance.[147] One of the windows incites the viewer to ascend from material things to the immaterial;[lviii] it portrays the Apostle Paul turning a millstone and the Prophets carrying sacks to it. The following are the verses about this scene:

> By turning the millstone, Paul, you separate flour from the bran.
> You reveal to us the inmost meanings of Mosaic Law.[lix]
> From so many grains comes true bread without bran,
> Everlasting food for the angels and us.[148]

These are the verses in that same window, where the veil is removed from Moses's face:

> What Moses veils, the teaching of Christ unveils.
> Those who unclothe Moses lay bare the law.[149]

---

145. For a description and history of the throne, see *Oeuvres* (ed. Gasparri), 1:232n263, and Crosby, *The Abbey of Saint-Denis, 475–1122*, 1:161–62. See also Anonymous, *A History and Description*, 35.

146. This was a lectern in the shape of an eagle.

147. For a detailed discussion of the stained glass windows in Saint-Denis, see Louis Grodecki, "The Style of the Stained Glass Windows at Saint-Denis," in *Abbot Suger of Saint-Denis* (ed. Gerson), 273–81.

148. This scene and inscription are portrayed today in the central medallion of the restored "Anagogical Window," located in the chapel of Saint Peregrinus in the ambulatory. See Is 47:2 for the inscription.

149. This scene and inscription are portrayed in the medallion located second from the bottom. See Ex 34:33–35 and 2 Cor 3:13–18 for the inscription.

In that same window, above the Ark of the Covenant, are these verses:

> The altar with the Cross of Christ is erected on the Ark of the Covenant.
> Life chooses to die there under a greater Covenant.[150]

Also in that same window, where the lion and the lamb break the seal of the book are these verses:

> He who is Almighty God, the Lion and the Lamb, unseals the book.
> The Lamb or the Lion becomes flesh joined to God.[151]

In another window, where the daughter of Pharaoh finds Moses in a basket are these verses:

> Moses is the child in the basket whom the royal
> Maiden, the Church, cherishes with motherly feelings.[152]

In the same window, where the Lord appears to Moses in the burning bush are these verses:

> Just as this bush appears to burn yet does not burn,
> So does he, full of divine fire, burn yet does not burn.[153]

In the same window, where Pharaoh is submerged in the sea with his cavalry are these verses:

> What happens to the good in baptism happened to Pharaoh's army,
> The ritual is similar, but the intent was different.[154]

---

150. This scene and inscription are contained in the top medallion of the window. Also seen are the symbols of the Evangelists: the man for Matthew, the lion for Mark, the ox for Luke, and the eagle for John.

151. This scene and inscription are seen in the second medallion from the top. The subject matter is taken from Rv 5:1–6.

152. "The Moses Window" is also located in the chapel of Saint Peregrinus in the ambulatory. The inscription and scene of finding Moses are portrayed in the bottom medallion of the restored window. See Ex 2:5–10 for this scene.

153. The burning bush medallion is the second to last one in the same window. See Ex 3:2–3 for this scene.

154. The crossing of the Red Sea medallion is in the middle of the window. See Ex 14:23 for this scene; for the comparison of this incident to Christian baptism, see 1 Cor 10:1–2.

Also in the same window, where Moses lifts up the bronze serpent, are these verses:

> Just as the bronze serpent slays all serpents,
> Thus Christ lifted up on the Cross slays all enemies.[155]

In the same window, where Moses receives the law on the mountain are these verses:

> The grace of Christ strengthens the law given to Moses.
> Grace gives life, but the letter of the law slays it.[156]

These windows were a marvelous piece of workmanship that was tremendously expensive because they were made of decorated glass and sapphire components. We employed a master craftsman to maintain and repair them, and also a skilled goldsmith to do the same for the gold and silver ornaments. They received stipends, as well as something they deemed extra, for example coins from the altar, and grain from the communal granary of the brothers; and in return they were to diligently take care of these treasures.

We also ordered seven candlesticks to be crafted with enamel and very fine gilding, because the ones that the Emperor Charles had given to the blessed Denis appeared to be ruined because of their age.[157]

We also acquired vessels made of gold and precious stones to be used in the service of the Lord's table to show our gratitude to blessed Denis; they supplemented those that the kings of the Franks and the church faithful had given for this service. Specifically, we had a new large gold chalice crafted out of one hundred forty ounces of gold and decorated with precious gems, such as hyacinths and topazes, to replace the one that had been pawned and lost during the time of our predecessor.[158]

---

155. The brazen serpent is the top medallion of the window. See Nm 21:9 for this scene.

156. The tablets of the law medallion is the second from the top. For the law given to Moses, see Ex 31:18. See also Madeline Harrison Caviness, "Suger's Glass at Saint-Denis: The State of Research," in *Abbot Suger of Saint-Denis* (ed. Gerson), 257–72.

157. The emperor here is Charles the Bald, who gave the above-mentioned silver candlesticks for the altar of the Trinity chapel on the northern side of the church; see Crosby, *The Abbey of Saint-Denis, 475–1122*, 1:185.

158. The chalice that has been lost may have been made of solid gold; see *Abbot Suger* (ed. Panofsky), 202–3.

In addition, we offered to the blessed Denis, along with some flowers from the empress's crown, another costly vessel made of prase sculpted in the shape of a ship that King Louis,[159] son of Philip, had pawned and lost for nearly ten years.[lx] After it had been offered for our possible purchase, we bought it with the consent of the king for sixty marks of silver. This vessel was extraordinary for the quality of its precious stone, its largely unblemished condition, and its decoration with the cloisonné work of Saint Eligius,[lxi] for which reason all goldsmiths considered it to be very valuable.

As a great token of his affection, the king gave us another vessel that resembled a ewer of beryl or crystal about the size of a pint;[160] his newly wed queen had given it to the Lord King Louis[161] during their first journey through Aquitaine.[lxii] We, however, bestowed it with great emotion upon our lords, the Holy Martyrs, for the sacrifice of the divine table. We inscribed on this same vessel, which had been decorated with gems and gold, the sequence of events surrounding this donation in the following short verses:

> His wife Eleanor gave this vessel to King Louis,
> Mitadolus gave it to her grandfather, the king gave it to me, and
> Suger gave it to the saints.[162]

We purchased for the divine services of that altar an expensive chalice from one solid piece of sardonyx composed of sard and onyx.[lxiii] The red sard of the stone stands out, in contrast to the blackness of onyx, in striated bands of color in such a way that one seems determined to overcome the distinctive quality of the other.

We added another vessel of similar material to the one above, but in the shape of an amphora, and these short verses were inscribed on it:

---

159. Louis VI.
160. The measure used here is a *justa*, a measure almost equivalent to a pint.
161. Louis VII.
162. Mitadolus has been identified with Imad al Dawla, the king of Saragossa, Spain (r. 1110–30). Mitadolus is the Latinized form of his Arab name; see *Oeuvres* (ed. Gasparri), 1:240n281. He gave this vessel to Eleanor's grandfather, William IX of Aquitaine.

> Since we should pour libations to God from vessels
> Of gems and gold, I, Suger, offer this one to the Lord.[lxiv]

We were also thrilled to add to the other vessels for that same divine service, a splendid large gallon vessel that Count Theobald of Blois sent to us in the same case in which the king of Sicily had sent it to him.[lxv]

We also placed there some small crystal vessels that we had assigned for the daily service of the altar in our own chapel.[163]

In addition, we adapted a porphyry vessel that a sculptor and polisher had beautifully handcrafted for the service of the altar; it had lain idle in a chest for many years. We modified its flagon design, using gold and silver, into the shape of an eagle, and then had these verses inscribed on it:

> This stone deserves to be encased in gems and gold,
> It was marble but encased in these it is more precious than marble.[lxvi]

We thanked Almighty God and the Holy Martyrs for all these treasures, because God did not hesitate to give generously to this most holy altar. For He wished us to be offered from childhood at it, under the authority of our holy rule, so that we might honorably serve Him.

Since we knew it was useful and honorable not to hide, but to publicly proclaim divine favors, we pointed out the increase of liturgical fabrics that the divine hand gave to this holy church during the time of our administration. We implore that on our anniversary they be displayed to appease the superiority of the divine majesty, to deepen the devotion of the brothers, and to set an example for succeeding abbots to emulate. However, late and infrequent penance is not enough to atone for my many serious mistakes or for my large number of sins, unless we rely on the intercession of the universal Church.

---

163. These crystal cruets have been lost; see *Oeuvres* (ed. Gasparri), 1:241–42n285.

ENDNOTES

i. Born in Italy, Denis was sent to Gaul with other missionary bishops to convert the province to Christianity. Denis became the first bishop of Paris. Under the persecution of Emperor Decius, he was beheaded there, along with his priest Rusticus and his deacon Eleutherius, according to legend, in the middle of the third century. These martyrs became the patron saints of the abbey of Saint-Denis. Denis himself later became the patron saint of France. See Gregory of Tours, *History of the Franks*, trans. O. M. Dalton, Oxford Medieval Texts [hereafter "OMT"] (Oxford: Clarendon Press, 1927), 2:20. See also below, appendix A (217–22).

ii. The Lendit Fair within the fortified town of Saint-Denis originally began on June 9, 1053, and was held in conjunction with the display of the abbey's relics of the passion of Christ—one of the nails used in the crucifixion and part of the crown of thorns. Louis VI started the Fair held out on the highway about halfway between Saint-Denis and Paris in 1111–12. This Fair opened on the second Wednesday in June and continued until June 23, the eve of the feast of Saint John the Baptist. Louis VI awarded the Fair to the abbey of Saint-Denis in 1124.

iii. The Latin word *serviens* is used here and can denote a servant or an armed peasant from the lowest rank of the warrior class who has enough money to supply his own weapons.

iv. A tallage is a tax paid by a tenant to his lord that could be paid in coin or in kind. This kind of tax was not abolished until the French Revolution.

v. Homage is the recognition by a vassal that he is holding an estate (manor) or fief in the name of a lord. There are mutual obligations formally stated that are involved in such ties. At times the ceremony of homage can be formal during which the vassal recognizes his service to a lord as his "man" and later swears an oath of fealty or allegiance to his lord. The types of ceremonies will vary.

vi. Three definitions of the Latin word *carruca* used here are provided by Niermeyer. It can mean "a wheeled plough," "a demesne arable field" belonging to the lord of the manor, and "as much land as can be ploughed by a wheeled plough in one season." The amount of land involved varies by region and period of time. In England it usually equaled a hide or about 120 acres. See J. F. Niermeyer and C. Van de Kieft, *Mediae Latinitatis Lexicon Minus*, vol. 1 (Leiden: Brill, 2002), 195.

vii. The *tensamentum* was a tax paid in coin or kind by a tenant to his lord in return for protection. See further Marjorie Chibnall et al., *King Stephen's Reign*, ed. Paul Dalton and Graeme J. White (Woodbridge: Boydell, 2008), 175. *Mortmain* is a legal right to the inalienable holding of land or real estate. In the Middle Ages this right was held by a church or an abbey, for the church or abbey never died according to medieval thought. This right meant a significant economic loss to a lord or to a secular community.

viii. Argenteuil, Val d'Oise, Île-de-France is located about seven miles west of Saint-Denis on the opposite bank of the Seine River. The town's name comes from the silver deposits (*argent* in French) that the Gauls utilized. The town grew up around the priory that was established there in the seventh century. Héloïse, who had the tragic romance with Peter Abelard, became its prioress in the early 1120s but was expelled in 1129.

ix. A medieval register of church immunities lists all the exemptions from legal obligation imposed upon it by custom, law, or by superior authority, which have been granted to either an ecclesiastical property or person. These immunities were not always honored, and those who do not honor them would be the defrauders mentioned here.

x. Hermenricus and his wife, Numma, founded the priory of Argenteuil during the reign of Clovis II (ca. 634–57), who was known as "the Lazy." Clovis succeeded his father Dagobert I and, like his father, was buried in the Church of Saint-Denis. Clovis gave the priory of Argenteuil to the abbey of Saint-Denis. See further *Oeuvres* (ed. Gasparri), 1:196n28. Suger is obviously not reviewing the foundation charter granted in the mid-650s, as indicated by the mention of King Pepin III "the Short" (714–68) here. The monks of Saint-Denis educated both Pepin and his brother Carloman. Wishing to be king of the Franks, Pepin asked the abbot of Saint-Denis to solicit the support of Pope Zachary for this purpose. Pope Zachary crowned him king of the Franks at Soissons in 751, making him the first Carolingian king. In 756 Pope Stephen II anointed Pepin, along with his two sons, Charles and Carloman, at Saint-Denis in a ceremony that established the traditional coronation rights of French kings. Pepin is buried at Saint-Denis, where all but three kings of France were also buried.

xi. Charlemagne's daughter Théorade was reputed to have been abbess of the priory of Argenteuil. She brought with her into the priory the "Seamless Robe of Jesus" that the Empress Irene of Constantinople gave to her father in about 800. However, other places also claim to possess this venerated relic.

xii. Louis the Pious was the only surviving son of Charlemagne and his wife, Hildegard, when he became king of the Franks and emperor of the Romans in 813. At that time he was anointed as co-king and co-emperor with his father, who died the following year leaving him as sole ruler. Louis died in 840; and his three sons, Lothair, Louis the German, and Charles the Bald, battled over the succession. The signing of the Treaty of Verdun in 843 that divided their father's kingdom and empire into three parts ended the dispute. The West went to Charles, the East to Louis, and the middle and Italy to Lothair.

xiii. These properties are as follows:
  1. Trappes, Yvelines, Île-de-France is located about twenty-six miles southwest of Saint-Denis.

2. Élancourt, Yvelines, Île-de-France is located about twenty-eight miles southwest of Saint-Denis.
3. Chavenay, Yvelines, Île-de-France is located about twenty-five miles west of Saint-Denis.
4. Bourdonné, Yvelines, Île-de-France is located about forty-two miles southwest of Saint-Denis.
5. Chérisy, Eure-et-Loir, Île-de-France is located about fifty-three miles southwest of Saint-Denis.
6. Montmélian is today part of Montefontaine, Oise, Picardy, which is located about twenty miles northeast of Saint-Denis.
7. Bondy, Seine-Saint-Denis, Île-de-France is located about eight miles southeast of Saint-Denis.
8. Montereau, Seine-et-Marne, Île-de-France is located about sixty-one miles southeast of Saint-Denis.
9. Melun, Seine-et-Marne, Île-de-France is located about forty miles southeast of Saint-Denis.

For the locations of these properties, see above, "The Possessions of the Abbey of Saint-Denis in the Twelfth Century," figure, 70.

xiv. The Roman emperor ruled a medieval political body that included Germany, northern Italy, and most of central Europe. The origin of the title of Roman emperor dates back to when Pope Leo III (r. 795–816) crowned Charlemagne (r. 800–814) "Emperor of the Romans" on December 25, 800. Charlemagne and his Germanic successors perceived themselves to be the inheritors of the Western Roman Empire as well as continuing the line of Roman emperors. The emperors from Charlemagne to Otto I (r. 962–73) called themselves *Romanum Imperator Augustus* or "August Emperor of the Romans." There was no Roman emperor from 924 to 962 because of civil strife inside the empire. However, Pope John XII (r. 955–64) crowned Otto I Emperor of the Romans in 962. Most historians argue that Otto I was the first emperor of what later became known as the Holy Roman Empire; Otto II (r. 973–83) was the first to call himself "Roman Emperor," and Frederick I Barbarossa applied the term "Holy" to the title in 1157. The princes of Germany chose successive Holy Roman Emperors. In 1356, Emperor Charles IV (r. 1355–78) issued the Golden Bull, which established the process by which future emperors of Germany were to be elected. According to the terms of the constitution, seven electors from various principalities in Germany would elect the emperor. The elected emperor of Germany assumed the title of Holy Roman Emperor and was crowned by the pope. Charles V (r. 1519–56) in 1530 was the last elected emperor to be crowned by the pope. The power of the Holy Roman Emperors was limited to their hereditary domains and the imperial cities of Frankfurt and Augsburg. Most political matters in the empire were decided by a Diet, a deliberative assembly that represented the various principalities. Although the numerous lords, princes, and kings in the empire were technically vassals of the Holy Roman Emperor and owed him service, they had de facto sovereignty in their own domains.

xv. The Vexin is an ancient county that dates from Carolingian times. It was divided into two parts in the treaty of Saint-Clair-sur-Epte in 911, with one belonging to the Normans and the other to the French. It was frequently fought over between the Angevins and the Capetians in medieval times. For the location of the Vexin, see the map below, "Normandy in the Twelfth Century," 142. Suger gave the details of this incursion into France by the German emperor Henry V (r. 1111–25, king of the Germans from 1106) in *The Deeds*, 127.

xvi. Suger here uses the word *hospitium*, the lord's right to food and lodging, which customarily might be taken a few times a year. This right entailed the same for his entourage, which could often be very large, and if taken too frequently, it imposed an impossible burden on medieval villeins. For these donations, see *Louis VI* (ed. Luchaire), no. 289 (135) and no. 315 (145–46), and *Louis VII* (ed. Luchaire), no. 111 (135–36), no. 137 (143), and no. 414 (233).

xvii. It is doubtful that Suger is referring to professional warriors here. These soldiers were probably peasants and commoners who had the duty of protecting the manors on which they lived. They were usually lightly armed and sometimes used axes, hoes, scythes, and other farming implements for weapons. At other times, the lord of the manor supplied them with their weapons. In this instance, Abbot Suger furnished their weapons because these manors belonged to Saint-Denis.

xviii. Pawning in medieval times was similar to what it is today. Something of value was put up to secure a loan of money and was not returned until the loan was repaid to the lender. In this case, the manor of Vernouillet was the pawn for a past monetary loan to the abbey of Saint-Denis. The lender who had held the manor is not known.

xix. The length of the mile used in medieval France was the Roman one, which was the equivalent of a thousand paces (the *milia passum*) or the distance between the fall of the same foot while walking (two thousand steps), about 1,620 yards today. The modern mile is 1,760 yards.

xx. On Amalric, count of Montfort and Évreux (ca. 1070–1137), see further Suger, *The Deeds*. Évreux, Eure, Upper Normandy is located about sixty-two miles west of Saint-Denis. Montfort is today Montfort-l'Amaury, Yvelines, Île-de-France and is located about thirty-six miles southwest of Saint-Denis.

xxi. Dagobert I (ca. 603/5–639) was the last Merovingian king to rule a united Frankish kingdom. He founded the abbey of Saint-Denis and was the first Frankish king to be buried in its church.

xxii. Demesne land was held by the manor's lord for his own use and support rather than rented or reserved for the use and support of the estate's villeins. The amount of demesne land varied from place to place but was at least a fifth to a third of the manor's arable land.

xxiii. Suger here called the manor of Monnerville "holy" because it now belonged to the abbey of Saint-Denis, and "inheritance" because, as Hugh of Méréville claimed in the next sentence, he had inherited the customary rights over the manor from his father, grandfather, and great-grandfather.

xxiv. Louis VII confirmed this renunciation by Hugh in favor of Saint-Denis in a charter dated 1144; see *Louis VII* (ed. Luchaire), no. 139 (144) and *Oeuvres* (ed. Gasparri), 1:79n83.

xxv. Hugh III of Le Puiset was a notorious enemy of Louis VI and rebelled against him at least three times (see Suger, *The Deeds*, 84). Hugh was the son of Evrard III of Le Puiset, who went on the First Crusade, and Alice of Corbeil. Hugh married Agnes of Blois. He went to Palestine in 1128 and disappears from all records. See further John L. La Monte, "The Lords of Le Puiset on the Crusades," *Speculum* 17 (January 1942): 100–118, here 101–2.

xxvi. Adam, abbot of Saint-Denis in 1099–1122, sent Suger to administer Toury in 1109 when he was in his late twenties. He discusses his administration and the conflict with Hugh III of Le Puiset in detail in *The Deeds*, 87–91.

xxvii. Saint Ivo, bishop of Chartres in 1090–1116, was a famous theologian and canon lawyer, and was one of the most learned men of his time. He studied along with Saint Anselm at Bec under Lanfranc, later archbishop of Canterbury. The chapter of Notre Dame mentioned in this sentence is the cathedral chapter of canons at Chartres. The Church of Saint Peter of Chartres then belonged to the Benedictine abbey of Saint-Père-en-Vallée, located down the hill south of the cathedral near the Eure River, whose abbot at that time was William I (r. 1102–29). Saint Ivo founded the Church of Saint-Jean-en-Vallée at Chartres in 1099–1101 and placed it under the Augustinian rule. The bishop of Orléans from 1096–1135 was John II; on John, a close friend of Louis VI, see further Suger, *The Deeds*. Saint-Aignan is a very beautiful church in Orléans that was originally built around 400 A.D. and later named for Saint Aignan, a bishop of Orléans who died in 453. The church was rebuilt in the eleventh century. The abbey of Saint-Benoît-sur-Loire at Fleury, Nièvre, Burgundy was founded in seventh century, but the church still standing today was dedicated in 1108; its abbot at this time was Boso, r. 1108–30. The archbishop of Sens was Daimbert (r. 1098–1122), who consecrated King Louis VI at Orléans in 1108 and caused a dispute with the church of Reims that claimed the right to crown French kings; see further Suger, *The Deeds*, 63–64.

xxviii. The villein's customary duties included working in and harvesting the crops of the lord's fields, digging ditches, repairing roads and bridges, paying taxes and rents in money or kind, and sometimes working in the lord's manor house.

xxix. Homage was a formal ceremony in which a vassal recognized someone as his lord. It often required kneeling before a lord and handing him an object that symbolized the fief being held in return for the vassal's homage. Service usually required the vassal's furnishing armed and equipped troops to the lord at least three times a year. Justice required that the vassal hold court and render good decisions in settling disputes. In this case, the young man and his successors would owe these obligations to the abbots of Saint-Denis as long as the contract between them remained valid.

xxx. Galeran, Viscount of Breteuil, was born about 1070 and died about 1130. *Oeuvres* (ed. Lecoy), 366, indicates in a charter of 1124 that Galeran gave a land in the region of Orléans to the king who then gave it to Saint-Denis. Breteuil, Eure, Upper Normandy is located about eighty-one miles west of Saint-Denis.

xxxi. See *Oeuvres* (ed. Gasparri), 1:200n121. The liberty that Saint-Denis enjoyed was the right to elect its abbot without the approval of the bishop of Paris.

xxxii. William I, duke of Aquitaine, established the abbey of Cluny in Burgundy in 910. It followed the Rule of Saint Benedict strictly and became another model for Western monasticism.

xxxiii. The abbey of Saint-Martin-des-Champs was originally founded during Merovingian times, but the Normans destroyed it in the late 900s. King Henry I of France rebuilt it in 1060, and it was given to Cluny in 1079. In medieval times it stood in the fields outside the city walls east of Paris (hence its name).

xxxiv. Prior Herveus of Saint-Denis assisted Suger in selecting the burial site for King Louis VI in the abbey church; see Suger, *The Deeds*, 159. He is also mentioned below in the *Life of Suger*, 192.

xxxv. Corbie Abbey was founded in Merovingian times (659/661). Corbie, Somme, Picardy is about eighty-three miles north of Saint-Denis. Robert, a monk of Saint-Denis, was abbot there from 1123–42.

xxxvi. The *Te Deum Laudamus* was an early Christian hymn of praise to the Father and the Son of the Trinity. It was sung at the end of Matins, the first and longest of the eight canonical hours, which was usually celebrated between midnight and 3 a.m., depending upon the season. The *Te Deum Laudamus* was also sung at other important liturgical celebrations.

xxxvii. For a listing of the treasures, decorations, shrines, altars, etc., of the abbey church, see Conway, "Abbey of Saint-Denis," 103–58, and M. Félibien, *Histoire de l'Abbaye Royale de Saint-Denys en France* (Paris: Frederick Leonard, 1706), and Anonymous, *A History and Description*.

xxxviii. Theobald (1090–1152), count of Blois and Chartres (1102–52) and count of Champagne (1125–52), was the son of Adela, a daughter of William the Conqueror. Theobald's brother Stephen became king of England. Theobald was often an enemy, sometimes an ally, of Louis VI; see Suger, *The Deeds*.

xxxix. The geographical divisions referred to here represent the middle and western parts of the Carolingian empire held by two of Louis the Pious's sons, Lothair and Charles the Bald, as formalized in the Treaty of Verdun in 843. For the possessions then held by Saint-Denis, see *Oeuvres* (ed. Gasparri), 1:201–2n135.

xl. These properties were all in northeastern France near the German border southeast of Metz. Arlange is still a farm; Ebersing is today called Vahl-Ebersing, and Salonnes retains its medieval name. They are in the Moselle department in the region of Lorraine.

xli. Metz (Moselle, Lorraine) is today a city in northeastern France just south of its border with Luxembourg; Guemines is today called Sarreguemines (Moselle, Lorraine) and is located on the German border; Blidestroff is today Kleinblittersdorf (Sarre, Sarrebrück, Germany), which is located on the Saar River (Sarre in French) that forms the border between Germany and France. Cochelingen is known today as Kuchlingen and is in the Saarland, Germany. See above, "The Possessions of the Abbey of Saint-Denis in the Twelfth Century," figure, 70.

xlii. See *Louis VII* (ed. Luchaire), nos. 167–68 (152–53), for the acts of 1146 in which the king determined that the abbey of Saint Peter of Chaumont belonged to Saint-Denis as well as his threat to the abbot to abandon his allegiance to the archbishop of Rouen.

xliii. King Henry I of England, youngest son of William the Conqueror and Matilda of Flanders, reigned in 1100–1135. He succeeded his brother William Rufus after William died in that untimely hunting accident in the New Forest. His governmental and tax reforms, for example the Rolls Series, helped make him a very successful ruler.

xliv. January 19. During his reign Dagobert I, king of Austrasia in 623–34 and king of the Franks in 629–34, gave a huge land holding in the area of Berneval-le-Grand to the abbey of Saint-Denis after he founded it.

xlv. Suger began this first addition at the western end of the abbey church, its narthex, about 1135 and completed it about 1140. For the iconography and the seventeenth and eighteenth century restorations of the western façade, see in *Abbot Suger* (ed. Gerson), the essays by Paula Lieber Gerson, "Suger as Iconographer: The Central Portal of the West Façade of Saint-Denis," 183–98, and Pamela Z. Blum, "The Lateral Portals of the West Façade of the Abbey Church of Saint-Denis: Archaeological and Iconographical Considerations," 199–227.

xlvi. Suger's work began at the main door of the western façade sometime in 1135–37, and this part of the church was consecrated on June 9, 1140. See Crosby, *The Abbey of Saint-Denis, 475–1122*, 1:77, 89, 92–93, 121, and *Oeuvres* (ed. Gasparri), 1:204n166. Charles Martel was the Mayor of the Palace for the Merovingian kings in 714–41. Pope Stephen II anointed his son Pepin the Short as king of the Franks in the Church of Saint-Denis in 754, an act that solidified his earlier seizure of the throne in 751 and subsequent coronation as the first Carolingian king. Charlemagne, son of Pepin the Short, was king of the Franks in 768–814; Pope Leo III crowned him emperor of the Romans at Rome in 800.

xlvii. King Louis VII took up the cross and pledged himself to go on a crusade to the East on Easter Sunday at the Council of Vézelay in 1146. Then, in February 1147 at the Council of Étampes, the king appointed Suger as one of his regents to govern the kingdom during his absence. Pope Eugenius III came to France in 1147 because of troubles in Rome and proceeded to Saint-Denis to celebrate the Easter services during which the pope named Suger as his apostolic vicar to assist him in governing the kingdom during King Louis VII's absence. See Odo, *De profectione*, 7–9; *Oeuvres* (ed. Gasparri), 1:219n218; and *Morigny* (ed. Cusimano), 156–62. See also below *Life of Louis VII*, X, 138nxxx, and *Life of Suger*, Bk. III, 198n34.

xlviii. Born about 1050, Guy of Burgundy was consecrated archbishop of Vienne by Pope Urban II in 1088; he was elected supreme pontiff at Cluny on February 21, 1119, and took the papal name Calixtus II. Queen Adelaide, the wife of King Louis VI, was his niece; see further Suger, *The Deeds*, 120. He died in 1124.

xlix. Born Gregorio Papareschi dei Guidoni, Innocent II succeeded to the papal throne in 1130 upon the death of Honorius II (r. 1124–30). The supporters of the antipope Anacletus II drove him from Rome, and Innocent fled to France. He received the support of Bernard of Clairvaux, Emperor Lothar III (r. 1125–37), and King Henry I of England (r. 1100–1135) and so was able to claim the papacy. Innocent was at Saint-Denis for Easter, April 19, 1131; see further Suger, *The Deeds*, 145–49, and *Morigny* (ed. Cusimano), 100–104.

l. Suger considers Charles the Bald to be the third emperor, with his grandfather Charlemagne and his father, Louis the Pious, being the first and second emperors, respectively. Charles was king of the West Franks in 843–77 and became emperor of the Romans in 875. He died in 877. For a detailed discussion of this altar, see *Abbot Suger* (ed. Panofsky), 186–88, and *Oeuvres* (ed. Gasparri), 1:220n222.

li. The cross of Saint Eligius is first mentioned in Hincmar's *Gesta Dagoberti*, written at Saint-Denis in the ninth century by someone in the entourage of Abbot Hilduin (r. 814–41). For a complete account of this cross, see the *Gesta Dagoberti*, 407, and *Oeuvres* (ed. Gasparri), 1:222–23n229.

lii. Ezek 28:13. These stones are some of the ones mentioned on the breastplate of Aaron (Ex 28:17), where each stone represents one of the twelve tribes of Israel. The sardonyx stands for the tribe of Reuben, the topaz for that of Simeon, the jasper for that of Benjamin, the chrysolite is the alternate stone for the tribes of both Simeon and Zebulun, the onyx stands for the tribe of Joseph, the beryl for that of Zebulun, the sapphire for that of Dan, the carbuncle for that of Levi, and the emerald for that of Judah. The diamond for the tribe of Naphtali, the hyacinth for that of Gad, and the agate for that of Asher are missing from Suger's list of precious stones.

liii. These critics may well be Saint Bernard of Clairvaux and his fellow Cistercians who abjure all ornamentation in their churches and services. See especially Bernard to Suger, in Bernard, *Letters*, no. 80 (110), and *Oeuvres* (ed. Gasparri), 1:226n237.

liv. Those present for the inspection of the holy relics were:
1. Faucon of Bothéon, archbishop of Lyons (r. 1139–42).
2. Samson of Mauvoisin, archbishop of Reims (r. 1140–61).
3. Hugh of La Ferté, archbishop of Tours (r. 1133–47).
4. Hugh of Amiens, archbishop of Rouen (r. 1130–64).
5. Jocelin of Verzy, bishop of Soissons (r. 1126–52).
6. Odo II, bishop of Beauvais (r. 1133–44).
7. Peter, bishop of Senlis (r. 1134–51).
8. Manasses II, bishop of Meaux (r. 1134–58).
9. The bishop of Rennes was either Hamelin (r. 1127–41) or Alain (r. 1141–56).
10. Donald, bishop of Alet (Saint-Malo, r. 1120–44).
11. Ives (Evenus), bishop of Vannes (r. 1137–43).

lv. This celebration that Charles decreed had been neglected for some time. Suger restored it and decreed that it be held on the day before the nones of each month, which would be the sixth day of March, May, July, and October and on the fourth day of the other months. See further *Oeuvres* (ed. Lecoy), Charter X, 353.

lvi. This cross has been called "the Cross of Charlemagne," but may have been among the gifts that Charles the Bald gave to the abbey. It disappeared after 1610. For a description of it and its history, see *Oeuvres* (ed. Gasparri), 1:230n255, and *Abbot Suger* (ed. Panofsky), 190.

lvii. "The Tree of Jesse Window" is located in in the chapel of the Virgin in the ambulatory in the eastern end of the church directly behind the altar of Saint Denis. For the biblical Jesse Tree, see Is 11:1. These trees trace the genealogy of Christ back to Jesse through the Virgin Mary. They were very popular in the stained glass windows of the twelfth and thirteenth centuries.

lviii. This window is called in *Abbot Suger* (ed. Panofsky), 193–94, "The Anagogical Window" and is located today in the chapel of Saint Peregrinus in the central section of the church's ambulatory. The window has also been called "The Allegories of Saint Paul Window"; see further Summer Crosby et al., *The Royal Abbey of Saint-Denis in the Time of Abbot Suger, 1122–1151* (New York: Metropolitan Museum of Art, 1981), 69 and 86.

lix. Mosaic Law refers to the first five books of the Hebrew Bible, known as the Torah, which include the books of Genesis, Exodus, Leviticus, Numbers, and Deuteronomy. Christian scholars refer to them as the Pentateuch, which is Greek for "five scrolls."

lx. Prase is a leek-green colored stone that is a variety of chalcedony. The empress mentioned here is probably Matilda (ca. 1102–67), daughter of King Henry I of England, who married Emperor Henry V of the Roman Empire in 1114. Following Henry V's death in 1125, she married Count Geoffrey the Handsome of Anjou in 1128. As Henry I's only surviving heir, she became embroiled in a civil war against her cousin, Stephen of Blois, for the throne of England that eventually passed to her eldest son, Henry II, in 1154. The vessel in the shape of a boat or gondola described here by Suger was stolen in 1804 and disappeared; see Conway, "Abbey of Saint-Denis," 126–27.

lxi. Cloisonné is the technique of applying vitreous enamel to an object that is set with precious stones, glass, or other materials. Saint Eligius was famous for crafting objects using this technique for Kings Clothar II and Dagobert I in the seventh century.

lxii. This ewer is preserved in the Louvre. Louis VII's wife was Eleanor of Aquitaine (1122–1204), the daughter of William X of Aquitaine and his heir. Suger himself had traveled to Bordeaux with the royal party when they married in July 1137; see Suger, *The Deeds*, 156–57; *Morigny* (ed. Cusimano), 125–27; and below, *Life of Louis VII*, VIII, 164–65nnxxvi–xxvii.

lxiii. This is the famous "Chalice of Suger," the cup of which seems to have been made in Alexandria, Egypt, about a century before Christ. The monastery's craftsmen added the base, handles, and rim made of gilded silver and precious stones. Once thought lost, it was rediscovered in 1922 and is today in the National Gallery of Art in Washington, D.C.

lxiv. This is the "Sardonyx Ewer of Suger" and is preserved today in the Louvre. For a description of this vessel, see *Oeuvres* (ed. Gasparri), 1:241n283. For the inspiration of the inscription, see Heb 9:11–14.

lxv. Count Theobald IV of Blois and Chartres (r. 1102–52; Theobald II as count of Champagne, r. 1125–52) was the older brother of King Stephen of England. The king of Sicily was Roger II (r. 1101–54).

lxvi. This is "Suger's Eagle," which is preserved in the Louvre. The porphyry body of the vessel dates to ancient Egypt or imperial Rome. Suger's craftsmen added the eagle head, spread wings, and the base formed by the eagle's claws and tail. The additions are in gilded silver and niello inlay.

[3]

The Illustrious King Louis [VII], Son of Louis [VI][i]

[I]

Louis, the illustrious son of the illustrious King Louis,[1] after he heard news of the sudden, tragic death of his father,[ii] took counsel and carefully put the affairs of the duchy of Aquitaine in order, and then rushed to prevent the plundering, discord, and insurrection that usually arises when kings die.[iii] He quickly returned to the city of Orléans, where he discovered the insanity of some fools who wished to destroy royal authority there by establishing a commune.[2] He fearlessly suppressed them and, in the process, wounded some of them.[3] From there he went back to Paris because it was his official residence, for as one reads in the ancient histories, the kings of the Franks customarily lived there. He governed superbly for a young man his age, considering the situation, while he managed

---

1. King Louis VII (r. 1137–80). On Louis VII, see also Marcel Pacaut, *Louis VII et son royaume* (Paris: SEVPEN, 1964), and Yves Sassier, *Louis VII* (Paris: Fayard, 1991). He was the son of King Louis VI "the Fat" (r. 1108–37).

2. In August 1137.

3. For the pardon Louis VII granted the inhabitants of Orléans for their insurrection, see *Études sur les Actes de Louis VII*, ed. Achille Luchaire (Brussels: Culture et Civilisation, 1964), no. 15 (103).

the kingdom and defended the Church.[4] The entire land deemed itself fortunate because a very noble offspring would inherit from a very noble and peacemaking father, and would vigorously defend the entire kingdom, favor the just, and reject the wicked. Everyone had seen how the Roman Empire and the English kingdom had suffered tremendous turmoil and had almost been destroyed because they lacked an heir to the throne.[iv] The more everyone heard how the inhabitants of those kingdoms suffered during those troubles, the more everyone appreciated the happy succession of the king to the kingdom, and the benefits each and every one of them enjoyed because of it.[v]

[II]

After Emperor Henry of the Romans[vi] died without an heir, we attended a very large, general assembly of nearly sixty thousand knights that was held at Mainz to choose his successor.[5] A huge dispute arose at this assembly when Duke Frederick of Germany strove to gain the kingdom through discord and the factional division of the realm because he was the nephew of the deceased Emperor Henry.[6] The archbishops of Mainz and Cologne,[7] as well as most of the magnates and great men of the realm opposed his claim, and turned instead to Duke Lothar of Saxony,[8] whom they crowned

---

4. Louis would have been about sixteen or seventeen years old at this time. For the birth year of Louis VII, see *Oeuvres* (ed. Gasparri), 1:244n17.

5. Mainz today is the capital city of the state of Rhineland-Palatinate in western Germany.

6. Frederick II "the One-Eyed" (1090–1147) was the second Hohenstaufen duke of Swabia and the nephew of Emperor Henry V. He was also the father of Emperor Frederick I Barbarossa.

7. Archbishop Adalbert I of Mainz (r. 1111–37) and Archbishop Frederick I of Cologne (r. 1100–1131) supported the election of Lothar III. Cologne today is Germany's fourth largest city and is located in the German Federal State of North Rhine-Westphalia. For the election at Mainz, see also Otto of Freising, *The Deeds of Frederick Barbarossa*, trans. Charles Christopher Mierow (New York: Columbia University Press, 1953), 48.

8. Duke Lothar III of Supplinburg of Saxony (1075–1137) was crowned German king in 1125 and Roman emperor as Lothar II in 1133. Saxony today is a federal state in east-central Germany that borders the countries of Poland and the Czech Republic.

with the royal diadem at Aachen, amid great jubilation among the clergy and people.[vii] However, this renowned coronation caused great harm to many when Duke Frederick was denied the throne of the realm. His parents, his brother Conrad[9] who would later succeed to the throne after Lothar's death, the rest of his faction, and Duke Frederick himself forced the realm to endure huge expenditures, wars, burnings, pillaging of the poor, destruction of churches, countless damages, and similar sufferings.[viii] Lothar accomplished many impressive feats, but the most eminent ones that are attributed to his chivalry, which are worthy of praise and admiration, were as follows. He gained the kingdom of the Germans without the legal right of inheritance and governed it forcefully. He subjected Italy to his authority and received the crown of the Roman Empire from Pope Innocent at Rome, despite the resistance of the Romans.[ix] Lothar traveled through the provinces of Capua and Benevento, and conquered Apulia by the sword.[10] He put the king of Sicily[x] to flight and seized the city of Bari with its surrounding countryside.[xi] He gained every trophy of victory, but while returning from those regions death, which awaits us all, caught up with him. Having been brought back to his native soil and to his own household in the duchy of Saxony, Lothar secured an honorable end to his great efforts.[11]

[III]

We also remember the same kind of chaos that occurred in the kingdom of the English over the same issue, following the death of its valorous and renowned King Henry.[xii] After Henry had lost his heir

---

9. Duke Conrad III of Franconia (1093–1152) was the brother of Duke Frederick II of Swabia. He succeeded Lothar III as king of Germany in 1137 and was crowned at Coblenz in 1138, thus becoming the first ruler of the Hohenstaufen dynasty to hold that title.

10. Capua, Caserta, Campania is a commune located about 152 miles south of Rome; Benevento, Benevento, Campania is a commune located about 144 miles southeast of Rome; Apulia is a region in extreme southeast Italy that forms "the heel" of Italy and borders the Adriatic Sea.

11. Lothar III died on December 4, 1137.

at sea,[xiii] his nephew, Count Stephen of Boulogne,[xiv] the younger brother of the Palatine Count Theobald, unexpectedly arrived in the kingdom.[12] When he seized Matilda's crown, Stephen did not take into consideration that the count of Anjou[13] had married the former empress of the Romans, who was the daughter of his own uncle King Henry,[14] and had sons with her.[xv] Stephen's actions created division among the barons, counts, and magnates of the kingdom, and ruined a wealthy and bountiful land through factional hatred among its inhabitants. This civil war destroyed nearly a third of the land through desolation, the plunder of property, and the slaughter of men throughout the entire kingdom.[xvi] All these wars brought some relief to the French who were rejoicing and celebrating the succession of an outstanding and extraordinary young man, while the other kingdoms were suffering terribly without an heir to the throne.

[IV]

Let us, however, return to our main topic, King Louis, a young man who by age fourteen or fifteen was developing in character and perseverance every day. He allowed his wife and mother, Adelaide,[xvii] to live with him in the palace, out of his highborn sense of nobility, and, for a while, shared with them the expenses and the gifts expected from royal generosity.[15] His mother, however, had a woman's tendency to nag and spent most of her time criticizing his assertiveness. After she wore down the king's patience over this issue, she pleaded with him, certain palace officials, and me to negotiate the return of her dowry so that she could live a peaceful, contented, and

---

12. Theobald (1090–1152) became count of Blois and Chartres as Theobald IV in 1102 and then count of Champagne as Theobald II in 1125. He helped his brother Stephen of Blois become king of England in 1135. The title "Palatine" here refers to a lord or count who possesses powers in his territory over justice and money that were usually held only by a king.

13. Geoffrey V Plantagenet (1115–51).

14. King Henry I of England (1068–1135).

15. Eleanor of Aquitaine (1122–1204) married Louis VII on July 25, 1135, in the cathedral of Saint Andrew in Bordeaux. See Ralph V. Turner, *Eleanor of Aquitaine* (New Haven, Conn.: Yale University Press, 2009), 39.

private life away from the troubles of the kingdom.[xviii] Count Ralph, likewise, requested that he return to his own affairs.[xix] Certain people are motivated by greed, the one and only concern that drives them, and so they became totally despondent, for, without appropriating their revenues, there would not be enough money available to meet the king's anticipated generosity as well as the needs of his administration. Therefore, after I had somewhat rebuked those nearly hopeless men, reminding them that France had never before been left abandoned, every one of them departed feeling very ashamed.

[V]

However, we, who are indebted to the kingdom and received benefits from his father, adhered to the king's just counsel without reservation. After we had the counts and castellans of the nearby and surrounding regions swear an oath of fealty to the king, we then persuaded him to come quickly to the city of Langres in the upper Burgundian marches that border the kingdom of the Lotharingians.[16] We also took it upon ourselves to order Count Theobald to rush to Auxerre to meet him. Our intention was to loyally bind the count to his lord by a sworn oath of fealty, as Louis held supremacy over everyone in the kingdom through fealty, sworn oath, and legal penalties. Since the king was young and had a tendency to procrastinate, he did not properly execute the affairs of the kingdom, and so everyone appealed to us to provide them with their exact maintenance. Theobald vowed that from then on he would loyally and faithfully honor his allegiance to Louis, and as we listened, Theobald tearfully gave thanks to God because the Lord King favored him with vassalian service, as a close intimate, and kindly forgave him for the traditional hostility of his ancestors. We hastened through the countryside of Autun to the city of Langres, which welcomed the king cordially, as though it were his own residence.[17]

---

16. Langres, Haute-Marne, Champagne-Ardenne is a commune located 186 miles southeast of Saint-Denis.

17. Autun, Saône-et-Loire, Burgundy is a commune located 190 miles southeast of Saint-Denis.

The king received the homage and fealty of the entire territory, with Count Theobald and us standing there in attendance. Having given his instructions and orders to all, the king returned to Paris, *and the land grew silent in his sight.*[18]

[VI]

In the following year, since the king had not completely subdued the duchy of Aquitaine after the sudden death of his father, news reached him from Poitiers[19] that the citizens there had formed a commune, fortified the city with a palisade of oak stakes that surmounted an embankment,[20] seized the city's fortress, and formed under their leadership an alliance with the remaining cities, castles, and strongholds of Poitou.[xx] When the king heard this news, he was consumed with rage and a desire for revenge against this egregious plot; and without delaying at all, he ordered Count Theobald to come to him immediately. The king summoned the count to advise and help him to avenge this great insolence of the Poitevins, telling him, "Noble count, set out at once, for I have placed myself and my kingdom under your protection, and I rely on you to restore rebellious Poitou to our dominion. This insult to our authority will have great repercussions on you if you show yourself incompetent in any way during this great threat to the kingdom." Fear of being greatly dishonored did not compel the count to act; he answered that he would do nothing more than consult with his barons for their advice. Although the king preferred to remain in the field, he returned to Paris and sent us to the count, as though we were one of his intimates, to give him a deadline for his response. However, we could not obtain from the count any money or any knights, even though he and a few of his men would have been enough. Taking advice from his friends and us, the Lord King took it upon himself to as-

---

18. 1 Mc 1:3.
19. The revolt in Poitiers began in 1138. Poitiers, Vienne, Poitou-Charentes is a city located 217 miles southwest of Saint-Denis in the west-central province of Poitou.
20. For a description of this same structure see Suger, *The Deeds*, 56, and *Oeuvres* (ed. Gasparri), 1:167n26.

semble two hundred elite knights, bowmen, and artillerymen, and headed for Poitou. Having summoned the barons of the region, he forced the Poitevins to surrender without shedding blood, dissolved the commune, and compelled its members to swear solemn oaths. He seized young men and young women from the most prominent citizens as hostages to disperse them throughout France.[xxi] When we followed him to Poitiers, for we had not been able to travel with him because of the feast of Saint Denis, crowds of people rushed up and threw themselves down not only at our feet but also at the hooves of our horses. They continually repeated their sorrowful pleas and wept bitterly for us to have mercy and intercede on their behalf with the Lord King for the release of their children. When I could no longer endure the deep sighing, groaning, and wailing of the young men and women, as well as their mothers who carried on as if their offspring were being slain in their wombs, I had a private and cordial meeting with the Lord King, who was glad to see us, and I explained to him briefly the reasons for all the grief and miseries that I had witnessed. The king was a young man of great nobility and gentleness, who clearly understood that the power of imperial majesty had its source in divine mercy.[21] He explained to us why such a harsh action was necessary and justifiable, even though some might consider it to be cruel, and then left to our decision and judgment whatever I thought needed to be done. Two days later I sensed feelings of remorse in the hearts of those aggrieved citizens. However, early on the morning that the king had ordered, the parents prepared two-wheeled carriages, pack animals, small carts, and asses to carry away their young men and women to different remote regions throughout the land. All had assembled in the square in front of the palace where, if you listened long enough, it seemed like you might actually be hearing the loud wailing of the dead in hell. This deafening noise ascended almost up to the heavens, and it continued to resound in the ears of the king, the magnates, and us. We were astonished how the sounds from the grieving, crying, tearing of cheeks, and beating of breasts, which resembled the wretched

---

21. For an explanation of the concept of imperial majesty and royal mercy, see *Oeuvres* (ed. Gasparri), 1:245n30.

sufferings in hell, reverberated up to the windows of the palace. So the gentle king took us aside and anxiously asked what he should do, because the two options he had troubled him. If he released the hostages, the city and the region would escape any penalty, or if he deported them as he had planned, he would be sanctioning a cruel act and resentment of the royal majesty. Since everyone disagreed on what advice to give him, we boldly proposed, in the presence of all, what seemed right to us: "Lord King," I said, "the King of kings and Lord of lords governs you and your kingdom, and if you show pity for such unforeseen misery and tremendous distress, the compassionate and forgiving Lord will, in His mercy, protect you and place this city and the other cities of Aquitaine under your authority. Do not worry; the more humane you become, the more the divine power shall increase the prestige of the royal majesty." Divine inspiration soon showed the king what to do, "Come with me to the windows," he said, "and tell everyone that as a gift of royal generosity, I will forgive the unlawful formation of a commune and will freely and safely return their young sons and daughters to them. Give them a stern warning never to do anything like this again; otherwise, a much more severe punishment will be inflicted upon them." I am happy to say, that when everyone heard this, their great sadness turned into joy, their sorrow into jubilation, and their unbearable grief into the aroma of precious perfumes.[22] This comparison is, indeed, a fitting one, since grief is similar to death, and joy and exaltation are similar to life; for someone who lives in misery does not live at all. By this act of royal clemency, which was both compassionate and noble, the king won the love and loyal service of all of Poitou, for no one there ever again thought about a commune or any kind of conspiracy.

[VII]

We were delighted to leave the city after such a serious crisis had been resolved, with many different complaints investigated and settled peacefully; and we then hurried to the Atlantic coast to a

---

22. Est 9:22. See also Neh 8:12 and Ps 30:11.

well-known castle called either "Heel of the world" or "A remarkable world," so named because of its location.[xxii] For to those who believed in such things, fate placed a high value on the place because of its ideal location, the abundance of its produce, and the natural defenses of its castle. The nearby ocean flowed up to the wall of the castle twice daily, which allowed the vessels of different merchants to carry inside on the gentle tide fish, meat, and other types of commerce right up to the tower gate two times a day. The king ordered Baron William of Lezay, a seditious and cunning man, to appear before him because William had usurped this castle for himself, while it was under the baron's custody.[23] Since the king had already severely reprimanded the baron for seizing Duke William's white falcons, known as gyrfalcons, the king now tried to force the baron to return them by threatening him with dire consequences, and he also strongly urged him to surrender the castle.[24] The baron called the bishop of Soissons and me aside and insisted that we invite the Lord King to come there and recover his castle.[25] Thus, the bishop and many other people persuaded the Lord King to rush there and quickly repossess the castle while it was being offered to him. However, a few others, who felt the same way we did, never believed that the bishop and the other people were acting out of treachery; but we knew it would be too dangerous for our lord and us to go inside the walls of the castle without first taking possession of its impregnable tower. We told the king about a similar incident to prevent him from going inside the castle. Once when King Charles of the Franks[26] was returning from an expedition in Lotharingia, Count Herbert of Vermandois[27] graciously welcomed him under the right of hospitality,

---

23. William of Lezay was baron and castellan of Talmont-by-the-Sea. Lezay, Deux-Sèvres, Poitou-Charentes is a commune located about 250 miles southwest of Saint-Denis. See also *Oeuvres* (ed. Gasparri), 1:245n34.

24. Duke William X of Aquitaine (1099–1137), the father of Eleanor of Aquitaine.

25. Jocelin of Vierzy, bishop of Soissons (1126–52), known as "the Red," was a friend of Suger. Suger dedicated his *Deeds of Louis the Fat* (Suger, *The Deeds*, 23–24) to Jocelin. See also ibid., 126 and 169n1. For the correspondence between Suger and Jocelin, see Bernard, *Letters*, no. 298 (366) and no. 301 (372).

26. Charles III the Simple (879–929). Charles was King of West Francia in 898–922 and King of Lotharingia in 911–919/23.

27. Herbert II of Vermandois (d. 943) was the count of Vermandois and Meaux

just as a vassal and friend is obliged to do.[xxiii] However, this treacherous enemy condemned the king and kept him imprisoned there for the rest of his life. As further evidence, we also heard how this very same Baron William of Lezay had played the identical trick, or something similar, on Duke William. The duke had been received there one night under the right of hospitality; but when he tried to leave the castle the next morning, he had trouble exiting through the gate that shut him and his men inside, and was compelled to leave behind the more noble men of his army as prisoners. When many in our party still wished to go to that castle rather than stay away, we adamantly opposed their reckless bravado. However, they sent their servants ahead to select lodging and purchase suitable provisions, and they followed after them as if the whole thing were a joke. But we put a stop to this foolish conduct, and scolded and derided them because these incompetent men had also sent their warhorses and warriors ahead and left themselves defenseless. It did not take long for Baron William to reveal his treachery, for with hardly any noise he captured the men in the advance party who had already come inside. Welcoming them at the gate, he let in and seized those men he deemed to be the most prominent, while shutting out those he did not want. The captives inside reacted violently and shouted to the men outside the gate to flee. The traitors opened the gates and chased those outside, intending to quickly capture, wound, or despoil them when, suddenly, although he arrived late, the Lord King rushed into battle with his forces. Having armed himself with chain mail, a helmet, and metal greaves, he engaged the pursuers, rescued his fleeing men, and took his revenge against the men of Poitou with his Frenchmen who were about the only troops with him. What a sight! The king cut off the feet of two of the Poitevin knights, but lacking stamina due to his young age, he hacked away at them slowly. The distress of the prolonged amputation, however, did not take long to demoralize those two knights. The king forced his enemies to flee, and pushed them back through

---

and the first to exercise power over the territory that would become the province of Champagne. Vermandois is a French county in the Picardy region that dates back to the Merovingian period.

the gate, even though he appeared ruthless; and, with the help of God, he punished the treason of those wicked men with a brutal and deserved vengeance. At the same time he unexpectedly rushed to attack, with a mighty hand and outstretched arm, a fortress that seemed impregnable. He smashed his way in with his armed men, burned down the entire fortress, and breaking privileges of immunity even its abbeys and churches, everything up to the precinct of the tower.[28] However, the conspirators who survived took refuge in the tower....[xxiv]

[A monk of Saint-Germain-des-Prés wrote the following chapters.][xxv]

[VIII]

He arranged a marriage with Eleanor.[xxvi] At that time Duke William of Aquitaine set out on a pilgrimage to the shrine of Saint James, and, while there, a bodily illness struck him down and he went the way of all flesh. The duchy of Aquitaine was thus deprived of its lord, who left behind no male heir. He had only two daughters, one named Eleanor and the other Alice.[29] Therefore King Louis married the elder sister, Eleanor, and held the entire Aquitaine in his possession,[xxvii] and gave the younger sister, Alice, in marriage to Count Ralph of Vermandois. The king, however, had one daughter, named Marie, with Eleanor.[30]

---

28. The abbey, founded in the eleventh century, was situated inside the castle of Talmont. See *Oeuvres* (ed. Gasparri), 1:246n38. For "outstretched arm," see Dt 26:8.
29. Alice (ca. 1125–93), also known as Petronilla, was the younger daughter of Duke William X of Aquitaine. She married Count Ralph of Vermandois in 1140; and they had three children: Elizabeth (1143–83), Ralph II (1145–67), and Eleanor (1148/49–1213).
30. Marie (1145–98) was the eldest daughter of Louis and Eleanor. She married Henry I of Champagne in 1164 and they had four children: Henry II (1166–97), Marie (d. 1204), Theobald III (1179–1201), and Scholastique (d. 1219). Marie retired to the nunnery of Fontaines-les-Nones near Meaux, after the death of Henry, and died there in 1198.

[IX]

He stormed the castle of Montjay. Not many days had passed before Gaucher of Montjay became swollen with the devil's pride and attempted to revolt against the king, but this insolent and arrogant man had not yet tried to create unrest in the kingdom.[31] The brave-hearted king, however, became very concerned about this threat; and after gathering his forces from wherever he could find them, he rushed against Montjay and destroyed the castle, along with the entire walled town.

[X]

The king and the other magnates take up their crosses. In that same year the Christians in the regions around Jerusalem suffered a major setback. Inspired by a satanic spirit, the Parthians [i.e., Turks] attacked the city of Edessa [in 1144] with a powerful army and captured it, but they suffered heavy casualties in doing so.[xxviii] This storming of the city made them exceedingly revengeful, and they threatened to slaughter all the Christians in the region. When the most devout King Louis learned about this disaster, he became filled with the fervor of the Holy Spirit, and his sense of religious duty stirred him to action.[xxix] To deal with this crisis, he convened a large assembly during the time of the Easter services that same year [i.e., 1146] at Vézelay,[32] where he gathered together archbishops, bishops, abbots, numerous magnates, and barons of his kingdom, among whom was Abbot Bernard of Clairvaux.[xxx] Bernard and the bishops attending this assembly preached about the land where Our Lord Jesus Christ was made flesh and suffered his Passion on the Cross for the redemption of the human race. Their preaching and admonitions inspired

---

31. Little is known about Gaucher of Montjay, but he is mentioned in a charter of Louis VII; see *Louis VII* (ed. Luchaire), no. 229 (172–73). See also *Morigny* (ed. Cusimano), 216n11, and Suger, *Vie de Louis* (ed. Molinier), 157n3. Montjay is today Montjay-la-Tour near Villevaudé, Seine-et-Marne, Île-de-France and is located about nineteen miles southeast of Saint-Denis.

32. Vézelay, Yonne, Burgundy is a commune located about 149 miles southeast of Saint-Denis.

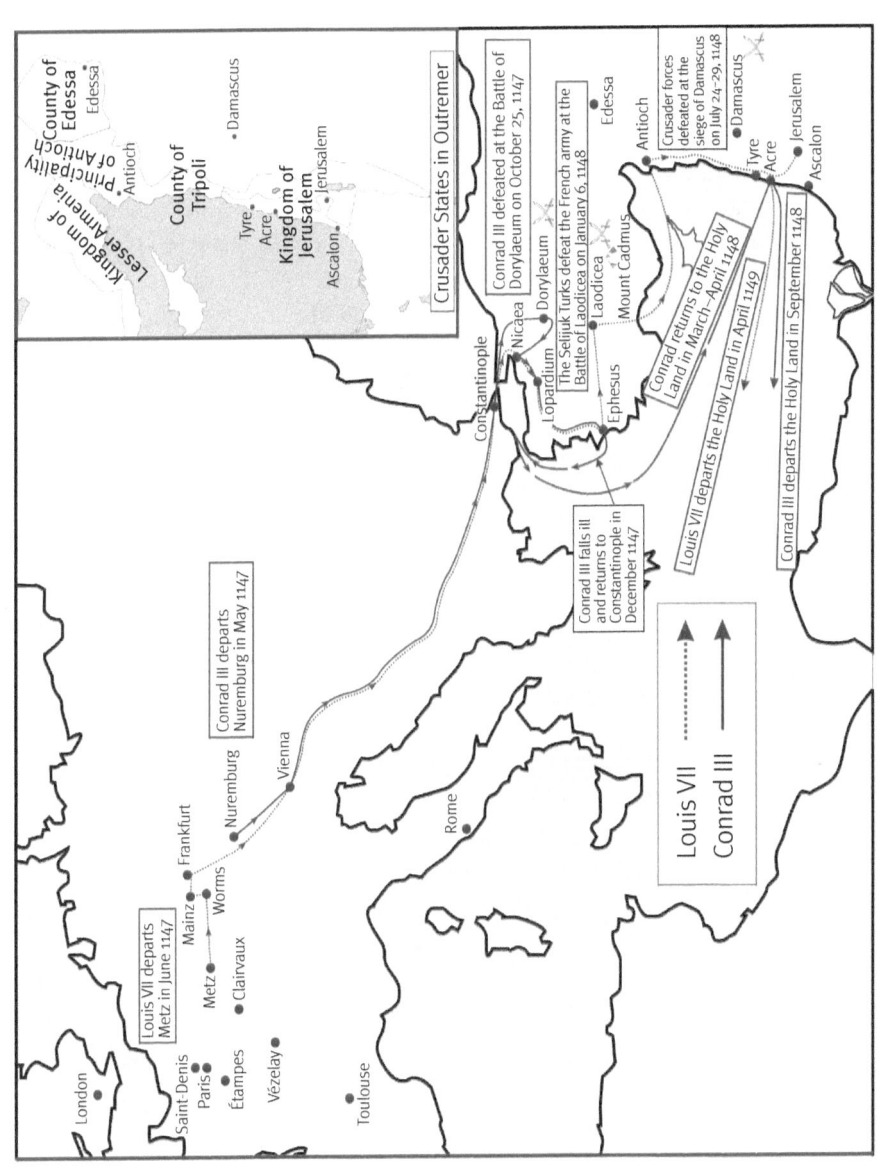

The Second Crusade

King Louis with divine grace; and burning with passion, he took up the cross, and after him his wife Eleanor.[xxxi] After witnessing this scene, the magnates standing nearby did the same. Those also taking up the cross after them were Bishop Simon of Noyon, Bishop Geoffrey of Langres, Bishop Arnulf of Lisieux, Abbot Herbert of Saint-Pierre-le-Vif at Sens, Abbot Theobald of Saint-Colombe, Count Alphonse of St. Egidius, Count Thierry of Flanders, Henry the son of the Palatine Count Theobald of Blois who was still alive at that time, Count William of Nevers and his brother Count Rainald of Tonnerre, Count Robert the brother of the king, Count Ivo of Soissons, Count Guy of Ponthieu, Count William of Warenne, Erchenbald of Bourbon, Enguerrand of Coucy, Geoffrey of Rançon, Hugh of Lusignan, William of Courtenay, Rainald of Montargis, Itier of Toucy, Gaucher of Montjay, Evrard of Breteuil, Dreux of Mouchy, Manasses of Bulles,[33] Anselm of Traînel and his brother Garin, William the Butler, William Aguillon of Trie, many other knights, and a countless number of foot soldiers.[xxxii] At the same time, Emperor Conrad of Germany[xxxiii] heard about the suffering of the Christians and took up the cross, as did Duke Frederick of Saxony,[xxxiv] who was his nephew and later became emperor. Count Amadeus of Moraine,[xxxv] the uncle of King Louis, and many other men in their retinues did the same. Then, the venerable Abbot Pons of Vézelay,[xxxvi] who revered the Holy Cross that the king and his companions had received, built a church to honor it at the spot on

33. Lisieux, Calvados, Lower Normandy is a commune located about 128 miles northwest of Saint-Denis. Tonnerre, Yonne, Burgundy is a commune located about 134 miles southeast of Saint-Denis. Ponthieu is one of the six counties that make up the province of Picardy. Coucy, Aisne, Picardy is a commune that contains the fortress of Coucy-le-Château-Auffrique, which was the power center of the lords of Coucy. It is located about seventy miles northeast of Saint-Denis. Rançon, Upper Vienne, Limousin is a commune located about 244 miles southwest of Saint-Denis. Lusignan, Vienne, Poitou-Charentes is a commune located about 233 miles southwest of Saint-Denis. Courtenay, Loiret, Centre-Val de Loire is a commune located about eighty-five miles southeast of Saint-Denis. Montargis, Loiret, Centre-Val de Loire is a commune located about seventy-nine miles southeast of Saint-Denis. Toucy, Yonne, Burgundy is a commune located about 109 miles southeast of Saint-Denis. Mouchy, Oise, Picardy is a commune located about thirty-nine miles north of Saint-Denis. Today it is known as Mouchy-le-Châtel. Bulles, Oise, Picardy is a commune located about fifty-four miles north of Saint-Denis.

the slope of the hill between Asquins[34] and Vézelay, where members of the assembly preached;[xxxvii] and the Lord has worked many miracles for the people of proper faith who have gathered in this church.

[XI]

The length of time the king carried the cross. Meanwhile, before King Louis set out for the regions of Jerusalem, he lingered in his kingdom for a whole year, from the Easter services when he took up the cross to the following Easter, including the days right up to Pentecost.[xxxviii]

[XII]

The death of Abbot Herbert of Saint-Pierre of Sens. While all of this was taking place, the burgesses of the city of Sens became extremely angry with Abbot Herbert of Saint-Pierre-le-Vif and brutally murdered him because he had dissolved their commune.[35] To avenge this act, the king had some of the murderers hurled off the tower of Sens and had others beheaded at Paris.[xxxix]

[XIII]

The king sets out for Jerusalem. In the year of the incarnation of the Lord 1146, the glorious King Louis wished to make the journey that he had vowed to undertake; and so he left the city of Paris a week after Pentecost, honorably surrounded by members of his retinue, as befit the occasion.[xl] After he departed, he endured many difficulties on the way before finally arriving at Jerusalem.[xli] After the king finished praying at the Sepulcher of the Lord and worshipped the Lord's Cross with proper reverence, he left those regions and came

---

34. Asquins, Yonne, Burgundy is a town located about two miles northeast of Vézelay and 146 miles southeast of Saint-Denis.
35. Herbert was abbot of Saint-Pierre-le-Vif in 1124–47. See L'Abbé H. Buvier, *Histoire de l'Abbaye de Saint-Pierre-le Vif de Sens* (Auxerre: Ch. Milon, 1891), 109.

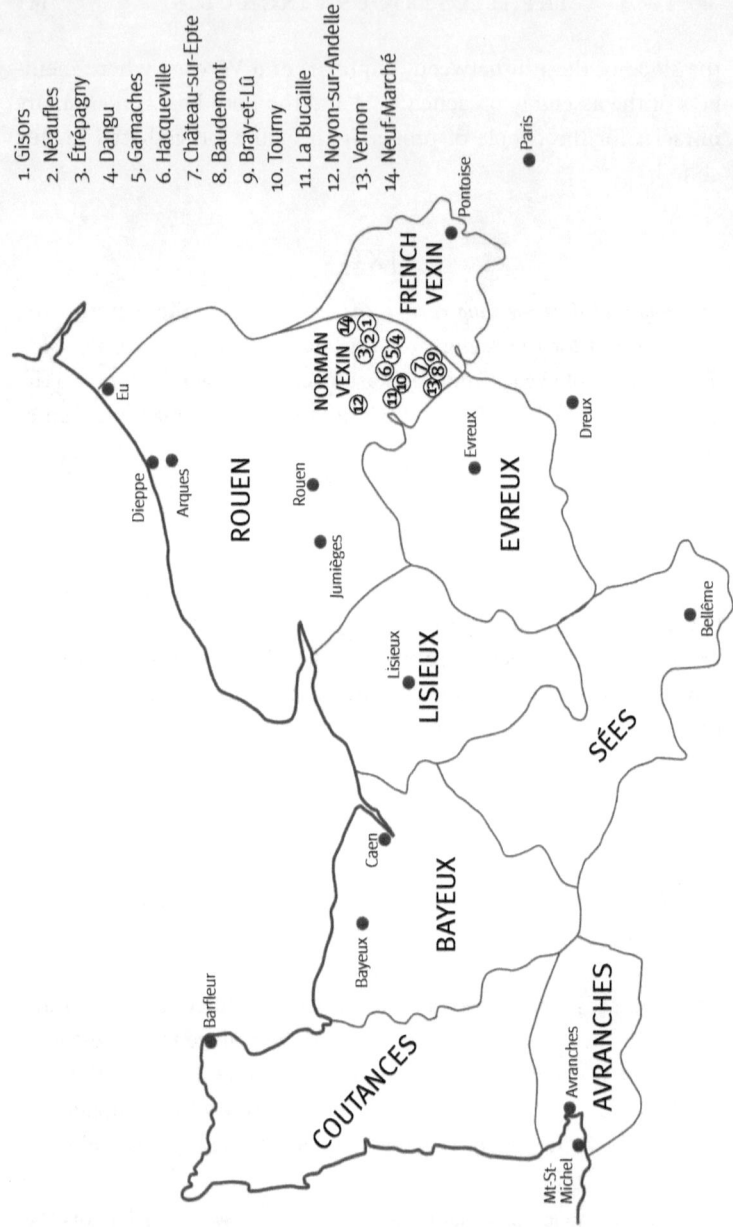

Normandy in the Twelfth Century

back to his own lands safe and sound.[36] After his return he fathered one daughter, named Alice, with his wife, Eleanor.[37]

[XIV]

The king restored Normandy to King Henry of the English. Count Geoffrey of the Angevins and his son Henry, who later reigned over the kingdom of the English, visited King Louis shortly after his return. They complained bitterly and showed how King Stephen of the English had unlawfully usurped their claim to the kingdom of England and the duchy of Normandy.[xlii] Then King Louis weighed all the evidence equitably and fairly, as befit the royal majesty, and decided to preserve and maintain the lawful rights of all. He attacked Normandy with a large army and seized it with a mighty hand. He returned it to Henry, the son of the count of the Angevins, and received Henry in liege homage for that land. With the consent of his father, Geoffrey, Henry gave to King Louis the Norman Vexin, free from all obligations, in return for the help given him.[xliii] The Norman Vexin lies between the Epte and Andelle Rivers, where the following castles and fortresses are located: Gisors, Néaufles, Étrépagny, Dangu, Gamaches, Hacqueville, Château-sur-Epte, Baudemont, Bray-et-Lû, Tourny, La Bucaille, and Noyon-sur-Andelle.[xliv] In this way, as has already been mentioned, King Louis acquired Normandy, and returned it to the treacherous Henry, for he did not foresee the treachery that Henry later plotted against him. What occurred, after a short time, is summed up by the common proverb, *the more someone lifts up a wicked man, the more likely he will rise up against his benefactor.*[38] After being made duke of Normandy by the king's hand, Henry became extremely arrogant and failed to appear in court when his Lord King Louis summoned him.[xlv] As a result the king became very enraged, and with his temper burning out of control from this serious provocation, he set out for Vernon with a

---

36. King Louis and his wife Eleanor returned to France in November 1149.
37. Alice, also known as Alix (1151–97/98), was the youngest daughter of Louis VII and Eleanor. She married Count Theobald V of Blois in 1164.
38. Ps 109:1–5.

large army. He stopped there for a few days to besiege the castle and then captured it by storm.³⁹ He also captured and took away from Henry the castle of Neuf-Marché.⁴⁰ Then that cunning Henry, duke of the Normans, realized that he could not possibly oppose the very powerful King Louis, and like a sly fox he reverted to his customary, deceitful tactics. In an effort to recover his losses, Henry pretended that he had been humbled, and falsely pledged that he would never again arrogantly step out of line against his Lord King. These false promises deceived King Louis, and being always too kind, he even now kindly forgave Henry and gave him back the two castles that he had just taken from him.[xlvi]

[XV]

The divorce of King Louis and Queen Eleanor.[xlvii] Sometime later, after a few years had passed, some of King Louis's relatives and kindred came to meet with him; and after telling him that he and his wife, Eleanor, were related by blood, they promised to swear to this relationship under oath. Upon hearing this news, the king no longer wished to be married to her in violation of Catholic law. Accordingly, Archbishop Hugh of Sens summoned both King Louis and Queen Eleanor to appear before him at Beaugency, and, at his request, they arrived there on the Friday before Palm Sunday.⁴¹ Also in attendance were Archbishop Samson of Reims, Archbishop Hugh of Rouen, and the archbishop of Bordeaux, including some of their suffragan bishops as well as a large number of magnates and barons

---

39. Vernon, Eure, Haute-Normandie is a town in the Norman Vexin located about forty-seven miles northwest of Saint-Denis. Louis VII besieged and captured its castle in July 1153.

40. Today Neuf-Marché, Seine-Marne, Haute-Normandie is located about fifty-two miles northwest of Saint-Denis, and the remains of the old Norman castle can still be seen there. Louis VII's allies, Count Henry of Champagne and Count Robert of Perche, besieged and captured the castle in 1153.

41. Beaugency, Loiret, Centre is a town located about 103 miles southwest of Saint-Denis. An assembly of French prelates met there in 1152 to determine whether Louis's marriage to Eleanor could be annulled on the grounds of consanguinity. The marriage was annulled on March 21, 1152. Hugh of Toucy was archbishop of Sens from 1142–68.

of the kingdom of France.[42] They all gathered together in the burg of Beaugency; and the king's relatives kept their promise, and swore under oath that the king and Queen Eleanor were closely related by blood, as was previously mentioned, and as a result their marriage was dissolved.[xlviii] After this had been done, Eleanor quickly demanded back her territory of Aquitaine, and Duke Henry of Normandy, who later became king of the English, did not waste any time marrying her. King Louis, however, arranged the marriages of his two daughters, whom he had fathered with Eleanor; he gave his elder daughter, Marie, to the Palatine Count Henry of Troyes, and the younger one, Alice, to Count Theobald of Blois, the brother of Count Henry.[43]

King Louis desired to live according to the divine law that prescribes that *a man should cling to his wife and become two in one flesh*.[44] He hoped to produce an heir who would succeed him and rule the kingdom of France, so he married Constance, the daughter of the king of Spain, and Archbishop Hugh of Sens anointed her as queen at Orléans and crowned the king at the same time.[45] After they had been married for a while, the king fathered with her one daughter, named Margaret. After receiving a dispensation from the Roman church, Margaret married the young Henry, the son of the English king and his wife Eleanor, and he was later associated with them on the throne of the English kingdom.[xlix] In addition, King Louis gave to his daughter, Margaret, as dowry the territory of Vexin, which King Henry of the English, father of the young Henry, had granted to King Louis free from obligations.[l]

---

42. Samson of Mauvoisin was archbishop of Reims in 1140–61; Hugh of Amiens was archbishop of Rouen in 1130–64; and Geoffrey of Loroux was archbishop of Bordeaux in 1136–58. Geoffrey had performed Louis and Eleanor's wedding ceremony in 1137.

43. Marie married Count Henry I of Champagne (1127–81) and Alice married his brother Count Theobald V of Blois (1130–91); the marriages took place in 1164. Both brothers went on crusades, Henry on the Second and Theobald on the Third where he died on January 20, 1191, at the siege of Acre.

44. See Mt 19:5, Mk 10:7–8, Eph 5:31, and 1 Cor 6:16.

45. Constance of Castile (ca. 1140–60) was the daughter of Alfonso VII (1105–57), king of Galicia, León, and Castile.

[XVI]

At that time Geoffrey of Gien[li] gave one of his daughters in marriage to Stephen of Sancerre.[lii] He believed that his clever plan could protect him from an attack by the count of Nevers.[liii] Geoffrey also gave Gien to his daughter as her dowry.[liv] When Geoffrey's son, Herveus, heard about this gift, he forbade the castle be given away like this, because it belonged to him by right of inheritance.[46] Geoffrey dismissed his son's objection and invested Stephen of Sancerre with the castle. For that reason Herveus went to the king and complained to him about how his father had disinherited him. He also protested loudly about Stephen, who had received, without his approval, a castle that he regarded as his inheritance, and who now held it without his consent. After hearing this complaint the king, who always *loved justice and fairness*, could neither allow Herveus to be deprived of his hereditary right nor allow such a great injustice to happen.[47] The king then gathered his army and rushed against the castle of Gien, which Stephen of Sancerre had fortified with his knights although he himself was not there. The king assailed the castle aggressively with his forces, captured it quickly, and then returned it to Herveus. With this issue settled, everyone returned to his own lands.[lv]

[XVII]

Queen Constance's tragic death while giving birth. The king fathered a daughter named Adelaide with Queen Constance who lived her final day during the very hour that she labored to deliver the child.[48] As a result the king and the entire kingdom mourned her deeply.

---

46. Herveus III (d. 1187) was the son of Geoffrey III of Donzy and Clemence, daughter of Duke Hugh II of Burgundy. He was lord of Gien as well as Donzy. He, too, went on the Third Crusade. Donzy, Nièvre, Burgundy is a commune located about 158 miles southeast of Saint-Denis. See Constance Bouchard, *Sword, Miter, and Cloister: Nobility and the Church in Burgundy, 980–1198* (Ithaca, N.Y.: Cornell University Press, 1987), 327–29. Herveus is also mentioned in a charter of Louis VII; see *Louis VII* (ed. Luchaire), no. 457 (247).

47. Ps 99:4.

48. Constance of Castile died on October 4, 1160, giving birth to her second child, Adelaide (Alix), and was buried in the Church of Saint-Denis.

[XVIII]

The king married Adela. The king's grief subsided a little after his magnates consoled him, and so he decided to heed the cautionary advice from his archbishops, bishops, and other barons of the kingdom and made plans to marry again. He never forgot that passage of scripture that says, "it is better to marry than to burn."[49] He also feared that without an heir his own descendants would no longer rule the kingdom of France. So he married Adela, the daughter of the Palatine Count Theobald of Blois, to safeguard his own interests and to protect the future of the state.[50] Theobald had already died and left behind four sons and five daughters as his descendants. They were the Palatine Count Henry of Troyes, Count Theobald of Blois, Count Stephen of Sancerre, Archbishop William of Sens, the duchess of Burgundy, the countess of Bar, who was the wife of William Gouet and formerly duchess of Apulia, the countess of Perche,[51] and finally his youngest daughter, Adela, whose status our Lord raised to such a degree that she held dominion over her brothers and sisters, to whom she had previously been subordinate.[lvi] Her character and determination were praiseworthy; wisdom emanated from her brilliantly; her beauty surpassed all others, and her moral purity was outstanding. Endowed and blessed with so many virtues, she was worthy to be elevated to the highest rank. As previously mentioned, Adela married the most serene King Louis in a solemn ceremony, and on the feast of Saint Brice in the Church of the Blessed Virgin Mary in Paris, Archbishop Hugh of Sens anointed her and crowned the king and her at the same time, as he celebrated Mass there that day.[52] Stephen, a canon

---

49. 1 Cor 7:9.

50. Louis married Adela of Champagne (ca. 1140–1206), the daughter of Theobald IV of Blois, on October 18, 1160, five weeks after the death of his second wife Constance.

51. Perche is a former province in northwestern France that contains the departments of Orne, Eure, Eure-et-Loire, and Sarthe. It is bordered by Normandy in the north. Bar, Meuse, Lorraine is a commune located about 164 miles east of Saint-Denis. Today it is known as Bar-le-Duc.

52. The coronation of Queen Adela was held at Notre-Dame of Paris on November 13, 1160. Saint Brice (ca. 370–444) was the fourth bishop of Tours and the successor of Saint Martin in 397.

of Sens, who later became archbishop of Meaux, read the epistle; and archdeacon William of Sens, who later became bishop of Auxerre, read the Gospel; Matthew, precentor of Sens, directed the choir; and Albert, cantor of Paris,[lvii] led the chant during the procession.

[XIX]

After these events had taken place, it was not long before ill will and greed increased and flourished from day to day. Nevelon of Pierrefonds[lviii] and Dreux of Mello,[lix] who had each married daughters of Dreux of Mouchy, began to feud with each other. Nevelon of Pierrefonds illegally seized half of the fief of Mouchy from Dreux of Mello that Dreux had obtained as part of his wife's dowry. Therefore Dreux brought his complaint before King Louis and humbly pleaded with the king to avenge this grievous, unjust act. After listening to Dreux's plea, the king wished to administer impartial justice to all, both the powerful and the weak. He assembled his army, marched against the castle of Mouchy, and captured it with a direct assault. He tore down its tower and walls, and returned to Dreux of Mello one-half of the holding of the castle that was his by legal right. Nevelon died a few days later, and the king then married off Nevelon's wife to Enguerrand of Trie,[lx] and gave him half of the holding of Mouchy, along with her.

[XX]

On the schism in the Roman Church. During that turbulent time, a disastrous schism arose in the Roman Church.[lxi] Following the death of its Pontiff, the cardinals, who were assisted by divine grace, unanimously elected Alexander III, of good memory, as high priest.[53] However, Victor, who was also called Octavian, became arrogant;

---

53. Pope Alexander III (r. 1159–81) was born Orlando of Siena from one of the city's leading families, but a later tradition claims that he was from the Bandinelli family of Bologna, where he probably studied. See Colin Morris, *The Papal Monarchy: The Western Church from 1050–1250* (Oxford: Clarendon Press, 1991), 192. The deceased pope was Adrian IV (r. 1154–59), who was born Nicholas Breakspear and is the only Englishman to have become pope.

and totally obsessed with earthly honors, he brazenly tried to usurp the papacy for himself.[54] He did so without proper canonical election by the Roman Church, for his clerical supporters were the only ones present at his unauthorized election. In fact, Victor lacked the support and vote of all but two of the cardinals and bishops; the rest of them unanimously agreed upon the Lord Pope Alexander.[lxii] The venerable Pope Alexander soon set out for the regions of Gaul and arrived at Montpellier.[lxiii] When the Lord King Louis heard news of his arrival, he sought advice as to what he should do; and the notable king then sent the Lord Abbot Theobald of Saint-Germain in Paris to meet with him.[lxiv] The abbot completed the instructions of the Lord King, and with the gratitude of the Lord Pope and the whole Roman Curia, Theobald then made plans to return home. On his way back he came down with a serious illness at Clermont.[55] He did not wish to linger any longer in a foreign region while sick; so he hastened to the Church of the Blessed Mary Magdalene at Vézelay where he had been raised from his youth, had received the habit of a monk, and had taken his vows. He arrived there on the third day before the feast of Saint Mary, but his illness grew worse, and he departed this world at that same church on the day after the feast of Saint Mary Magdalene.[56] Hugh, a monk of Saint Mary at Vézelay, replaced him as abbot in the year of our Lord 1162.[57]

---

54. Antipope Victor IV (r. 1159–64) was born Octavian of Monticelli. He was also elected pope following the death of Adrian IV, but was never recognized outside the Roman Empire. See John of Salisbury, *Historia Pontificalis*, trans. Marjorie Chibnall, Nelson's Medieval Texts [hereafter "NMT"] (New York: Thomas Nelson and Sons, 1956), 75–78, and Arnulf to the archbishops and bishops of England, in Arnulf of Lisieux, *The Letters of Arnulf of Lisieux*, ed. Frank Barlow, Camden (Third Series) 61 (London: Royal Historical Society, 1939), no. 28 (38).

55. Clermont, Puy-de-Dôme, Auvergne is a commune located about 276 miles south of Saint-Denis. Today it is known as Clermont-Ferrand.

56. The feast of Saint Mary Magdalene is July 22.

57. Theobald died on July 24, 1162, and was buried in the Church of Saint Mary Magdalene in Vézelay. Hugh of Monceaux (d. 1182) became the next abbot of Saint-Germain-des-Prés in 1162.

[XXI]

King Louis supported Pope Alexander, as did other rulers of kingdoms who followed his example. At the same time as King Louis, the entire kingdom of France recognized Pope Alexander as their shepherd. As news of this support spread quickly throughout the kingdoms, the emperors of Constantinople and Spain, the king of England, the king of Jerusalem, the king of Sicily, the king of Hungary, and all the kings of Christendom followed the example of King Louis and acknowledged Pope Alexander with due reverence.[lxv] The one exception was Emperor Frederick of Germany who ranted and raged, in his usual tyrannical manner, and supported the schismatic Octavian, contrary to all laws and legal rights.[58] Frederick recognized him as pope while Octavian lived; but after he died, the despicable emperor substituted, as his successor, Guido of Cremona, who was one of the two cardinals who were partisans of the schismatic Octavian.[lxvi] At Guido's urging, the emperor set out for Rome to destroy it, but many of his men were slaughtered there, not by the might of the Romans or other mortal men, but solely by divine retribution. It is wonderful to relate that the Lord stretched his hand of revenge over the army of this most wicked tyrant, and unleashed upon them a torrential rainstorm from the turbulent sky. Thus, the invincible sword of divine power struck down a countless host of knights and foot soldiers, and they ended their lives in an inglorious death.[lxvii] Among those who perished was the son of the Emperor Conrad, as well as Archbishop Reginald of Cologne, whose body had been cut to pieces and lay bloated in the rushing water.[59] The archbishop's men preserved his body in salt and carried it back to Cologne. The emperor, however, lifted the siege out of fear of the divine scourge and arrived in Tuscany as a fugitive. He left there; and while he crossed through Lombardy, the inhabitants of this region courageously drove him out. He then hastened to Susa, but fled

---

58. Fredrick I Barbarossa (r. 1155–90).

59. Reginald of Dassel was archbishop of Cologne in 1159–67. See Otto, *Deeds*, 337n13 (Otto of Freising was the half-brother of Emperor Conrad III).

secretly from there with a few companions and crossed the Alps.⁶⁰ However, he had lost a great number of his bishops and barons in the siege at Rome. Frightened and distressed, the emperor did not dare linger in Italy too long; so, he marched back into Germany in shameful retreat.^{lxviii}

[XXII]

The king attacked the count of Clermont and his allies. Since evil deeds were growing day by day, King Louis needed to assert royal authority to provide for the kingdom and protect his subjects from attacks. Unless the royal power became actively engaged in protecting the state, the strong would endlessly oppress the weak. The true story about what had actually happened at that time finally became clear when the devil animated the count of Clermont, his nephew Count William of Le Puy,⁶¹ and the viscount of Polignac,⁶² and they devoted themselves to worthless lives of banditry.^{lxix} They pillaged churches, harassed pilgrims, and persecuted the poor. The bishops of Clermont and Le Puy, in addition to the abbots of that region, could no longer withstand their tyranny, but they and their vassals did not have the power to oppose these men.^{lxx} So, they came before King Louis to seek his judicious advice and to plead their case against these tyrants. They told him about the savage attacks on churches, and sincerely petitioned and encouraged him to avenge the poor and the imprisoned. After hearing about the vile deeds of these tyrants, the dutiful king immediately assembled his army, took up the rod of revenge, which was an easy decision to make, and went to war against those enemies. Fighting against them ag-

---

60. Susa, Turin, Piedmont is a commune in northwestern Italy situated near the French border at the foot of the Alps. It is located about 461 miles northwest of Rome.

61. Count William VIII "the Old" ruled the episcopal county of Clermont in Auvergne from 1155 to 1182. William VII "the Young" was the count of the episcopal county of Clermont in Auvergne (r. 1143–55) and was the son of Count Robert III of Auvergne. His uncle, Count William VIII "the Old," dispossessed him of the county in 1155. Le Puy, Upper Loire, Auvergne is a commune located about 349 miles south of Saint-Denis.

62. Viscount Pons III of Polignac (r. 1142–73). Polignac, Haute-Loire, Auvergne is a town located about 330 miles south of Saint-Denis.

gressively as befit his royal majesty, he attacked them with the edge of his sword, and took captive those he routed. He took away the captives with him, and imprisoned them for a long time until they promised and swore a firm oath that they would never again harass churches, the poor, and pilgrims.[63]

[XXIII]

The king took revenge on behalf of the monks of Cluny. Not too long later, news of a despicable deed, unheard of in our times, circulated throughout various parts of the realm. Count William of Chalon, who followed in the footsteps of the devil, dared provoke the Lord by flagrantly persecuting the church of Cluny.[64] To carry out his tyrannical cruelty he assembled countless numbers of brigands, commonly called Brabantines, who had no respect for God or any desire to act righteously.[65] Relying on his criminal henchmen, William set out to plunder and loot the church of Cluny. The monks serving God in that church had no sword or shield to protect themselves; but clad only in divine armor and clerical vestments, they carried relics of the saints and crosses as they marched out, with a great multitude of people, to confront the tyrant. However, William's wicked mob of henchmen stripped the monks of their sacred vestments; and like ravenous wild beasts that pounce on carcasses they viciously slaughtered five hundred or more burghers of Cluny as if they were sheep.[lxxi] News of this unprecedented crime traveled throughout different regions and came to the attention of the most just King Louis. He took this violation against a holy church very seriously, and the ever-increasing passion of the Holy Spirit motivated him to exact revenge against this extremely barbarous slaughter. What else can I say? He assembled by royal edict a heavily armed

---

63. Louis VII captured and imprisoned Viscount Pons III and his brother Heraclius in 1169.

64. Little is known about Count William II of Chalon except that he died in 1174. See Bouchard, *Sword*, 314. Chalon-sur-Saône, Saône et Loire, Bourgogne-Franche-Compté is a city located about 219 miles southeast of Saint-Denis.

65. The Brabantines were inhabitants of the duchy of Brabant that was established in the Roman Empire in 1133. Today it is a province of the Netherlands.

band of warlike Frenchmen, and with their support he rushed against the tyrant to destroy him. The insidious count of Chalon, however, learned of the king's approach and did not have the courage to await his arrival; so he abandoned his land and fled. Then, as the king quickly advanced and traveled through the districts of the province of Cluny, widows who had just lost their husbands, virgins, and fatherless children went out to meet him. Weeping and wailing, they threw themselves at his feet and sorrowfully revealed to him the depth of their pain, imploring his royal majesty with heartfelt pleas to mercifully help them with his counsel and aid. Their misfortunes nearly moved this just king and his entire army to tears, and made them even more determined to destroy that evil band of men. It was not uncommon to see orphans clinging to their mothers' breasts and young girls pathetically weeping and crying out with no parents to console them, and the screaming of babies was echoing everywhere. Need I say more? The king continued his mission and fearlessly took his army into the land of the wicked count of Chalon; and encountering no opposition, he captured with the edge of his sword the city of Chalon, Mount St. Vincent, and all the tyrant's land.[66] He gave the central part of this land to the duke of Burgundy and transferred the remaining part to the count of Nevers.[67] The king was able to capture some of those Brabantines who had showed contempt for the divine will by following the precepts of the devil; so the king hanged them from gallows to avenge the Church of God. One of them offered a huge bribe to save his life, but his attempt failed, and he met the same fate as the others. Having won a great victory, the king returned home satisfied that he had exacted a suitable revenge for the horrific massacre and persecution that the holy Church of God had suffered at Cluny.

---

66. Mont-Saint-Vincent, Saône, Burgundy is a town located about 251 miles southeast of Saint-Denis.
67. King Louis captured Count William's fortifications at Chalon and laid waste to his lands as far as the Saône River. The king delivered Count William's lands to Duke Hugh III of Burgundy (1142–92) and Count William IV of Nevers (ca. 1130–68). See Hugh of Poitiers, *The Vézelay Chronicle*, trans. John Scott and John O. Ward (Binghamton, N.Y.: MRTS, 1992), 309–10n3.

[XXIV]

Since it is the duty of the royal majesty to defend the churches of God from its persecutors behind his protective shield, this most kindhearted king did not want the churches to lack justice through his negligence and thus be laid waste by plunderers. After he nobly avenged the damages done to the church of Cluny, he likewise freed the church of Vézelay from attacks by its enemies.[lxxii] The burghers of Vézelay had formed their own commune and arrogantly rebelled against their lord abbot and his monks, and unmercifully harassed and attacked them for a long time. The burghers all swore an oath that they would no longer be subject to the authority of the church, and they did this with the assent and advice of the count of Nevers, who was an enemy of the church of Vézelay.[lxxiii] The burghers launched savage attacks against the abbot and the monks, and forced them to fortify the towers of the monastery for their own defense. The burghers outside unleashed a relentless rain of arrows and projectiles hurled from ballistas, and held the defenders shut inside for so long by force of arms that they ran out of bread to eat and survived by eating only meat. Some of the monks stood on guard during the night, while others rejuvenated their exhausted bodies by getting a little sleep.[lxxiv] After the defenders endured a tremendous amount of suffering, the abbot realized that those evil men would never let up their sacrilegious acts but would increase their attacks against them. Therefore, the abbot, escorted by some of his friends, secretly left the monastery and hastened to King Louis, who had stopped momentarily at Corbie.[68] The abbot lodged his complaint before the king, explaining to him how the commune of Vézelay had undeservedly harassed the church. After hearing the abbot's report, the king, who was always inclined to protect churches, sent the bishop of Langres[69] to the count of Nevers, who supported

---

68. Corbie, Somme, Picardy is a town located about eighty-three miles northeast of Saint-Denis.

69. Bishop Geoffrey of La Roche (r. 1139–63). He was the fourth cousin of Bernard of Clairvaux and the first abbot of Fontenay. He went on the Second Crusade with King Louis VII in 1147. He retired in 1161 to the monastery at Clairvaux and died there in 1165. See Bouchard, *Sword*, 396.

the commune, and ordered him to restore peace to the church and dissolve the commune.[lxxv] The count, however, did not obey the royal command or stop the men of Vézelay from continuing their perverse deeds. When the king learned about the count's defiance, he felt obligated to put an end to this great affront; he gathered his host into a united force and rode against the count. The count heard about the king's approach and sent the bishop of Auxerre to the king with the message that he would obey the king's orders about the commune.[70] The count then met the king at the castle of Moret[71] and gave him his word that he would no longer support the commune, but would instead dissolve it completely.[lxxvi] The king took the count at his word, disbanded his forces, and accompanied him to Auxerre, where the assembled burghers of Vézelay swore a solemn oath to bind themselves to the dictates of Abbot Pons and his successors; and they also pledged to dissolve the commune and never form it again. The king then ordered the burghers to pay Abbot Pons 40,000 *solidi*; and in this way, peace was restored to the church.[lxxvii] After a few years had elapsed, however, Count William of Nevers began again to disrupt the peace of that church when he started complaining that the church owed him certain customary services that Abbot William and the monks of Vézelay denied they owed him.[72] So the count set aside any reverence for God and withheld food supplies from the monks. Lacking provisions they went on foot to King Louis, appeared before him in Paris, threw themselves on the ground, and tearfully lodged a complaint about the injustices the count had done to them. The king sympathized with the monks' tearful lament and restored lasting peace to the church of Vézelay.[lxxviii]

---

70. Bishop Alain of Auxerre (r. 1152–67).

71. Moret-sur-Loing, Seine-et-Marne, Île-de-France is a town located about fifty-eight miles southeast of Saint-Denis.

72. Abbot William of Mello was abbot of Vézelay in 1161–71. He was from the noble family of Mello and was the uncle of William of Mello and Rainald, the almoner of Vézelay. He had earlier been abbot of Saint-Martin of Pontoise. See Hugh of Poitiers, *Vézelay*, 230n3, and Bouchard, *Sword*, 431.

[XXV]

The divine bounty bestowed upon the most pious King Louis a much deserved reward for the many virtuous deeds related above, as well as the countless other acts of justice that he performed under the inspiration of the divine majesty for the church of Vézelay and many others, and for the frequent times he took revenge against the enemies of the church of Cluny and numerous other churches. Divine grace rewarded the king when he fathered a son with the noble Queen Adela; and this noble offspring was born on a Saturday in the year 1165 after the incarnation of the Lord while Matins was being celebrated on the octave of the Assumption of the Blessed Virgin Mary.[73] A messenger spread the joyful news of this birth, and upon arriving at Saint-Germain-des-Prés, related the happy story at the exact hour when the monks started singing the prophetical canticle: *Blessed is the Lord, the God of Israel, for he has visited and redeemed his people*, which made it obvious that this coincidence was the result of divine intervention.[74] News of this long-anticipated child spread everywhere and filled every Frenchman with great joy, since all of them had waited a long time for a male heir from the line of King Louis to succeed him. This heir would inherit the throne of the royal majesty after the death of his illustrious father, and *the Lord granted them their wish, and they were not cheated out of what they desired*.[75] On Sunday, the day after the birth of the royal child, his father King Louis had his son baptized. Bishop Maurice of Paris put on his priestly vestments at the king's request and performed the ceremony, and he solemnly gave the royal child new spiritual life through baptism in the church of Saint-Michel-de-Platea.[76] His godfather, Abbot Hugh of Saint-Germain in Paris, held the baby boy in his arms over the baptismal font.[77] Abbot Herveus (Ernisius) of

---

73. The son is the future King Philip II Augustus who was born on August 21/22, 1165. He was king of France in 1180–1223.

74. Lk 1:68.

75. Ps 77:29–30.

76. Actually a chapel attached to the royal palace in the Ilê-de-la-Cité. See Suger, *Vie de Louis* (ed. Molinier), 177n6. Maurice of Sully was bishop of Paris (r. 1160–96).

77. Abbot Hugh VI of Saint-Germain-des-Prés (r. 1162–82) had been a monk at

Saint Victor,[lxxix] and Odo, formerly abbot of Sainte-Geneviève,[78] were also his godfathers. His godmothers were two Parisian widows, as well as Constance, the sister of King Louis and wife of Count Raymond of Saint-Gilles.[lxxx]

The End

ENDNOTES

i. Suger began writing the *Life of Louis VII* towards the end of his life. He appears to have been working on it as late as 1147–48, but did not complete the work before his death in 1151. A monk from the abbey of Saint-Germain-des-Prés continued the *Life* and ended it around the year 1162, with the birth and baptism of Louis's son and successor, Philip Augustus. While accompanying the king to the Holy Land on the Second Crusade, Odo of Deuil, who succeeded Suger as abbot of Saint-Denis, claimed that his own history of that crusade developed from the notes he was making for Suger's biography of Louis VII. See Odo, *De profectione*, 2–4, and Grant, *Abbot Suger*, 36–37.

ii. Louis VI fell ill of dysentery and diarrhea in the forest of Yvelines in late July 1137 and was taken to Paris, where he died on August 1. For the death of Louis VI, see Suger, *The Deeds*, 157–59; *Orderic Vitalis* (ed. Chibnall), 4:490n4; *Morigny* (ed. Cusimano), 128; and *Louis VI* (ed. Luchaire), no. 590 (268) and no. 595 (270).

iii. In accordance with the arrangements made by his father Louis VI and Duke William X of Aquitaine, Prince Louis had traveled to Bordeaux, with a royal entourage, to marry Eleanor of Aquitaine and claim her vast dowry. He was in Poitiers when the news reached him of his father's death. Suger, *The Deeds*, 157, includes Suger in this expedition to Bordeaux, but *Morigny* (ed. Cusimano), 205n5, surprisingly does not mention him. See Suger, *The Deeds*, 156; *Morigny* (ed. Cusimano), 124–26 and 204n4; and Grant, *Abbot Suger*, 140.

iv. The Roman Empire was a medieval political body that consisted of Germany, northern Italy, and much of central Europe, and was ruled by Frankish and later German kings for almost a thousand years following the coronation of Charlemagne (r. 800–814) by Pope Leo III (r. 796–816). The term "Holy" was not used until 1157, when Frederick I Barbarossa called it the "Holy Empire"; the term "Holy Roman Empire" did not come into popular use until 1254. Emperor Francis II (r. 1768–1835) dissolved the Holy Roman Empire in 1806, following his defeat by Napoleon at the Battle of Austerlitz.

Vézelay. He is mentioned in several acts of Louis VII, see *Louis VII* (ed. Luchaire), no. 457 (246–47). See also Suger, *Vie de Louis* (ed. Molinier), 177n7.

78. Odo of Sully, abbot of Sainte-Geneviève (r. 1148–ca. 1154, d. 1173). He is mentioned in a charter of Louis VII dated 1149. See *Louis VII* (ed. Luchaire), no. 244 (177). See also Suger, *Vie de Louis* (ed. Molinier), 178n1.

v. Louis VI's eldest son Philip was killed on October 13, 1131, after he was thrown from his horse. Pope Innocent II consecrated Louis VI's second son, the ten-year-old Prince Louis, as associate king at the Council of Reims on October 25, 1131. For this coronation of Louis VII, see Suger, *The Deeds*, 149–50; *Morigny* (ed. Cusimano), 104–12; *Orderic Vitalis* (ed. Chibnall), 6:420–2, 446, 490; Peter the Venerable to Pope Innocent II, in *The Letters of Peter the Venerable*, ed. Giles Constable (Cambridge, Mass.: Harvard University Press, 1967), no. 97 (1:257–58); *Louis VI* (ed. Luchaire), no. 476 (220–21); and Grant, *Abbot Suger*, 136–37. Prince Louis and his new bride, Eleanor of Aquitaine, were declared joint rulers of France at a coronation ceremony at Bordeaux in 1137; see Suger, *The Deeds*, 157; *Morigny* (ed. Cusimano), 124–26.

vi. Emperor Henry V (1086–1125), the last ruler of the Salian dynasty, was king of Germany (1099–1125) and Roman Emperor (1111–25). He entered Italy with an army in 1110 for his coronation by Pope Paschal II. Henry arrested Pope Paschal, kept him imprisoned at Città Castellana twenty-five miles north of Rome, and forced the pope to allow him the authority to invest churchmen. Henry used this new authority to appoint Adalbert as archbishop of Mainz on August 15, 1111. The Investiture Controversy ended when Henry V signed the Concordat of Worms with Pope Calixtus II (r. 1119–24) in 1122. See also *Morigny* (ed. Cusimano), 197n5.

vii. Emperor Henry V died childless and sent the imperial insignia to his wife, Matilda, the daughter of King Henry I of England. Both *Orderic Vitalis* (ed. Chibnall), 6:360, and Otto, *Deeds*, 47–48, state that Archbishop Adalbert of Mainz induced Matilda to turn over the imperial insignia to him to avoid a possible imperial schism, and called an assembly of princes at Mainz in August 1125 to elect the next ruler of Germany. The first election took place on August 24. Forty men were chosen from among the princes; then these forty men were narrowed down to three candidates: Frederick II of Swabia, Lothar III of Saxony, and Leopold, duke of Austria. Frederick of Swabia was the favorite of the electors, but Adalbert, who was an enemy of Henry V, opposed his election because Frederick was Henry's nephew. Adalbert posed questions to Frederick in the second election that took place on September 1 that made the duke appear unfavorable to the electors. The next day Frederick of Swabia and many of the secular nobles who supported him were absent, and (according to Otto, *Deeds*, 48) Adalbert "persuaded all the princes who were present to select Lothar, duke of Saxony." The supporters of Frederick of Swabia protested the vote and attempted to walk out of the assembly. Adalbert shut and locked the doors and forced Frederick's supporters to vote for Lothar to make his election appear unanimous. The assembled princes did homage to Lothar and the bishops swore fealty to him before they adjourned the assembly; Frederick and his brother Conrad protested this election. Lothar was crowned king of Germany at Mainz on September 13, 1125. See also, Otto of Freising, *The Two Cities: A Chronicle of Universal History to the Year 1146 A.D.*, trans. Charles Christopher Mierow, ed. Austin P. Evans and Charles Knapp (New York: Columbia University Press, 1928),

423–24; *Orderic Vitalis* (ed. Chibnall), 6:360n7 and 365nn2–3. For Suger's role in this election, see *Oeuvres* (ed. Gasparri), 1:159n7.

viii. Lothar declared Frederick of Swabia an outlaw and enemy of the empire because he refused to accept the results of the imperial election. Frederick and his brother Conrad began an almost ten-year civil war against Lothar. Lothar besieged Nuremberg in 1127, and Frederick attacked and seized Speyer in 1128. The armies of Duke Henry the Proud and Lothar won a string of victories over the Hohenstaufen forces in both Germany and Italy; they captured Speyer (1129), Nuremberg (1130), most of Rome (1132), and Ulm (1134). In 1133, Pope Innocent II crowned Lothar Roman emperor in Rome. Frederick and Conrad were pardoned at Bamberg in 1135 and had their lands restored to them. In return, they recognized Lothar as emperor and promised to assist him in an Italian campaign against the forces of the antipope Anacletus II. Lothar II and Archbishop Adalbert both died in 1137. Conrad was elected king of the Romans in 1138. For an account of the warfare between Duke Frederick II of Swabia and Lothar III of Saxony, see Otto, *Deeds*, 48n89, and *Two Cities*, 424; Suger, *The Deeds*, 181–82n22; *Morigny* (ed. Cusimano), 200n1; and *Orderic Vitalis* (ed. Chibnall), 6:364–66.

ix. Papal Chancellor Haimeric of La Châtre called a papal election the day after Pope Honorius II died on February 14, 1130. This assembly hastily elected Gregorio Papareschi, the cardinal deacon of San Angelo, as Pope Innocent II (r. 1130–43) without waiting for the customary three days to elapse after the burying of a pope. A major schism developed in the Roman church when Peter, the cardinal bishop of Porto, assembled another faction of cardinals and elected Peter Leo as antipope Anacletus II on February 23, 1130; on that same day, cardinal Bishop John of Ostia consecrated Innocent II as pope in the Church of Santa Maria Novella. The majority of Romans, who supported Anacletus, forced Innocent out of Rome, and he fled to France, where he had the support of St. Bernard of Clairvaux. Innocent's election was confirmed at the Council of Étampes in 1130 (Suger, *The Deeds*, 146–47, and *Morigny* [ed. Cusimano], 100). Innocent and Anacletus both tried to get the support of King Lothar III of Germany. Anacletus offered to crown Lothar as Roman emperor in return for his support, but Bernard of Clairvaux and the priest Norbert of Xanten urged Lothar to support Innocent, which he did at the synod of Würtzburg in 1130. Lothar and Innocent met at Liège in 1131 and the German king recognized Innocent as pope and promised him an escort back to Rome (Suger, *The Deeds*, 147, and *Morigny* [ed. Cusimano], 104). Lothar gathered a small army in 1132 and entered Rome, and Pope Innocent crowned him Roman emperor on June 4, 1133, in the Lateran (Bernard to Emperor Lothair, *Letters*, no. 142 [210–11]). Lothar returned to Germany, and the supporters of Anacletus forced Innocent out of Rome a second time. He took refuge at Pisa (Bernard to the People of Pisa, *Letters*, no. 132 [201–2]). Innocent convened the synod of Pisa in 1135 at which he excommunicated both Anacletus and King Roger II of Sicily, who supported Anacletus (Bernard to Emperor Lothair, *Letters*, no. 143 [211]). Lothar returned with another army in 1136 and fought Roger II in southern Italy. Lothar had tremendous military success against Roger and pushed him back into Sicily; however, the German army threatened to mutiny and Lothar was forced to return home. He died on the trip back to Germany on December 3, 1137. For the papal schism and the war with Roger of Sicily, see Bernard to King Louis VI, *Letters*, no. 133 (202–3); Bernard to Pope Innocent II, no. 137 (205); and Bernard to Pope Innocent II, no. 239 (317); *Morigny* (ed. Cusimano), 96–98, 100, 196nn2–3; Otto, *Two Cities*, 425; *Orderic Vitalis* (ed. Chibnall), 6:393n3, 418–20, 424; and Peter the Venerable to Pope Innocent II, *Letters*, no. 62 (1:192), Peter the Venerable to Gilo of Tusculum, no. 66 (1:196), and Peter the Venerable to King Roger of Sicily, no. 90 (1:231).

x. The king referred to here is Roger II of Sicily (1095–1154), the Norman ruler of southern Italy and Sicily. Roger was only nine years old when he inherited Sicily from his brother Simon in 1105. He began his rule there in 1112. Roger wished to unite the Norman conquests in southern Italy with the Kingdom of Sicily, so he captured the cities of Calabria in 1122 and Apulia in 1127. Pope Honorius II opposed the union of Apulia and Sicily because it threatened papal influence in the south. Honorius preached a crusade against Roger II and gained the support of Robert II of Capua and Roger's brother-in-law, Ranulf II of Alife. Honorius's coalition against Roger failed and the pope was forced to invest him at Benevento as Duke of Apulia, Calabria, and Sicily in August 1128. Baronial resistance to Roger in Naples, Bari, and Salerno collapsed; and by September 1129, Sergius VII of Naples, Robert of Capua, and most of the barons in southern Italy recognized Roger's claims.

xi. Roger II supported Anacletus's claim to the papacy, and as a reward for this support, Anacletus anointed Roger as King of Sicily (*Orderic Vitalis* [ed. Chibnall], 6:418). Roger was crowned on December 25, 1130, in Palermo. Roger's support of Anacletus plunged him into a ten-year war against the backers of Innocent. Bernard of Clairvaux organized a coalition against Anacletus that included King Louis VI of France, King Henry I of England, and King Lothar III of Germany (Suger, *The Deeds*, 147, and *Morigny* [ed. Cusimano], 112–14). Lothar III entered Italy in 1132 and waged a fairly ineffectual campaign, even failing to capture the city of Milan (Otto, *Two Cities*, 426). Lothar returned to Germany after his coronation as Roman emperor at Rome in 1133, leaving most of Rome in the hands of Anacletus's supporters. At the insistence of Pope Innocent, Pisa, Genoa, the Byzantine emperor John II Comnenus (1118–43), Lothar, and Duke Henry the Proud of Bavaria led two imperial armies into Italy in 1136 to engage Roger II in southern Italy. The armies of Lothar and Henry the Proud met at Bari, which they captured in 1137, and continued their advance south. Lothar won another victory at San Severino and invested Ranulf II of Alife as Duke Apulia in August 1137. Lothar had managed to liberate all of southern Italy and push Roger back into Sicily. Lothar's German soldiers grew tired of fighting and revolted in the summer of 1137; this ended Lothar's hope of conquering Sicily. Lothar left Italy but died while crossing the Alps on December 4, 1137. His body was boiled to prevent decomposition and his bones were buried in the Church of Saints

Peter and Paul in Königslutter near Brunswick. For Roger II of Sicily and the war with Lothar, see Otto, *Two Cities*, 426; *Orderic Vitalis* (ed. Chibnall), 6:366–67n6 and 432–34n5; and Suger, *The Deeds*, 54 and 182n23.

xii. The king mentioned here is King Henry I (r. 1100–1135), who was the fourth son of William I the Conqueror. After his death, a period of civil war occurred in England that lasted from 1135 to 1154. The conflict began as the result of a succession crisis at the end of King Henry's reign because his only son and heir, William Adelin, drowned in the *White Ship* accident of 1120. Henry wished to install his only surviving, legitimate child, Matilda, as his successor. Matilda's cousin Stephen of Blois seized the throne with the assistance of his younger brother, Bishop Henry of Winchester, and many of the Anglo-Norman barons. As a result, Stephen's reign was plagued by a ferocious civil war against the English barons who supported Matilda. Matilda invaded England in 1139 and was supported by her half-brother, Robert of Gloucester. See H. L. Warren, *Henry II* (Berkeley: University of California Press, 1973), 18 and 23.

xiii. On November 20, 1120, King Henry I commandeered a boat, known as the *White Ship*, to transport his legitimate heir, William Adelin, from Barfleur in Normandy to England. Accompanying William were Henry's illegitimate son, Richard of Lincoln, as well as Henry's illegitimate daughter, Countess Matilda FitzRoy of Perche. Amid excessive drinking by crew and passengers, the ship set sail at night on November 25, struck a rock off the coast of Normandy, and capsized. All but two of the three hundred people on board drowned, including William Adelin. As a result of William's death, England entered a period of civil war and anarchy. See *Orderic Vitalis* (ed. Chibnall), 6:294; *The Anglo-Saxon Chronicle*, trans. Michael Swanton (New York: Routledge, 1996), 249; William of Malmesbury, *Gesta Regnum Anglorum*, ed. and trans. R. A. B. Mynors, OMT (Oxford: Clarendon Press, 1998), 2:758; and Henry of Huntingdon, *Historia Anglorum*, ed. and trans. Diana Greenway, OMT (Oxford: Clarendon Press, 1997), 466n190 and 594. For poems regarding the *White Ship* disaster, see *Orderic Vitalis* (ed. Chibnall), 6:302–4, and Henry of Huntingdon, *Historia*, 466.

xiv. Count Stephen of Boulogne (ca. 1092/96–1154) is also known as Stephen of Blois. He was the count of Boulogne by right of his wife. Stephen was the grandson of William the Conqueror, and was king of England from 1135 until his death. His reign is marked by the Anarchy, a civil war with his cousin and rival, Empress Matilda. Boulogne, Pas-de-Calais, Nord-Pas-de-Calais is a city located about 150 miles north of Saint-Denis.

xv. Empress Matilda (1102–67), also known as Maude, was the eldest child of King Henry I of England and his first wife Matilda of Scotland. She married Emperor Henry V of Germany at Wörms in January 1116 and had no children with him. After Henry V died in 1125, Matilda returned to Normandy in that same year, and married Count Geoffrey V Plantagenet (1115–51). Geoffrey was count of Anjou,

Touraine, and Maine by inheritance in 1129 and became Duke of Normandy by conquest in 1144. He married Matilda on June 17, 1128, in Le Mans and had three sons with her: Henry (1133–89), Geoffrey (1134–58), and William (1136–64). The eldest son, Henry Plantagenet, ruled as count of Anjou and Maine, duke of Normandy and Aquitaine, and count of Nantes after his father's death. He became King Henry II of England in 1154 and died in 1189. He married Eleanor of Aquitaine on May 18, 1152. Geoffrey became the count Nantes as Geoffrey VI in 1156, and William became viscount of Dieppe in 1156.

xvi. The civil war between Stephen and Matilda caused tremendous human and material destruction in south and southeastern England; however, it is difficult to determine the full extent of the depredations that the English people endured. For a comprehensive account of the civil war, see Jim Bradbury, *Stephen and Matilda: The Civil War of 1139–1153* (Gloucestershire: Sutton Press, 2005), and Edmund King, *King Stephen*, English Monarchs Series [hereafter "EMS"] (New Haven, Conn.: Yale University Press, 2010). See also *Orderic Vitalis* (ed. Chibnall), vol. 6; Gesta Stephani, ed. and trans. K. R. Potter, OMT (Oxford: Clarendon Press, 1976); Henry of Huntingdon, *Historia*; Florence of Worcester, *The Chronicle of Florence of Worcester*, trans. Thomas Forester (New York: AMS Press, 1968), 249; John of Worcester, *The Chronicle of John of Worcester*, ed. and trans. P. McGurk, OMT (Oxford: Clarendon Press, 1998), 3:216–18; Gervase of Canterbury, *The Historical Works of Gervase of Canterbury*, ed. William Stubbs (London: Longman and Co., 1880), 1:94–95; and Bernard to King Stephen, *Letters*, no. 197 (267), and Bernard to Queen Matilda, no. 198 (267–68). For the suffering and privation of the English people during the civil war, see *Anglo-Saxon Chronicle*, 264–65.

xvii. Adelaide of Maurienne (1092–1154) was the mother of King Louis VII. She was the daughter of Humbert II of Savoy and Gisela of Burgundy, and was a niece of Pope Calixtus II. Adelaide married King Louis VI on August 3, 1115, in Paris and bore him eight children. She married Matthew I of Montmorency (d. 1160) following the death of Louis VI in 1137. Adelaide died in 1154 and was buried in the cemetery of the Church of Saint Peter at Montmartre; her tomb was later destroyed during the French Revolution. For Adelaide of Maurienne, see Suger, *The Deeds*, 120, 147, 150, and *Morigny* (ed. Cusimano), 54, 64, 82, 112.

xviii. King Louis VII was young and inexperienced, and made some unwise decisions. One of those was to allow his mother, Adelaide of Maurienne, to live at court, where her relationship with Queen Eleanor and Suger immediately became strained. According to Turner, *Eleanor*, 56, widowed queens were supposed to retire from court and live a quiet life on their dower lands. Adelaide had enjoyed the power that she had possessed as consort to her husband, Louis VI, and expected to continue to influence her son. She allied herself with Count Ralph of Vermandois in an attempt to maintain her power at court, and they both provoked a confrontation with King Louis VII over the money he spent on Queen Eleanor and her entourage. Fearing that her dower lands would be jeopardized, Adelaide complained about the lavish spending habits of her son for his wife; so she insisted that she be given full possession of her lands. Suger and Eleanor, however, opposed Adelaide and Count Ralph's designs. Grant, *Abbot Suger,* 145, says that Louis's quarrel with his mother strained his relationship with his uncle, Count Amadeus of Savoy, who refused to provide the king assistance for an expedition into Berry, Aquitaine, or eastern Burgundy in 1137/38. Suger wrote to Peter the Venerable and urged him to try to resolve the tension between Count Amadeus and King Louis (Peter the Venerable to Count Amadeus, *Letters,* no. 68 [1:199]). Adelaide demanded permission to leave Paris and settle on her estates at Compiègne, and Count Ralph likewise asked to retire to his lands. Adelaide's second marriage was to Lord Matthew I of Montmorency, but in 1153 she retired to the abbey of Montmartre in Paris, where she died on November 18, 1154. See also Sassier, *Louis VII,* 86. For Adelaide's dower lands in Compiègne, see *Oeuvres* (ed. Gasparri), 1:244n20, and *Louis VII* (ed. Luchaire), no. 303 (197) and no. 638 (301).

xix. Count Ralph I of Vermandois (r. 1117–52) was the son of Hugh the Great and Countess Adela of Vermandois, and was the first cousin of King Louis VI. Ralph became the royal seneschal of Louis VI, following the fall of Stephen of Garland in 1127. He became one of Louis VI's staunchest supporters in the 1130s, and was a witness to several royal charters. Suger tried to weaken the influence of the "old counselors," such as Adelaide of Maurienne and Ralph, at the court of Louis VII, which caused a contentious relationship between Suger and Ralph. Ralph left the court shortly after the departure of Adelaide, which left the post of seneschal vacant for a period of time. For Ralph of Vermandois's relationship with Kings Louis VI and Louis VII, see Suger, *The Deeds,* 130, 157, 193n8; *Morigny* (ed. Cusimano), 108, 126, 160, 201n9; and *Oeuvres* (ed. Gasparri), 1:163n21.

xx. The citizens of Poitiers revolted and proclaimed a commune in 1138, but the exact date of the uprising has been debated. *Oeuvres* (ed. Gasparri), 1:167n25, says that the revolt occurred in spring 1138. Turner, *Eleanor,* 326n79, says other scholars have placed it in September. Louis VII saw the proclamation of the Poitevin commune, the fortification of the city, and its attempted federation with neighboring towns, as affronts to royal power. The situation worsened when the nobles in the Vendée region, who possessed heavily fortified castles, rose in revolt at the same time. See Sassier, *Louis VII,* 89–90; Turner, *Eleanor,* 60; and *Oeuvres* (ed. Gasparri), 1:169n29 and 245n27.

xxi. Louis VII marched to Poitiers with a force of two hundred knights, a contingent of archers, and siege engines. This show of force outside Poitiers's walls must have caught its defenders unprepared, and they surrendered to the king. Louis ordered the commune dissolved and enacted severe reprisals against the town's leading citizens by demanding that they surrender a hundred of their children, both boys and girls, to be sent off as hostages to remote locations throughout the kingdom. Louis then left Poitiers and put down the uprising in the Vendée region. See Turner, *Eleanor,* 60n79, and Sassier, *Louis VII,* 93.

xxii. An uprising in the Vendée region occurred simultaneously with the revolt in Poitiers in 1138. The Vendée is a department in the Pays-de-la-Loire region in west-central France situated on the Atlantic Ocean. For the etymology of the phrase *Talus mundi*, see *Oeuvres* (ed. Gasparri), 1:245n33. Today it is the commune of Talmont-sur-Gironde, Charente-Maritime, Poitou-Charentes located about 332 miles southwest of Saint-Denis.

xxiii. Charles III was the third son of King Louis II the Stammerer and his second wife, Adelaide of Paris. Robert of Neustria, the brother of Duke Odo, led the Frankish nobles in a rebellion against Charles in 923 that resulted in the coronation of Odo as king. Charles fled to Lotharingia and returned with a Norman army, but Robert defeated him near Soissons on June 15, 923. Charles was captured and imprisoned in a castle near Péronne under the custody of Herbert II of Vermandois. Charles died in captivity on October 7, 929. See *Oeuvres* (ed. Gasparri), 1:246n37. For hospitality, see below, Glossary, 252.

xxiv. William of Lezay lost all of his possessions after this fight, and may have been killed in the battle. Ebles of Mauléon (ca. 1120–90) became castellan of Talmont; and Lezay, along with its dependent lands, was transferred to Hugh VII "the Brown" of Lusignan (1065–1151). Hugh was one of the nobles from the Lusignan family who went on the Second Crusade with King Louis VII. For Hugh VII, see Sidney Painter, "The Lords of Lusignan in the Eleventh and Twelfth Centuries," *Speculum* 32 (January 1957): 27–47, here 38–40. For Ebles of Mauléon, see Bélisaire Ledain, "Savary de Mauléon et le Poitou à son époque," *Revue poitevine et des confins de la Touraine et de l'Anjou* 9 (January 1892): 101–37, here 129–36.

xxv. Saint-Germain-des-Prés is located in the sixth arrondissement of Paris. Childebert I (r. 511–88) built the original abbey, which became the official burial place of the Merovingian kings of Neustria. It is located about seven miles south of Saint-Denis. For this anonymous monk of Saint-Germain-des-Prés, see Suger, *Vie de Louis* (ed. Molinier), xxxv–xxxvi.

xxvi. Duke William X of Aquitaine (1099–1137) made a pilgrimage to the tomb of Saint James at Compostela (Santiago, Spain) in 1137. He took his two daughters with him as far as Bordeaux, where he installed them in the castle of l'Ombrière. They would rejoin him on his return trip (Turner, *Eleanor*, 21). William became fatally ill at Compostela and died of suspected food poisoning on April 9, 1137. On his deathbed, he expressed his wish that King Louis VI be the guardian of his daughter Eleanor to find a suitable husband for her. Suger (*The Deeds*, 156) says the duke turned over his land and his daughter to King Louis VI "for the purpose of marriage" without specifically designating her to be married to Prince Louis, the future Louis VII; and it was only later that Louis VI met with his advisers and chose Prince Louis to marry Eleanor. *Orderic Vitalis* (ed. Chibnall), 6:480–82, and *Morigny* (ed. Cusimano), 124, relate that Duke William specifically designated her to marry Prince Louis and so made him the heir to all his lands. King Louis VI lay gravely ill at Béthizy in spring 1137 when the legates of Duke William arrived to offer Eleanor in marriage to Prince Louis. See also *Morigny* (ed. Cusimano), 204n3 and 205n7; and Turner, *Eleanor*, 39.

xxvii. *Morigny* (ed. Cusimano), 124–26, tells us that Louis VI assembled a very noble host of five hundred or more knights that included Count Theobald of Blois, Count Ralph of Vermandois, Suger, Geoffrey of Lèves (bishop of Chartres), Count William of Nevers, and Count Rotrou of Perche to escort Prince Louis to Bordeaux to marry Eleanor. The royal train left on June 18 and the wedding of Louis and Eleanor of Aquitaine took place on July 25, 1135, in the cathedral of Saint-André in Bordeaux, with Archbishop Geoffrey of Loroux (r. 1135–58) officiating. Louis VII was crowned duke of Aquitaine on August 8, 1137, at Poitiers. See *Morigny* (ed. Cusimano), 204–5n4 and 205n7; *Louis VI* (ed. Luchaire), no. 589 (268); Turner, *Eleanor*, 44–45; *Oeuvres* (ed. Gasparri), 1:244n19.

xxviii. Edessa was the northernmost of the four Crusader states established in the east following the First Crusade in 1101. It was the smallest and least populated and therefore was exposed to frequent attacks by surrounding Muslims, including the Seljuk Turks. Imad ad-Din Zengi (1085–1146) led the Turks and laid siege to Edessa in 1144, using siege engines and sappers, and took the city on December 24 after only four weeks. The citizens tried to take refuge in its citadel, but the archbishop had ordered the doors of the castle barred, so they crowded together in the main square. The Turks flooded into the city through a breach in its protective wall and slaughtered thousands of them before Zengi arrived to restore order. Zengi divided the remaining citizens into the Armenian and Greek Christians and the Roman Christians. He pardoned the Armenian and Greek Christians but slaughtered all the Roman Christian men and sold their women and children into slavery. The fall of Edessa threatened the continued existence of the remaining Crusader states and control of the holy sites. The fall of Edessa led to the calling of the Second Crusade. See Odo, *De profectione*, 6; Jonathan Phillips, *The Second Crusade: Extending the Frontiers of Christendom* (New Haven, Conn.: Yale University Press, 2007), 46–48; and John J. Robinson, *Dungeon, Fire, and Sword: The Knights Templar in the Crusades* (New York: M. Evans and Company, 1991), 77–78.

xxix. Louis VII's crusading piety resulted from a war with Count Theobald II of Champagne (IV of Blois) in 1142 that had been caused by a divorce. Eleanor of Aquitaine pressured Louis VII to allow Ralph of Vermandois to repudiate his wife, Eleanor, Count Theobald's sister, to marry Petronilla (Alice), the younger sister of Queen Eleanor. Ralph's brother, Bishop Sampson of Noyon, and Bishop Peter of Senlis had Ralph's marriage dissolved on the basis of consanguinity. Theobald complained to Pope Innocent II (r. 1130–43), who sent a papal legate to the Council of Lagny (1142), where the legate declared Ralph's first marriage still valid. He then excommunicated the bishops who dissolved the marriage and placed the county of Vermandois under interdict (Bernard to Louis VII, RHF, no. 57 [15:586–87]). In retaliation, Louis invaded Champagne and burned Vitry in January 1143 (Bernard to Louis VII, RHF, no. 58 [15:587–88]). Louis's troops set fire to the castle, and the fire quickly spread and consumed most of the village. The panicked villagers had crowded into the central church, which was soon engulfed in flames. The burning roof collapsed on them, killing all thirteen hundred villagers who had taken refuge there. This incident caused Pope Innocent II to place France under interdict, and it also aroused the ire of Bernard of Clairvaux. Louis was anxious to make amends; and on Christmas 1145 he assembled his leading nobles at Bourges. It was here that the king announced his decision to take the cross and lead a French army to Jerusalem; he then called on his vassals to take the crusader vow with him. There was little response to Louis's call, and it appeared there would be no crusade. In response to this situation, Pope Eugenius III (r. 1145–53), at the urging of Bernard of Clairvaux, issued the papal bull, *Quantum praedecessores*, directly to Louis and the barons of France in December 1145, insisting that they take up the cross. See Odo, *De profectione*, 6; Robinson, *Knights Templar*, 79; and Jim Bradbury, *The Capetian Kings of France, 987–1328* (London: Continuum Books, 2007), 153–54.

xxx. Pope Eugenius III was unable to leave Rome and entrusted Bernard of Clairvaux to preach the Second Crusade at a great assembly at Vézelay on Palm Sunday. The town's basilica could not accommodate the multitudes that showed up, so a high platform was erected in a field outside of town. In one of his most eloquent sermons, Bernard promised total absolution from sin to anyone who took up the cross and eternal bliss to those who gave up their lives for Christ. So many volunteers came forward that Bernard ran out of premade crosses to issue to the crusaders and ordered that his own red cloak be cut into strips to make more crosses. Louis VII and Eleanor took the cross at Vézelay on March 31, 1146. See Odo, *De profectione*, 6; Otto, *Deeds*, 73–74; Grant, *Abbot Suger*, 156; Bradbury, *Capetian Kings*, 154; Robinson, *Knights Templar*, 79–80.

xxxi. On February 16, 1147, a great council was held at Étampes to elect regents who would govern the kingdom in Louis's absence. Bernard of Clairvaux dominated the election and declared for Suger, who was reluctant to accept it without papal sanction, which Bernard arranged. Louis VII chose Ralph of Vermandois and Archbishop Samson of Reims to be co-regents. Pope Eugenius III left Rome for Viterbo, Italy, in January 1147 and joined Louis VII at the abbey of Saint-Denis on June 11 during the Lendit Fair, where a magnificent ceremony was performed. In the presence of Pope Eugenius, King Louis prostrated himself before the altar of Saint-Denis in the presence of his wife Eleanor, his mother and dowager queen Adelaide of Maurienne, his court, and many leading magnates of France. Pope Eugenius gave Louis the pilgrim's scrip or wallet, and Suger presented him with the *oriflamme*. This marked the official start of the Second Crusade. Suger was opposed to Louis going on crusade because of the enormous cost of the undertaking and the fear that his enemies would use his absence to threaten the kingdom. See Odo, *De profectione*, 12 and 14–18; *Morigny* (ed. Cusimano), 158–60; see below, the *Life of Suger*, Bk. III, 197n98; Bernard to Suger, Bernard, *Letters*, no. 405 (476–77); Grant,

THE ILLUSTRIOUS KING LOUIS   167

Abbot Suger, 157–58; Bradbury, *Capetian Kings,* 154; and Robinson, *Knights Templar,* 81–82.

xxxii. The French nobles and ecclesiastics going on the Second Crusade included:
1. Simon of Vermandois, bishop of Noyon (r. 1123–48), who died in 1148 on the return trip from Palestine.
2. Geoffrey of la Roche, bishop of Langres (r. 1139–63).
3. Bishop Arnulf of Lisieux (r. 1141–84).
4. Abbot Herbert of Saint-Pierre-le-Vif at Sens (d. 1147).
5. Abbot Theobald of Sainte-Colombe at Sens, who took the cross at Vézelay on March 31, 1146, and died in Asia Minor on April 7, 1146/47.
6. Alphonse of St. Giles (1103–48), who was count of Toulouse and duke of Narbonne as Alfonso I (r. 1112–48), and was also known as Alphonso-Jordan after his baptism in the Jordan River. He took the cross at Vézelay on March 31, 1146, and died at Caesarea in 1148; he was rumored to have been poisoned either by Eleanor of Aquitaine or Melisende, the mother of King Baldwin III of Jerusalem.
7. Thierry of Alsace, count of Flanders (ca. 1099–1168), who took the cross at Vézelay on March 31, 1146.
8. Henry I (1127–81), count of Champagne, was the son of Theobald II of Blois; he took the cross at Vézelay on March 31, 1146.
9. William III (b. ca. 1107–d. 1161), count of Nevers, who escaped death in a shipwreck on the return voyage from the Holy Land.
10. Count Rainald II of Tonnere (r. 1147–48), who was the younger brother of Count William III of Nevers; Rainald took the cross at Vézelay on March 31, 1146, and died in the Holy Land in captivity (see Bouchard, *Sword,* 347n198).
11. Robert I, count of Dreux (b. ca. 1123–d. 1188), who was the fifth son of King Louis VI and brother of Louis VII. Robert took the cross at Vézelay on March 31, 1146, and fought at the siege of Damascus in 1148.
12. Ivo II of Nesle, count of Soissons in 1146–78 (see Odo, *De profectione,* 98n22).
13. Guy II, count of Ponthieu (b. ca. 1120–d. 1147), who took the cross at Vézelay on March 31, 1146, and died at Ephesus.
14. Count William III of Warenne, who was also the earl of Surrey (r. 1138–48) and a supporter of Stephen in the English Civil War; he took the cross at Vézelay on March 31, 1146, and was part of the royal guard killed at the Battle of Mount Cadmus on January 6, 1148.
15. Count Erchenbald VII of Bourbon (also known as Archibald), who was count of Bourbon from an unknown date until his death in 1171; he was allied to the French crown through his marriage to Agnes of Savoy, aunt of Louis VII (see Odo, *De profectione,* 28n21).
16. Enguerrand II of Coucy, who died in Palestine in 1148/49.

17. Geoffrey of Rançon (d. 1190s), who was one of the principal barons of Poitou; he began his association with Louis VII and Eleanor by hosting them at his castle after their wedding; Geoffrey was the head of Eleanor's army on the Second Crusade and bore the blame for the disastrous defeat at Mount Cadmus.
18. Hugh VII of Lusignan (1065–1151), who announced his intention to go on the crusade at Bourges and followed King Louis VII to the Holy Land.
19. William of Courtenay, who was the son of Miles of Courtenay (d. 1127) and Ermengarde of Nevers.
20. Rainald, lord of Courtenay and Montargis (1096–after 1161), who later quarreled with King Louis, who in turn seized his lands; Rainald then went to England and became a favorite of King Henry II.
21. Itier III of Toucy (1100–1147/49), who died on this crusade to the Holy Land.
22. Gaucher II of Montjay, the lord of Châtillon, who formed a close friendship with the king's brother Robert I of Dreux on the Second Crusade that led to the marriage of his son, Guy II, to Robert's daughter, Adele. Gaucher was part of the royal guard killed at the Battle of Laodicea on January 6, 1148. See Theodore Evergates, *The Aristocracy in the County of Champagne, 1100–1300*, The Middle Ages Series (Philadelphia: University of Pennsylvania Press, 2007), 177.
23. Evrard III, count of Breteuil, who is a somewhat obscure figure mentioned in two acts of the king; he was part of the royal guard that was killed at the Battle of Laodicea on January 6, 1148. See Odo, *De profectione*, 52n37 and 122, and *Louis VII* (ed. Luchaire), no. 17 (104), no. 200 (163), and no. 229 (172–73).
24. Dreux II, lord of Mouchy-le-Châtel, who was the son of a supporter of King Louis VI (see Suger, *The Deeds*, 30 and 102).
25. Manasses of Bulles, the count of Dammartin, who is another obscure figure and a member of the royal guard killed at the Battle of Laodicea on January 6, 1148; Manasses also appears in a letter that Louis VII wrote to Suger (Louis VII to Suger, RHF, no. 47 [15:500]), requesting that the abbot preserve the property of Manasses of Bulles for his brother, Rainald of Bulles, who was still in the East.
26. Anselm of Traînel, who was later the butler of Count Henry the Liberal of Champagne (see Suger, *Vie de Louis* [ed. Molinier], 159n15); nothing else is known about his brother Garin.
27. William de la Tour of Senlis, who was the butler of King Louis VII in 1137–42.
28. William Aguillon II of Trie-Château, who died on this crusade in 1147.

xxxiii. King Conrad III of Germany (1093–1152) heard Bernard of Clairvaux preach at Speyer in 1146 and agreed to join Louis VII on the Second Crusade. Conrad set off for the Holy Land in May 1146 and was joined by the king of Poland, the king of Bohemia, and his heir, Duke Frederick of Swabia, along with a number of German nobles and bishops. The German contingent took an overland route through Hungary and Byzantine territory in the Balkans, and arrived at Constantinople on September 10, 1146. Conrad decided to engage the Turks before the French forces arrived and ignored the warning of the Byzantine Emperor, Manuel I Comnenus, to follow the safer coastal route through Christian territory to the Holy Land. Instead Conrad marched eastward through Asia Minor, where the Turks ambushed his forces near Dorylaeum. At the second Battle of Dorylaeum on October 25, 1147, the Turks routed the Germans, and a wounded Conrad and a few of his followers barely escaped alive. Near Laodicea on November 16, 1147, the Turks ambushed another German force, which was led by Bishop Otto of Freising; the majority of Otto's forces were killed, captured, or sold into slavery. The remnants of the German army arrived at Nicaea, where many of them deserted and returned home; the rest later joined up with Louis VII's forces at Lopadium. Conrad fell gravely ill at Ephesus and had to return to Constantinople to recover. He then sailed to Acre and traveled to Jerusalem. He took part in the ill-fated siege of Damascus, but his forces failed to arrive for the attack at Ascalon. Conrad grew disaffected with his French allies and returned to Germany. See Otto of Freising, *Deeds*; Odo, *De profectione*; and Angus Konstam, *Historical Atlas of the Crusades* (London: Mercury Books, 2002), 106. See also above, "The Second Crusade," figure, 139.

xxxiv. Frederick I Barbarossa (1122–90), the nephew of King Conrad III, became duke of Swabia (mistakenly called Saxony here) in 1147 and Roman Emperor in 1155. For Frederick's involvement in the Second Crusade, see Otto, *Deeds*, 75, 79–81, 102, and Odo, *De profectione*, 47n18, 91n6, 102.

xxxv. Count Amadeus III of Savoy and Moraine (1095–1148) was the uncle of Louis VII, and he also participated in the Second Crusade. Amadeus attempted to sail from Asia Minor to Antioch, but fell ill in Cyprus. He died at Nicosia on May 1, 1148, and was buried there in the Church of Saint Croix. See Odo, *De profectione*, 78n37, and Phillips, *Second Crusade*.

xxxvi. Pons of Montboissier, abbot of Vézelay (1138–61), was the brother of Peter the Venerable of Cluny and Abbot Jordan of La Chaise-Dieu. See Bouchard, *Sword*, 431.

xxxvii. Abbot Pons founded a church at the spot on the hill outside Vézelay where Bernard of Clairvaux preached the Second Crusade, and dedicated it as the Church of the Holy Cross. The platform on which Bernard preached was kept there as an object of veneration.

xxxviii. King Louis VII took up the cross and pledged himself to participate in the crusade on Easter Sunday, March 31, 1146, at the Council of Vézelay. He was still in France the following year and celebrated Easter services with Pope Eugenius on April 20, 1147, at Saint-Denis. It was at this time that Louis received papal sanction to take up the cross. While at the abbey, the pope also consecrated the large golden crucifix that Suger erected over the shrine of Saint Denis. For the visit of Pope Eugenius III to Saint-Denis in 1147, see Odo, *De profectione*, 114–16; and for the golden crucifix, see above, *The Administration*, XXXII, 102–4. See also *Oeuvres* (ed. Gasparri), 1:219n218, and Grant, *Abbot Suger*, 158.

xxxix. In 1146 the citizens of Sens formed an association, with the consent of King Louis VII, and adopted the charter of liberties of Soissons. It was then common practice for one town to adopt the charter of liberties of another town. When Abbot Herbert of Saint-Pierre-le-Vif realized that he no longer had jurisdiction over the city, he pleaded his case to Pope Eugenius III, who was still in France, and the pope convinced King Louis to dissolve the commune. When Herbert returned to Sens, the citizens formed an angry mob and broke down the doors of the monastery at Saint-Pierre-le-Vif and murdered Herbert and his nephew. Royal troops then seized the city and apprehended the principal perpetrators of the murder. Some of them were executed without a trial, others were forced to jump from the tower of Saint-Pierre, and the rest were taken to Paris, where they were beheaded. See Geoffroy of Courlon, *Chronique de l'Abbaye de Saint-Pierre-le-Vif*, ed. M. G. Julliot (Sens: C. Duchemin, 1876), 477–78; Achille Luchaire, *Les communes françaises a l'epoque des capetiens directs* (Paris: Hachette, 1890), 282; and Arthur Giry and André Réville, *Emancipation of the Medieval Town* (New York: H. Holt and Company, 1907), 23–24.

xl. Louis VII and the French contingent began the journey to the Holy Land with an army of about fifteen thousand about a month after Conrad III had departed for the East. They left from the abbey church of Saint-Denis in June 1147 and stopped briefly at Metz, and from there followed the same overland route through Hungary and Byzantine territory in the Balkans that Conrad had taken. Louis had in his retinue an impressive array of French nobility that included:

1. Eleanor of Aquitaine, his wife.
2. Raymond of Poitiers (1115–49), who was the Prince of Antioch and Eleanor's uncle; Raymond was killed in the Battle of Inab during an expedition against Nur ad-Din Zengi.
3. Thierry of Alsace (1099–1168), who was the count of Flanders.
4. Reginald I "the One-Eyed" (ca. 1080–1149), who was the count of Bar. He drowned in the Mediterranean Sea sometime before March 10, 1149, on his return voyage from the Holy Land.
5. Amadeus III (1095–1148), who was the count of Savoy.
6. William V of Montferrat (ca. 1115–91), who was the marquis of Montferrat.
7. William VII "the Young," who was the count of Auvergne (r. 1145–55).
8. Armies from Lorraine, Brittany, Burgundy, Aquitaine, and a force from Provence led by Alphonse I of Toulouse also joined Louis's army. In addition, Louis took with him a monk from Saint-Denis, Odo of Deuil (1110–62), as his personal chaplain. Odo later wrote a history of the Second Crusade (see Odo, *De profectione*, 4), and he also succeeded Suger as abbot of Saint-Denis in 1151. See the *Gesta Eugenii III Papae*, RHF, 15:424–25.

xli. The French crusaders encountered many problems and difficulties on their way to the Holy Land. Louis VII found himself in a diplomatic conflict with the Hungarian king, Géza II (1130–62), when Géza learned that the French were hiding Boris, the pretender to the Hungarian throne, among their ranks. Louis ignored Géza's demand that he turn Boris over to him, and instead escorted the pretender out of Hungary and into Byzantine territory. The French army was then plagued by food shortages and encountered a population that had been made hostile by the German crusaders of Conrad III, who had preceded them. They reached Constantinople only to learn that Emperor Manuel I Comnenus did not intend to keep the agreement that he had made with Louis VII earlier. Manuel had negotiated a truce with the Turks. He did not provision the French crusaders with proper amounts of food and water as he had promised, he refused to reinforce the French army with Byzantine troops, and had the French swear to return to him any territory they captured from the Turks. Sometime before March 10, 1149, the French army was shipped across the Bosporus to Asia Minor, short of water and provisions. It met up with the remnants of Conrad's army at Nicaea and followed the coastal route south to Ephesus in December 1147, where they learned that the Turks were preparing to attack them. The French and Turks fought a small skirmish outside Ephesus that ended with a French victory. Louis next marched south to Laodicea in January 1148, where the Turks attacked again, inflicting heavy losses on the French. The Turks employed a scorched earth policy against the French that denied them much needed food and water. Lacking an adequate amount of horses, Louis decided to commandeer ships at Adalia and sail his forces to Antioch, but storms delayed the ships for months, and there were not enough of them to carry his entire army. Louis and his retinue boarded the ships and the rest of the army marched overland to Antioch; the Turks and sickness, however, almost completely destroyed the French army. Louis battled storms and rough seas and arrived in Antioch on March 19, 1148. He arrived in Jerusalem in early summer 1148 and attended the Council of Jerusalem with Conrad III on June 24. Following the disastrous attack on Damascus in July, Louis remained in Jerusalem visiting holy sites until summer 1149. See Odo, *De profectione*; Louis VII to Suger, RHF, no. 52, 15:501–2; Robinson, *Knights Templar*, 83ff.; Grant, *Abbot Suger*, 170; and Bradbury, *Capetian Kings*, 153.

xlii. King Henry I of England named his daughter, Matilda, as his heir in 1127 and married her to Count Geoffrey of Anjou in 1128. When Henry I died in 1135, Matilda's cousin Stephen of Blois rushed to England and usurped the throne, with the support of the Anglo-Norman barons. Geoffrey sent Matilda to Normandy to claim the title Duchess of Normandy in Stephen's absence. He also supported his wife's claim to the English throne and invaded Normandy on her behalf in 1135. Stephen traveled to Normandy in 1137 and made an alliance with Louis VI, who promised to recognize Stephen's son and heir, Count Eustace IV of Boulogne (ca. 1127–53), as duke of Normandy in return for Stephen's fealty to him. The Norman barons supported Stephen overwhelmingly, and Geoffrey remained in Normandy fighting them while Matilda invaded England in 1139. Geoffrey used this period to increase his gains in Normandy. Matilda's capture of Stephen at Lincoln in 1141 and his subsequent imprisonment crushed the morale of the Norman lords, who began turning over key strongholds to Geoffrey. He captured the Avranchin and Mortain in 1142 and the Cotentin in 1143. Geoffrey took Rouen in 1144 and then proclaimed himself duke of Normandy. The last stronghold, Arques, fell to him in 1145, giving him complete control of Normandy. See Henry of Huntingdon, *Historia*; Florence of Worcester, *Chronicle*; Robert of Torigni, *The Chronicle of Robert of Torigni*, ed. Richard Howlett, Rolls Series 4 [hereafter "RS"] (London: Eyre and Spottiswoode, 1889).

xliii. Louis VII supported Stephen of Blois and his son and heir, Count Eustace IV of Boulogne (ca. 1127–53), in the civil war against Matilda and Geoffrey. Louis arranged the marriage of his sister Constance (1124–76) to Eustace in 1140. Geoffrey of Anjou supported the claim of his son, Henry Plantagenet, to the duchy of Normandy and throne of England. Following his return from the crusade in 1149, Louis VII became very concerned about Geoffrey's growing power in Normandy. Geoffrey began to threaten the northern borders of the Aquitaine in 1149–51 when he attacked the castle of Montreuil-Bellay, which belonged to Louis's seneschal in Poitou, Gerard III of Bellay. Geoffrey made Henry duke of Normandy in 1150, and Louis responded by proclaiming Eustace as the rightful duke of Normandy. Louis and his brother Robert of Dreux began preparation for an invasion of Normandy in 1151 to remove Henry from the duchy. Louis fell seriously ill before hostilities began, and Geoffrey convinced Henry to make peace with Louis. Geoffrey and Henry met with Louis in September 1151 and negotiated a peace agreement. Henry did homage to Louis for Normandy and turned over to him disputed lands in the Norman Vexin, and in return Louis recognized Henry as duke of Normandy. See *Gesta Stephani* (ed. Potter), 226 and 230; Arnulf to Robert of Chesney, bishop of Lincoln, Arnulf, *Letters*, no. 4 (6–7) and no. 6 (9); Suger to Count Geoffrey of Anjou and Empress Matilda, *Oeuvres* (ed. Lecoy), no. 15 (264); Grant, *Abbot Suger*, 284nn39 and 42; and Bradbury, *Capetian Kings*, 158–59.

xliv. The castles mentioned here are:
1. Gisors, Eure, Haute-Normandie, which is a town located about thirty-seven miles northwest of Saint-Denis. The original keep is still visible atop a large motte.
2. Néaufles, which is today the town of Néaufles-Saint-Martin, Eure, Haute-Normandie and is located about forty-four miles northwest of Saint-Denis; the donjon of the castle is still visible today.
3. Étrépagny, Eure, Haute-Normandie, which is a town located about forty-seven miles northwest of Saint-Denis; its castle no longer exists.
4. Dangu, Eure, Haute-Normandie, which is a town located about forty-two miles northwest of Saint-Denis; two castles were built there in the twelfth century, part of one remains today.

5. Gamaches, Eure, Haute-Normandie, which is today known as Gamaches-en-Vexin, a town located about forty-six miles northwest of Saint-Denis; its castle no longer exists.
6. Hacqueville, Eure, Haute-Normandie, which is a town located about forty-seven miles northwest of Saint-Denis. Its remains are still visible and it has one of the best-preserved shell keeps in Normandy.
7. Château-sur-Epte, Eure, Haute-Normandie, which is a town located about forty-one miles northwest of Saint-Denis whose castle remains are still visible.
8. Baudemont, Val-d'Oise, Eure, which is a rural area located about three miles to the southwest of Bray-et-Lû and forty miles northwest of Saint-Denis; there is no trace of its castle today.
9. Bray-et-Lû, Val-d'Oise, Île-de-France, which is a town located about thirty-eight miles northwest of Saint-Denis; its castle no longer exists.
10. Tourny, Eure, Haute-Normandie, which is a town located about forty-seven miles northwest of Saint-Denis; its castle no longer exists.
11. La Bucaille, Eure, Haute-Normandie, which is located about thirty-four miles northwest of Saint-Denis; its castle no longer exists.
12. Noyon-sur-Andelle, which is today Charleval, Eure, Haute-Normandie and is located about fifty-nine miles northwest of Saint-Denis; its castle no longer exists.

See Christopher Gravett, *Norman Stone Castles: Europe, 950–1204* (Oxford: Osprey Publishing, 2004), 52–56, and Charles Coulson, "The French Matrix of Castle- Provisions of the Chester-Leicester Convention," *Anglo-Norman Studies* [hereafter "*ANS*"] 17 (1994): 65–86. For the location of these castles, see above, "Normandy in the Twelfth Century," figure, 142.

xlv. As part of the peace settlement of 1151, Duke Henry of Normandy had performed homage to Louis and recognized the king as his feudal lord; see John Gillingham, "Doing Homage to the King of France," in *Henry II: New Interpretations*, ed. Christopher Harper-Bill and Nicholas Vincent (Woodbridge: Boydell, 2007), 63–84. Relations between the two deteriorated when Henry married Eleanor of Aquitaine on May 18, 1152, eight weeks after Louis VII had his marriage to Eleanor annulled. Henry's marriage to Eleanor was seen as an insult to Henry's liege lord and a direct violation of feudal protocol. It also threatened the inheritance rights to the Aquitaine of Louis's two daughters, Marie and Alice, through their mother Eleanor. Louis summoned Henry to appear at his court in 1152 to deal with this issue, and Henry promptly ignored him. See Warren, *Henry II*, 42–45; Marjorie Chibnall, "Anglo-French Relations in the Work of Orderic Vitalis," in *Essays in Medieval History Presented to G. P. Cuttino*, ed. J. S. Hamilton and Patricia J. Bradley (Woodbridge: Boydell, 1989); and Gillingham, "Doing Homage."

xlvi. Louis VII organized a coalition against Duke Henry of Normandy that included King Stephen of England, Eustace of Boulogne, Count Henry of Champagne,

Count Robert of Perche, and Henry's brother, Geoffrey of Anjou. Fighting broke out along the Norman borders in 1153. After capturing the castles of Vernon and Neuf-Marché in July 1153, Louis's forces then attacked the Aquitaine. Henry countered this move by attacking the Vexin and Anjou, where he captured one of his brother Geoffrey's castles. Louis became sick and had to withdraw from the campaign, and Geoffrey was forced to come to terms with Henry. Peace talks were initiated between Louis and Henry in August 1154. Henry bought back the two castles of Vernon and Neuf-Marché for a sum of two thousand marks of silver. See John Hosler, *Henry II: A Medieval Soldier at War, 1147–1189* (Leiden: Brill, 2007), 48. See also Robert of Torigni, *Chronicle*, 174–75 and 180; and John Gillingham, "The Meetings of the Kings of France and England, 1066–1204," in *Normandy and Its Neighbors, 900–1250: Essays for David Bates*, ed. David Crouch and Kathleen Thompson (Turnhout: Brepols, 2011), 17–42.

xlvii. Louis and Eleanor were incompatible from the start. Louis was highly intelligent, reserved, and awkward around company; Eleanor was vibrant and had a zest for revelry, parties, and romance. There was already talk of a separation by 1143; and Gervase of Canterbury, *Works*, 1:149, later noted the discord between them in 1152. Eleanor's relationship with her uncle, Raymond of Antioch, during the Second Crusade was a major source of contention between her and Louis. Eleanor spent long hours alone conversing with Raymond, and she supported his military strategy over that of her husband. Eleanor's excessive affection toward her uncle fueled speculation of an illicit relationship between them. Louis became furious at her behavior and ordered her to leave Antioch and go with him to Jerusalem, a command she disobeyed. Louis and Eleanor took separate ships back to France in 1149, and the marriage appeared to be doomed. Pope Eugenius III tried in vain to reconcile them. To make matters worse, Eleanor had produced no male heir for Louis; she bore him only two daughters, Marie and Alice. It was Louis who took the initiative to end the marriage despite Suger's bitter objections. See John of Salisbury, *Historia Pontificalis*, 52–53, 60–62. See also Turner, *Eleanor*, 104–7, and Bradbury, *Stephen and Matilda*, 157.

xlviii. The annulment of marriages for reasons of consanguinity was quite common among the nobility in the twelfth century. The terms "divorce" and "annulment" were used interchangeably in the historical literature to describe Louis's action toward Eleanor. See also Warren, *Henry II*, 43–44.

xlix. Margaret (1157–97) was the eldest child of King Louis VII and Constance. She married Henry the Young (1155–83), the second of five sons born to King Henry II and Eleanor of Aquitaine, on November 2, 1160. Henry was crowned in 1170 during Henry II's lifetime and was known as "Henry the Young" to distinguish him from his father. He died of dysentery in 1183, while fighting his brother Richard in the Limousin. Henry the Young was not counted in the numerical succession of English monarchs because he died before his father. Margaret then married King Béla III of Hungary (ca. 1148–96) in 1186 and was widowed a second time in 1196. She died at St. John of Acre in 1197 on a pilgrimage to the Holy Land.

l. Henry II had granted Louis VII disputed lands in the Norman Vexin in 1151. In August 1158 Henry arranged the betrothal of his eldest son, Henry the Young, to Margaret, the daughter of Louis VII and Constance. Her dowry was to include all of the Norman Vexin above the Epte River. In a treaty signed by Louis VII and Henry II in May 1160, the Vexin could only be gained through a successful marriage between Henry the Young and Margaret; and if the marriage occurred within three years, Henry II would gain the Vexin to the benefit of his son. The Knights Templar were to occupy the castles of Gisors and Néaufles as guarantors of the treaty. On November 2, 1160, Henry the Young and Margaret married. However, Henry II seized the castles of Gisors and Néaufles, and then attacked Blois in 1161, which further alienated King Louis VII. The two monarchs were reconciled in September 1162 through the mediation of Pope Alexander III at Toucy on the Loire River. Sporadic warfare continued in Normandy, Flanders, and Brittany between Henry II and Louis VII in 1162–69. Louis and Henry negotiated another treaty on January 6, 1169, at Montmirail in Perche. According to this treaty, (1) Henry paid homage to Louis and his son Philip for Normandy; (2) Henry the Young paid homage to Louis for Anjou, Maine, and Brittany; (3) Richard paid homage to Louis for Aquitaine and Poitou and was married to Louis's daughter Alice, by Constance of Castile. For details of the treaty, see Robert of Torigni, *Chronicle*, 240–41; Gervase of Canterbury, *Works*, 1:207–8; John of Salisbury to Bishop Bartholomew of Exeter, *Letters*, no. 288 (2:636–38); and John Hosler, *Henry II*, 56–65. See also Lindsay Diggelman, "Marriage as Tactical Response: Henry II and the Royal Wedding of 1160," *English Historical Review* 119 (2004): 954–64.

li. Lord Geoffrey III of Donzy and Gien (1100/1105–57) was the son of Lord Herveus II. For Geoffrey, see Hugh of Poitiers, *Vézelay*, 121–22, and Bouchard, *Sword*, 327. Gien, Loiret, Centre is a town located 114 miles south of Saint-Denis; Donzy, Nièvre, Burgundy is a town located about 132 miles southeast of Saint-Denis.

lii. Stephen I of Sancerre (1133–90) became count of Sancerre in 1151 following the death of his father, Count Theobald II of Champagne. Stephen was the third son of Theobald as well as the younger brother of both Count Henry I of Champagne and Count Theobald V of Blois. Stephen married Alice, the daughter of Geoffrey of Donzy, in 1153. Stephen died at the siege of Acre in 1190.

liii. William III (ca. 1110–61) became count of Nevers in 1148. Louis VII insisted that the conflict between William and Geoffrey of Donzy be settled by a judicial duel in January 1150. William feared that Louis favored Geoffrey and begged Suger to support his cause. See Grant, *Abbot Suger*, 277–78, and William of Nevers to Suger, RHF, no. 99 (15:519–20).

liv. Geoffrey of Donzy had given his daughter Alice in marriage to Lord Anselm II of Traînel (r. 1152–85), a close companion of Count Henry I of Champagne. As dowry, Geoffrey gave the castle of Neuilly and half of the town of Oulchy, and in return Anselm agreed to pay Geoffrey a reverse dowry. The wedding took place at Donzy in 1153 but was not consummated, perhaps because the bride was too young; and Anselm returned to his lands immediately after the wedding. Stephen of Sancerre took advantage of this situation and married Alice with the lands of Gien as her dowry and took her to the castle of Saint-Aignan. Anselm, deprived of his dowry, complained to Count Henry, who had arranged the marriage in the first place, to make right this matter. Henry appealed his case directly to Louis VII to right this wrong by force. See *Feudal Society in Medieval France: Documents from the County of Champagne*, ed. Theodore Evergates (Philadelphia: University of Pennsylvania Press, 1993), 38–39. Traînel, Aube, Champagne-Ardennes is a commune located about seventy-three miles southeast of Saint-Denis.

lv. Other sources report that Louis VII and Count Henry of Champagne laid siege to the castle of Saint-Aignan instead of the castle of Gien in 1153 and captured it. In the settlement that followed, the castle of Neuilly and half of the town of Oulchy were returned to Anselm of Traînel, a familiar of Count Henry; and Stephen kept Alice and the castle of Saint-Aignan. See RHF, 12:128, note a; Suger, *Vie de Louis* (ed. Molinier), 165n5, and *Feudal Society in Medieval France* (ed. Evergates), 39.

lvi. Theobald (1090–1152) became count of Champagne in 1125 as Theobald II. He married Matilda of Carinthia (d. 1160/61), the daughter of Duke Englebert of Carinthia (d. 1141) in 1123; and despite the somewhat confused list of offspring and marriages presented in the text, Theobald and Matilda had the following children:

1. Count Henry I of Champagne (1127–81).
2. Count Theobald V of Blois (1130–91).
3. Stephen I of Sancerre (1133–91).
4. William of Blois (1135–1202), known as "White Hands," who became bishop of Chartres in 1165, archbishop of Sens in 1169, and archbishop of Reims in 1175.
5. Adelaide (Adela) of Champagne (ca. 1140–1206), who married King Louis VII.
6. Isabelle of Champagne, who married both Duke Roger III of Apulia (1118–48) and William IV of Gouet (d. 1170).
7. Marie of Champagne, who married Duke Odo II of Burgundy and later became abbess of Fontevraud.
8. Agnes of Champagne (d. 1207), who married Renaud II of Bar (d. 1170).
9. Margaret of Champagne, who became a nun at Fontevraud.
10. Matilda, who married Count Rotrou IV of Perche (1135–91).

lvii. Hugh was archbishop of Sens in 1143–68; Stephen of La Chapelle was bishop of Meaux in 1162–71; William of Toucy was the younger brother of Archbishop Hugh of Sens. He joined the chapter of Sens in 1141 and served there as archdeacon and became bishop of Auxerre in 1167–81; except for this passage, Matthew of Sens and Albert of Paris remain obscure.

lviii. Nevelon II of Pierrefonds (1060–ca. 1147) was the son of Nevelon I of Chérisy and Aremburge of Milly. He married Heddiva (Basilie) of Mouchy, daughter of

Dreux IV of Mouchy. Pierrefonds, Oise, Picardy is a town located about forty-five miles northeast of Saint-Denis.

lix. Dreux IV of Mello (1138–1218) was the son of Dreux III of Mello and Eustachie of Lusignan. He married Ermengarde of Mouchy (b. 1132), the daughter of Dreux IV of Mouchy, in 1162. He went on the Third Crusade in 1191. Mello, Oise, Picardy is a town located about thirty-three miles north of Saint-Denis; and Mouchy-le-Châtel, Oise, Picardy is a town located about forty miles northwest of Saint-Denis.

lx. Enguerrand II "Aiguillon" of Trie (ca. 1110–66) married Heddiva (Basilie) of Mouchy. Enguerrand has been identified with Enguerrand of Chaumont, son of Drogo (Dreux) of Chaumont, who was mentioned by Suger in his account of the capture of the castle of Andelys. Trie, Hautes-Pyrénées, Midi-Pyrénées is a commune in Gascony located about 493 miles southwest of Saint-Denis. Today it is known as Trie-sur-Baïse. See *Orderic Vitalis* (ed. Chibnall), 6:218n2, and Suger, *The Deeds*, 114–16.

lxi. The origin of the schism lay in the political situation in Italy during the twelfth century. The Normans under King William I of Sicily (r. 1154–66) had recently united Sicily with southern Italy. The German kings through their title as Roman Emperor had controlled the cities that lay in the old Kingdom of Italy in the north, but these cities began to fragment and declare themselves independent communes in the eleventh century. Frederick I Barbarossa (1122–90) was elected Roman Emperor in 1155 and tried to reimpose his rule over them, which led to four invasions of Italy by his forces in 1154–74. The Papal States were caught in the middle of this conflict, and its boundaries and right to exist were disputed both by the Normans in the south and the Roman Emperor in the north. The situation became even more complex when the Romans elected their own commune in 1144, and proclaimed self-rule and independence from the authority of the pope. The popes had traditionally relied on the German emperors to protect the Papal States, but the erosion of imperial power in northern Italy caused the papacy to turn to the Normans in the south. Pope Adrian IV turned to William I for military support and signed the Treaty of Benevento (June 18, 1156) that recognized William's rule over most of southern Italy in return for an annual cash payment and military help against the Roman commune. This agreement shocked many cardinals who opposed unifying southern Italy under a single king who might threaten the security of the Papal States. For the reign of Pope Adrian IV see *Gesta Adriani IV Papae*, RHF, 15:661–66. See also Rupert Matthews, *Popes: Every Question Answered* (New York: Metro Books, 2013), 159–60, and Morris, *Papal Monarchy*, 190–91.

lxii. The division among the cardinals over Adrian IV's new pro-Norman policy played itself out in the papal election of 1159. Orlando of Siena headed those cardinals who supported the Norman policy of Adrian IV, and Octavian of Monticelli led those who favored an imperial alliance. Negotiations for the selection of a new pope began three days after the funeral of Adrian IV; and on September 4, 1159, the rival groups of cardinals elected two popes: Orlando of Siena as Alexander III and Octavian of Monticelli as Victor IV. Thus, in less than a century, there began a third major papal schism, following those of 1080–1100 and 1130–88. Victor IV had only the support of about nine members of the thirty-one-member College of Cardinals, with those favoring him later dropping to five. Riots broke out between the two sides, and Alexander took refuge in the Vatican fortress next to Saint Peter's. Next, he fled to the castle of Ninfa where he was consecrated pope on September 20, 1159; he then excommunicated Victor. Emperor Frederick I assembled a council at Pavia on February 5, 1160, to settle the issue, but Alexander refused to attend on the grounds that the papacy was above adjudication. Frederick invited about fifty bishops from imperial territories in Germany and Italy to the council, and it voted in favor of Victor IV. Alexander responded to the decision of the council by excommunicating Frederick and releasing all of his subjects from their allegiance to him. Political support for Alexander came mostly from the Kingdom of Sicily and Lombardy. For this papal schism, see RHF, 15:720; Hugh of Poitiers, *Vézelay*, 227–29; Archbishop Theobald to King Henry II, in John of Salisbury, *Letters*, no. 116 (1:190–92); and Morris, *Papal Monarchy*, 193–94.

lxiii. Shortly after the Council of Pavia, Alexander began soliciting the support of both Louis VII and Henry II. He sent the papal legates William of Pavia, Henry of Pisa, and Otto of Carcere Tulliano into France and England where he enjoyed Cistercian support for his cause. Louis VII, Henry II, and the bishops of the realm met at Toulouse in October 1160 and declared Alexander as pope. Alexander and his cardinals fled to France and arrived there in April 1162. On May 19, 1163, he convened the Council of Tours, at which he renewed his excommunication of Emperor Frederick Barbarossa. Montpellier, Hérault, Languedoc-Roussillon is a city in southern France situated on the Mediterranean Sea and is located about 478 miles south of Saint-Denis. For Alexander's letters to Louis VII and Henry II, see RHF, vol. 15. See also Morris, *Papal Monarchy*, 194. For Pope Alexander III's arrival in France and the Council of Tours, see Robert Somerville, *Pope Alexander III and the Council of Tours* (Berkeley: University of California Press, 1977), 1–3; for the pope's support of the traditional rights of the monastery at Vézelay and the non-support of him by the monks of Cluny, see Hugh of Poitiers, *Vézelay*, 228–29.

lxiv. Hugh of Poitiers, *Vézelay*, 240, states that Theobald took his clerk Cadurcus with him to see Pope Alexander III. Theobald is also mentioned in an act of Louis VII in 1146; see *Louis VII* (ed. Luchaire), no. 169 (153).

lxv. These were: (1) Emperor Manuel I Comnenus of Constantinople (r. 1143–80), (2) King Alfonso II of Spain (r. 1164–96), (3) King Henry II of England (r. 1154–89), (4) King Baldwin III of Jerusalem (r. 1143–63), (5) King William I of Sicily (r. 1154–66), and (6) King Géza II of Hungary (r. 1141–62). Louis VII later became disenchanted with Pope Alexander III because he received the king's delegation "with less enthusiasm than they (the delegates) had hoped for" (see Hugh of Poitiers, *Vézelay*, 240), and they returned to Vézelay. Pope Alexander learned of the king's anger

THE ILLUSTRIOUS KING LOUIS   179

and met with him at Souvigny in 1162, but the meeting failed to reconcile the two. King Louis instructed Count Henry of Champagne in August 1162 to contact Emperor Frederick Barbarossa and begin negotiations to end the schism. Count Henry tried to trick King Louis into accepting terms favorable to the emperor, but the king was saved from this deception when Archbishop Rainald of Cologne, Count Henry's chancellor, revealed to the king the true nature of the negotiations between Count Henry and the emperor. King Louis and the pope were able to reconcile their differences in February-March 1163. See Hugh of Poitiers, *Vézelay*, 240–45, and Martha G. Newman, *The Boundaries of Charity: Cistercian Culture and Reform, 1098–1180* (Redwood City, Calif.: Stanford University Press, 1996), 205–8.

lxvi. The antipope Victor IV (Octavian) died on April 20, 1164, in Lucca, and on the same day a small group of cardinals, who supported Emperor Frederick I Barbarossa, elected Guido of Cremona, a former elector of Alexander III, as antipope Paschal III, with his seat at Viterbo. Paschal died in 1168 and another supporter of the imperial cause, abbot Giovanni of Struma, was elected antipope Calixtus III (r. 1168–78). After the defeat of Emperor Frederick in northern Italy, Pope Alexander III was able to return to Rome in 1178; but he lost favor with some nobles who expelled him again in 1179. They then set up Lando Di Sezze as Innocent III (r. 1179–80), the last of the four antipopes during the schism. Cremona, Cremona, Lombardy is a commune in northern Italy located about 323 miles north of Rome. For Paschal III, see John of Salisbury, *Historia Pontificalis*, 45–47; Hugh of Poitiers, *Vézelay*, 246; and Otto, *Deeds*, 338.

lxvii. Emperor Frederick I Barbarossa launched his fourth invasion of Italy in 1166 in an attempt to destroy the Lombard League that supported Pope Alexander III, and to end the schism. He sent Rainald of Cologne and Christian of Mainz with their forces to Rome. The Romans engaged them at Tusculum at the Battle of Monte Porzio on May 29, 1166. But the Romans suffered a crushing defeat: about nine thousand were killed and another three thousand, taken prisoner. Frederick then attacked Rome, burned the Leonine part of the city, captured the Vatican fortress, and had Paschal III seated as pope on July 22, 1167. Frederick's victory was short-lived as floodwaters caused the sewers in the street to overflow, which brought about a plague in August 1167 that killed many of his troops and leaders. This misfortune caused Frederick to withdraw from Italy. See Otto, *Deeds*, 337n11 and 338. See also Morris, *Papal Monarchy*, 195.

lxviii. Frederick left Rome in August 1167 and made a perilous journey back into Germany. He reached Pavia on September 12; he was forced to take refuge inside of the city and was besieged there for some time. On December 1, 1167, his enemies began to coalesce against him; the League of Cremona joined with the League of Verona and recreated the Lombard League. Frederick took hostages before leaving Pavia and then traveled to the town of Susa near Savoy. There the citizens trapped Frederick and his men inside the town, and he escaped only by disguising himself in servant's clothing and slipping out at night. Taking only five men with him,

Frederick left Susa, crossed the Alps into Burgundy, and finally reached safety in Saxony in 1168. He led another invasion into Italy in 1174, but his army was defeated at the Battle of Legnano on May 29, 1176. Frederick now decided to come to terms with Pope Alexander III; on July 24, 1177, at Venice he formally renounced antipope Calixtus III and recognized Alexander III as the legitimately elected pope. The schism came to an end with the calling of the Third Lateran Council in March 1179 where a decree was issued that required the consent of two-thirds of the cardinals for the election of a new pope. See Otto, *Deeds*, 337n11; John of Salisbury to Nicholas of Mont-Saint-Jacques, *Letters*, no. 239 (2:452–56), and John of Salisbury to Archdeacon Baldwin of Totnes, no. 272 (552); John Hosler, *John of Salisbury: Military Authority of the Twelfth-Century Renaissance* (Leiden: Brill, 2013), 162–64; and Morris, *Papal Monarchy*, 197.

lxix. For decades the counts of Polignac had robbed and plundered tenants and travelers in their lands through arbitrary demands and seizures. Seizures from pilgrims and merchants on the roads of Le Puy had been repeatedly condemned and renounced, and Louis VII twice had to make punitive expeditions into Auvergne. In 1173 Bishop Aldebert III of Mende (r. 1151–87) complained to Louis VII that the bishop of Le Puy, Pierre III of Solignac (r. 1159–90), and Count Pons III of Polignac had agreed to divide the plunder between them. See *Louis VII* (ed. Luchaire), no. 600 (289). See also Thomas N. Bisson, *The Crisis of the Twelfth Century: Power, Lordship, and the Origins of European Government* (Princeton, N.J.: Princeton University Press, 2009), 309–10; Coulson, "French Matrix," 72–73; and Sassier, *Louis VII*, 339–43.

lxx. Stephen VI of Mercoeur was bishop of Clermont in Auvergne in 1151–69; and Pierre III of Solignac was bishop of Le Puy in 1159–90. The bishops of Le Puy were counts under the sovereignty of the kings of France and served them in the episcopal county of Clermont in Auvergne. However, the bishops were either under the domination of the counts of Polignac or were fighting them over the right to coin money, which had been given to the bishops of Le Puy in 924. The counts of Polignac had their own mint and needed regional control over the currency there in order to debase it. See Sabine Baring-Gould, *A Book of the Cevennes* (London: John Long, 1907), 31–33.

lxxi. William II of Chalon (d. 1174) and his son, William the Younger, invaded Cluniac lands in 1166 at the instigation of Emperor Frederick I Barbarossa. William the Younger (d. ca. 1190) captured the Cluniac castle of Lourdon, and Brabançon mercenaries under his command indiscriminately attacked the monks of Cluny in procession, sacked the church, and slaughtered five hundred of the inhabitants of Cluny. King Louis VII, assisted by Duke Hugh III of Burgundy (1142–92) and Count William IV of Nevers (ca. 1130–68), intervened on behalf of the monks. See Hugh of Poitiers, *Vézelay*, 309–10n3 and 314.

lxxii. There were two primary reasons for the violence committed against the monastery of Vézelay. The first was the immunity granted to the monastery in its foundation charter around 860, which stated that only the church of Rome had authority over it, its possessions, and revenues. By the twelfth century the monastery possessed lands and churches in Autun, Auxerre, Nevers, Mâcon, Clermont, Bourges, Poitiers, Saintes, Sens, Noyon, and Beauvais. The abbots and monks of Vézelay had seigniorial control and legal jurisdiction in these towns, which became a source of contention between them and the townsmen in them as well as the region around them. The neighboring lords, particularly the counts of Nevers, tried to exploit this division in an effort to wrest the seigniorial rights and immunity privileges away from Vézelay by inciting uprisings and violence in the abbey's possessions. The counts of Nevers wished to acquire the lucrative revenues from Vézelay that included (1) the profits from administering justice over the inhabitants of Vézelay (including the right to administer justice in the courts of the count), (2) exemption from abbatial tolls on commercial traffic, (3) the right to impose their own tolls on the main roads leading into Vézelay, (4) pilgrimage revenues, (5) the right of hospitality for themselves and their retinues whenever they visited the monastery, and (6) the right to tax the abbots' buyers and sellers in the lands under direct control of the counts. Abbots Pons of Montboissier (r. 1138–61) and William of Mello (r. 1161–71) spent most of their abbacies resisting these claims made by Counts William III and William IV of Nevers. Second, Henry of Burgundy, bishop of Autun (r. 1148–70), claimed that he should exercise spiritual authority over Vézelay, which included the consecration of churches and chapels, the ordination of priests and monks, the administration of abbey revenues, and supervision over the general operation of the monastery during an abbatial vacancy. Bishop Henry of Autun frequently allied himself with the counts of Nevers against the claims of the abbots of Vézelay. For a discussion of the comital rights over these possessions, see Hugh of Poitiers, *Vézelay*, 3–4, 6–7n2, 23–24, 66.

lxxiii. Count William III (r. 1148–61) stirred up the burghers in Vézelay by telling them that abbot Pons was abusing his seigniorial authority and right of advocacy, and was treating them unjustly. The burghers rose up in revolt in 1152, absolved their allegiance to Abbot Pons, recognized the authority of Count William, and established an independent commune. They plundered the church, assailed the monks, and forced Abbot Pons to flee Vézelay and take refuge in the Cluniac monastery at Souvigny. Count William then selected the leaders and magistrates of the commune from among the burghers. See Hugh of Poitiers, *Vézelay*, 184.

lxxiv. Prior Hilduin and some monks were besieged in the fortress of the monastery. They were joined by some of the abbot's peasants, archers, fishermen, and carters who had climbed the ramparts by rope at night. The fortress garrison consisted of only about one hundred men and was opposed by five thousand of the rebel burghers. The burghers failed to take the fortress by assault, but the garrison did not have a sufficient store of food and other necessities to maintain a prolonged siege. See Hugh of Poitiers, *Vézelay*, 204-5.

lxxv. King Louis VII summoned Count William III and the burghers of Vézelay to Auxerre in December 1154 and negotiated a truce between the abbot and the count. Hostilities soon resumed, and Abbot Pons once again was forced to flee Vézelay and go to the king, who was then at Corbie. The king summoned the parties to meet at Soissons. The Council of Soissons met in June 1155, and the king decreed "a general peace for ten years to be extended to all churches, cultivators of the soil, and merchants." See Hugh of Poitiers, *Vézelay*, 199.

lxxvi. King Louis met Count William III at Moret in 1155 where the count agreed to dissolve the commune, return all property to Abbot Pons, and bring to justice those involved in the plundering and sacking of church property. See Hugh of Poitiers, *Vézelay*, 209-10.

lxxvii. Count William III did not fulfill the promise he made to the king at Moret. Instead of arresting those involved in the looting of church property in Vézelay, he sent warning for them to leave the town and go into hiding. The rebellious burghers dispersed across the countryside and into the woods where they engaged in banditry along the roads leading into Vézelay. Abbot Pons returned to Vézelay with an army of bowmen, ballista-operators, and foot soldiers. The abbot arrested the remaining burghers who stayed behind and destroyed their property. Count William, dressed as a pilgrim of Saint Denis, went to the king for forgiveness, asking him to spare the lives of the exiled burghers, and promised to bring the guilty men to justice. King Louis was moved by the pleas of the count and arranged a meeting at Auxerre in late October 1155. The king, Abbot Pons, Count William, and the burghers were in attendance at Auxerre; and the king made the burghers swear an oath to pay forty thousand *solidi* for damages and destroy all fortifications and outworks by November 30, 1155. See Hugh of Poitiers, *Vézelay*, 209.

lxxviii. The count referred to here is William IV of Nevers (r. 1161-68) who ordered Abbot William of Mello to appear in his court in 1163 for not paying his salt duties. Abbot William refused to appear, so Count William broke into the monastery and ordered heralds to summon all of the abbey's men to present themselves before him. The count ordered all of them to renounce their allegiance to Abbot William and swear fealty to him. Abbot William complained to both Pope Alexander III and King Louis; and the king summoned a conference at Sens on December 31, 1164. King Louis ordered that Count William delay his summons of Abbot William to a later date. See Hugh of Poitiers, *Vézelay*, 249. The last sentence of this passage in the text is misleading because, after a decision was reached at Sens, Count William, his mother Countess Ida, and Hugh Letard continued to plunder and harass the monastery of Vézelay. See Hugh of Poitiers, *Vézelay*, 252.

lxxix. Abbot Herveus (Ernisius) of Saint Victor (r. 1162-72) was a worldly man who was probably an Englishman. He spent lavishly on unnecessary projects and caused much strife within the monastery by appointing favorites to offices. He was finally removed from office by papal sanction in 1172. He is mentioned in several charters of Louis VII; see *Louis VII* (ed. Luchaire), no. 467 (250), no. 577 (282), and no. 634 (299–300). See also Richard of Saint-Victor, *The Book of the Patriarchs, The Mystical Ark, Book Three of the Trinity* (New York: Paulist Press, 1979), 4 and James Walsh, *The Pursuit of Wisdom and Other Works by the Author of the Cloud of Unknowing*, trans. Grover A. Zinn (New York: Paulist Press, 1988), 13.

lxxx. Constance (ca. 1124–76) was the younger sister of Louis VII. She married Count Eustace IV of Boulogne in 1140; he died in 1153. In 1154 she took as her second husband Count Raymond V of Toulouse (ca. 1134–94), sometimes known as Raymond of Saint-Gilles. Saint-Gilles, Gard, Languedoc-Roussillon is a commune in southern France located about 464 miles south of Saint-Denis.

[4]

The Life of Suger

WILLIAM, to his fellow monk Geoffrey[i]

I seemed to have had no free time to write when you were at hand, but after my departure I immediately remembered your request and the promise I made to you. So when I had time, I picked up a pen and began writing something about our Suger that you might find pleasant and that would benefit many people. When I reflect on the virtues of this venerable man and recall his words and deeds, I truly consider him an excellent example of how future generations should conduct their lives. Along with you I saw first-hand for a while how he lived his private life, and so I fear that I would be guilty of ingratitude if I did not praise everything I can remember about him in my writing, especially since I was privileged to enjoy his friendship and experience his generosity.

Even if envy demands silence, virtues, by their very nature, cannot be hidden from the sight of everyone; and virtues are not diminished, even when they have been hidden. A day will finally come that will shed light on any good deeds that the jealousy of the times has kept hidden and suppressed.[1] There is one thing, how-

---

1. Medieval society and its monasteries were ridden with factional strife. As an important figure in both church and state, Suger had rivals and enemies in both spheres.

ever, that I ask from you. Do not expect me to follow any particular order in what I am going to write about him. Although I promised to write just a few things about his countless deeds, I could hardly recall any of them. Since you know all of them better than I do, you should be the one to write about them.[2] However, I will do what I can because you wish and request it, and I think it is the least that I can do for you.

First Book

Our Suger seemed divinely ordained to preside over this very important abbey and to glorify the entire kingdom of the French. Once promoted to higher office, he alone advanced not only one family of monks, but also all the orders of the Church.[3] One is pleasantly surprised at this man because nature placed a beautiful and remarkable spirit in such a short, little body. However, nature wished to show plainly through him that a very beautiful spirit can hide under any type of surface, and that virtue can arise anywhere. Thus, we know that a short body does not weaken a spirit, but that a vigorous spirit enhances a body. I am aware that a false supposition about him had become embedded in the hearts of some people,[4] but I wish to make clear that he was absent and far away when he was chosen to preside over the abbey.[ii] He never suspected it would happen, and was even unwilling to accept the position; but he was not allowed to refuse it, or live his life in obscurity.

Our Suger's strength of character and learning, as well as his renowned friendship with men of high rank, thrust him into the public eye; but, more than anything else, divine stewardship had prepared this vessel for honor in his Church. He had attracted so much notice that, even if he were hidden in the most out of the way places, his intrinsic honesty would still single him out and the

---

2. This type of modesty seems to have been a necessary convention for medieval writers.
3. Suger became abbot of Saint-Denis in 1122.
4. This false supposition probably refers to the initial opinion of King Louis VI that Suger's election as abbot of Saint-Denis would cost Louis his personal confidant and adviser; but Suger continued to play those roles during his abbacy.

virtues that he had demonstrated since boyhood would reveal him. So much light shone around him from his preeminent and profound wisdom that he could not remain in the shadows, even if he wished to.[5] Everyone marveled at his remarkable self-control over his emotions when all the turmoil of the world was pressing down upon him; he smiled at whatever the public usually feared or desired; and although he was placed in this world, his better part still clung to the heavens.

He presided over the monastery and the royal court at the same time; and he performed each office in such a way that the court did not prevent him from his care of the monastery, nor did the monastery excuse him from the royal councils. The king revered him like a father, and respected him as a teacher, because of his superb and sound advice.[iii] Prelates stood up when he approached, and he was the first among them to sit down. Every time the king summoned the bishops to attend an assembly to obtain their advice on the urgent business of the kingdom, they unanimously insisted that Suger alone answer for them because of his tested and proven wisdom. Just as Job testified about himself, *they dared add nothing*, to his words, *for his eloquence spilled over all of them drop by drop*.[6] The cry of the orphan and the plea of the widow reached the king through our Suger, who always intervened on their behalf, and sometimes he even ordered what should be done.[7] Who among the oppressed and the injured did not have him as an advocate if his case was legitimate? When he rendered decisions he never deviated from what was right for any price, nor did the person involved ever sway his judgment, nor did he care for gifts or seek rewards.[8] Who did not admire such a personality as his that was uncorrupted by greed, humble amid success, calm during the chaos of the times, and un-

---

5. The above two sentences are similar to the thoughts expressed in Mt 5:14–16.
6. Job 29:22.
7. On intervening, see above, *Life of Louis VII*, VI, 132–34. Jas 1:27 defines pure religion in the eyes of God as coming to the aid of orphans and widows. Suger followed this biblical injunction seriously.
8. Suger asserts the same about himself in his letter of 1150 to Bishop Henry, the clergy, and people of Beauvais; see Suger to Bishop Henry of Beauvais and the people of Beauvais, *Oeuvres* (ed. Lecoy), no. 23 (279).

deterred by danger? His spirit was larger than anyone could have imagined would fit in such a small body.

His rivals held this illustrious man in contempt because of his humble origins,[iv] but these blind and ignorant men did not realize that whatever related to his greater praise or glory had made them nobler than their having been born of noble parents. However, Plato says that every king has had humble origins in his lineage and every man of humble origins has had kings.[v] The changing times have jumbled all things together, and fortune has turned them upside down.[9] The soul makes men noble, and this certainly applies to our Suger in such a way that the following has accurately described him: "The soul that contemplates truth knows what should be shunned or pursued; it determines the value of things not from common opinion but from their nature; it involves itself in the entire world and focuses its attention on all its actions; it is very beautiful in splendor; it is healthy and firm in strength; it is unperturbed and undaunted; no force can break it and no chance occurrences can lift it up or weigh it down."[vi] This was indeed Suger's spirit. Whenever this sincere and honest man attempted to abandon the court and the administration of the kingdom in order to retire to nobler activities, the good fortune that had placed him at the summit of affairs did not allow it, nor did it permit him to grow old in the style of his origins that, as he confessed, he wished to have happened.

The principal matters of the kingdom were burdensome to him, but public or private duties never kept him away from divine service. When he met the brothers for prayer or when he celebrated the Divine Office with the residents of his household, he did not listen in silence to the chanting of the psalms as some usually do, but he was always eager to chant or read them aloud. I often admired his ability to remember everything he had learned as a young man, and as a result there was no one in any monastic office able to compare himself to him. One would suppose that he knew nothing else, nothing except the things he had learned; but he was very well versed in the liberal arts and could discuss books of logic or rhetoric in great de-

---

9. Seneca, *Ad Lucilium epistulae morales*, V, 44.4; available at www.thelatinlibrary.com/Seneca.html.

tail, not to mention topics of theology that he continued to study as he grew old. Our Suger knew every reading of Divine Scripture so well that no matter what part he was asked about, he immediately gave a learned and suitable response. His retentive memory allowed him to recall passages from the pagan poets, and he could recite to us from memory as many as twenty or thirty verses of Horace if they had a good message.[10] Once he grasped something, it never faded from his penetrating mind and prolific memory.

Why should I mention that he became famous as the greatest orator of his times when everyone already knows this? Actually, just like Marcus Cato, he was a talented man and expert speaker.[11] Our Suger possessed eloquence in two languages, his native tongue and Latin; and whenever he gave a speech, you would have thought he was reading rather than speaking. He also had a superb knowledge of history; he could immediately and without hesitation recount the deeds of any French king or prince you happened to name. He described the deeds of King Louis in a splendid style, and also began to write about his son, Louis, but died before he could finish this work.[12] For who knew their deeds better than he or who could write them with greater accuracy? He was an intimate of both kings, who kept nothing secret from him. They never opened a council without him, and the palace seemed empty when he was not there. From the time the kings first summoned him to the royal councils until the day he died, the kingdom always flourished; and having expanded its boundaries and subjugated its enemies, it grew larger and more prosperous.[13] But he felt that the kingdom would immediately be shaken by his absence after he was no longer involved in its af-

---

10. Quintus Horatius Flaccus, commonly called Horace in English, was a Roman poet (65–8 B.C.).

11. There were two famous Roman statesmen and orators with the name Marcus Cato: Cato the Elder (234–149 B.C.) and Cato the Younger (95–45 B.C.). The author is probably referring to the Elder Cato here.

12. See Suger, *The Deeds*, for King Louis VI, as well as above, *Life of Louis VII*, for King Louis VII.

13. Suger was present at the royal court as early as 1104 when he overheard King Philip (r. 1060–1108) give his son Louis advice concerning the castle of Montlhéry; see Suger, *The Deeds*, 40.

fairs.[14] Without his counsel, he knew that a large part of the realm, the duchy of Aquitaine, would be severed from the kingdom.[vii]

Our Suger possessed a special virtue amid his other ones. If he heard an accusation against any of his subjects, he did not immediately rush to judgment, but wisely suspected the motives of the accusers. He considered it unjust to discipline a person until he conducted a thorough investigation into the charge, and would punish sinners not because they had sinned but to prevent them from sinning again. He proved to be so fair when administering discipline that no one in his right mind doubted his compassion or his reluctance to punish. As a shepherd he reprimanded them, as a father he mentored them. He did not readily remove his officials from their duties without the existence of irrefutable evidence proving them guilty of wrongdoing. He used to say that nothing was more detrimental to the state than when those, whom you remove from office, take away with them whatever they can, and their replacements quickly steal everything before the same thing happens to them.

However, many ignorant or envious men who did not know him well tried to smear this man's outstanding reputation by impugning his character. These insults, like the words of Solomon, were *like goads and like well-fixed nails*, and like the blessed Job, *the light of his face was never cast down*.[15] These men considered him too harsh and rigid, and his firmness made them think he was too savage. In fact, his close friends and his intimates had a totally different perception of him. When among his close associates, he was amiable and somewhat playful; but having fun never made him lose his composure just as sadness never made him depressed. His role was that of good parents who sometimes mildly admonish their children, sometimes scold them, and sometimes threaten them with the rod. Our Suger never took away rights of inheritance for a first offense unless the accused had committed a considerable number of serious crimes, or unless he feared that the accused would do something far worse in the future than his present crime; and he never administered capi-

---

14. For Suger's role in the diplomatic affairs of the Anglo-Norman world, see Lindy Grant, "Suger and the Anglo-Norman World," *ANS* 19 (1996): 51–68.

15. Eccl 12:11; Job 29:24.

tal punishment until all other remedies had been exhausted. This wise man used the legal authority granted to him humanely and soundly, and that is why the French and foreign people celebrate his name today.

Who among the Christian kings was not astonished after hearing about our Suger's high ideals? Who among them did not desire to enjoy his conversation and be guided by his counsel? Did not the renowned King Roger of Sicily send letters of petition and entreaty as well as gifts to him?[viii] Did not King Roger afterwards plan to meet him after he learned of his desire to leave for the crusade?[16] Did not the powerful King Henry of the English also boast about being our Suger's friend and rejoice in being his intimate?[17] Did not King Henry choose him to mediate and negotiate a binding peace with King Louis? Every time our Suger visited King Henry to discuss peace between both kingdoms, the king did not follow his usual protocol, but rushed outside the royal palace to greet and embrace him. King Henry valued his conversation more than any kind of treasure. Even the pious King David of the Scots sent him gifts, along with personal letters, as well as the teeth of a sea monster of extraordinary size and value.[18] With God as my witness, I once saw the king of the French cordially assisting our Suger who was sitting on a humble footstool with the magnates gathered around them.[19] Our abbot was giving orders as if to subordinates, and they were hanging on every word he said with undivided attention. After the audience ended, our Suger wanted to escort the king out, but the king did not permit him to move from his place or rise from his seat. I have mentioned all this so that his rivals would know, and his detractors would hear, about his status among kings, and how much respect the magnates had for him.

Count Theobald of Blois, a devotee of religion, honored our Suger

---

16. Suger planned another crusade to the East in 1150 that never took place.

17. Henry I was king of England in 1100–1135. See Suger to Count Geoffrey of Anjou and Empress Matilda, *Oeuvres* (ed. Lecoy), no. 15 (265), where Suger discusses his intimacy with Henry and subsequent peace negotiations that Suger held with Louis VI on Henry's behalf.

18. King David I of Scotland (1080–1153) was prince of the Cumbrians in 1113–24, earl of Northampton and Huntingdon, and king of the Scots (1124–53).

19. King Louis VII (1137–80).

in every way and chose him as his only advocate with the kings of France.[ix] How often did Geoffrey, count of the Angevins and duke of the Normans, send messengers to him with flattering and solicitous petitions?[20] How often did Count Geoffrey himself, despite his sharp temper and wild, forceful disposition, write him humble letters in which he placed our abbot's name before his own?[21] Although both of these dukes were the most powerful magnates of their time, they thanked him for the peace that existed between them and especially attributed to him the harmony between their domains. And I wonder whether this quotation would be a more fitting accolade for our Suger than for any of the abbots that preceded him: *And in a time of violence he provided reconciliation.*[22]

Second Book

I appear to have already written more about this venerable man than his rivals would have desired, for a lot of them become ill when they read about his deeds even though they are very true. I suspected this might happen, but I will not remain content with what I have already written. I will happily add as much as I can recall from my memory of him, for I want those who do not know him to know him completely, if that were possible, and those who already know him to become reacquainted with him. I am certain that many people will appreciate whatever attempt I make to praise him. I do not claim to know all his achievements and eminent virtues, and I certainly know less than those before me who were his close associates for a long time, but few of them appear to be alive today. The gray hair on his head was already turning white when he allowed me the privilege to share in his greatness. Why would I not thank him as much as possible? Why would I not always stand up out of respect at the mention of his great name? He admitted an

---

20. Geoffrey V Plantagenet (1113–51) was count of Anjou, Touraine, and Maine in 1129–51 and duke of Normandy by conquest in 1144–51.

21. For the correspondence between Geoffrey and Suger, see Suger to Count Geoffrey of Anjou and Empress Matilda, *Oeuvres* (ed. Lecoy), no. 15 (264–66); Suger to Count Geoffrey of Anjou, no. 17 (267–68, 291–92, 310); and Count Geoffrey of Anjou to Suger, RHF, no. 29 (15:493–94).

22. Sir 44:17.

outsider who was a totally undeserving stranger into his inner circle and frequently invited him to sit at his table. The point I wish to stress here is that one's status meant nothing to him.

The public business of the kingdom or the needs of the Church frequently required that this illustrious man be away from the monastery. So he delegated competent brothers who were inflamed with divine zeal to instruct and provide role models, in his absence, for the flock entrusted to him. The family origins or the native lands of the brothers he selected did not concern him, but he promoted those whose way of life he admired. For example, he put in charge of our congregation Herveus, a man of great sanctity and remarkable simplicity but who was not well educated.[x] Our abbot realized that knowledge too often makes one arrogant, while charity always confirms one's faith.

Crowds of people from every social or religious rank flocked to him, no matter whether he was at home or abroad. What a sight! Some of them carried away something beneficial for their bodies, others for their souls. No one departed from him disappointed, no one empty-handed. Monastic communities, both far away and nearby, can testify to how generous he was to the poor, and how merciful to the sick. No one can adequately describe how charitable he was to everyone—foreigners, as well as his own countrymen. Is not that remarkable work of glass in a Parisian church visible proof of his extraordinary generosity?[23] That is certainly one example, but not the only one. There still exists in many places a large number of works of this kind that he did, not out of a sense of duty, but out of kindness. Did anyone ever come to him demanding justice who did not depart from him pleased? He either satisfied the wishes of those seeking help, or he suitably placated them with the expectation of a better outcome. He considered it most noble to take everything upon himself, and to ask for nothing in return.

Our Suger was appointed shepherd of only one monastery; but, at the same time, he was constantly worried and greatly concerned about all churches, no matter where they were located in the king-

---

23. *Oeuvres* (ed. Lecoy), 472 (index), identifies this stained glass as being in the Church of Notre-Dame in Paris.

dom. He guided some of them by offering advice, others with a benefice that supplied food, and, more than anything else, he made sure that their religious devotion did not become lax. He supplied grain to needy churches and constructed workshops for others. It was a beautiful sight for both angels and men when everyone leaned on this one man, as though he were a sturdy column; and all drew from him, as though he were a bountiful source. All understood that he served them, as well as supervised them, and that he daily attended to the well-being of each and every one of them.

Good Jesus, how much energy and spirit he had! When he approached, tyrants fled, the sons of darkness hid themselves, and the sons of light and the day rushed to him.[24] When the kingdom fell into disorder, and, as often happens, wars break out, he was the foremost proponent of harmony and the most vigorous restorer of peace. He was Caesar in spirit, Cicero in speech, a suppressor of rebellions, and a vanquisher of seditions. One could accurately say about this man: "while he was alive, we were all of one mind; after he died, trust among us broke down."[25]

If I may say something bold but true, his wisdom and passion were so great that I believe the entire world would not have been a challenge for him to govern. I would be exaggerating in my statements about him if his intentions and solemn promises did not support my assertions; and he would have finished the work he had begun, had not envious death been jealous of his successful deeds. When the two powerful kings of the French and the Romans united their armies and gathered provisions from all over the West, I do not know why God did not allow them to be successful.[26] Our Suger, bolstered by divine favor and a unique talent in which he excelled, had already valiantly tried to accomplish this, just as the following narrative will show. But I fear that I may diminish the grandeur

---

24. 1 Thes 5:5.

25. Virgil, *Georgics*, 4:212–13; available at www.thelatinlibrary.com/verg.html. See also Seneca, *De Clementia*, 4.1; available at www.thelatinlibrary.com/sen/sen.clem.shtml.

26. Emperor Conrad III and King Louis VII fought as allies against the Turks in the Second Crusade of 1147–49, but their endeavor ultimately failed miserably. See above, *Life of Louis VII*, XIII, 142–43.

of these events if I described them with my unpolished and simple pen. Nonetheless, let us now mention still more about his lifestyle and habits, even though everyone already agrees that his daily life, and nearly all of his words, are worthy of the highest praise.

Fate assigned our Suger a short and slender body, but constant work depleted a great deal of his strength. He reached old age, with the help of God, by eating frugally, avoiding the type of food that stimulates the appetite, and taking good care of himself. His food was neither too coarse nor too refined. He never complained about its quality or its preparation. He only nibbled from the dishes placed in front of him, and sent out what was left to the poor; and because of this, I never saw him refreshed. He never ate meat until his body required it during an illness, when his friends insisted that he eat it. He did not drink wine unless he diluted it with a lot of water, and in the summer he often drank only water. He obtained all kinds of favors, but there was one privilege he absolutely shunned. After he came to power, he grew no fatter than he was as a simple monk; but if I may speak candidly, nearly all the other abbots usually became fat in their cheeks and stomachs immediately after the laying on of the hands, no matter how slim they had been previously. Since he needed little sleep, he took every occasion during the summer and winter to read, or listen to a lengthy reading after the evening meal, or to instruct those sitting with him by telling famous stories. The reading was from the approved books of the Fathers or sometimes from Church histories. When he was in a light-hearted mood, he told about his own deeds, or the deeds of other brave men that he had seen or learned about; and several times he talked until midnight. As a result, he only slept for a short time in a bed that was not too hard or too soft. He totally avoided anything that appeared ostentatious in his wardrobe or lifestyle. He felt that pretense was unworthy of good men, and as the Stoic said, he thought it dishonorable to follow the perverse road of ambition.[27]

After he had solemnly celebrated the office of Matins, our Suger awakened from sleep after a short rest and hastened each day to the

---

27. This is a theme of Seneca's letter 92, "On the Happy Life," in his *Moral Letters to Lucilius*.

church. Before he ascended the altar there, he humbly prostrated himself in front of the tombs of the Martyrs and offered himself completely to God in his prayers, while flooding the floor beneath him with tears.[28] Thus, the venerable priest devoutly and reverently proceeded to offer the Communion hosts of salvation. Who can adequately describe the remorse that burned within him as well as the abundance of tears and sighs he usually poured forth when he held the true presence of God during the most holy sacrifice? During the Nativity of the Savior, the Resurrection, or other major feast days, it was amazing how devoutly joyful, and joyfully devout he was—joyful in his speech, and devout in his heart. As a result, he would not permit any worldly affairs to distract him or allow anything sad to be mentioned, insisting that the day pass joyfully and be spent only praising God. On those days when night descended suddenly and caught him as usual solemnly engaged in the praises of Vespers, he said that it did not matter whether divine praise was finished during the night or the day, for both the night and the day belong to Him. He also said that the celebration of the liturgy should not be shortened for any reason. This man, just as he had read in Scripture, *stationed the singers before the altar; and to their song he added sweet melodies and gave beauty to the celebrations, and he adorned his time until the end of his life.*[29]

He treated the infirm brothers, whom he had fathered spiritually in Christ Jesus, just as if he had begotten each one of them in the flesh. He provided physicians to care for them at great expense; and if I may get right to the point, he doubled the annual revenues for this purpose by his efforts.[30] I am the least worthy of the many brothers who experienced his charity, but it was I who benefitted more than the others from his benevolence. Indeed, no one has more abundantly experienced his kindness, no one more lavishly his generosity than I have. For this reason I have not related all the

---

28. The martyrs were Saint Denis and his two companions, Rusticus and Eleutherius, who were beheaded for their Christian faith at Paris around 250 A.D. during the persecution of the Roman emperor Decius.

29. Sir 47:11–12.

30. See also *Oeuvres* (ed. Lecoy), Charter X, 350.

events as they unfolded, in order to avoid appearing boastful about my close relationship with this great man, and to prevent my uncultivated and lengthy prose from boring my audience. May the Lord repay him on my behalf, and may He look favorably upon his works of mercy. But everyone is convinced that the Lord has already rewarded His servant, washed away his sins, praised his courage, and increased his glory forever.

Our Suger had other noble and honorable achievements. He hired all kinds of craftsmen, stonemasons, carpenters, painters, blacksmiths or metal casters, goldsmiths, and jewelers from every part of the kingdom, and every one of them was skilled in his craft. He commissioned them to adorn the shrine of the Martyrs with wood, stone, gold, gems, and every precious material, and to restore an old, narrow, and dark church into a new, spacious, and light-filled one. Hope did not disappoint him, nor did fortune abandon him in his task. The splendid works speak volumes to anyone desiring to know how the resources helped what he wanted to do, and how fortunate he really was. He decorated the church with a large amount of expensive furnishings—gold and silver vessels, onyx and sardonyx cruets, green gems, crystals, all kinds of precious stones, purple hangings, long garments woven in gold, and pure silk apparel. He added highly admirable works of glass or marble, and increased the number of sacred vessels.

There are many letters addressed to him from prominent men; and among those who wrote frequently were Abbots Peter of Cluny and Bernard of Clairvaux, who were both well renowned for their lifestyle and learning, which were matched only by their eloquence. [xi] Both men offer enough evidence to show how respected our Suger and his reputation were among all men, both near and far. In addition, Father Bernard, beloved of God, wrote a short letter to the Supreme Pontiff Eugenius that was full of praises for our Suger.[31] He maintained that in the presence of Caesar, our Suger acted as though he were a member of the Roman Curia, and in the presence of God, as though he were a member of the heavenly court, just like

---

31. For this letter to Pope Eugenius III (r. 1145–53), see Saint Bernard to the Pope, *Oeuvres* (ed. Lecoy), no. 4 (419).

the most holy David who entered and departed the house of God in both capacities. On one occasion the abbot of Cluny inspected the works and buildings of our Suger, as well as the very small cell that this man, a philosopher of the highest degree, had built for himself to live in. Abbot Peter then moaned deeply in this cell and is said to have uttered this opinion: "This man shames us all, for he does not build for himself, as we do, but only for God." Our Suger built nothing for his own use during his entire administration, except for that humble cell attached to the church, a cell that was barely ten feet wide and fifteen feet long. He built the cell for himself ten years before his death, so that he could reflect upon his entire life that he admitted had been wasted too much on worldly affairs. He spent his free time there reading, doing penance, or meditating. He retreated to it to avoid the confusion of the world and evade all crowds. There, as was said about the wise man, he was never less alone than when he was alone, for he focused his attention on all the greatest men in whatever age they lived.[32] He conversed with them and learned with them. He used straw instead of feathers to sleep on in his cell; and in the place of soft linen, he lay upon a coarse woolen garment that he hid during the day with a fine rug. I must warn the reader that I am omitting a large number of his virtues because I want to be brief, and to honor the promise that I made earlier to give a short narration.

Third Book

At that time the most Christian King Louis of the French departed for Jerusalem wearing the cross of the Lord;[33] and so the bishops and the magnates of the kingdom convened a general council, primarily to determine whether to entrust the most pressing issues and the governance of the realm to the magnates or to the lead-

---

32. Cicero, in his *De Officiis*, trans. Walter Miller (London: William Heinemann, 1938), 3.1, quoted Cato the Elder, who used this expression about Scipio Africanus.
33. King Louis VII took up the cross at Vézelay on Easter Sunday, 1146, and along with nobles and knights of the realm departed France from Metz in June 1147 on the Second Crusade. See above, *Life of Louis VII*, XIII, 141–43.

ing churchmen.[xii] As it turned out under divine inspiration, the unanimous choice of all fell on our illustrious Suger, and they pressured him to take on the administration and care of the state, even though he was unwilling, and was somewhat opposed to the decision. He turned down this honor, no matter how right it was, because he believed it was more of a burden than an honor, and he did not accept the position until Pope Eugenius, who was present for the king's departure, forced him to take it.[34] He could not resist the pope nor would it have been right for him to do so.[35] Let no one believe that the king set out on the crusade because our abbot advised or wanted it. The king, in fact, undertook it out of pious intentions and his love of God, although the events turned out very differently from what he had hoped. Besides, our abbot was a prudent and foresighted man, who neither suggested nor approved of the undertaking when he heard about it. He initially tried in vain to prevent it, but he could not check the king's strong desire for it. Therefore, he decided to defer to the king's wishes because he did not want to lessen the king's devotion, or uselessly offend its supporters.[xiii]

After the king had set out on the crusade and our eminent Suger had taken charge of royal affairs, brigands suddenly emerged everywhere in the kingdom, and openly exposed their factions that had been in the making for a long time. It appeared to our Suger that the king's absence gave them the freedom to become lawless. Some of them plundered the possessions of the churches and the poor with unabashed violence, while others committed robbery from hidden places.[36] A new commander was immediately girded with two swords to avenge those who had been violated. One sword represented secular and royal authority, and the other spiritual and ecclesiastical authority; and the Supreme Pontiff divinely entrusted both of these swords to our Suger.[37] In a short time he suppressed

---

34. Eugenius III (Bernard of Pisa) was pope in 1145–53.
35. See also Grant, *Abbot Suger*, 157.
36. For a thorough account of Suger's regency, see ibid., 156.
37. Pope Saint Gelasius I (r. 492–96) first introduced the doctrine of the Two Powers or Swords in the late fifth century. He used it against the Eastern Roman emperor Anastasius I (r. 491–518), claiming that the spiritual power superseded the temporal one. See also Lk 22:38 and Eccl 4:12.

the reckless plans of those wicked men and, with a powerful stroke, reduced their plots to empty threats. He was so imbued with divine favor through all of these crises that he was able to win bloodless victories over the enemy and keep the entire kingdom intact.[xiv] Thus, this valiant man, outwardly a lion and inwardly a lamb,[xv] peacefully fought the battles of the kingdom with Christ as his leader. You could see men from the distant parts of the kingdom, Limousin, Berry, Poitou, and Gascony, who found it in their best interests to place themselves under his protection.[38] He satisfied them so completely in every way, sometimes with aid, sometimes with advice, that they could not have expected anything more from a king.

He guided the kingdom as a good father would his family and undertook much more than he had agreed to do. He restored royal palaces and rebuilt ruined walls and towers. Did not the king find every part of the palace and the royal buildings in better condition upon his return? And to prevent the kingdom from suffering any loss of prestige during the king's absence, he gave the knights their customary stipends and on the prescribed days their livery or royal gifts. Everyone knows that he dispensed all these benefits from his own generosity rather than from the king's treasury or the state's. He either sent all the money that he released from the royal treasury to the king on his pilgrimage, or saved it for him, believing that, while the king was far away, he had many expenses and that, upon his return, what he saved for him would be needed.[xvi]

By his decree, ecclesiastical offices were either given or revoked from individuals, and bishops-elect were consecrated and abbots ordained upon his approval. Bishops recognized his authority over them, and obeyed and deferred to him without any envy or shame. When he summoned them they assembled, and when he dismissed them they returned home rejoicing that they had found a clergyman who, alone, could take care of the kingdom for all of them.[xvii]

The Supreme Pontiff was so grateful for our Suger's enormous

---

38. Limousin is a region in west-central France; Berry is a province in central France; Poitou is a province in west-central France whose western side borders the Atlantic Ocean; and Gascony is an area in the extreme southwest portion of Aquitaine whose southeastern end borders the Pyrenees mountains.

integrity and wisdom, that any decision he made on behalf of the French was approved at Rome; and whatever initiative he brought before the pope was confirmed there. Pope Eugenius wrote to our Suger as one would to a close friend, and his encouragement often strengthened him, for the pope never gave him a direct order or command but, in fact, made only polite requests. Our Suger faithfully fulfilled everything required of him, and the pope worked with the authority granted our abbot; and those things that could not be settled at Rome often found a satisfactory solution in our Suger's presence. One can obtain a great appreciation of the tremendous respect, esteem, and trust they had for each other after reading the letters and correspondence they frequently exchanged.[xviii]

The king's brother returned from Jerusalem ahead of the king; and the common people, who are easily stirred up to revolt, flocked to him and bid him a long life with royal power.[39] Some members of the clergy also began to cajole and shamefully flatter him; and trusting in his royal blood, they incited this man to commit illicit acts because they preferred different policies in the kingdom.[40] We shall not reveal the names of those involved to avoid harming any of them intentionally. However, our just Suger, like a courageous lion, prevented the government entrusted to him from being thrown into chaos, after he heard about Robert's arrogance that resembled the treachery of the Greeks unleashed when the military camps of God lay before them.[41] Therefore, our Suger sought the advice of the king's vassals and did not stop countering Robert's schemes until he skillfully checked all of his insolence and forced him to make suitable reparations. No doubt our Suger had such great dedication and perseverance in the pursuit of truth and justice that, if required, he would have happily given his life to attain them. After careful

---

39. Count Robert I of Dreux (ca. 1123–88) was the fifth son of King Louis VI and his wife, Adelaide of Maurienne. He went on the Second Crusade and fought in the siege of Damascus along with King Louis VII in 1148. See above, *Life of Louis VII*, X, 140.

40. The events of Robert's insurrection are obscure. For a discussion of the insurrection, see Grant, *Abbot Suger*, 172–74.

41. For numerous examples of Greek treachery against the crusading armies of Louis VII and the German emperor Conrad III, see Odo, *De profectione*.

consideration of the courage he displayed in his actions, I have concluded that the safety of the king and his return should be especially attributed to him. For he decided that the clergy and the people should donate alms and say frequent litanies for the king's safety. He was so concerned about his return that he continually asked him in private and public correspondence to do so, and he implied that it was the desire and anxious wish of everyone for him to come back, and argued that it would be pointless for him to delay.[42]

Therefore it should surprise no one that this man habitually performed only good acts. It should surprise no one, I say, that he had to endure evil accusations and outright lies from detractors, for even our Savior was not immune from such slander. Rumors circulated everywhere that every day easily turned evil deeds into good ones and good deeds into evil ones. Some rumors about this man were told to the king that confused his naive mind and swayed him for a while, from his own opinions, into believing the sentiments of the detractors. However, when the entreaties of his own vassals and those of others had brought about the king's welcome return, he learned that the Roman Pontiff was coming to greet him as he approached Rome.[43] The pope immediately began their conversation by making a special point to commend the splendid merits of our abbot to the king. Thus the pope totally silenced the tongues of the detractors, and proved that those men were liars who tried to disgrace this distinguished man and darken his splendor. As a result, their jealousy only enhanced his reputation, rather than damaged it. The king learned the truth about our Suger and discovered how loyal he had been from both his deeds and the testimony of the pope. If the king held this man in high regard before he set out, he had good reason now to esteem and honor him even more on his return, after all suspicions had been removed. Why would the king not admire him? Why would he deny our Suger every honor when he valiantly and loyally managed the most important affairs entrusted to him, and returned the kingdom to the king at peace and intact? Why would

---

42. See Suger to Louis VII, *Oeuvres* (ed. Lecoy), no. 11 (258–60), and RHF, no. 69 (15:509–10).

43. Louis VII and Pope Eugenius III met at Tusculum on July 9, 1149.

the king not trust him more than all the others, when he had proved himself more faithful than anyone else? The king sincerely esteemed and loved him, and our Suger's death demonstrated how much he loved him.[44] Many people know the king showed his gratitude to him while our abbot was alive, and even after he died. From that time forward the people and the king referred to him as the father of the fatherland, and likewise everyone praised and conferred on him the highest titles of honor.[45] Many people believed that this level of good fortune was all that he could attain, and that he could not rise to any higher level of success. However, just as there is no limit to the depths that evil men can descend, similarly there is no end or limit of success that men of virtue can achieve.

This illustrious man endured mental anguish every single day over the lack of valor displayed along the route of that crusade. He thought it shameful that some in that powerful French army died miserably by the sword or famine, and that he had to witness others return home in disgrace. He worried that the glory of the Christian name would be lost in the East during that calamitous time; and that the holy places would be surrendered to the infidels and be trampled under their feet. The king of Jerusalem and the patriarch of Antioch sent him letters from across the sea that tearfully pleaded with him to send them help.[46] They claimed that after the prince had been killed, that the Saracens enclosed the Cross of the Savior within the walls of Antioch, and that the city was on the verge of surrendering unless it were quickly relieved.[47] At the same time Pope Eugenius, out of respect for our abbot, sent him apostolic letters that implored and ordered him to use his authority and the wisdom that God gave him to rescue the Eastern Church, and to do what he could

---

44. Suger died on January 13, 1151, and was buried in the abbey church on January 15; the king was present at the funeral services.

45. The Roman Senate awarded this title to distinguished Romans and emperors, including Cicero, Julius Caesar, and Caesar Augustus, as well as many later emperors.

46. Baldwin III was king of Jerusalem in 1143–63; Aimery of Limoges was the Latin patriarch of Antioch in 1140–96.

47. See Emperor Manuel to Pope Eugenius III, RHF, no. 25 (15:440–41), and Stephen Runciman, *A History of the Crusades* (London: Folio Society, 1994), 2:201–2. Raymond of Poitiers, the Prince of Antioch in 1136–49, was killed in the battle of Inab on June 29, 1149, against the forces of Nur al-Din.

to repair the disgrace incurred by the Christians.[48] The dire situation stirred our Suger into action, especially after an apostolic command had urged him, and papal authority had backed him; and he wholeheartedly planned to assist those in danger and avenge the insult that those wicked Saracens had made upon the Cross. He decided not to trouble the king of the French or the knights who had not fully recovered after their recent return. Therefore, he summoned and convened the bishops to discuss the business of the kingdom, encouraging and inspiring them to anticipate with him the glory of victory that had eluded the most powerful kings. He tried in vain three times to motivate them, but only found traces of fear and cowardice in them; but he still believed it important to attain that praiseworthy goal on his own, after the others had abandoned the idea.[xix] He would clearly have preferred to conceal his noble endeavor for a while because of its uncertain outcome, or to avoid appearing arrogant; but, in truth, the large amount of preparation made that impossible. He next took pains to send ahead to Jerusalem, through the knights of the Holy Temple,[xx] the necessary expenses for this great undertaking from the revenues that his own labor and expertise had acquired for the monastery. Thus no one should be offended by his using this money, when one considers the total increase of revenues for the possessions of the church his zeal had earned, the number of estates he acquired, and the number of churches he added during his administration. He did everything, to all appearances, as if he were preparing others to conduct everything on his behalf; in truth, however, if he had continued to live, he would have set out on his own initiative and undertaken this adventure. He hoped that the Almighty would help him, Who usually bestowed victory on worthy men, whether they are few or many, considering that in such cases, intention is more important than troops, and wisdom is more essential than weapons.[49]

Our Suger continually desired to wage this holy combat while trying to decide whether to make this journey himself; but the

---

48. For these letters of April and June 1150, see Pope Eugenius III to Suger, *Oeuvres* (ed. Lecoy), 313–14, and RHF, no. 65 (15:457) and no. 71 (458–59).

49. Eccl 9:18.

Most High Observer of hearts, who believes that intention is just as worthy as action, decided, I say, to crown His champion before the battle and spare this glorious old man, who had already waged all kinds of battles for Him. He was stricken with a light fever while God was summoning him to His side. My Geoffrey, we watched this elderly man, who was still strong and vigorous in spirit, wrestle for a while with the illness in his small, weakened body. We often saw him sacrificing the sacred host while being held upright by others until his illness grew worse, diminished his strength, and confined him to his bed. I could not watch this scene without a heavy heart, nor speak about it without choking up. When he realized that he was being called home and his final day was at hand, he submitted to the will of the Creator with a calm and cheerful spirit. He said he was happy, because he would soon escape from this pit, so to speak, into a place that is free and sublime. Did not his spirit foresee his impending death when he set out that same year to pray at the tomb of the distinguished confessor of Tours?[50] Was he not seeking permission to die when he remarked to us that this was going to be his final farewell to the saint? He was even seen at the tomb of the saint offering, with his usual generosity, a silken garment of outstanding workmanship.

Our Suger seemed very annoyed that someone else would have to undertake his devout plan, and worried that he would do it without enthusiasm. He, therefore, selected one of the most renowned magnates of the French, a courageous man who had physical strength and a great deal of experience in warfare, to guarantee that his sworn vow would be carried out.[51] He wanted to send in his place a capable man to lead the way because he was being called to the Heavenly Jerusalem. Our Suger invested him with the cross, assigned him the task of fulfilling his vow, and gave him permission to use the money that he had sent ahead to cover the expenses—an

---

50. The tomb of Saint Martin of Tours (316–97) was a popular destination for pilgrimages. Martin was buried at Tours in central, western France where he was bishop from 371 to his death.

51. Unfortunately the text leaves this French magnate unnamed. He may have been William of Courtenay, who was about to depart on crusade at this time; see *Oeuvres* (ed. Gasparri), 2:350n70, and *Louis VII* (ed. Luchaire), no. 261 (183).

amount sufficient for him and a large contingent of knights to fight the infidels for a long period of time in order to avenge their crimes against heaven.

Then, from that day forward, he began to joyfully wait for his final hour. He never lost his composure at the end, because he had already lived a full life before his death; and although he enjoyed living, dying did not trouble him. He died without regret because he knew better things awaited him after his death; and he believed that a good man's departure from this life was not the same as someone being banished or driven out against his will. He remained cheerful in the face of death; and as God is my witness, he was less annoyed about death than about our attempts to reassure him that he would continue to live. Amazingly, he viewed his own end with the same confidence and courage that one usually shows towards someone else's death; and he could not have come to terms with it so joyfully had he not spent a long time preparing for it. Whereas some people seek to live, our Suger sought to die because, by living well, he felt that he had lived long enough, for he never cared about how long he lived but how well he lived. The sickness lingered for four months or more, and he thanked the Almighty for not taking him too quickly, but for leading him little by little toward the much-needed rest for a worn-out man. He became acutely aware that the day of the Lord's Nativity was eminent, and began pleading with the Lord insistently to put off his death a little while longer, until the feast days had passed, for he did not want festive days to be turned into days of sorrow because of him. The Lord appeared to have clearly heard his request, because after the holy days had been completed, he departed to the Lord on the octave of the Epiphany, and he is surely now celebrating perpetual post-octave days with Him.[52] This man, who usually enjoyed the feast days of the Lord or the saints more than other men, without doubt, now deserves to celebrate everlasting feast days.

Hear me, Geoffrey, while I wish to obey you, I have left myself open to the vicious ridicule and denunciation from many people. I

---

52. In other words, an eternal celebration. Suger died at Saint-Denis on January 13, 1151.

know that there will be no shortage of those who will accuse me of presumption in undertaking to ornament this noble subject matter with exceptional praises. I have put off the task for a long time, hoping that someone else would repay this great man for his merits. However, since some might do it halfheartedly, I have decided to write about him in some form or other, rather than earn the reputation of being ungrateful or neglectful. Someone may think that I have not written enough about his merits, but he should understand that I have chosen to be brief out of consideration for modern readers. Anyone who complains that my writing exaggerates too much should read the royal deeds that our Suger wrote;[53] and he should read, if he likes, the letters addressed to him from all over the world;[54] and he would then learn how much I have failed to match the eminence of the events. I believe that I have only laid the foundations upon which more lofty structures will one day rise, and have cut down, out of a thick forest, the rough, unfinished timber that someday the hands of skilled artisans will shape.

I have produced the letter that you requested about his death that will reveal more information about it to anyone wanting to know.[55] The letter will reveal how a man, who lived a praiseworthy life, passed away gloriously; and it will describe his honorable funeral rites and list the renowned persons who attended his burial. Finally, how privileged we both are to have had the opportunity to serve him while he lived, and then after he died to spread precious balms over his lifeless body with our hands. There is only one thing left for us to desire. We ask that this man, who used to pray with us, remember and pray for us now; and may we, who have rejoiced in his company, be strengthened by his prayers. If I knew him at all, even though he is now imbued with eternal joy, he is still fulfilling the duty of his title. While he lived among us, he brought petitions before lofty princes on behalf of his subjects; and our Suger is still

---

53. See Suger, *The Deeds*.

54. Information on these letters is given in *Oeuvres* (ed. Lecoy), 285; *Oeuvres* (ed. Gasparri), 2:99–154; and RHF, vol. 15.

55. See *The Circular Letter* that follows. William also wrote it at the request of his fellow monk Geoffrey.

intervening on behalf of his devout suppliants before the throne of God. He took great care of the brothers, even though the burdens of his body oppressed him, and now that the shackles of his flesh have been broken, what else can we believe except that he has escaped and found complete freedom? There is no doubt that the Lord mercifully considered the prayers of a man who paid close attention to, and diligently carried out, the commands of the Lord.

The Circular Letter of the Monastery of Saint-Denis Concerning the Death of Abbot Suger

TO ALL THE FAITHFUL located everywhere in Christ, the humble community of Saint-Denis sends greetings, and may eternal consolation in heaven be obtained for everything demanded in the present.[56]

We feel that it is appropriate to relate to your holy congregation the glorious passing from this world of the most reverend Abbot Suger of pious memory in order to obtain your deepest condolences and receive, from your charity, some comfort and relief from the sorrow that constantly overwhelms us. We all owe each other compassion because we are all individual members united under one head.[57] He was a father whose energy and zeal should be made known to almost the whole world, although every generation knew and recognized him for his exceptional wisdom. However, we have worried about appearing ungrateful and neglectful for the immense benefits and merits of so great a father. Yet there is no way we can fully describe all his extraordinary deeds or accolades on this small page, because a large volume and outstanding skill would be required to produce a work that could describe all of them; for his merits truly

---

56. William began writing this circular letter almost immediately after the death of Suger in 1151 for the purpose of announcing and describing his death and funeral to other church entities; see Grant, *Abbot Suger*, 43. It was composed before his *Life of Suger*.

57. William uses the Latin *caput* here, whose exact meaning is unclear in this context; he may be referring to the pope, because his Letter is addressed to all the faithful in Christ.

overshadow his fame, and his pious acts far exceed the praise for them. For who can relate the story of his life adequately in a eulogy? Who can sufficiently admire his high ideals from the time of his youth, and his wisdom in both ecclesiastical and secular affairs? No one can adequately portray his attentiveness to divine worship and his determination to beautify his church. His primary intention and desire was to raise the noble monastery of Saint-Denis to the highest honor and prestige, to reform its religious life, to enrich the church's revenues, to enlarge it with additions, and to adorn it with beautiful objects. The evidence of all this is clearer than light and will endure until the end of time. Therefore, one can honestly and cheerfully sing to the Lord: *I have loved the beauty of your house, Lord, and the dwelling place of your glory.*[58] His brilliant mind, eloquent speech, knowledge of letters, and skill in speaking and writing, both all together and individually, so shone forth in him that no one could determine which of these qualities he excelled in the most; however, his most extraordinary talent appeared to be his ability to write as smoothly, effortlessly, and almost as quickly as he could speak. He was fortunate to be born with a superior ability to remember things and with an exceptional skill to understand what was important and should be kept in mind. Thus, he could easily recall the time and place of any memorable statement, or anything that he had once heard, or that he himself had said. He had such incredible moderation that no one could decide whether he was more abstemious before or after he had eaten his meal.

To make a long story short, one example alone proves how much power or influence he had in the whole kingdom. Upon departing for Jerusalem, King Louis took the advice of the bishops and the great men of the realm, and specifically entrusted the governance of the kingdom to our Suger's proven fidelity and expertise. With the help of God he managed and governed the realm so well for nearly two years that he handed back the kingdom entrusted to him in sound condition when the king returned. The Supreme Pontiff Eugenius often deferred to our Suger's expert judgment to settle seri-

---

58. Ps 25:8.

ous issues arising in the kingdom that were brought to the pontifical court. Although he did not want to but was required to do so, he attended the assemblies of kings and princes and confessed that the only reason he endured this mental anguish was to help orphans, widows, poor people, and those suffering injustices.[59] He especially appeared before the king at the appropriate times in support of the church over which he presided, or the other churches in the kingdom.

Therefore, the great deeds of this magnificent man lulled our minds into believing that he, who was so deserving of life, would live forever, and for that reason we received a blow that we were not prepared to deal with. If we could put our sense of duty in perspective, we would have rejoiced because we had such a father, rather than grieve that we outlived him; for we know that one day we will follow him in death. He was not snatched away from us, but delivered from life's perils; he did not lose his life, but gladly exchanged it. But no one can avoid death; so when the illness that took his life began to torment this venerable man, he begged the brothers, who had to hold him up with their hands, to escort him into an assembly of the community. There, after words of encouragement, he prostrated himself at the feet of everyone present as they wept and sighed. Like all men, he feared the judgment of the Lord as he humbly submitted himself to the judgment of the brothers, and tearfully asked them to mercifully forgive him if he had offended or neglected them in any way. All the brothers did so most willingly, amid great reverence and a flood of tears. He also freely and mercifully forgave every errant brother judged to be associated with some kind of wrongdoing and released him from whatever punishment he had incurred. He restored to favor everyone present or far away and returned him to his previous office and rank. Finally, he strove with many prayers and pleaded as much as he could to be completely relieved of his pastoral duty; but it was impossible for him to get the brothers to agree with his request. A short time later his illness appeared to weaken him more seriously, and both

---

59. Jas 1:27 exhorts the reader to help widows.

the doctors and he agreed that his death was imminent. He then summoned into his presence the venerable lord bishops of Soissons, Noyon, and Senlis, his close associates, to witness and advise him as he put his household in order and allow their mediation to strengthen him to die with peace of mind.[60] The bishops humbly attended to him every day as he tearfully confessed to them, both individually, and sometimes all of them together, everything that weighed on his conscience. He trusted these men completely, and devoutly finished whatever they asked him to do; and they took turns administering to him the sacraments of the body and blood of the Lord for nearly fifteen consecutive days before his death.

Our Suger focused his total attention on the Lord; and each day and night he diligently devoted himself to reciting, in order, the psalms and the litanies of the saints. He continually urged all the brothers to strive for harmony and to remain united above all else, and make every effort to avoid scandal, seditions, or schisms. He carefully warned them to work toward maintaining order, the divine worship, and the veneration of the saints. Then this beloved father and eminent pastor died, while reciting the Lord's Prayer and the Apostles' Creed, on the Ides of January, in the seventieth year of his life, nearly sixty years after receiving the monastic habit, and in the twenty-ninth year of his abbacy.[61] He died, I say, after a long virtuous life, as the saints in heaven rejoiced, and the faithful on earth of every sex, age, rank, or class mourned and wept. With God assenting, six venerable bishops, many abbots, and other monks attended his burial and very dignified funeral rites that befit his prestige and the majesty of the place; and they solemnly committed his soul to God and his body to earth with devout prayers. The most

60. Jocelin of Vierzy was bishop of Soissons from 1126 until his death in 1152. An opponent of Abelard, he was a French theologian who built the cathedral of Soissons. Soissons, Aisne, Picardy is a commune located about fifty-eight miles northeast of Saint-Denis. Baldwin II of Boulogne was bishop of Noyon in 1148–67. Noyon, Oise, Picardy is a commune located about sixty miles northeast of Saint-Denis. Peter I was bishop of Senlis from 1134 until April 1151. Senlis, Oise, Picardy is a commune located about twenty-seven miles northeast of Saint-Denis.

61. Suger was born in 1081; he entered the abbey of Saint-Denis as an oblate at age ten, became abbot in 1122, and died there on January 13, 1151.

Christian King Louis had been away for a long time when he received the very sad news of our Suger's death; and because of their longstanding friendship and affection for each other, he suspended all his current business and hastened to attend the funeral, along with the magnates of the realm. Out of religious devotion, the king forgot his royal dignity and wept bitterly the entire time our abbot was being buried. One thing is certain; this man who had lived his whole life gloriously could not end it in any other way. Thus, heaven ordained that the bishops consecrate his death, and that the king honor his burial with his presence. The Master of the Sacred Temple was also there with a large company of knights from his order; and with prayers, tears, and all other means possible they commended to the Lord a soul precious to them.[62]

How can we go on without him? Can we now be comforted without this man who customarily consoled the grieving, made people happy, and drove away sorrow? How can we now live without such a great companion, such a great consoler of our cares and hardships? His illness showed how valuable he was when healthy. We did not realize what we had until we lost it. He alone calmed anxiety within our household and settled public concerns at the same time. He was our comfort at home and brought us honor abroad. We should not be upset about his passing, because in death he paid nature's common debt; but what he gained from Christ in grace was unique. However, will we ever be able to think about, or remember him, without tears and remorse, although all in heaven are rejoicing with him because he has trampled death under foot and now has received his eternal reward? Can we ever forget so great a father or remember him without shedding tears of gratitude? But these recollections, although sorrowful, lift our spirits. If we start to mourn him, we will appear doubtful of his salvation. However, if we shed no tears, we can justifiably be accused of disrespect and ingratitude. We could have endured it better if we could have thought about his death be-

---

62. Evrard of Barres became preceptor of the Templars in France in 1143 and Master of the Temple in Jerusalem in 1147 until he resigned the office in 1151 and became a monk at Clairvaux. See Odo, *De profectione*, for his participation in the Second Crusade.

forehand. We were terrified to contemplate anything like that about him, not because we were unaware of his condition, but because we had learned to think only happy thoughts about him. But he was snatched away to prevent illness from changing his heart, because his soul was pleasing to God. Surviving to ripe old age, he fell asleep in the Lord and was placed beside his patron saints. Dust has returned to dust, but his soul has fled among the stars, to be crowned and joined to the rank of the elect by Him whom he served while in the flesh, and fought for with unwavering faith.[63]

> While I recall his merits and manner of life,
> As much as I know and remember of his virtues,
> Although I remain silent and hide things known to me,
> Still a day will come and bring them to light.
> The essence of goodness, its power, can never be hidden.
> Things long obscure will be revealed to the public eye.
> A model of living this man to mortals has been,
> Justly, I believe, from heaven guided and given.
> I marvel at the huge spirit in such a body,
> So many good things in a small, frail vessel.
> But nature wished this one man to prove
> That virtue can be covered by any skin at all.
> In speech Tullius,[64] in merits Cato,[65] in courage Caesar,[66]
> He guided kings with counsel, kingdoms with strength.
> What Cato, what Scipio[67] once did for Rome,
> This one man alone did for his native land.
> What praises, what honors, what sort of triumph,
> Father Abbot, can your flock shout again for you?
> O most worthy Suger, what can we say that is
> Worthy of your merits? Our praise will be brief,
> But heaven and earth applaud you for those merits,

---

63. "Dust returning to dust" is a reference to Gn 3:19.
64. Marcus Tullius Cicero, the famous Roman orator of the first century B.C.
65. Marcus Cato the Elder (234–149 B.C.).
66. Julius Caesar (100–44 B.C.), Roman general and statesman who conquered Gaul.
67. Scipio Africanus (236–183 B.C.), Roman general who defeated Hannibal in North Africa in the Second Punic War.

And all Gaul celebrates your fame.
Seven stars[68] smiled at your birth,
Providence and power were propitious for them.
Generous nature furnished you its treasures,
And philosophy opened her bosom to you.
Fortune did not deny you joyful success;
The Fates[69] habitually gave you every good they had.

ENDNOTES

i. William and Geoffrey were both monks of Saint-Denis and intimates of Abbot Suger. William had led a faction opposed to the new abbot of Saint-Denis, Odo of Deuil, during the two years of turmoil at the abbey following the death of Suger. Odo transferred William to the priory of Saint-Denis-en-Vaux in Poitou; and it was while in exile there that William began writing this biography in summer 1152, completing it in autumn 1154. See Grant, *Abbot Suger*, 43–44. The phrase *post discessum* used in the first sentence of the text is ambiguous, for it is not clear whether William or Geoffrey has departed from the abbey. William certainly departed from the abbey; and we have chosen to translate the sentence as such, but whether Geoffrey also departed is not clearly known.

ii. In 1122 King Louis VI had sent Suger to meet Pope Calixtus II (r. 1119–24) in Apulia in southern Italy concerning some affairs of the kingdom; he was returning home from this embassy when he learned he had been elected abbot. See Suger, *The Deeds*, 121–23.

iii. King Louis VI and Abbot Suger appear to have had an association and friendship from boyhood in the 1090s at the abbey of Saint-Denis where Louis grew up. For Louis's presence at the abbey as a boy, see above, *The Administration*, XXXIII, 108, and Suger, *The Deeds*, 162n8.

iv. Suger often refers to himself, too, as being humble in birth. Modern research, however, indicates that he was related to the minor nobility; see John F. Benton, "Suger's Life and Personality," in *Abbot Suger and Saint-Denis* (ed. Gerson), 3. How-

---

68. The classical planets are the five planets visible to the naked eye (Mercury, Venus, Mars, Jupiter, and Saturn), plus the sun and the moon.

69. The Roman Fates were a triad of deities known as the *Parcae* or *Fatae*, who represented the destinies to which mortals were subject. Originally goddesses of birth, the Parcae were known respectfully as Nona ("nine-month birth"), Decuma ("ten-month birth"), and Morta ("still-birth"). They later assumed the same duties as the Greek Fates: Clotho, Lachesis, and Atropos. Nona spun the thread of life; Decuma measured the thread; and Morta cut the thread when a person reached his allotted day.

ever, the social status of minor nobility may indeed have been "humble" for the abbot of one of the most prestigious monasteries in France.

v. Plato, *Theaetetus*: "Every man has had thousands of progenitors, and among them have been rich and poor, kings and slaves." The quotation from Plato is found in Seneca, *Ad Lucilium epistulae morales*, V, 44.4; available at perseus.uchicago.edu.

vi. We have not been able to locate this quotation, but it is an outstanding example of Stoicism and its debt to Neo-Platonism, as seen in the writings of Seneca.

vii. Louis VII lost the Aquitaine when he had his marriage to Eleanor annulled on March 21, 1152, by the French prelates assembled at Beaugency. The author indicates here that Suger had counseled the king against this annulment. See also above, *Life of Louis VII*, XV, 144–45.

viii. Roger II the Young (1095–1154). He ruled as Grand Count of Sicily in 1105–30 and as king of the Norman Kingdom of Sicily in 1130–54. He added Calabria to the kingdom in 1122 and Apulia in 1127. See *Oeuvres* (ed. Lecoy), 292–93, for a mention of the letter that Roger addressed to Suger, and 245 for the response that Suger sent him. For the complete text of both letters see Roger II to Suger, RHF, no. 34 (15:495), and Suger to Roger II, no. 35 (15:495).

ix. Theobald IV was the count of Blois and Brie (1102–52) and count (II) of Champagne (1125–52). Blois, Loir-et-Cher, Centre-Val de Loire is a city located about 122 miles southeast of Saint-Denis. For the letters he wrote to Suger, see Count Theobald of Blois to Suger, RHF, no. 17 (15:490) and no. 56 (15:503), and Count Theobald of Blois to Suger and Ralph of Vermandois, RHF, no. 65 (15:507–8) and no. 73 (15:511).

x. For Herveus, see Suger, *The Deeds*, 159. Before he departed for the Aquitaine for the marriage of Louis VII to Eleanor, Suger had entrusted Herveus to oversee the burial of King Louis VI in the Church of Saint-Denis if the king were to die while the abbot was away, as happened. For Herveus, see also above, *The Administration*, XVIII, 88. See also *Oeuvres* (ed. Lecoy), no. 7 (340), no. 8 (343), and no. 9 (348), where his name appears as a witness to charters.

xi. Peter the Venerable was born about 1092 in the Auvergne region of France and died as abbot of the Benedictine abbey of Cluny on December 25, 1156. Bernard of Clairvaux was born in 1090 at Fontaine-lès-Dijon, France and died on August 21, 1153, as abbot of the Cistercian abbey of Clairvaux, which he founded in 1115. Pope Alexander III canonized him as a saint on January 18, 1174. He was one of the most prolific writers of his time. Today Clairvaux is in Ville-sous-la-Ferté, Aube, Champagne-Ardenne, which is a commune located about 150 miles southeast of Saint-Denis. For their letters to Suger, see Peter the Venerable to Suger, *Letters*, no. 109 (1:271–72); and Bernard to Suger, *Letters*, no. 80 (110). See also RHF, no. 21 (15:644–45), nos. 22–24 (15:645–46), and no. 26 (647).

xii. This assembly opened at Étampes on February 16, 1147, and chose Abbot Suger, along with Count Ralph I of Vermandois (1085–1152), after Count William II of Nevers (1080s–1148) declined appointment, to administer the kingdom in the absence of the king during this crusade. Samson of Mauvoisin, archbishop of Reims (r. 1140–61), was later added as a third regent, probably to placate the archbishops and bishops of the realm, for Suger was a Benedictine monk and abbot. However, Samson was not very active as regent. For this assembly, see *Morigny* (ed. Cusimano), 158–60; Odo, *De profectione*, 12–14 and 20n1; and above, *Life of Louis VII*, X, 138n41.

xiii. Suger did not oppose the idea of a crusade, but only the king's departure from the realm. He correctly predicted, as the next paragraph indicates, that disorder in the kingdom would occur during Louis VII's absence.

xiv. *Oeuvres* (ed. Gasparri), 2:334n52, gives a list of Suger's supporters in the struggles against the rebels: Counts Theobald of Blois, Geoffrey of Anjou, William of Nevers, Thierry of Flanders, as well as Archbishops Geoffrey of Bordeaux and Peter of Bourges.

xv. The lion symbolizes ferocity while the lamb represents gentleness. The two are not found lying with each other anywhere in scripture, but both are found there signifying characteristics of God, with the lamb specifically representing Jesus Christ.

xvi. For Suger's maintenance of the royal buildings and his meeting the financial obligations during the absence of the king on crusade, see Suger's letter to King Louis VII, *Oeuvres* (ed. Lecoy), no. XI (258–60).

xvii. The author may be referring here to the Council of Reims that Suger was instrumental in convening in mid-March 1148. For this Council, see *Morigny* (ed. Cusimano), 160, and Grant, *Abbot Suger*, 162–63.

xviii. See *Oeuvres* (ed. Lecoy), Suger to Pope Eugenius III (various letters); RHF, vol. 15; and for this pope's letters to him, see Eugenius III to Suger, RHF, vol. 15 (various letters).

xix. For this assembly, see Suger's letter of 1150 to Abbot Peter the Venerable of Cluny in *Oeuvres* (ed. Lecoy), no. 18 (268–69). The letter indicates that the first assembly was held at Laon in March 1150. Apparently nothing resulted from it. Thus, a second assembly occurred at Chartres after Easter on May 7. A third assembly took place in July at Compiègne. See *Oeuvres* (ed. Gasparri), 2:346n65. For the meetings at Laon and Chartres, see Grant, *Abbot Suger*, 279–80. For the letters to Suger from Bernard of Clairvaux, Peter the Venerable of Cluny, Archbishop Humbert of Lyons, Archbishop Geoffrey of Bordeaux, and Bishop Alain of Rennes giving excuses for their inability to attend the meeting at Chartres, see *Oeuvres* (ed. Lecoy), 311–12.

xx. See Bernard to Suger, RHF, no. 93 (15:614). The Knights Templar were a monastic military order founded in the 1120s to protect the pilgrimage routes to Jerusalem in the Holy Land from marauders and highwaymen. Under pressure from King Philip IV, who seized their monetary resources in France, Pope Clement V disbanded the order in 1312.

Appendix A

Legends and Myths of Saint Denis in the Early Literary and Historical Records

The story of Saint Denis's life and the history of the abbey itself are filled with legend and myth. Much of what is known about the life, martyrdom, and miracles of the saint and the foundation of the abbey comes from hagiographical and historical literature written in the fifth, sixth, and ninth centuries. The five extant sources are the *Passio sanctorum martyrum Dionysii episcopi, Rustici et Eleutherii*; the *Vita Genovefae virginis Parisiensis*; Hilduin's *Areopagitica sive Sancti Dionysii vita*; and Hincmar's *Gesta Dagoberti I regis Francorum* and his *Miracula sancti Dionysii*. These works were mainly intended to promote Denis's role as the apostle of France and spiritual protector of the French monarchy, as well as enhance the importance of the abbey through association with him. These early writings also established a close relationship between the monarchy and the abbey that began during the reign of King Dagobert and lasted throughout the Middle Ages.[1]

Denis was one of seven bishops whom Pope Fabian (r. 236–50) sent to Gaul to convert its pagan population to Christianity in the third cen-

---

1. For a detailed account of the relationship between the abbey of Saint-Denis and the monarchy, and the development of the cult of Saint Denis, see Gabrielle M. Spiegel, "The Cult of Saint Denis and Capetian Kingship," in *The Past as Text: The Theory and Practice of Medieval Historiography* (Baltimore, Md.: Johns Hopkins University Press, 1997), 138–62; Elizabeth M. Hallam, *Capetian France, 987–1328* (London and New York: Longman, 1980), 174–79, and Crosby, *The Abbey of Saint-Denis, 475–1122*, 1:41–52.

tury. Assigned to Paris, Denis became the city's first bishop. He established a religious community there that became a center for missionary activity in Gaul. Denis and his apostles angered the local pagan priests, who then reported them to the Roman authorities during the persecutions of the Emperor Decius.[2] Gregory of Tours wrote that Denis was one of many Christians whom the Roman authorities tortured in 251.[3] Condemned to death, Denis and his two companions, Rusticus and Eleutherius, were taken to the outskirts of Paris to the village of Catulliacum and beheaded. Catulliacum was in the area where the abbey church of Saint-Denis stands today.[4]

The earliest of the extant sources associated with the life and martyrdom of Saint Denis is the *Passio sanctorum martyrum Dionysii episcopi, Rustici et Eleutherii*, written at the end of the fifth century.[5] It incorrectly claimed that Pope Clement I (r. 92–99) sent Denis to France in the first century, instead of the third; and it is the first work to establish the authenticity of Denis's role as the apostle of France.[6] It is also the first to identify Rusticus and Eleutherius as Denis's companions and to describe their martyrdom.[7] The *Passio* stated that, after the execution of the three martyrs, a pagan woman stole their bodies and buried them in a field that she had been sowing. A commemorative shrine was later built over the spot where they were buried.[8]

The *Vita Genovefae virginis Parisiensis* is a biography of Saint Genevieve, composed in about 520.[i] According to the *Vita*, Saint Genevieve, sometime in the fifth century, replaced the shrine over the graves of the Holy Martyrs with a church where many miracles occurred.[9] This is the earliest mention of a church built there. In addition, Gregory of Tours in the sixth century wrote about "guardians," who were attached to a basilica there that contained holy relics.[ii]

The most important sources recounting the life of Saint Denis, however, are the ninth-century works of Hilduin and Hincmar. Built upon the

2. Emperor Decius (r. 249–51).
3. Gregory of Tours, *History of the Franks*, 20.
4. Crosby, *The Abbey of Saint-Denis, 475–1122*, 1:39.
5. Spiegel, *The Chronicle Tradition of Saint-Denis*, 139.
6. Spiegel, *Chronicle Tradition*, 139. On Clement sending Denis, see *Passio Dionysii episcopi, Rustici et Eleutherii*, in PL 88:580.
7. *Passio*, 88:581.
8. Ibid., 88:582. Later texts identify this woman as Catulla.
9. *Vita Genovefae virginis Parisiensis*, ed. B. Krusch, MGH, SRM (Hanover: Impensis Bibliopolii Hahniani, 1862), 3:222–25.

narratives of the *Passio* and the *Vita Genovefae*, they resulted in a biographical story of Saint Denis filled with legend and miraculous events. King Louis I ("the Pious," r. 814–40) commissioned Hilduin in 835 to write a biography of Saint Denis, which he titled the *Areopagitica sive Sancti Dionysii vita*.[iii] In it, Hilduin attempted to determine the actual date that Denis was sent to France, as well as describe the origin of the monastery of Saint-Denis. Although he took great license with the historical record, he produced a narrative that appeared to be plausible and convincing.

Louis I had instructed Hilduin to use all the available Greek and Latin sources available to him to write his *Areopagitica*.[10] The Greek writings of Pseudo-Dionysius the Areopagite were among those that Hilduin used. In one of them Dionysius, a Syrian Neo-Platonist living in around the year 500, falsely identified himself with Dionysius the Areopagite, whom Saint Paul converted to Christianity in the first century, presumably in order to give greater credibility to his writing. Thus, Hilduin became the first writer to merge the identity of Saint Denis, the third-century martyr, with both Dionysius the Areopagite of the first century and the Neo-Platonist Pseudo-Dionysius of the sixth century. He identified them as the Dionysius associated with the abbey of Saint-Denis, believing all three to be the same person.[11]

Hilduin wrote that Denis was born in a suburb of Athens called Areopagus. One day the apostle Paul gave a sermon there about judgment day and the resurrection of the dead, and on this day Denis converted to Christianity.[12] Paul later baptized him, taught him Christian doctrine, and appointed him bishop of Athens.[iv] When Denis learned that Emperor Nero had ordered Paul's arrest in Rome, he hastened there; but Paul had already been crucified by the time he arrived. While in Rome, Pope Clement I commissioned him to be an apostle to France, and upon arriving there Denis founded a church at Arles and then traveled north to Paris.[13] Hilduin did not mention Rusticus and Eleutherius accompanying Denis to Gaul, but mentioned them later in the work engaging in missionary activity and being martyred.

Hilduin stated that one of Denis's converts in the region of Paris was a nobleman named Lisbius, who offered Denis his house and the land next

---

10. *Ludovici Pii Epistolae*, Louis to Abbot Hilduin of Saint Denis, no. 12, in PL 104:1326–28.
11. Spiegel, *Chronicle Tradition*, 142, and Hallam, *Capetian France*, 175.
12. Acts 17:19–34.
13. Hilduin, *Areopagitica sive Sancti Dionysii vita*, in PL 106:26–27, 38–40.

to it to build a church. Denis established a religious community there whose primary function was to conduct missionary work among the local pagan population. However, his proselytizing incurred the wrath of the pagans, who turned him over to the Roman authorities during the time when the Emperor Domitian (r. 81–96) had ordered a general persecution of Christians. The provost Sisinnius arrested Denis and his followers and asked them to recant their Christianity; and when they refused, Denis, Rusticus, and Eleutherius were tortured and thrown into prison.[14]

According to Hilduin, on the night before their execution, Jesus Christ appeared outside the cell window of the Holy Martyrs and comforted them.[15] The next morning Roman authorities led them to a hill outside of the city called Montmartre, which Hilduin said was formerly called *Mons Mercurii*; and there Denis, Rusticus, and Eleutherius were beheaded.[16] Then occurred one of the most famous events in the legend of Saint Denis; Denis picked up his severed head and walked six miles, in the company of a host of angels, to the site where he wished to be buried, singing hymns to God the entire way.[17]

Archbishop Hincmar wrote the *Gesta Dagoberti I regis Francorum* in the ninth century.[v] In it, he recounted the numerous favors and gifts that King Dagobert (of the Franks, r. 629–34) gave to the Church of Saint-Denis and the miracles associated with Denis.[18] The miracles Hincmar described in the *Gesta Dagoberti* provide the rationale for King Dagobert's extraordinary devotion to the abbey of Saint-Denis and his generosity to it, in the forms of material wealth, donations, and privileges, which included the proceeds of the Lendit Fair.

These miraculous stories, dating back to the reign of King Dagobert, served to further Saint Denis's role as spiritual protector of individuals and the French monarchy. They also engendered the close relationship that existed between the monarchy and the abbey of Saint Denis that lasted throughout the Middle Ages.[19]

14. Ibid., 106:40.
15. Ibid., 106:45–46.
16. Ibid., 106:50.
17. Ibid., 106:45–46.
18. Hincmar also wrote the *Miracula sancti Dionysii* that told of even more miracles associated with Saint Denis than those mentioned in the *Gesta Dagoberti*. See A. Luchaire, "Etudes sur quelques manuscrits de Rome et de Paris, *Les Miracula Sancti Dionysii*," Bibliothèque de la Faculté des Lettres 8 (Paris: Ancienne Librairie Gerner Baillière, 1899), 20–29.
19. Spiegel, *Chronicle Tradition*, 144.

There are two miracles in the *Gesta Dagoberti* that emphasize Saint Denis's protective role. One day the young prince Dagobert was pursuing a serf with his dogs, when the serf hid himself in the small shrine that housed the relics of the Holy Martyrs to evade detection. The dogs followed the serf to his hiding place, but were unable to enter the shrine even though the door was open. Dagobert stood in awe at this miracle.[20]

In the second miracle, Dagobert himself sought the protection of Saint Denis. Dagobert wanted to avenge an insult that Sadrigesilus, the duke of Aquitaine, had done to him; so he ordered his servants to flog the duke and to shave off his beard. When Dagobert's father, King Clothar II (r. 613–29), learned of Sadrigesilus's humiliation, he ordered Dagobert's arrest. Like the serf he had earlier chased, Dagobert fled from his father's sergeants and took refuge in the shine that housed the relics of the Holy Martyrs. The sergeants, like the dogs, were unable to enter the shrine.

In another story, Dagobert fell asleep in the shrine and had a dream about Denis, Rusticus and Eleutherius, in which Denis stepped forward and offered Dagobert protection if the prince promised to honor them by remodeling their tombs.[21] When Dagobert became king, he kept his promise to the Holy Martyrs and constructed a new church. He adorned it with beautiful objects, then exhumed their bodies and transferred their remains to the new basilica.[22]

Thus, Dagobert constructed the first basilica of Saint-Denis out of gratitude for the protection that the saint gave him as a young man, thereby establishing the special relationship between the monarchy and the abbey. The basilica has undergone several renovations,[vi] the greatest of which began in the 1130s under Abbot Suger. His reconstruction of the basilica helped usher in the Gothic style of cathedral building in Europe.

These stories about Saint Denis's life and the history of the abbey are rich in legend, miraculous occurrences, and anachronistic events. This kind of narrative culminated with the *Gesta Dagoberti* in the ninth century. They all established Saint Denis as the patron saint of France and so enhanced the fame and reputation of the abbey that it became the official necropolis of the French kings, queens, and nobility, as well as a place of veneration that made it the most important pilgrimage destination in northern France.[23]

20. Hincmar, *Gesta Dagoberti*, 401.
21. Ibid., 402–3.
22. Ibid., 406. For the other miracles that occurred at Saint-Denis, see 411.
23. For the literary tradition and legends of Saint Denis, see also Crosby, *The Abbey of Saint-Denis, 475–1122*, 1:24–40.

ENDNOTES

i. Saint Genevieve was born at Nanterre around 420. When she was about seven years old, she promised Saint Germain of Auxerre that she would embrace the celibate religious life, and at age fifteen she took vows of virginity before Bishop Villicus of Paris and became a nun. Following the death of her parents, Genevieve moved to Paris and lived in partial seclusion with her grandmother. She died around 500, and her feast day is January 3.

ii. Gregory mentions the "guardians" or *custodies* as being associated with a basilica, which commonly housed the relics of saints, rather than a simple church (*ecclesia*). See Gregory of Tours, *Liber in Gloria martyrum*, ed. B. Krusch, MGH, SRM (Hanover: Impensis Bibliopolii Hahniani, 1885), 1:85–86.

iii. Hilduin (775–840) was the bishop of Paris and chaplain to King Louis I the Pious (r. 814–40). The king appointed him abbot of Saint-Denis in 815.

iv. Hilduin, *Areopagitica sive Sancti Dionysii vita*, in PL 106:18–20. Peter Abelard in the twelfth century discovered Hilduin's error while living at Saint-Denis following his mutilation. He saw a passage in Bede's *Commentaries* on the Acts of the Apostles that said Dionysius was the bishop of Corinth, not Athens. See *Historia calamitatum*, in *Abelard and Heloise: The Story of His Misfortunes and The Personal Letters*, trans. Betty Radice (London: Folio Society, 1977), 39.

v. Hincmar (806–82) was raised at the monastery of Saint-Denis under the tutelage of Hilduin. He became archbishop of Reims in 845 and was a close associate and adviser to King Charles the Bald (r. 843–77).

vi. The church was rebuilt as one of the first great Carolingian abbeys and was dedicated in the presence of Charlemagne on February 24, 775. It officially became a royal abbey when Charles the Bald assumed the title of lay abbot in 867 to protect it from Norman raids. See Crosby, *The Royal Abbey of Saint-Denis, 1122–1151*, 1:13.

Appendix B

The Early Royal Banners of France

The Oriflamme and the Vexillum

The first banner associated with the abbey of Saint-Denis was the *oriflamme*, the origin of which can be traced back to Charlemagne.[i] Pope Leo III (r. 795–816) had allegedly presented Charlemagne with this banner in recognition of his imperial status over the Roman people.[ii] He carried the banner into battle affixed to a lance, for a legendary angelic prophecy spoke of a knight armed with a golden lance whose tip produced flames of "great marvel," which would rid the Holy Land of the Saracens.[1] The legend of the golden lance with the flame emanating from its tip was referred to in *The Song of Roland* as the "orie flambe."[2] *The Song of Roland* also relates that the battle cry of Charlemagne's army was *Montjoie!*, and from that time on, his battle standard was associated with both names.[iii] In the tenth century, Hugh Capet transferred Charlemagne's banner from Aachen to the abbey of Saint-Denis, where the name *oriflamme* became the popular name for the standard. The *oriflamme* retained a religious significance until the eleventh century,

---

1. Barbara W. Tuchman, *A Distant Mirror: The Calamitous 14th Century* (New York: Random House, 1978), 148.
2. *The Song of Roland*, trans. C. K. Scott Moncrieff (London: Folio Society, 2010), 120. *Oriflamme* is a French term that is derived from the Latin *aurea flamma* or "golden flame." For the origin and religious significance of the *oriflamme*, see Crosby, *The Abbey of Saint-Denis, 475–1122*, 1:50–52, and for the *vexillum*, see Crosby, *The Royal Abbey of Saint-Denis: From Its Beginnings to the Death of Suger, 475–1151*, 11–12.

when it began to take on a more secular character and represent the kingdom as a whole.³

The banner housed in the abbey of Saint-Denis, known as the *vexillum*, was that of the county of Vexin. The counts of the Vexin held their land as vassals of the abbey of Saint-Denis, and as such they became the abbey's temporal defenders. After King Philip I seized the Vexin in 1082,⁴ the *vexillum* became associated with the monarchy, and the king of France replaced the counts of the Vexin as defenders of the abbey.[iv] King Louis VI greatly enhanced the fame and reputation of the *vexillum* in 1124, when the German Emperor Henry V was preparing to invade France. To meet this threat, King Louis went to the abbey, approached the altar of Saint Denis, declared the saint to be the special protector of the kingdom, and offered gifts and prayers to him.[v] He then took the *vexillum* from the saint's altar[vi] and invited "all of France to follow him."⁵ Thus began the tradition of kings taking the sacred banner into battle, which continued throughout the medieval period.⁶

At some point, the *vexillum* of Saint-Denis became identified with the *oriflamme* of Charlemagne, although Abbot Suger never referred to the banner of Saint-Denis as anything but the *vexillum*; and Odo of Deuil referred to it by that same name when describing a ceremony Louis VII staged at Saint-Denis before setting off on the Second Crusade.⁷ However, William the Breton referred to the *vexillum* of Saint-Denis as the *oriflamme* at the end of the twelfth century.⁸ From that time on, the *oriflamme* had certainly become the common name for the banner kept at Saint-Denis, and a war cry emerged relating to both banners: *Montjoie, Saint-Denis!*[vii]

The *oriflamme* has been described as being made of orange-red silk

---

3. Stephen Wilson, *Saints and Their Cults: Studies in Religious Sociology, Folklore and History* (Cambridge: Cambridge University Press, 1983), 153–54.

4. See Augustin Fliche, *Le règne de Philippe I, roi de France, 1060–1108* (Paris: Société Françoise D'Imprimerie et de Librairie, 1912). See also Conway, "Abbey of Saint-Denis," 116.

5. Suger, *The Deeds*, 128.

6. The earliest known battle standard in France, however, was that of Saint Martin of Tours. It was a blue banner that was housed in Marmoutier abbey near Tours, and was believed to be the half of the blue cloak that Saint Martin kept for himself when he gave the other half to the beggar.

7. Odo, *De profectione*, 16.

8. *Oeuvres de Rigord et de Guillaume le Breton, Tome Second: Philippide de Guillaume le Breton*, ed. François Delaborde (Paris: Libraire Renouard), 318–19.

with green fringes, and flown from a golden lance or a silver gilt staff with green tassels.[9] Red was chosen as the color because, according to legend, the banner was dipped in the blood of Saint Denis shortly after he was beheaded. Surviving descriptions of the *oriflamme* indicate that the banner underwent changes through the centuries, as newer versions emerged that bore little resemblance to older ones, with the exception of their red color.

The *oriflamme* was carried at the head of the king's forces when they engaged the enemy in the field,[viii] and remained the visible symbol of French national unity for almost three hundred years.[10] The *oriflamme* was replaced in the fifteenth century by the flag of Joan of Arc, which had a white background and a gold fleur-de-lis with religious images depicting the annunciation of the Virgin Mary and the crucifixion of Christ.

ENDNOTES

i. There are several other ideas as to the origin of the *oriflamme*. Some believed that it descended from heaven as a gift God sent to France to ensure perpetual victories. Others trace its origin to Clovis, and mark its significance equal to that of the Holy Grail. It was also said that King Charles VII (r. 1422–61) returned it to heaven. See Crosby, *The Abbey of Saint-Denis, 475–1122*, 1:50.

ii. Gabriel Spiegel says that the banner was originally called "Romane." The *Nova Gesta Francorum*, written at Saint-Denis in the twelfth century, also refers to the banner as *Romane* (Bibliothèque nationale, lat. 11793, fol. 27v). However, the name *Montjoie* given in *The Song of Roland* became the preferred name. See Spiegel, *Chronicle Tradition*, 153 and 263n53.

iii. There are several hypotheses as to the origin of the term *Montjoie!*; one is that it refers to stone markers or cairns that were set up along roadsides. The name for these cairns may have derived from a Germanic battle cry, *mund gawi*, roughly meaning "hold the line." The later Latin term for these markings was *mons Jovis*, which from 1200 onward became known in French as *Montjoie*. Another hypothesis maintains that the term is connected to *Mons Gaudii*, an expression coined by medieval pilgrims journeying to Rama, just to the northwest of Jerusalem, where they would get their first glimpse of the city. See *The Song of Roland* and L. H. Loomis, "The Oriflamme of France and the War Cry Montjoie," in *Studies in Art and Literature for Bella da Costa Greene*, ed. Dorothy Eugenia, Miner. (Princeton, N.J.: Prince-

---

9. Descriptions of the *oriflamme* can be found in William the Breton's *Philippide, the Regista Delphinalia* of 1456, and in the inventory of the treasury of Saint-Denis made in 1536.

10. *Abbot Suger* (ed. Panofsky), 5.

ton University Press, 1954), 67–82, and Crosby, *The Abbey of Saint-Denis, 475–1122*, 1:51–52.

iv. Philip I transferred the rights of the counts of the Vexin to the crown, following the death of Simon, the last count of the Vexin, in 1088. See John Woodward and George Burrett, *A Treatise in Heraldry, British and Foreign: With English and French Glossaries* (Edinburgh: W. and A. K. Johnston, 1892), 2:658, and Crosby, *The Abbey of Saint-Denis, 475–1122*, 1:50–51.

v. Louis VI issued a charter in 1124, in which the king recognized that the Vexin was held in homage to the Holy Martyrs, and that the counts of the Vexin had carried the *vexillum* into battle as the guardian of the abbey of Saint-Denis. See *Louis VI* (ed. Luchaire), no. 348 (160).

vi. The original banner stood on one side of the altar of Saint Denis and a replica of the original stood on the other side. The replica was probably the one that was taken into battle. See Bradbury, *Capetian Kings*, 144.

vii. According to Crosby, *The Abbey of Saint-Denis, 475–1122*, 1:51–52, "Montjoies" were common battle cries in the Middle Ages throughout France and England. He states that *Montjoies* were natural landmarks that served as boundaries between two territories, and thus were military objectives as well as meeting places; and the banners and standards of the army were placed on them. Thus, the *Montjoie* originally had no national significance as a war cry; therefore, some name had to be attached to it to delineate a specific *Montjoie*. For the dukes of France, and later for the Capetian kings, the name was "Saint-Denis!"; for the dukes of Burgundy, it was "Saint André!"; for the dukes of Bourbon, "Notre Dame!"; for the kings of England, "Saint George!" and "Notre Dame!" See also Wilson, *Saints*, 153.

viii. The *oriflamme* is recorded as being carried into six battles between the thirteenth and fifteenth centuries, four of which the French lost: the Battle of Bouvines in 1214 (won); the Battle of Mons-en-Pevele in 1304 (lost); the Battle of Crécy in 1346 (lost); the Battle of Poitiers in 1356 (lost); the Battle of Roosebeke in 1383 (won); and the Battle of Agincourt in 1415 (lost). When the *oriflamme* was displayed on the battlefield, it indicated that the French army would give no quarter, for its red color symbolized blood. The standard bearer was called the *porte-oriflamme*, and carrying it became an important office and great honor. The duty was very dangerous because the standard bearer was expected to die rather than let it fall into enemy hands.

Appendix C

French Kings and Queens Buried in the Abbey of Saint-Denis

The cathedral of Saint-Denis,[1] located about eight miles north of Paris, became the official burial place of the French monarchy in the seventh century.[i] Through the centuries, the royal tombs in Saint-Denis have been arranged and rearranged, as well as plundered and restored, and the remains of those buried in them scattered and recovered. To date there are forty-two kings, thirty-two queens, sixty-three princes and princesses, and ten great barons buried in Saint-Denis. The number of royal tombs increased over the centuries by the transferal of the remains of monarchs to Saint-Denis from other abbeys around France, such as Sainte-Geneviève, Saint-Germain-des-Prés, and Royaumont. The number of royal tombs and monuments has also changed over the centuries from the destruction and despoliation during the Hundred Years' War and the French Revolution.[ii]

There was no systematic arrangement for the royal tombs until the reign of King Louis IX (r. 1226–70). He enlarged the north and south transepts of the church in 1263/64 and ordered the remains of earlier kings and queens, who were buried at other churches in simple graves, to be exhumed, placed in boxes, and buried in tombs at Saint-Denis. Louis also commissioned the production of sixteen stone effigies that

---

1. The basilica of Saint-Denis was given cathedral status in 1966.

were placed over their tombs,[2] and instructed that the tombs of eight kings and queens from the Merovingian and Carolingian dynasties be arranged in the south transept, and eight from the Capetian dynasty in the north one. The tombs of Kings Louis VIII and Philip Augustus were given an honorary position in the center of the church. Louis IX issued a proclamation stating that only legitimately crowned kings and queens could be buried at Saint-Denis, and that royal children were to be buried at the abbey of Royaumont. Philip IV the Fair, the grandson of Louis IX, revoked this proclamation; and thus today there are nobles and aristocrats resting alongside the monarchs in Saint-Denis.

The cathedral of Saint-Denis and many other abbeys throughout France suffered tremendous destruction and despoliation during the French Revolution, as the revolutionaries sought to eradicate all vestiges of the French monarchy and the institution that became synonymous with the Old Régime—the Catholic Church. During the period of the National Convention, monasteries and churches were closed and turned into "Temples of Reason." King Louis XVI and Queen Marie Antoinette were both guillotined in 1793, and their bodies thrown into a common grave with other victims of the Reign of Terror. The Committee of Public Safety issued a decree in 1792, ordering that the metal tomb markers, metal monuments, and plaques in Saint-Denis be melted down and used to make armaments. Its ostentatious tombs were also to be destroyed.[3]

The executions of King Louis XVI and Queen Marie Antoinette exacerbated public hatred of the Old Régime, and the royal tombs in Saint-Denis became a primary target of this rage. The National Convention issued another decree on August 1, 1793, that ordered the destruction of all royal tombs there. The revolutionaries entered the church and began systematically opening and pillaging the tombs. On the first day, the vault of the Bourbon monarchs was opened and their tombs plundered and pillaged.[iii] The lead and bronze coffins were melted down for military use, and the tombs were stripped of gold crowns, jewels, ornaments, and anything else of value. Fifty tombs were either partially or completely destroyed, and the monuments were removed and thrown outside into a garden located behind the north transept. Obeying a de-

---

2. The effigies of Odo and Hugh Capet were destroyed during the French Revolution; thus there are only fourteen of the sixteen effigies commissioned by Louis IX extant today.

3. The two royal tombs lost were those of Charles II the Bald and Charles VIII.

cree issued October 15, 1793, the revolutionaries took the remains of deceased kings, queens, and aristocrats, and threw them into nearby pits filled with quicklime. Some people took macabre souvenirs, such as the shoulder blade of Hugh Capet (d. 996) and a snippet of the beard of Henry IV (d. 1610). Dom Germain Poirier, a Benedictine monk and keeper of the archives at Saint-Denis, has left us a detailed account of the despoliation of the royal tombs that took place in 1792–93.[iv]

The survival of the monuments of Saint-Denis and of other abbeys from the ravages of the French Revolution can be credited primarily to the effort of the archaeologist Alexandre Lenoir (1761–1839). The National Constituent Assembly, at Lenoir's urging, created the Commission of Monuments in 1791 to determine which monuments were of historical or artistic value and thus worthy of preservation, and designated the monastery of the Petits-Augustins to be used as a repository to house them.[v] The Assembly put Lenoir in charge of finding these works of art and transporting them there. Lenoir's persistence and boundless dedication were responsible for the preservation of more than 1,200 historic and artistic treasures.[vi] On August 15, 1795, Lenoir converted the Petits-Augustins into a public museum, which became known as the Museum of National Monuments. Many of the objects brought there were returned to their original locations under Lenoir's direction. The museum had an impact on public sentiment and brought a renewed awareness of the importance and uniqueness of France's historical past. By 1795, public sentiment began to reject the iconoclasm of 1793 and turned to a renewed awareness and appreciation for the art of the Middle Ages.

The cathedral of Saint-Denis remained in dilapidated condition from 1793 to 1805. Emperor Napoleon I reopened the church in 1805 and commissioned restorations. In 1806 he had the church reconsecrated and declared the official sepulcher of the emperors. Napoleon was an enemy of the Bourbon kings and insisted that their remains be left in the mass graves. After Napoleon's exile to the island of Elba in 1815, the victorious powers at the Congress of Vienna restored the Bourbon monarchy in the person of Louis XVIII. He ordered an intensive search for the remains of the Bourbon monarchs. The remains of Louis XVI and Marie Antoinette were discovered on January 21, 1815, and buried in the crypt of Saint-Denis. King Louis's royal ordinance in December 1816 closed Lenoir's Museum of National Monuments and ordered all its artifacts returned to their original locations at government expense.

Napoleon's Hundred Days interrupted Louis's search for his royal ancestors, but following Napoleon's exile to St. Helena, Louis once again resumed the search for all royal remains. In 1817 the mass graves were reopened; however, it was impossible to positively identify the remains of all the individuals inside. Therefore, Louis ordered the remains to be placed in a small room in the crypt of Saint-Denis and enclosed by two marble plates that were inscribed with the names of those persons whose tombs remained unaccounted for. Under Louis's direction, royal monuments in other churches that had escaped destruction during the French Revolution, and those that Lenoir had preserved at the Museum of National Monuments, were then transferred to Saint-Denis. Louis had the remains of Louis VII, previously buried at the abbey of Barbeau, interred in the ossuary in the crypt of Saint-Denis, along with some of the other unidentified remains. The remains of the Bourbon monarchs that could be identified were interred in the Bourbon vault. Louis XVIII died on September 16, 1824, and was buried in the center of the crypt, near the graves of Louis XVI and Marie Antoinette.

The Funeral Monuments and the Crypt of Saint-Denis

Saint-Denis contains a collection of more than seventy funeral monuments, statues,[4] and recumbent effigies. The monuments and statues constitute an eclectic collection that showcases changing artistic styles through the centuries. The tomb monuments of the Merovingian and Carolingian monarchs were covered with ordinary slabs of carved stone. The monument of Dagobert, built in the thirteenth century, is an ornate marble structure that resembles the façade of a Gothic cathedral, with miniature sculptures adorning its interior and exterior. Art historians consider the lifelike recumbent effigies of the Valois kings as the first examples of realism in funeral sculpture. The nave and ambulatory contain impressive monuments that reflect the influence of the Italian Renaissance. The funeral monuments of Louis XII and Anne of Brittany, Francis I and Claude of France, and Henry II and Catherine de Medici are impressive structures that represent some of the best examples of French Renaissance art.[5]

---

4. Today there are only fourteen statues left in Saint-Denis.
5. For a more detailed description of the funeral monuments, tombs, and statues,

The crypt of Saint-Denis is composed of four distinct parts: the archaeological crypt, Suger's crypt, the Bourbon Chapel, and the royal ossuary. The archaeological crypt is named for the excavations done there by Sumner McKnight Crosby in the 1930s. His discovery of human and animal remains that date back to the fourth century has led some scholars to believe that this part of the crypt might possibly have been the original burial place of Saints Denis, Rusticus, and Eleutherius. Some of the sarcophagi Crosby found there date to the fifth century; thus, this discovery provides supporting evidence that members of the Frankish aristocracy were buried at Saint-Denis. Suger constructed another crypt in the twelfth century from the remains of the old Carolingian crypt. The central part of the crypt, called the Bourbon Chapel, contains the graves of the last Bourbon kings and queens, which are capped with black marble gravestones. Louis XVIII had the remains of Louis XVI and Marie Antoinette transferred from the cemetery of the Chapelle expiatoire in Paris on January 21, 1815, and buried in this crypt.[6] The Bourbon Chapel contains a series of cenotaphs created in the nineteenth century in honor of the Bourbon kings. There are many small alcoves in the wall and in one of them is the mummified heart of King Louis XVII in a clear crystal urn. The royal ossuary, situated in the Bourbon Chapel, is a small vault on the left-hand side of the entrance into the crypt that contains the bones of all the kings and queens exhumed from mass graves dug during the French Revolution. These bones could not be positively identified and thus were placed together in the ossuary, with the kings on one side and the queens on the other. The ossuary is sealed with large slabs of black marble containing a long list of the names of those believed to have been buried inside.

---

see Anonymous, *A History and Description*, and Alain Erlande-Brandenburg, *The Abbey Church of Saint-Denis: The Royal Tombs*, vol. 2 (Paris: Éditions de la Tourelle, 1984); and Elizabeth A. R. Brown, *The Oxford Collection of the Drawings of Roger De Gaignières and the Royal Tombs of Saint-Denis*, Transactions of the American Philosophical Society 78 (Philadelphia: American Philosophical Society, 1988).

6. This cemetery is located near the Church of La Madeleine in the eighth arrondissement.

French Kings, Queens, and Aristocrats Buried in the Abbey of Saint-Denis

The following is a complete list of everyone buried in Saint-Denis. Certain names are preceded by bracketed numbers that correspond with the numbers on the sketch map, "Royal Tombs in the Abbey of Saint-Denis" (figure facing), to show the location of the extant tombs and monuments of the French kings and queens buried in Saint-Denis.

The Merovingian Dynasty

[1] **Clovis I** (*d. 511*). Clovis, queen Clotilde, and their two murdered grandsons were originally buried the abbey church of Sainte-Genevieve. King Louis IX commissioned Clovis's monument and recumbent effigy, which were constructed at some point in 1220–30. They are located in the upper part of the central chevet, next to the monument of Childebert. Clovis's remains were transferred to Saint-Denis in the mid-eighteenth century.

[2] **Childebert I** (*d. 558*). He was initially buried in the abbey church of Sainte-Croix-et-Saint-Vincent (the royal necropolis of the Neustrian kings until 675, later named Saint-Germain-des-Prés). His monument and recumbent effigy were made sometime before 1163 and are located next to that of Clovis I in the upper part of the chevet. King Louis XVIII had Childebert's remains transferred to Saint-Denis in 1816.

Arégund (*ca. 515/20–ca. 580*). She was the wife of King Chlothar I (497–561). Her tomb was discovered in 1959; she might be the first royal personage buried at Saint-Denis.

[3] **Fredegund** (*d. 596*). She was the wife of King Chilperic I (539–84) and was first buried in the abbey church of Saint-Germain-des-Prés. Her remains were transferred to Saint-Denis in the early nineteenth century. Her tomb is situated in the upper part of the central chevet, just below that of Clovis I and Childebert.[7]

---

7. Fredegund's tomb in Saint-Germain-des-Prés was covered with an ornate limestone slab with the outline of her head, belt, and clothing carved in bas-relief. The outline contains hollowed lines highlighted with inlays of stones and gilded copper. The funeral slab stone escaped the despoliations of the French Revolution and was later placed in Saint-Denis.

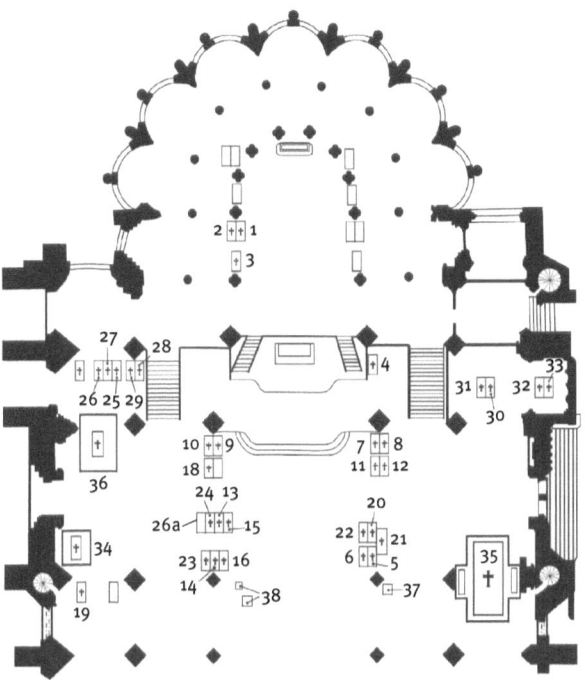

Royal Tombs in the Abbey of Saint-Denis

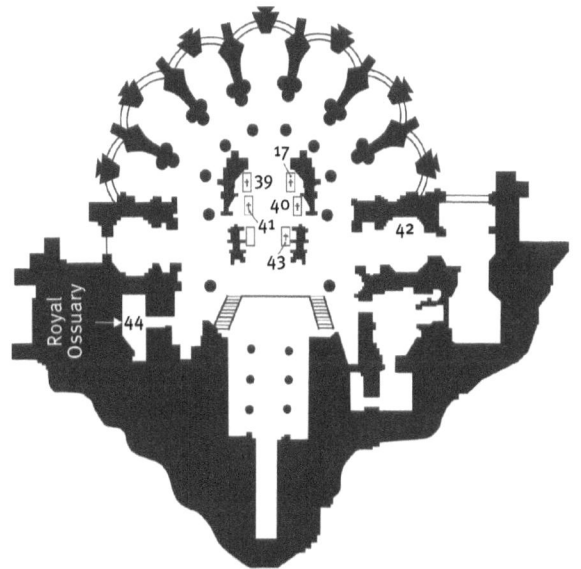

Royal Tombs in the Crypt

[4] Dagobert I (*d. 639*). He was the first Frankish king to be buried at Saint-Denis, which led to its being the official burial place of the French monarchs. His monument, which dates from 1258, is located on the upper-right side of the nave, just below the main altar.

Nanthild (*d. 642*). She was the second wife of King Dagobert I. A statue of her appears on the base of Dagobert's monument next to the head of his recumbent figure.

[5] Clovis II (*d. 657*). King Louis IX commissioned his recumbent effigy in the thirteenth century. It is located in the south transept, next to that of Charles Martel. A statue of Clovis II also appears on Dagobert's monument next to the feet of his recumbent figure.

Chlothar III (*d. 691*). There is no extant monument or effigy for him in Saint-Denis.

The Pepinid/Carolingian Dynasty

[6] Charles Martel (*d. 741*). King Louis IX commissioned his recumbent effigy in the thirteenth century. It is located in the south transept next to that of Clovis II.

[7] Pepin the Short (*d. 768*). His recumbent effigy is located next to that of his wife, Bertha. King Louis IX commissioned both effigies in the thirteenth century; they are located in the south transept.

[8] Bertha of Laon "the Younger" or "Broadfoot" (*d. 783*). She was the wife of King Pepin the Short. Her recumbent effigy is located in the south transept next to her husband's.

[9] Carloman I (*d. 771*). The son of Pepin the Short, Carloman was originally buried at Reims. King Louis IX transferred his remains to Saint-Denis in the thirteenth century and commissioned his recumbent effigy, which is located in the north transept, next to that of Ermentrude, the wife of Charles the Bald.

Charles II the Bald (*d. 877*). Originally buried at the abbey church of Nantua, France, his remains were transferred to Saint-Denis at some later date. His monument and brass memorial plaque were destroyed during the French Revolution.

[10] Ermentrude (*d. 869*). She was the wife of Charles the Bald. King Louis IX commissioned her recumbent effigy in the thirteenth century, which is located in the north transept, next to that of Carloman I.

[11] **Louis III** (*d. 882*). King Louis IX commissioned his recumbent effigy in the thirteenth century. It is located in the south transept next to that of Carloman II.

[12] **Carloman II** (*d. 884*). His recumbent effigy is located in the south transept, next to that of Louis III.

The Capetian Dynasty

King Odo or Eudes (*d. 898*). His monument and effigy were destroyed during the French Revolution, and there is no extant monument or effigy for him in Saint-Denis.

Hugh Capet (*d. 996*). His monument and effigy were destroyed during the French Revolution, and there is no extant monument or memorial for him in Saint-Denis.

Adelaide of Aquitaine (*d. 1004*). She was the wife of Hugh Capet and was supposedly buried at Saint-Denis. There is no extant monument or effigy for her in Saint-Denis.

[13] **Robert II the Pious** (*d. 1031*). His recumbent effigy is located in the north transept.

[14] **Constance of Arles** (*d. 1032*). She was the wife of Robert II the Pious. Her effigy is located in the north transept between that of Louis X and Louis VI the Fat.

[15] **Henry I** (*d. 1060*). Louis IX commissioned his recumbent effigy in the thirteenth century, and it is located in the north transept above that of Louis VI.

Matilda of Frisia (*d. 1044*). She was the first wife of King Henry I. There is no extant monument or effigy for her in Saint-Denis.

[16] **Louis VI the Fat** (*d. 1137*). Louis IX commissioned his recumbent effigy in the thirteenth century, and it is located in the north transept.

[17] **Louis VII** (*d. 1180*). He was originally buried at the Cistercian abbey of Notre-Dame-de-Barbeau in Melun, but Louis XVIII had his remains transferred to Saint-Denis in 1817. His tomb is in the crypt below the chevet.

[18] **Constance of Castile** (*d. 1160*). She was the second wife of King Louis VII. Her recumbent effigy is located in the north transept.

236 KINGS AND QUEENS BURIED IN SAINT-DENIS

Philip II Augustus (*d. 1223*). His tomb was destroyed during the Hundred Years' War, and there is no extant monument or effigy for him in Saint-Denis.

Louis VIII the Lion (*d. 1226*). His monument was destroyed during the Hundred Years' War, and there is no extant monument or memorial for him in Saint-Denis.

Louis IX "Saint Louis (*d. 1270*). His monument was destroyed during the Hundred Years' War, and there is no extant monument or effigy for him in Saint-Denis.

Marguerite of Provence (*d. 1295*). She was the wife of King Louis IX, and there is no extant monument or effigy for her in Saint-Denis.

[19] **Louis of France** (*d. 1260*). He was the eldest son of King Louis IX and Queen Marguerite of Provence. He acted as titular regent of France in 1252–54 while his mother and father were in Egypt on the Seventh Crusade. He was originally buried at Royaumont Abbey because of his father's decree that reserved burial rights at Saint-Denis only for those who were legally crowned king. King Louis XVIII ordered his remains transferred to Saint-Denis in 1817, and his monument is located in the north transept.

[20] **King Philip III the Bold** (*d. 1285*). He was originally buried at Narbonne in October 1285, but his remains were transferred to Saint-Denis in December 1285. His tomb is located in the south transept next to that of Philip IV the Fair.

[21] **Isabella of Aragon** (*d. 1271*). She was the wife of King Philip III. Her monument is located in the south transept.

[22] **Philip IV the Fair** (*d. 1314*). His recumbent effigy is located in the south transept.

[23] **Louis X the Quarreler** (*d. 1316*). His recumbent effigy is located in the north transept.

[24] **John I the Posthumous** (*d. 1316*). He was the son of Louis X and was the only person to be the king of France since birth. His reign of only five days, as an infant, was the shortest of any monarch in French history. His monument is located in the north transept.

[25] **Philip V the Long** (*d. 1322*). His recumbent effigy is located in the north transept with those of Charles IV and Jeanne of Évreux.

[26] **Charles IV the Fair** (*d. 1328*). His recumbent effigy is in the north transept.

[26a] **Jeanne of France** (*d. 1349*). She was the daughter of Louis X and the wife of Philip III of Navarre. Her monument is in the north transept; her veils completely hide her effigy.

[27] **Jeanne of Évreux** (*d. 1371*). She was the wife of King Charles IV. Her monument is located next to her husband's in the north transept.

The Valois Dynasty

[28] **Philip VI the Fortunate and Valois** (*d. 1350*). His monument is located in the north transept.

Joan of Burgundy "the Lame" (*d. 1348*). She was the first wife of Philip VI. There is no extant monument or effigy for her in Saint-Denis.

Blanche of Évreux (*d. 1398*). She was the second wife of Philip VI. There is no extant monument or effigy for her in Saint-Denis.

[29] **John II the Good** (*d. 1364*). His monument is located in the north transept.

Joan I, Countess of Auvergne (*d. 1360*). She was the wife of King John II. There is no extant monument or effigy for her in Saint-Denis.

[30] **Charles V the Wise** (*d. 1380*). His monument is located in the south transept.

[31] **Joanna of Bourbon** (*d. 1378*). She was the wife of King Charles V. Her heart was buried in the convent of Cordeliers, her entrails in the royal necropolis of the convent of the Celestines in Paris, and the rest of her remains interred at Saint-Denis. Her original tomb and effigy were destroyed during the French Revolution. Her reconstructed recumbent effigy is located in the south transept, next to that of her husband, Charles V.

[32] **Charles VI the Beloved or Mad** (*d. 1422*). His monument with that of his wife, Isabeau of Bavaria, is located in the south transept.

[33] **Isabeau of Bavaria** (*d. 1435*). She was the wife of King Charles VI. Her monument is with that of her husband in the south transept.

Charles VII (*d. 1461*). There is only a bust of him, located in the south transept.

Marie of Anjou (*d. 1463*). She was the wife of King Charles VII, and only a bust of her remains in the south transept next to that of her husband.

Charles VIII (*d. 1498*). His heart is buried at Notre-Dame-de-Cléry, and his body interred at Saint-Denis. A silver effigy was melted down during the French Revolution; there is no extant monument or effigy for him.

[34] **Louis XII** (*d. 1515*). He and his wife, Anne of Brittany, are buried in an impressive marble monument built around 1531, which is located in the north transept.

[34] **Anne of Brittany** (*d. 1514*). She was the wife of both King Charles VIII and King Louis XII. Her monument is located in the north transept with her second husband, Louis XII.

[35] **Francis I** (*d. 1547*). The massive monument of Francis I and his wife, Claude, is located in the south transept. The urn containing Francis's heart, which was originally buried at Hautes Bruyères abbey in the Yvelines, is located right behind his monument.

[35] **Claude of France** (*d. 1524*). She was the wife of King Francis I and is buried with him in the south transept.

[36] **Henry II** (*d. 1559*). He was buried alongside his wife, Catherine de' Medici, in Saint-Denis. The original bronze urn[8] containing his heart and the bronze bases of his and Catherine's tomb were destroyed during the French Revolution. The tomb of Henry and Catherine is located in the north transept.

[36] **Catherine de' Medici** (*d. 1589*). She is buried with her husband Henry II in the north transept.[9]

---

8. The surviving urn dedicated to him is a replica made in the nineteenth century, and can be found today in the Louvre.

9. Catherine's husband, Henry II, died in 1559; and she commissioned a new chapel to be constructed at Saint-Denis in his honor. Construction of the domed circular chapel began in 1563, and the structure was attached to the north transept of the basilica. Completed in 1573, the two-story chapel was known as the Valois Mausoleum. It was abandoned in 1585 and demolished in 1719.

[37] **Francis II** (*d. 1560*). He was originally buried in the Church of the Celestines in Paris, but his remains were later transferred to Saint-Denis. There is a monument dedicated to him in the south transept that contains his embalmed heart.

Charles IX (*d. 1574*). There is no extant monument or effigy for him in Saint-Denis.

[38] **Henry III** (*d. 1575*). His heart was buried in the collegiate church of Saint-Cloud and his body at Saint-Denis. His body was disinterred during the French Revolution and thrown into a common grave. A monument containing his embalmed heart is in the north transept.

[39] **Louise de Lorraine-Vaudémont** (*d. 1601*). She was the wife of King Henry III. Louise was originally buried at the convent of the Capuchins in Paris, but King Louis XVIII ordered her remains to be interred in the ossuary in the crypt of Saint-Denis in 1817.

The Bourbon Dynasty

[44] **Henry IV** (*d. 1610*). His remains are in the Bourbon vault or ossuary in the crypt below the north transept. There is no extant monument or effigy for him in Saint-Denis.

[44] **Margaret of Valois** (*d. 1615*). She was the wife of King Henry IV and was buried in the chapel of the Valois at Saint-Denis. Her casket has disappeared, and it is not known whether it was placed somewhere else during renovation work, or if it was destroyed during the French Revolution. Today what is believed to be her remains are in the ossuary in the crypt. There is no extant monument or effigy for her in Saint-Denis.

[44] **Marie de' Medici** (*d. 1642*). She was the second wife of King Henry IV. Her remains are located in the ossuary in the crypt. There is no extant monument or effigy for her in Saint-Denis.

[44] **Louis XIII** (*d. 1643*). His remains are located in the ossuary in the crypt. There is no extant monument or effigy for him in Saint-Denis.

[44] **Anne of Austria** (*d. 1666*). She was the wife of King Louis XIII. Her remains are located in the ossuary in the crypt. There is no extant monument or effigy for her in Saint-Denis.

[44] Louis XIV (*d. 1715*). His remains are located in the ossuary in the crypt. There is no extant monument or effigy for him in Saint-Denis.

[44] Maria Theresa of Spain (*d. 1683*). She was the first wife of King Louis XIV. Her remains are located in the ossuary in the crypt. There is no extant monument or effigy for her in Saint-Denis.

[44] Louis XV (*d. 1774*). His remains are located in the ossuary in the crypt. There is no extant monument or effigy for him in Saint-Denis.

[44] Maria Leszczyńska (*d. 1768*). Her heart was buried at the Church of Notre-Dame-de-Bonsecours in Nancy. Her remains are located in the ossuary in the crypt. There is no extant monument or effigy for her in Saint-Denis.

[40] Louis XVI (*d. 1793*). His body and that of Marie Antoinette were thrown into a mass grave following their executions in 1793. Louis XVIII "discovered" their remains in the Madeleine cemetery in 1815. The tombs of Louis XVI and Marie Antoinette are located in the Bourbon Chapel in the crypt. Statues of them kneeling side by side were made around 1830 and are located in the ambulatory.

[41] Marie Antoinette (d. 1793). Her remains are in the crypt of Saint-Denis next to the remains of her husband.

[42] Louis XVII (d. 1795). He was sentenced to prison by the National Convention in 1792 and died there in 1795. His body was buried in an unmarked grave in the cemetery of Saint Marguerite. In 1814 his heart was placed in a crystal vase in the crypt below the south transept.

[43] Louis XVIII (d. 1824). He was the last French king to be buried at Saint-Denis,[10] and his tomb is located in the Bourbon Chapel in the crypt.

---

10. There is an empty tomb that anticipated the death of Charles X, who was never buried at Saint-Denis. He died in exile in Gorizia, Italy in 1836, and was buried in the Church of the Annunciation of Our Lady, located at the Franciscan monastery of Kostanjevica in Nova Gorica, Slovenia.

ENDNOTES

i. Saint-Denis was never used for the coronations of kings, but was commonly used to crown queens. Royal coronations of kings were performed in the cathedral of Reims. Pepin the Short was anointed at Saint-Denis in 751 but was not crowned there. Only three kings were not buried in Saint-Denis: Philip I (1060–1108); Louis VII (1137–80); and Louis XI (1461–83). Philip was buried at the abbey of Saint-Benoît-sur-Loire; Louis VII was buried at the Cistercian abbey of Barbeau, and Louis XI was buried at the basilica of Notre-Dame de Cléry. Louis VII's remains were later transferred to the crypt at Saint-Denis.

ii. The monuments of Philip II Augustus, Louis VIII, Saint Louis IX, and Joanna of Bourbon were lost during the Hundred Years' War; those belonging to Odo, Charles II the Bald, Hugh Capet, and Charles VIII were destroyed during the French Revolution.

iii. The tomb of Henry IV was the first of the Bourbon tombs to be pillaged and that of Louis XV was the last. Louis's remains were removed at eleven o'clock on Wednesday, October 16, 1793, about the exact time that Marie Antoinette was beheaded. See Alexandre Lenoir, "Historical Notes on the Disinterments executed in 1793 at the Abbey of St. Denis," *Fraser's Magazine for Town and Country* 32 (July 1845): 93–99.

iv. According to the record left by Dom Poirier, the exhumations and despoilment of the royal tombs occurred as follows: Henry IV (October 12, 1793); Louis XIII, Louis XIV, and Marie de Medici (October 14, 1793); Louis V and Charles V (October 16, 1793); Charles VI, Isabeau of Bavaria, Charles VII, Marie of Anjou, Marguerite of Valois, Francis II, and Charles VIII (October 17, 1793); Henry II, Catherine de Medici, Charles IX, Henry III, Louis XII, Anne of Brittany, Louis X, John I the Posthumous, and Charles the Bald (October 18, 1793); Philip IV the Fair, Dagobert, and Nanthild (October 19, 1793); Francis I and Claude of France (October 20, 1793); Philip V and Philip VI the Fortunate/Valois (October 21, 1793); and Charles IV (October 24, 1793). The tomb of Abbot Suger was plundered on October 22, 1793, and his remains were thrown into the common trench. For more detail and first-hand accounts about the plundering of the tombs and the discarding of their remains, see *Forum consacré aux tombeaux royaux de la basilique de Saint-Denis*, "La destruction et la violation des tombeaux royaux et princiers en 1792–1793," available at saintdenis-tombeaux.forumculture.net, and *Forum consacré aux tombeaux royaux de la basilique de Saint-Denis*, "Profanateurs et témoins lors de la violation des tombeux royaux en 1793," available at saintdenis-tombeaux.forumculture.net. See also "Biographie de Dom Poirier," in *Dictionnaire Historique, Histoire Abrégée* (Lille: Chez L. Lefort, 1833), 10:508–9.

v. The monastery had a church, a cloister, two large courts, and a massive garden. The largest and oldest monuments were housed in the church. Other objects ranging from fragments of famous buildings to contemporary stained glass were arranged by period and housed in separate rooms that were decorated in the artistic style of that period. Chapels, sepulchers, columns, fountains, and sarcophagi were placed in the garden. Façades from various chateaux were brought here, where some of them still remain. The monastery of Petits-Augustins is today the École nationale supérieure des Beaux-Arts. See Alexandra Starta, *The Museum of French Monuments 1795–1816: "Killing Art to Make History"* (Farnham: Ashgate, 2013).

vi. Lenoir was so passionate about preserving France's historical past that he once received a bayonet wound when he threw himself between the tomb of Cardinal Richelieu and a frenzied mob that wished to plunder it. See Alexandre Lenoir, *Musée impérial des monuments français: histoire des arts en France, et description chronologique des statues en marbre et en bronze, bas-reliefs et tombeaux des hommes et des femmes célèbres, qui sont réunis dans ce Musée* (Paris: Hacquart, 1810).

Appendix D

Terms of Measurement and Money in Suger

bushel Equivalent to four pecks or eight gallons in dry measure.

carruca Could mean "a wheeled plough," "a demesne arable field" belonging to the lord of the estate, or "as much land as can be ploughed by a wheeled plough in one season." The amount of land involved varies by region and period of time. In England, it usually equaled a hide, or about 120 acres.

denarius Derived from a Frankish silver coin issued in the late seventh century, a denarius was a monetary unit equivalent to one-twelfth of a solidus; 240 denarii equaled a pound.

justa A measure almost equivalent to a pint.

librum Derived from a Roman unit of weight, the librum (livre or pound) was a monetary unit that could be divided into twenty solidi.

millia passum A Roman term equivalent to one thousand paces, or 0.915 of a modern mile.

mine Twenty-four mines equal one modius.

TERMS OF MEASUREMENT AND MONEY

modiolus   A short measure of a modius, used when measuring grain. Suger indicates that twenty-five modioli did not equal four modii as his abbey measured them (see 78n39).

modius   Derived from a Roman term, a unit of dry measure roughly equivalent to a peck, which was eight dry quarts; in liquid measure, it was equivalent to about nine quarts.

peck   Equivalent to one modius or eight dry quarts.

sextarius   Roughly equivalent to a pint (liquid and dry); in dry measure, about one-sixteenth of a modius.

shilling   The English shilling was equivalent to one-twentieth of a pound, or twelve pence (pennies).

solidus   Derived from the Roman coin first issued by Emperor Constantine, the French medieval solidus was a monetary unit equal in value to one-twentieth of a pound (livre) and could be divided into twelve denarii (derniers). The solidus later became the English shilling and the French sous.

Glossary of Medieval Words in the Selected Works of Abbot Suger of Saint-Denis

advocacy   The position of a lay protector or legal representative of a monastery, known as an advocate, who pleads, intercedes, or defends another person or a monastery. Advocates were often lords who acted as patrons of a monastic institution and vowed to protect a monastery or church from secular enemies.

almoner   A castle's servant or a religious household official in charge of dispensing alms (money, food, clothing, or other things of value) to the poor.

almonry   The almonry was the place or room in an abbey, church, or other church building where alms were distributed.

alms   Charity in the form of money, food, clothing, or other things of value given out for the relief of the poor. Giving alms was considered a moral and religious obligation.

alpha   The first letter of the Greek alphabet, used to indicate the beginning of all things. When joined with the Greek letter omega, it is a representation of God (Rv 1:8 and 22:13).

altar-frontal   Also known as an antependium, it is a decorative piece made of textile, metalwork, stone, or other material used to adorn an altar, lectern, pulpit, or table.

ambulatory   A semicircular processional aisle behind the main altar at the eastern end of a cathedral or basilica. The ambulatory often includes numerous altars of saints situated in curved, radiating chapels in its outer walls.

amphora A pitcher used to hold wine or water (see Lk 22:10).

anathema A form of excommunication that excludes a person from church services and from receiving the eucharist.

annuity Also known as a corrody; a pension in the form of lodging, money, or both granted to a lay person by a monastery, often at the request of the king, abbot, or patron of the monastic house, who had the right to billet retired servants and retainers on the monastic estate.

annulment A legal procedure by the church that cancels the marriage contract between a man and a woman, and declared that the marriage never existed and thus was never valid. A common reason or excuse for annulments in the Middle Ages was consanguinity, or being married to a blood relative.

apostolate The position of authority of an apostle or religious leader whose duty is to propagate a religious doctrine; the dignity or authority of the pope as head of the Apostolic See.

apostolic Of or pertaining to the twelve apostles; relating to the pope as the successor of Saint Peter.

appendage A separate piece of land held by a larger estate.

apse A semicircle or polygonal east end of a church, which terminates in the chancel that contains the main altar.

archbishop The title given to a bishop who presides over an important or special diocese in a region.

arpent A unit of length and a unit of area. In area, it is the equivalent of about 0.85 modern acres; in length, it is about 190 feet, which is the measurement of one side of a square arpent.

aspergil (aspergillum) A device used to sprinkle holy water during a religious service, it has a handle with a perforated ball at the end of it. It is dipped into a bucket of holy water, called an aspersorium.

ballista A siege weapon that fired a large bolt, spear, or other projectile.

baron One of the lower hereditary titles of the European nobility; comes from the later Latin *baro*, meaning "man, servant, soldier, or mercenary."

basilica An oblong church that has a central nave, side aisles, and a domed recess at one end.

benefice An ecclesiastical office or reward that guarantees a fixed amount of property or income for performing clerical duties.

beryl A transparent pale green, blue, or yellow mineral used as a gemstone; it was one of the gems that decorated the walls of the New Jerusalem in heaven (Rv 21:19).

bishop An ordained and consecrated member of the Christian clergy entrusted with a position of authority and oversight of a diocese and its churches.

burg A Germanic term used for any fortified place or walled city.

burgess (burgher) A citizen of a burg, medieval town, or commune, who was usually a member of the upper-middle class.

butler A household servant in charge of the cellar, who was responsible for ordering, supervising, and serving from the butts or casks of wine, beer, and ale.

candelabrum An ornamental branched candleholder that held several candlesticks.

canon A clergyman who is a member of the staff of a cathedral or its chapter; a member of certain orders of Roman Catholic clergy that live together communally like monks or nuns.

cantor A monk or clerk whose liturgical role is to lead the choir.

capital The carved or molded top part of a column or pillar.

carbuncle A term for any red gemstone, but most often used of the red garnet.

castellan The overseer of a lord's castle who was in charge of its domestic staff, garrison, and defenses, and protector of the castle's lands.

cathedral The central church of a diocese that is the seat of the bishop; from the Latin *cathedra*, meaning "seat."

chalcedony A form of silica composed of intergrowths of quartz and moganite, which is a polymorph form of quartz.

chalice The vessel from which the consecrated water and wine of the eucharist is drunk during Communion.

chancellor An officer in the secretarial office (chancery) of a king or bishop who was responsible for the production of official documents.

chapter The daily assembly of a monastic community at which the Rule was read, sins and transgressions confessed, and business transacted; it is also the term for a body of clergy serving a cathedral that advises the bishop and presides over a diocese during the vacancy of a bishop.

charter of liberties A document outlining the rights and privileges given by a lord or king to a person or town. The person or town often paid a large sum of money to gain independence from its lord or king.

cherub A winged angelic figure that is mentioned throughout the Old Testament, but only once in the New Testament, in reference to the Ark of the Covenant (Heb 9:5). According to *The Celestial Hierarchy*, written by the Pseudo-Dionysius the Areopagite, cherubs are the second-highest ranking angels in the first order, below only the seraphim.

chevet The east end of the church containing the radiating chapels, choir, main altar, and apse; it is from the French word *chevet*, meaning the "head" (of a bed).

chrism Oil mixed with balsam that is consecrated by a bishop. It is used in the anointing rites of the church, such as baptism, the ordination of bishops, and the consecration of churches and altars.

chrysolite A green or yellow-green gemstone; it was one of the gemstones that decorated the walls of the New Jerusalem in heaven (Rv 21:19).

churchwarden A member of the laity who oversaw the accounts, building maintenance, poor lists, and other miscellaneous duties of a church. He was usually chosen by the clergy of the church.

cloisonné Enamel work in which different colors in the design are separated by strips of flattened wire placed on a metal backing; from the French word *cloisons*, meaning "partitions."

cloister A place of seclusion in a monastery or convent; a covered passage around an open courtyard in a monastery or convent, usually having a row of columns on the side next to the courtyard.

commune A town or city whose citizens band together for mutual protection against lawless nobles or bandits. Sometimes the king or a lord allowed the commune to draw up a charter of self-government or liberties.

concordat An agreement or treaty made between the Vatican and a secular government that recognizes the rights and privileges of the Catholic Church in that government's area of jurisdiction.

consanguinity The state of being of the same kinship, or "blood relationship," with another person, resulting from descent from the same ancestor.

consecration The solemn act of declaring holy or sacred a person or secular object, such as an altar, church, or the eucharist, for the service of God.

cope An ecclesiastical vestment worn by a priest or bishop in ceremonial processions. It is a semicircular, sleeveless, hoodless cape or cloak made of silk, brocade, or embroidered fabric that rests on the shoulders, and is fastened at the chest with an ornamented broach.

count The title for a member of the upper nobility above the rank of baron, but sometimes used interchangeably with the title of duke. The count functioned as the overlord of a county, but he could sometimes be subject to a king and had to provide him with soldiers when needed; however, some counts could be totally independent of a king's jurisdiction.

crenellation A pattern along the top of a fortified wall, most often in the form of multiple, regular, rectangular spaces through which arrows or other weaponry could be fired.

crosier An ornate staff resembling a shepherd's crook, which is held by bishops or mitered abbots to symbolize their role as shepherds of Christ's flock. It is carried in liturgical functions and religious processions.

crypt Underground chamber beneath the chancel of a church that sometimes contains coffins, sarcophagi, or religious relics. It often has a chapel with an altar.

curia An assembly, council, or court where important secular or religious decisions are made.

demesne Land on a manor belonging to a lord, who held it for his own use. The villeins or serfs, who had no right of tenure to it, worked the land for the lord's benefit.

dependency Describes the relationship between a lord and his vassal, usually with the vassal's obligation to his lord spelled out in a contract. The term may also apply to the relationship between an abbey (motherhouse) and a new monastic community (daughter house) that has been founded to administer outlying ecclesiastical estates.

diadem The crown or ornamental headband, symbolic of honor, royalty, or dignity, usually made of metal or fabric fillet. It can either be simple or adorned with jewels, and is worn low on the forehead.

dormitory Sleeping area of monks in a monastery.

dowry The wife's share of her family's fortune that she brings to her marriage; the husband administers it, but the bride regains it on his death or their divorce.

dropsy Also known as edema; it is an abnormal accumulation of fluid in a bodily organ or its tissues in the cavities of the body, which is accompanied by swelling and inflammation.

duke A high-ranking member of the nobility below the rank of a monarch. He ruled entire duchies or provinces. The title was sometimes used interchangeably with that of count.

emerald A bright green gem consisting of a variety of beryl. It was one of the gemstones that decorated the New Jerusalem in heaven (Rv 21:19).

enclosure An area on a manor that was separated by a hedgerow or natural barrier from the fields to keep the farm animals away from the crops. Monastic enclosure or cloister kept the monks and nuns separate from the affairs of the world. They did not leave the enclosure without special permission of the bishop or their superior. Generally, it was an area of the monastery where outside people, especially those of the opposite sex, did not enter.

endowment An income or property given to a church, monastery, or institution.

Epiphany A Christian feast, celebrated on January 6, which commemorates the disclosure of Christ as the Son of God to the Magi, who represent the non-Christian world.

ewer A large jug with a wide mouth that is used for washing the priest's hands during the celebration of the Mass and other church services.

fallow Farmland left for a period of time without any crops being planted on it in order to restore the land's fertility or avoid surplus production; the practice was common in the medieval three-field system of agriculture.

fealty An oath taken by a vassal to his lord in which the vassal promised to fulfill his duties of service and aid to him. The oath usually took place with the hand of the vassal resting on a Bible or saint's relics.

fief Land or an estate given by a lord to his vassal in exchange for service to him, including military service. The ceremony of exchange included an oath of fealty and an act of homage performed by the vassal in front of his lord.

flagon A large jug, pitcher, or pouring vessel in which wine, beer, or ale is served. It is often embellished with enamel, intaglio, inlay, or gold and silver adornments.

font A basin containing holy water that is usually placed at the rear of the church or at the start of the central nave. The water is used for baptism, religious services, and consecration ceremonies.

forfeiture The act of a lord recovering a fief that he granted to a tenant or vassal, who violated his solemn oath or the compact he had made with the lord.

gradual A hymn or responsorial chant usually performed during the celebration of the eucharist or after the reading of the epistle; a book containing all the choral parts of the Mass.

greave Armor that protected the shin or leg.

habit A distinctive set of garments worn by religious orders, most commonly black, white, or brown.

Hagia Sophia A former Christian basilica in Constantinople (Istanbul) built by Emperor Justinian in 537 and converted into a mosque in 1453 by the Turks; Greek for "Holy Wisdom."

Holy of Holies The tabernacle or small house-like structure on top of the main altar that stores the consecrated hosts to be distributed during Communion. The hosts are believed to be the body of Jesus, which is consumed by those taking the sacrament. The hosts are placed in a ciborium, which is the bowl or container that is kept inside the tabernacle.

homage A public ceremony where a vassal kneels before his lord, places his hands between his lord's, and swears to become the lord's "man," meaning that he owes him fealty, service, and duty.

hospitality An obligation that a vassal owed to his lord that required him to provide the lord and his retinue with lodging, food, and entertainment, often at great expense to the vassal.

hyacinth A yellowish-red to red-brown variety of the zircon gem; it is one of the gems that decorated the walls of the New Jerusalem in heaven (Rv 21:19).

ides A day in the Roman calendar that marked the middle of the month, from which other dates were calculated. The ides fell on the fifteenth during the months of March, May, July, and October, and on the thirteenth in the other months.

immunity A special right or exemption granted to a person or entity to free them from certain obligations or liabilities.

investiture A formal ceremony that placed someone in an office or gave him official rank; a religious ceremony performed to invest abbots and bishops with the symbols of their office, such as their rings and staffs; a ceremony during which a vassal received his fief from his lord by being given a stick, a piece of turf, a knife, or some other symbolic object.

jasper An opaque reddish-brown variety of quartz; one of the gemstones that decorated the walls of the New Jerusalem in heaven (Rv 21:19).

judicial duel Also known as trial by combat; the practice originated in Germanic law to settle legal disputes in the absence of witnesses.

Based on the idea that God is always on the side of right, the two litigants fought a battle to determine on whose side divine favor fell. In essence, the winner won the dispute. It was also possible to name a champion to fight on one's behalf.

knight   A warrior who performed military service to a king or other nobleman. In return, the knight held land or received livery and maintenance.

Lateran Council   A church council or synod called directly by the pope and held in the Lateran Palace in Rome. The council dealt with political, doctrinal, and liturgical issues of the Catholic Church.

Lendit Fair   A fair conducted within the fortified town of Saint-Denis that was first held on June 9, 1053, in conjunction with the display of the abbey's relics of the passion of Christ—one of the nails used in the crucifixion and part of the crown of thorns. Louis VI started the fair, which was held out on the highway about halfway between Saint-Denis and Paris in 1111–12. This fair opened on the second Wednesday in June and continued until June 23, the eve of the feast of Saint John the Baptist. Louis VI awarded this fair to the abbey of Saint-Denis in 1124.

Levite   The members of the tribe of Levi, the third son of Jacob and Leah. God chose the priests of the tribe to perform duties at the Tabernacle and teach the word of God to the people. The Levites also functioned as assistants to the priests in the Temple.

liege homage   The act of a vassal who performs his pledge of primary allegiance to a principal lord, even though he holds fiefs from multiple lords.

livery and maintenance   The practice of a lord providing clothing and food to his vassal on numerous occasions.

madder   A red coloring obtained from the root of a plant, used in dyeing fabric and tenting yarn for cloths and tapestries.

magnate   A nobleman of the highest rank, who had great influence, power, or wealth. The magnates were the primary vassals of a king and often advised him at court.

manor A large estate of a lord where serfs or villeins lived, worked the land, and provided services to the lord. They often paid him various kinds of rents.

mark Scandinavian in origin, the mark was equivalent to eight ounces of silver or about two-thirds of the English pound.

Matins The first and longest of the eight canonical hours, Matins was usually celebrated between midnight and 3 a.m., depending upon the season. It was expanded into an all-night service, called a *pervigilium*, on special occasions, such as the eve of great feasts. It was commonly called Vigils or Nocturns during the Middle Ages.

miter A tall headdress that tapers to a point at the front and back with a deep cleft in between; it is worn by bishops and senior abbots as symbols of their office.

mortmain The legal right to the inalienable holding of land or real estate. In the Middle Ages, this right was held by a church or an abbey, for the church or abbey never died, according to medieval thought. Mortmain meant a significant loss of revenue for a lord or secular community.

motte A hill or mound of earth, sometimes artificially constructed, on which a castle or other defensive structure was built. The defensive structure often included a courtyard, called a bailey, within its walls.

narthex The main entrance area or vestibule of a cathedral, basilica, or church located at its western end.

nave The long central space in a cathedral, basilica, or church that accommodates most of the congregation. It often has a central aisle and is separated from the two side aisles by rows of columns or pillars.

niello A black-colored mixture of copper, silver, and lead sulphides used as an inlay on engraved or etched metal.

octave The eighth day or a period of eight days, counting inclusively, that follows a liturgical festival.

omega The last letter of the Greek alphabet, used to indicate the end of all things. It is a representation of God when joined to the Greek letter alpha (Rv 1:8 and 22:13).

onyx A gemstone of solid black, or banded black and white, chalcedony.

oratory A small chapel in a church used for prayer or meditation.

orphreys An embroidered panel, usually of a vertical rectangular shape, either sewn to or worn over ecclesiastical copes, chasubles, and vestments. The panel was often jeweled and bordered with fringe and lace, depicting holy scenes, symbols, or saints and their attributes.

Paraclete A Greek word that literally means, "a counselor at one's side." John used this word in the New Testament when he described the Holy Spirit as another "Paraclete" who teaches (Jn 14:16), reminds the disciples of what Jesus taught (Jn 14:26), witnesses for Jesus (Jn 15:26), and instructs about sin (Jn 16:7–8).

patriarch Any one of the bishops of the Eastern Orthodox sees of Constantinople, Alexandria, Antioch, and Jerusalem, as well as the heads of various Eastern churches.

pawn An object or property left with a pawnbroker as security in return for a money loan; the pawnbroker can sell the item if the loan is not repaid.

porphyry A reddish, igneous rock containing crystals of either feldspar or quartz.

portico A porch or walkway covered by a roof, which is supported by columns, at the entrance of a building.

pound Originating in Anglo-Saxon England, the pound was a monetary unit equivalent to one pound of silver; it could be divided into 240 silver pennies.

prase A translucent, light green variety of chalcedony.

prebend A benefice in the form of stipend paid from the revenues of a church or parish to a prebendary, a senior member of the clergy who has a role in the administration of a cathedral.

precentor A church dignitary who is responsible for the choir and leads the congregation in singing.

protomartyr A term that describes the first Christian to be martyred in a country or among a particular group; the term Protomartyr refers to Saint Stephen, the first martyr of the Christian church.

provost A steward or bailiff on a medieval manor or an officer of a medieval administrative district.

refectory The dining hall of a monastery.

relic A holy or revered object, such as a bone, strand of hair, body part, article of clothing, or object thought to belong to a deceased saint or holy figure, usually preserved in a container called a reliquary.

reverse dowry Money or other valuables paid by the bridegroom or his family to the family of the bride.

royal majesty A term used to describe the stately and lofty power of sovereign monarchs.

ruby A deep red precious stone that is a variety of corundum (aluminum oxide).

sapper A person who digs tunnels (called mines) under the walls of a fortification in order to weaken or destroy its walls.

sapphire A bright blue precious stone that is a variety of corundum (aluminum oxide); one of the gemstones that decorated the walls of the New Jerusalem in heaven (Rv 21:19).

sardonyx A gemstone that contains alternating bans of yellow or reddish-brown sard and onyx, a stone that comes in a variety of banded colors; both are varieties of chalcedony.

schism A formal division into opposing groups within an organization, movement, or church over political or doctrinal issues.

seigneurial A term that refers to a lord.

seneschal An official in a noble household who made all domestic arrangements, supervised the servants, and sometimes administered justice.

sepulcher A small room cut into rock or a monument made of stone used as a place of burial. The most famous is the Holy Sepulcher in Jerusalem, where Jesus was said to have been buried.

seraphim Winged angelic figures who, according to *The Celestial Hierarchy* written by Pseudo-Dionysius the Areopagite, are considered to be the highest ranking in the first order of angels.

sergeant Soldier beneath the rank of knight who fought either mounted or on foot, and who had enough money to supply his own weapons.

side aisles A pair of walkways on the north and south sides of a church, which are set off from the nave by a row of columns or arches.

steward A servant who supervised the lord's household or estate.

straw tribute An obligation whereby a vassal must provide his lord with a prescribed amount of straw to cover flooring or to construct thatch roofs; it was known as *paleagium*.

suffragan A bishop appointed to assist another bishop in the administration of a diocese.

synod A church council called to decide an issue of doctrine or administration.

tallage A tax paid by villeins to their lord for the use of land on the manor; the amount paid was based on the amount of land held. It later came to mean any tax imposed by a lord on his dependents.

Te Deum Laudamus "Thee, O God we praise"; the *Te Deum Laudamus* was an early Christian hymn of praise to the Father and the Son of the Trinity. It was sung at the end of Matins, the first and longest of the eight canonical hours. It was also sung at other important liturgical celebrations and special occasions, such as the election of a pope, the consecration of a bishop, church, or altar, the publication of a peace treaty, the coronation of a king, etc.

tenant A vassal holding a fief from his lord. The tenant owed his lord homage and fealty, aid, goods and services, and various payments.

Terce The third of the canonical hours, recited around 9 a.m.

tithe An annual tax paid to the church in the amount of one-tenth of all income or one-tenth of the value of all crops and livestock.

toll Money payments made for using roads and rivers.

topaz A precious stone derived from aluminum and chlorine that can be colorless, wine red, yellow, pale grey, or blue brown; it was one of the gemstones that decorated the walls of the New Jerusalem in heaven (Rv 21:19).

vassal A person who has entered into a mutual obligation contract with a lord, in which he promises to provide military and other services to his lord in return for certain privileges from the lord, such as a grant of land called a fief.

vault A roof of a church or cathedral that contains a succession of load-bearing arches that support the weight of the roof; the most common type of vault in Gothic architecture was the ribbed vault.

Vespers The sixth of the canonical hours, which is the sunset or evening prayer said between 4 and 6 p.m., depending on the season of the year.

villein A tenant completely subject to the lord of a manor, to whom he owes dues and services for use of the land.

viscount An official or administrator who assisted counts or dukes. Their primary duties were to collect taxes, administer justice, and serve as castellans. In England, they became the equivalent of a sheriff.

Glossary of Medieval Latin Words in the Selected Works of Abbot Suger of Saint-Denis

abbas, -atis (*m.*)   abbot

abbatia, -ae (*f.*)   abbey, abbacy (office or dignity of an abbot)

abbatissa, -ae (*f.*)   abbess

abstulo, -ere   to take away

accomodo, -are   to lend one's ear, lend

advocatio, -onis (*f.*)   ecclesiastical advowry or office of advocate (see *advocatus*); payment to a lord for protection, position of the protector of an abbey or church

advocatus, -i (*m.*)   patron or lay protector of an abbey or church, representative of an abbey or church at court, advocate or counselor

aedifico, -are   to build, strengthen, confirm in faith

ala, -ae (*f.*)   aisle (of a church)

anaglyphus, -a, -um   carved in relief, embossed, or engraved

angaria, -ae (*f.*)   oppressive service or obligation imposed by a lord on his tenants, toll, unlawful service, unjust duty

animositas, -atis (*f.*)   courage, boldness, valor

annona, -ae (*f.*)   grain, annual grain rent or tax

apex, -icis (*f.*)   letter, letter by a person of high standing

apostolicus, -a, -um   papal, episcopal, apostolic (pertaining to an apostle)

apparatus, -us (*m.*)   armaments, equipment, furnishings

appendicium, -ii (*n.*)   appendage, property belonging to a domain or manor

aquaria, -ae (*f.*)   fishing rights, office of ewery (person in a household responsible for the water and the vessels for drinking or washing of a person)

arca, -ae (*f.*)   treasure chest, money box

ariditas, -atis (*f.*)   dryness, drought, scanty food supply

armarium, -ii (*n.*)   archives

arripio, -ere   to set out on a journey

artifex, -ificis (*m./f.*)   artisan, artist

atavus, -i (*m.*)   great-grandfather

athleta, -ae (*m.*)   champion

atrium, -ii (*n.*)   churchyard, cemetery

auctoritas, -atis (*f.*)   royal authority, order or ordinance, royal charter

aula, -ae (*f.*)   church, nave of a church, large hall

aurifaber, -bris (*m.*)   goldsmith

aurifex, -icis (*m.*)   worker in gold, goldsmith

aurifrisium, -ii (*n.*)   orphreys, gold embroidery on clerical vestments

avena, -ae (f.) oats

balista, -ae (*f.*)   crossbow, siege engine for hurling projectiles, ballista

balistarius, -ii (*m.*)   artilleryman

beneficium, -ii, (*n.*)   favor or gift, benefice, an ecclesiastical estate, property, office, or source of revenue for clerics

beri(y)llus, -i (*m.*)   beryl; precious stone of varying colors, mainly green or greenish blue; cut glass or crystal

bibliotheca, -ae (*f.*)   scriptures, Bible

biblus, -i (*m.*)   register, text

birota, -ae (*f.*)   two-wheeled carriage

bos, bovis (*m./f.*)   ox, cow

bubul(c)us, -i (*m.*)   ploughman

bubus   dative or ablative plural of *bos*

caespes, -itis (*f.*)   sod of turf, piece of land, areas of land

calceamentum, -i (*n.*)   shoe or shoes

cambiatio, -onis (*f.*)   money exchange

camera, -ae (*f.*)   chamber, small room, vault, small vaulted room, workshop

camerula, -ae (*f.*)   small room or compartment

campipars, -partis (*f.*)   lord's share of the crop in return for a grant of farmland to a manorial tenant

candelabrum, -i (*n.*)   candlestick

canis, -is, -e   being gray or white (from *caneo, -ere*)

canonica, -ae (*f.*)   prebend of a canon, canonry, chapter of canons

capitellum, -i (*n.*)   capital or top of a column

capitulum, -i (*n.*)   assembly of monks in chapter, usually in a place designated in the monastery for that purpose; the assembly can be of several houses held by a church

cappa, -ae (*f.*)   large cloak, cap, hood

caput, -itis (*n.*)   head, principal abbey, main seat of a religious community

caput ecclesiae   choir part of a monastic church, chevet

carbunculus, -i (*m.*)   carbuncle, precious stone of a deep red color

carretula, -ae (*f.*) small cart

carruca, -ae (*f.*) wheeled plow, demesne field; amount of land that can be plowed by a wheeled plough in a season

carta, -ae (*f.*)   charter

castellum, -i (*n.*)   castle, fortification built up around an abbey or episcopal see, fortified town; *see also castrum*

castrum, -i (*n.*)   burg, walled town or settlement (some grew up around monasteries), castle; *see also castellum*

catalogus, -i (*m.*)   list

cathedra, -ae (*f.*)   king's, bishop's, or abbot's throne or seat; dignity of a bishop or abbot

causa, -ae (*f.*)   legal position or rights

censualis, -is, -e concerning rent payment, a tenant owing rent, a lease requiring rent

census, -us (*m.*) tax, annuity, customary duties, rent, payment for military service (all paid in money or kind)

ci(y)clas, -adis (*f.*) long garment or robe, cape-like cloak

circuitus, -us (*f.*) circuit, circle

claustrum, -i (*n.*) cloister

clausus, -us (*m.*) enclosed place

cœnobium, -ii (*n.*) monastery, convent

colonus, -i (*m.*) landholder, serf, villein

comitatus, -us (*m.*) court dignitaries, great men around a king or emperor, warrior companions

communia, -ae (*f.*) commune

commutatio, -onis (*f.*) exchange contract

condescendo, -ere to help, show good will, contribute

conductus, -us (*f.*) passage-money, safe conduct, transport, escort

confinium, -ii (*n.*) border, boundary, frontier area

confirmo, -are to confirm, bestow by means of a charter or pledge

consilium, -ii (*n.*) counsel, advice; imperial, royal, or church council

consistorium, -ii (*n.*) consistory, solemn assembly of clergymen

consuetudinarius, -a, -um customary

consuetudo, -inis (*f.*) customary right held by a lord over a tenant, customary service owed by a tenant to the lord; customary tax, agricultural good, or other product owed by a tenant to the lord

contractus, -us (*m.*) agreement, contract

conventus, -us (*m.*) religious community of men or women, assembly of the community

coquina, -ae (*f.*) kitchen

corpus, -oris (*n.*) nave of a church

cri(y)stallum, -i (*n.*) crystal

crisolitus, -i (*m.*) chrysolite or olivine; a green-colored precious stone

crux collateralis (*f.*) transept arms

cultor, -oris (*m.*)   manorial manager, steward

cultura, -ae (*f.*)   somewhat large amount of arable land in a manorial field

cultus, -us (*m.*)   worship, cultivation

cumulus, -i (*m.*)   roof, ridge of a roof, vault, mass, or webbing (of a vault)

cuprum, -i (*n.*)   copper

curia, -ae (*f.*)   courtyard, court of a lord, manorial court

curticula, -ae (*f.*)   small courtyard, farmyard, garden

curtis, -is (*f.*)   courtyard, walled farmyard or homestead, manor, estate

dapifer, -i (*m.*)   seneschal, steward, bailiff

decima, -ae (*f.*)   tithe, one-tenth, usually paid to the church from an agricultural product

decurio, -onis (*m.*)   court official

defensabilis, -is, -e   easily defended, fortified

defero, deferre   to honor

defossum, -i (*n.*)   pit

denarius, -ii (*m.*)   money, cash

desertum, -i (*n.*)   wilderness, desert

ditio, -onis (*f.*)   authority, sovereignty, rule

divina, -orum (*n.*)   sacraments, divine worship, or service

dolium, -ii (*n.*)   font, basin, cask

domesticus, -i (*m.*)   household resident, vassal without a fief in a household, inmate in a religious house

dominica, -ae (*f.*)   demesne

dominicatura, -ae (*f.*)   holding, demesne, lord's demesne, dependency, mother abbey

dominicum, -i (*n.*)   church building, demesne land, possession of a lord

dominium, -ii (*n.*)   power, dominion, authority

domus, -us (*f.*)   household, house or residence, court, monastery, farm

dormitorium, -ii (*n.*) dormitory

eleemosyna, -ae (*f.*) alms, almonry, act of mercy, free gift to a church, church endowment

encyclicus, -a, -um circular, general, encyclical

exactio, -onis (*f.*) collection of a tax, exaction, action to collect something due

exactor, -oris (*m.*) tax collector or sheriff

exemplum, -i (*n.*) text, transcript

exercitus, -us (*m.*) host, army, military expedition

exhibitio, -onis (*f.*) fulfillment of a promise, example, display

exorcizo, -are to exorcize, bless

expugnatio, -onis (*f.*) attack, assault, taking by storm

f(ph)iala, -ae (*f.*) cruet, vial

faber, -bri (*m.*) blacksmith

factio, -onis (*f.*) plot, scheme, faction

familiaris, -is (*m.*) intimate

familiariter intimately, submissively

famulatus, -us (*m.*) allegiance, service, obedience

famulor, -ari to serve God, usually in some form of monastic life; to perform homage, serve, enslave

fatigo, -are to take the pains of going abroad, travel

fautor, -oris (*m.*) accomplice, supporter, member of a faction

feodatus, -i (*m.*) vassal, someone holding a fief

feodum, -i (*n.*) fief, fee, holding

fidelis, -is (*m.*) vassal, retainer

fides, -ei (*f.*) fealty, loyalty, faith

firmitas, -atis (*f.*) stronghold, fortress

forisfactum, -i (*n.*) (forisfactio, -ionis) forfeiture, wrong, injury, penalty

forma, -ae (*f.*) terms, charter, legal formula

frons, -ontis (f.)   front, front part, façade

furca, -ae (f.)   gallows

furnus, -i (m.)   oven

fusilis, -is, -e   cast, molten, liquid

fusor, -oris (m.)   founder, metal caster

g(w)arantia, -ae (f.)   madder (a plant that produces red dye)

galea, -ae (f.)   helmet

gallina, -ae (f.)   hen

gallus, -i (m.)   rooster

gazofilacium, -ii (n.)   treasury, treasure-chest, treasure-room (usually of a church)

gemmarius, -ii (m.)   jeweler

gens, -tis (f.)   band of retainers or followers, mercenary or hired man

gentilicus, -a, -um   pagan, heathen

glans, -dis (f.)   oak stake

graduale, -is (n.)   the Gradual

grafio, -onis (m.)   sheriff in Anglo-Norman usage, reeve

granchia, -ae (f.)   granary, barn, storehouse, grange, farm with outbuildings belonging to a lord

gregarius, -ii (m.)   common or ordinary knight, who is not noble

guerra, -ae (f.)   war, private war, quarrel

habitaculum, -i (n.)   dwelling place, abode

hominium, -ii (n.)   homage, right of homage

homo, -inis (m.)   man, people, retainer, vassal

honor, -oris (m.)   honor, high office, benefice, or fief

horreum, -i (n.)   granary, barn

hospes, -itis (m.)   tenant, villein, guest, visitor

hospitium, -ii (n.)   right of lodging

hostia, -ae (f.)   host, sacrifice

immunitas, -atis (*f.*)   privilege of immunity or freedom from obligations

imperium, -ii (*n.*)   royal power or authority

importunitas, -atis (*f.*)   urgency, pressing matter

inclusorius, -a, -um   cloisonné

incrementum, -i (*n.*)   increase, gain, profit, extension, acquisition

indictum, -i (*n.*)   public fair, charter

intitulo, -are   to entitle, list, record

jaspis, -idis (*f.*)   jasper, opaque crystalline quartz, usually green in color

jugum, -i (*n.*)   measure of land, yoke of land, half a plough-land (about sixty acres)

jumentum, -i (*n.*)   beast of burden

justa, -ae (*f.*)   decanter or flagon, just amount or allowance of a beverage (usually alcoholic)

justitia, -ae (*f.*)   justice, suit, plea, right, or jurisdiction

lacrima, -ae (*f.*)   penance

lagena, -ae (*f.*)   gallon-sized vessel with neck and handle, large pitcher

lan(e)a, -ae (*f.*)   woolen garment, coarse wool

lat(h)omus, -i (*m.*)   stonecutter

latrunculus, -i (*m.*)   brigand, highwayman, thief

lavacrum, -i (*n.*)   washing, baptism, baptismal font

lectica, -ae (*f.*)   reliquary

leuga, -ae (*f.*)   league

libatorium, -ii (*n.*)   pouring vessel, vessel for pouring libations

libertas, -atis (*f.*)   franchise, exemption, charter of liberties

libra, -ae (*f.*)   pound (either money or weight)

ligius, -a, -um   liege

lignarium, -ii (*n.*)   rick or stack of wood, money payment to a lord in lieu of a supply of wood

lignarius, -ii (*m.*)   carpenter, woodworker

locellus, -i (*m.*)   reliquary, small place, manor, monastery

lorica, -ae (*f.*)   suit of chain mail

lucrum, -i (*n.*)   crop, produce, money, interest from money lent

macellum, -i (*n.*)   butcher stall or shop, meat market

maceria, -ae (*f.*)   wall, garden wall

magister, -istri (*m.*)   master craftsman, foreman, manorial officer, household official

major, -oris (*m.*)   steward, mayor

mando, -are   to send, dispatch, order

mansa (mansus), -ae (*f.*)   manor, estate

mansio, -onis (*f.*)   dwelling

manus, -us (*f.*)   possession

marchia (marca), -ae (*f.*)   march, borderland, frontier

marsupium, -ii (*n.*)   purse, pouch

matricularius, -ii (*m.*)   churchwarden

matrimonium, -ii (*n.*)   dowry, marriage

matrina, -ae (*f.*)   godmother

medietas, -atis (*f.*)   one-half, one-half of a holding

membrus, -a, -um   pertaining to a daughter church or subordinate church

mercatus, -i (*m.*)   commerce, trade goods, merchandise

miles, -itis (*m.*)   professional warrior, soldier, knight

ministerialis, -is (*m.*)   person of the ministerial class, such as an household or court official; officer; monastic obedientiary; or servant

ministerium, -ii (*n.*)   public office or agency, duty, service, administrative district

modiolus, -i (*m.*)   small measure (twenty-five do not equal a bushel)

modius, -ii (*m.*)   old Roman unit of measurement; as a dry measure (e.g., for grain), equivalent to a peck; as a liquid measure (e.g., for wine or olive oil), nine quarts

molendinum, -i (*n.*)   mill

monasticus, -a, -um   monastic

mortua manus (*f.*)   mortmain; land held by the church, called the "dead hand" because the church paid no tax on it or never relinquished it; death tax paid by a tenant's heirs allowing them to inherit his assets; lord's right to inherit from a tenant who dies without heirs

municipium, -ii (*n.*)   town wall, walled town, castle, fortress

munificentia, -ae (*f.*)   donation, gift, munificence

munitio, -onis (*f.*)   stronghold, fortified place

musivum, -i (*n.*)   mosaic

natio, -onis (*f.*)   region, territory, people

navis, -is (*f.*)   nave of a church, vault

nomen, -inis (*n.*)   title, name

novitas, -atis (*f.*)   newness of an office

nundina, -ae (*f.*)   fair, tournament connected to a fair

obedientia, -ae (*f.*)   obedientiary, such as the sacristan, cellarer, infirmarian, almsgiver, etc.; office or other ministry

obryzeus, -a, -um   of fine gold, pure gold

obryz(i)um, -i (*n.*)   fine gold, pure gold

ocrea, -ae. (*f.*)   metal leggings

officina, -ae (*f.*)   workshop, building, office

officium, -ii (*n.*)   divine service, liturgical prayers or hours

olosericus, -a, -um   of pure silk

oni(y)x, -ychis (*m./f.*)   onyx, translucent quartz with parallel layers of different color

operatura, -ae (*f.*)   covering, roof, lining

oppidanus, -i (*m.*)   castellan, person living in a castle, member of a castle's garrison

oppidum, -i (*n.*)   town, walled or fortified town

oratorium, -ii (*n.*)   oratory, chapel

pagus, -i (*m.*)   countryside, district, region, parish paleagium, -ii (*n.*)   straw tribute

palatium, -ii (*n.*)   palace; imperial, royal, or ecclesiastical court

palea, -ae (*f.*)   straw, chaff

palagium, -ii (*n.*)   fee to moor a boat

palliatura, -ae (*f.*)   textiles, precious fabrics

palliatus, -a, -um   draped, veiled

pallium, -ii (*n.*)   altar frontal; altar covering, cloth, or hanging; garment, draperies, tapestries, textiles

Pantera, -ae (*f.*)   square in the burg of Saint-Denis

parens, -entis (*m./f.*)   relative

parifico, -are   to equalize

parochialis, -is, -e   of a parish, parochial

pastor, -oris (*m.*)   shepherd, head of a community of Christians

pater, -ris (*m.*)   father, pope, bishop, abbot

patria, -ae (*f.*)   land, territory, county, principality

patrinus, -i (*m.*)   godfather

patrocinium, -ii (*n.*)   protective power of a saint or relic, relic of a saint

pax, pacis (*f.*)   peace, kiss of peace, accord, agreement, checking of violent action

pedagium, -ii (*n.*)   "right to walk," toll paid by travelers

peregrinor, peregrinatus sum   to go on a pilgrimage, go on a crusade

phiala (fiala), -ae (*f.*)   censer, small vessel for liquids that can be closed

phlegma, -atis (*f.*)   mucus, slime

pi(n)ctor, -oris (*m.*)   painter

pignus, -oris (*n.*)   relic

pistorium, -ii (*n.*)   bake house

pistorus, -i (*m.*)   baker

placitum, -i (*n.*)   claim, plea, lawsuit, contract, agreement

plancatus, -us (*n.*)   floor, floorboards

platea, -ae (*f.*)   square, open area, plot or space, highway, main road, courtyard

pluma, -ae (*f.*)   feathers

podium, -ii (*n.*)   prop or support

populares, -um (*m.*)   common people

porticus, -us (*f.*)   narthex, vestibule of a church, portico

portio, -onis (*f.*)   portion or share of ecclesiastical revenue

possessio, -onis (*f.*)   estate, possession, property

praeambulus, -i (*m.*)   herald, forerunner

praebenda, -ae (*f.*)   money, income or food allowance granted to a cleric or church official

praeceptio, -onis (*f.*)   precept, order, rule

praeceptum, -i (*n.*)   royal charter or edict, command

praelatio, -onis (*f.*)   preferment, authority; headship, especially of a religious community

praelatus, -i (*m.*)   church dignitary, abbot, prior

praepositura, -ae (*f.*)   office of provost, district under the jurisdiction of a provost, bailiff, steward, reeve

praepositus, -i (*m.*)   provost, bailiff, steward, reeve

praevaricatio, -onis (*f.*)   sin, transgression

prasius (prasinus), -a, -um   green-colored

praterium, -ii (*n.*)   cloister

princeps, -ipis (*m.*)   king, territorial prince

privilegium, -ii (*n.*)   charter, privilege, special right

procer, -eris (*m.*)   great man of the realm, lay magnate

procuratio, -onis (*f.*)   compulsory provision of food

procurator, -oris (*m.*)   fiscal officer, manorial officer, steward, proctor in church courts

professio, -onis (*f.*)   taking of monastic vows

GLOSSARY OF MEDIEVAL LATIN WORDS 271

professus, -us (*m.*)   monk who has taken vows

promptuarium, -ii (*n.*)   storeroom, storehouse

propositum, -i (*n.*)   monastic community

proprium, -ii (*n.*)   estate, landed property

propugnaculum, -i (*n.*)   rampart, fortress, bulwark

providentia, -ae (*f.*)   management, provision, care, maintenance

querimonia, -ae (*f.*)   suit, claim, action

reclamatio, -onis (*f.*)   act of recovery, reclamation, appeal to a higher authority

redditus, -us (*m.*)   revenues, returns, gift, dues, taxes, profits

redemptio, -onis (*f.*)   relief, amount of money paid for appointment

refectio, -onis (*f.*)   pittance, gift to a religious congregation for extra food and wine on special feast days or other important occasions

refectorium, -ii (*n.*)   refectory, dining hall, guest chamber

refugo, -are   to put to flight, drive back

regio, -onis (*f.*)   kingdom, realm, county, region

regnum, -i (*n.*)   kingdom, realm, throne, domain

regula, -ae (*f.*)   rule, code of monastic discipline

replico, -are   to recount, reveal, unfold

rusticus, -i (*m.*)   villein, serf, peasant as opposed to a person free of obligations

sacramentum, -i (*n.*)   sworn oath

sagittarius, -ii (*m.*)   bowman, archer

sanctimonialis, -is (*m./f.*)   monk, nun

sapphirus, -i (*m.*)   sapphire, precious stone of a deep blue color

sardius, -ii (*m.*)   sardonyx, hard translucent quartz that is orange-reddish in color

satelles, -itis (*m.*)   military retainer below the class of knights, followers, companions

sauma (sagma), -atis (*n.*)   load on a beast of burden, pack-saddle

scedula, -ae (*f.*) small leaf inserted in the register or chronicle of a monastery

scrinium, -ii (*n.*) case, chest, case for books, papers or scrolls, shrine, reliquary

sedes, -is (*f.*) residence, throne, seat, ecclesiastical see, office of abbot

serviens, -entis (*m.*) servant, sergeant, serf

servitium, -ii (*n.*) service in general, service as a vassal to a lord

sextarius, -ii (*m.*) sixth part of a measure; a pint (liquid and dry); as a dry measure, a sixteenth part of a modius

smalta(i)tus, -a, -um enameled

smaragdus, -i (*m.*) emerald, gem of a deep green color that is a variety of beryl

solarium, -ii (*n.*) upper room or story, loft, attic, gallery

solidus, -i (*m.*) about twelve pennies or pence, or one-twentieth of a pound

stagnum, -i (*n.*) pond

statio, -onis (*f.*) garrison service

suffraganeus, -a, -um suffragan, pertaining to the subordinate clergy or a subordinate

suggero, -ere to bring before a person

summa (sagma), -ae (*f.*) packsaddle, load for a beast of burden

superliminare, -ris (*n.*) lintel

suppletio, -onis (*f.*) supplementary payment

Symbolus, -i (*m.*) Apostles' Creed

synaxis, -is (*f.*) assembly, meeting for prayer, monastic chapter, Mass, Communion

tabula, -ae (*f.*) altar-frontal, panel or board, table, altar table

tabulatum, -i (*n.*) flooring, story, board

tallia, -ae (*f.*) tallage, exaction or impost in kind or money, tax paid by a tenant to his lord

tapeta, -ium (*n.*) tapestries, draperies, coverlets, hangings

tensamentum, -i (*n.*)   payment in coin or kind by a tenant to his lord in return for protection

terra, -ae (*f.*)   land, arable land, tenement, estate, kingdom, principality

testitudo, -inis (*f.*)   vaulted room, vaulted hall, nave

textus, -us (*m.*)   text, gospel book, office, charter

theca, -ae (*f.*)   reliquary, side chapel, chest, money box, depository

theloneum, -i (*n.*)   toll house, toll, transport, or market fees

topazius, -ii (*m.*)   topaz, transparent crystal that is yellow to brownish-yellow in color

torcularium, -ii (*n.*)   wine press

tristega, -ae (*f.*)   tower, usually of three stories, used in sieges; scaffolding

tropheum, -i (*n.*) trophy, triumph, victory

tunna, -ae (*f.*) cask

turris, -is (*f.*)   tower

unanimitas, -atis (*f.*)   title addressed to both clergy and laymen, complete sympathy

unio, -onis (*m.*)   large pearl

usus, -us (*m.*)   right of possession

vadimonium, -ii (*n.*)   pledge (of security), pawn, mortgage

valens, -entis   valuable, productive, healthy (participle from *valeo*)

vallis, -is (*f.*)   pit, hollow place

vallum, -i (*n.*)   rampart, wall, embankment

valva, -ae (*f.*)   opening of a door, leaf of a door, door (usually used in the plural)

vectigal, -is (*n.*)   revenue, rent, other payments from dependent persons to lords, transport duties or services

venatio, -onis (*f.*)   hunting rights

venditio, -onis (*f.*)   sale, toll on a sale

vestis, -is (*f.*)   tapestry, hanging textile, cloth, altar cloth, vestment

viatura, -ae (*f.*)   jurisdiction as agent or overseer of a lord

villa, -ae, (*f.*)   village, town, township, homestead or farmstead, estate, manor, burg (settlement outside a castle)

vitrea, -ae (*f.*)   window-pane, stained-glass window

vivarium, -ii (*n.*)   fish pond, fish preserve

volvo, -ere   to vault

zelus, -i (*m.*)   jealousy, hatred

Selected Bibliography

Primary Sources

Arnulf of Lisieux. *The Letters of Arnulf of Lisieux*. Edited by Frank Barlow. Camden (Third Series) 61. London: Royal Historical Society, 1939.
Bernard of Clairvaux. *The Letters of St. Bernard of Clairvaux*. Translated by Bruno Scott James. Chicago: Henry Regnery, 1953.
Biblia Sacra Iuxta Vulgatam Versionem. Edited by R. Weber and R. Grayson. Fourth edition. Stuttgart: Deutsche Bibelgesellschaft, 1994.
Boso, Cardinal. *The Life of Alexander III*. Translated by G. M. Ellis. Oxford: Basil Blackwell, 1973.
Bouquet, M., and L. Delisle, eds. *Recueil des Historiens des Gaules et de la France*. 24 vols. Paris, 1869–1904.
Cicero. *De Officiis*. Translated by Walter Miller. London: William Heinemann, 1938.
Cusimano, Richard, trans. *A Translation of the Chronicle of Morigny, France, c. 1100–1150*. Lewiston, N.Y.: Edwin Mellen Press, 2003.
Delaborde, H.-François, ed. *Oeuvres de Rigord et de Guillaume le Breton, Tome Second: Philippide de Guillaume le Breton*. Paris: Libraire Renouard, 1885.
Dufour, J., ed. *Recueil des Actes de Louis VI, roi de France (1108–1137)*. Edited under the direction of Robert-Henri Bautier. Paris: Academie des Inscriptions et Belles-Lettres (distributed by Boccard), 1992–94.
Eusebius of Caesarea. *The History of the Church*. Translated by G. A. Williamson. Edited by Andrew Louth. London: Folio Society, 2011.
Florence of Worcester. *The Chronicle of Florence of Worcester*. Translated by Thomas Forester. New York: AMS Press, 1968.
Gasparri, Françoise, ed. *Suger: Oeuvres*. 2 vols. Paris: Les Belle Lettres, 2008.
Geoffroy of Courlon. *Chronique de l'Abbaye de Saint-Pierre-le-Vif*. Edited by M. G. Julliot. Sens: C. Duchemin, 1876.

Gervase of Canterbury. *The Historical Works of Gervase of Canterbury.* 2 vols. Edited by William Stubbs. London: Longman and Co., 1880.
Gesta Adriani IV Papae. RHF 15. Paris: Victor Palmé, 1840.
Gregory of Tours. *History of the Franks.* 2 vols. OMT. Translated by O. M. Dalton. Oxford: Clarendon Press, 1927.
———. *Liber in Gloria martyrum.* Edited by B. Krusch. MGH. SRM 1. Hanover: Impensis Bibliopolii Hahniani, 1885.
Henry of Huntingdon. *Historia Anglorum.* Edited and translated by Diana Greenway. OMT. Oxford: Clarendon Press, 1997.
Hilduin. *Areopagitica sive Sancti Dionysii vita.* PL 106.
Hincmar. *Gesta Dagoberti I regis Francorum.* Edited by B. Krusch. MGH. SRM 2. Hanover: Impensis Bibliopolii Hahniani, 1888.
Hugh of Poitiers. *The Vézelay Chronicle.* Translated by John Scott and John O. Ward. Binghamton, N.Y.: MRTS, 1992.
John of Salisbury. *Historia Pontificalis.* Translated by Marjorie Chibnall. NMT. New York: Thomas Nelson and Sons, 1956.
———. *The Letters of John of Salisbury.* NMT. Vol. 1. Edited by W. J. Milor and H. E. Butler. Revised by C. N. L. Brooke. New York: Thomas Nelson and Sons, 1955.
———. *The Letters of John of Salisbury.* OMT. Vol. 2. Edited by W. J. Milor and C. N. L. Brooke. Oxford: Clarendon Press, 1979.
John of Worcester. *The Chronicle of John of Worcester.* OMT. Vol. 3. Edited and translated by P. McGurk. Oxford: Clarendon Press, 1998.
Krusch, B., ed. *Vita Genovefae virginis Parisiensis.* MGH. SRM 3. Hanover: Impensis Bibliopolii Hahniani, 1862.
Lecoy de la Marche, A. ed. *Oeuvres Complètes de Suger.* Paris: Jules Renouard, 1868.
Lucan. *Pharsalia.* Available at www.thelatinlibrary.com/lucan.html.
Luchaire, Achille, ed. *Études sur les Actes de Louis VII.* Brussels: Culture et Civilisation, 1964.
———, ed. *Louis VI le Gros: Annales de sa vie et de son règne (1081–1137).* Geneva: Mégaritis Reprints, 1979.
Ludovici Pii Epistolae. In PL 104. Paris: Garnier, 1864.
Migne, J.-P., ed. *Patrologia Latina.* 217 volumes. Paris: Garnier, 1844–55.
Odo of Deuil. *De profectione Ludovici VII in orientem.* Edited and translated by Virginia Gingerick Berry. New York: W. W. Norton and Company, 1948.
Orderic Vitalis. *The Ecclesiastical History of Orderic Vitalis.* Vol. 6. Edited and translated by Marjorie Chibnall. Oxford: Oxford University Press, 2002.
Otto of Freising. *The Deeds of Frederick Barbarossa.* Translated by Charles Christopher Mierow. New York: Columbia University Press, 1953.
———. *The Two Cities: A Chronicle of Universal History to the Year 1146 A.D.* Translated by Charles Christopher Mierow. Edited by Austin P. Evans and Charles Knapp. New York: Columbia University Press, 1928.

Ovid. *Metamorphoses*. Available at www.thelatinlibrary.com/ovid.html.
Passio Dionysii episcopi, Rustici et Eleutherii. In PL 88.
Peter Abelard. *Historia calamitatum*. In *Abelard and Heloise: The Story of His Misfortunes and The Personal Letters*, translated by Betty Radice. London: Folio Society, 1977.
Peter the Venerable. *The Letters of Peter the Venerable*. Vol. 1. Edited by Giles Constable. Cambridge, Mass.: Harvard University Press, 1967.
Pseudo-Dionysius. *The Celestial Hierarchy of Dionysius the Areopagite*. Translated by John Parker. London: Skeffington and Son, 1894.
Potter, K. R., ed. and trans. *Gesta Stephani*. Notes by R. H. C. Davis. OMT. Oxford: Clarendon Press, 1976.
Richard of Saint-Victor. *The Book of the Patriarchs, The Mystical Ark, Book Three of the Trinity*. Translated by Grover A. Zinn. New York: Paulist Press, 1979.
Robert of Torigni. *The Chronicle of Robert of Torigni*. Edited by Richard Howlett. RS 4. London: Eyre and Spottiswoode, 1889.
Scott Moncrieff, C. K., trans. *The Song of Roland*. London: Folio Society, 2010.
Seneca. *Ad Lucilium epistulae morales*. Available at www.thelatinlibrary.com/seneca.html.
———. *De clementia*. Available at www.thelatinlibrary.com/sen/sen.clem.shtml.
Suger. *The Deeds of Louis the Fat*. Translated by Richard Cusimano and John Moorhead. Washington, D.C.: The Catholic University of America Press, 1992.
———. *Libellus Alter de Consecratione Ecclesiae Sancti Dionysii*. In *Oeuvres Complètes de Suger*, edited by A. Lecoy de la Marche. New York: Georg Olms, 1979.
———. *Liber de Rebus in Administratione Sua Gestis*. In *Oeuvres Complètes de Suger*, edited by A. Lecoy de la Marche. New York: Georg Olms, 1979.
———. *Vie de Louis le Gros par Suger suivie de L'Histoire du Roi Louis VII*. Edited by Auguste Molinier. Paris: Alphonse Picard, 1887.
———. *Vie de Louis VI le Gros*. Edited by Henri Waquet. Paris: Les Belle Lettres, 1929.
Swanton, Michael, trans. *The Anglo-Saxon Chronicle*. New York: Routledge, 1996.
Virgil. *Georgics*. Available at www.thelatinlibrary.com/verg.html.
William of Malmesbury. *Gesta Regum Anglorum*. Vol. 1. OMT. Edited and translated by R. A. B. Mynors. Oxford: Clarendon Press, 1998.
William of Saint-Denis. *Circular Letter of the Monastery of Saint-Denis Concerning the Death of Abbot Suger*. In *Oeuvres Complètes de Suger*, edited by A. Lecoy de la Marche. New York: Georg Olms 1979.
———. *Sugerii Vita*. In *Oeuvres Complètes de Suger*, edited by A. Lecoy de la Marche. New York: Georg Olms, 1979.

Secondary Sources

Anonymous. *A History and Description of the Royale Abbaye of Saint Denis with an Account of the Tombs of the Kings and Queens of France and Other Distinguished Persons Interred There*. Ann Arbor: University of Michigan Library, 2009.

Baring-Gould, Sabine. *A Book of Cevennes*. London: John Long, 1907.

Benton, John F. "Suger's Life and Personality." In *Abbot Suger and Saint-Denis: A Symposium*, edited by Paula Lieber Gerson, 3–15. New York: Metropolitan Museum of Art, 1986.

Bisson, Thomas N. *The Crisis of the Twelfth Century: Power, Lordship, and the Origins of European Government*. Princeton, N.J.: Princeton University Press, 2009.

Blum, Pamela Z. "The Lateral Portals of the West Facade of the Abbey Church of Saint-Denis: Archaeological and Iconographical Considerations." In *Abbot Suger and Saint-Denis: A Symposium*, edited by Paula Lieber Gerson, 199–227. New York: Metropolitan Museum of Art, 1986.

Bouchard, Constance Brittain. *Sword, Miter, and Cloister: Nobility and the Church in Burgundy, 980–1198*. Ithaca, N.Y.: Cornell University Press, 1987.

Bradbury, Jim. *Stephen and Matilda: The Civil War of 1139–1153*. Gloucestershire: Sutton Press, 2005.

———. *The Capetians: Kings of France, 987–1328*. London: Continuum Books, 2007.

Brown, Elizabeth A. R. *The Oxford Collection of the Drawings of Roger de Gaignières and the Royal Tombs of Saint-Denis*. Transactions of the American Philosophical Society 78. Philadelphia: American Philosophical Society, 1988.

Bur, Michel. *Suger: Abbé de Saint-Denis, Régent de France*. Paris: Perrin, 1991.

Burkhofer III, Robert F. *Day of Reckoning: Power and Accountability in Medieval France*. Philadelphia: University of Pennsylvania Press, 2004.

Buvier, L'Abbé H. *Histoire de l'Abbaye de Saint-Pierre-le-Vif de Sens*. Auxerre: Ch. Milon, 1891.

Caviness, Madeline Harrison. "Suger's Glass at Saint-Denis: The State of Research." In *Abbot Suger and Saint-Denis: A Symposium*, edited by Paula Lieber Gerson, 257–72. New York: Metropolitan Museum of Art, 1986.

Chibnall, Marjorie. "Anglo-French Relations in the Work of Orderic Vitalis." In *Essays in Medieval History Presented to G. P. Cuttino*, edited by J. S. Hamilton and Patricia J. Bradley, 5–19. Woodbridge: Boydell, 1989.

———. "Introduction." In *King Stephen's Reign, 1135–1154*, edited by Paul Dalton and Graeme J. White, 1–10. Woodbridge: Boydell, 2008.

Constable, Giles. "Suger's Monastic Administration." In *Abbot Suger and Saint-Denis: A Symposium*, edited by Paula Gerson, 17–32. New York: Metropolitan Museum of Art, 1986.
Conway, W. Martin. "The Abbey of Saint-Denis and Its Ancient Treasures." *Archaeologia or Miscellaneous Tracts Relating to Antiquity* 66 (February 1915): 103–58.
Cosner, Madeleine Pelner. *The Medieval Wordbook*. New York: Facts on File, 1996.
Coulson, Charles. "The French Matrix of Castle-Provisions of the Chester-Leicester Convention." *ANS* 17 (1994): 65–86.
Crosby, Sumner McKnight. *The Abbey of Saint-Denis, 475–1122*. Vol. 1. New Haven, Conn.: Yale University Press, 1942.
———. *The Royal Abbey of Saint-Denis: From Its Beginnings to the Death of Suger, 475–1151*. Edited and completed by Pamela Z. Blum. New Haven, Conn.: Yale University Press, 1987.
Crosby, Sumner McKnight, et al. *The Royal Abbey of Saint-Denis in the Time of Abbot Suger, 1122–1151*. New York: Metropolitan Museum of Art, 1981.
Dalton, Paul, and Graeme J. White, eds. *King Stephen's Reign*. Woodbridge: Boydell, 2008.
De Feller, François-Xavier. *Biographie de Dom Poirier*. In *Dictionnaire Historique, Histoire Abrégée*, vol. 10, edited by François Marie Pérennès. Lille: Chez L. Lefort, 1833.
Diggelman, Lindsay. "Marriage as Tactical Response: Henry II and the Royal Wedding of 1160." *English Historical Review* 119 (2004): 954–64.
Erlande-Brandenburg, Alain. *The Abbey Church of Saint-Denis: The Royal Tombs*. Vol. 2. Paris: Éditions de la Tourelle, 1984.
Evergates, Theodore. *The Aristocracy in the County of Champagne, 1100–1300*. The Middle Ages Series. Philadelphia: University of Pennsylvania Press, 2007.
Félibien, M. *Historie de l'Abbaye Royale de Saint-Denis en France*. Paris: Frederic Leonard, 1706.
Feudal Society in Medieval France: Documents from the County of Champagne. Edited by Theodore Evergates. Philadelphia: University of Pennsylvania Press, 1993.
Fliche, Augustin. *Le règne de Philippe I, roi de France (1060–1108)*. Paris: Société Françoise D'Imprimerie et de Librairie, 1912.
Gerson, Paula Lieber. "Suger as Iconographer: The Central Portal of the West Facade of Saint-Denis." In *Abbot Suger and Saint-Denis: A Symposium*, edited by Paula Lieber Gerson, 183–98. New York: Metropolitan Museum of Art, 1986.
Gillingham, John. "Doing Homage to the King of France." In *Henry II: New Interpretations*, edited by Christopher Harper-Bill and Nicholas Vincent, 63–84. Woodbridge: Boydell, 2007.
———. "The Meeting of the Kings of France and England, 1066–1204."

In *Normandy and Its Neighbors, 900–1250: Essays for David Bates*, edited by David Crouch and Kathleen Thompson, 17–42. Turnhout: Brepols, 2011.

Giry, Arthur, and André Réville. *Emancipation of the Medieval Town*. New York: H. Holt and Company, 1907.

———. *Abbot Suger of St-Denis: Church and State in Early Twelfth-Century France*. London: Longman, 1998.

Grant, Lindy. "Suger and the Anglo-Norman World." *ANS* 19 (1996): 51–68.

Gravett, Christopher. *Norman Stone Castles: Europe, 950–1204*. Oxford: Osprey Publishing, 2004.

Grodecki, Louis. "The Style of the Stained-Glass Windows at Saint-Denis." In *Abbot Suger and Saint-Denis: A Symposium*, edited by Paula Lieber Gerson, 273–81. New York: Metropolitan Museum of Art, 1986.

Hallam, Elizabeth M. *Capetian France, 987–1328*. London: Longman, 1980.

Hosler, John. *Henry II: A Medieval Soldier at War, 1147–1189*. Leiden: Brill, 2007.

———. *John of Salisbury: Military Authority of the Twelfth-Century Renaissance*. Leiden: Brill, 2013.

King, Edmund. *King Stephen*. EMS. New Haven, Conn.: Yale University Press, 2010.

Konstam, Angus. *Historical Atlas of the Crusades*. London: Mercury Books, 2002.

Ledain, Bélisaire. "Savary de Mauléon et le Poitou à son époque." *Revue poitevine et des confins de la Touraine et de l'Anjou* 9 (January 1892): 101–37.

Le Monte, John L. "The Lords of Le Puiset on the Crusades." *Speculum* 17 (January 1942): 100–118.

Lenoir, Alexandre. *Musée impérial des monuments français: histoire des arts en France, et description chronologique des statues en marbre et en bronze, bas-reliefs et tombeaux des hommes et des femmes célèbres, qui sont réunis dans ce Musée*. Paris: Hacquart, 1810.

———. "Historical Notes on the Disinterments Executed in 1793 at the Abbey of St. Denis." *Fraser's Magazine for Town and Country* 32 (July 1845): 93–99.

Loomis, L. H. "The Oriflamme of France and the War Cry Montjoie." In *Studies in Art and Literature for Bella da Costa Greene*, edited by Dorothy Eugenia Miner. Princeton, N.J.: Princeton University Press, 1954.

Luchaire, Achille. *Les communes françaises a l'epoque des capetiens directs*. Paris: Hachette, 1890.

———. "Etudes sur quelques manuscrits de Rome et de Paris, *Les Miracula Sancti Dionysii*." Bibliothèque de la Faculté des Lettres 8. Paris: Ancienne Librairie Gerner Baillière, 1899.

Matthews, Rupert. *Popes: Every Question Answered*. New York: Metro Books, 2012.
Morris, Colin. *The Papal Monarchy: The Western Church from 1050–1250*. Oxford: Clarendon Press, 1991.
Newman, Martha G. *The Boundaries of Charity: Cistercian Culture and Reform, 1098–1180*. Redwood City, Calif.: Stanford University Press, 1996.
Niermeyer, J. F., and C. Van de Kieft. *Mediae Latinitatis Lexicon Minus*. 2 vols. Leiden: Brill, 2002.
Pacaut, Marcel. *Louis VII et son royaume*. Paris: SEVPEN, 1964.
Painter, Sidney. "The Lords of Lusignan in the Eleventh and Twelfth Centuries." *Speculum* 32 (January 1957): 27–47.
Panofsky, Erwin. *Abbot Suger: On the Abbey Church of St.-Denis and Its Art Treasures*. Edited and translated by Erwin Panofsky. Princeton, N.J.: Princeton University Press, 1948.
Phillips, Jonathan. *The Second Crusade: Extending the Frontiers of Christendom*. New Haven, Conn.: Yale University Press, 2007.
Poirier, Dom Germain. "La destruction et la violation des tombeaux royaux et princiers en 1792–1793" (1796). Available at saintdenis-tombeaux.forumculture.net.
"Profanateurs et témoins lors de la violation des tombeux royaux en 1793." *Forum consacré aux tombeaux royaux de la basilique de Saint-Denis*. Available at saintdenis-tombeaux.forumculture.net.
Robinson, John J. *Dungeon, Fire, and Sword: The Knights Templar in the Crusades*. New York: M. Evans and Company, 1991.
Runciman, Stephen. *A History of the Crusades*. Vol. 2. London: Folio Society, 1994.
Sassier, Yves. *Louis VII*. Paris: Fayard, 1991.
Somerville, Robert. *Pope Alexander III and the Council of Tours*. Berkeley: University of California Press, 1977.
Spiegel, Gabrielle M. *The Chronicle Tradition of Saint-Denis: A Survey*. Brookline, Mass.: Classical Folia Editions, 1978.
———. "The Cult of Saint-Denis and Capetian Kingship." In her *The Past as Text: The Theory and Practice of Medieval Historiography*. Baltimore, Md.: Johns Hopkins University Press, 1997.
Starta, Alexandra. *The Museum of French Monuments 1795–1816: "Killing Art to Make History."* Farnham: Ashgate, 2013.
Strickland, Matthew. *War and Chivalry: The Conduct and Perception of War in England and Normandy, 1066–1217*. New York: Cambridge University Press, 1996.
Tuchman, Barbara W. *A Distant Mirror: The Calamitous 14th Century*. New York: Random House, 1978.
Turner, Ralph V. *Eleanor of Aquitaine*. New Haven, Conn.: Yale University Press, 2009.

Verdier, Philippe. "Some New Readings on Suger's Writings." In *Abbot Suger and Saint-Denis: A Symposium*, edited by Paula Lieber Gerson, 159–62. New York: Metropolitan Museum of Art, 1986.

Waldmann, Thomas G. "Abbot Suger and the Nuns of Argenteuil." *Traditio* 41 (1985): 239–72.

Walsh, James. *The Pursuit of Wisdom and Other Works by the Author of the Cloud of Unknowing*. New York: Paulist Press, 1988.

Warren, H. L. *Henry II*. Berkeley: University of California Press, 1973.

Wilson, Stephen. *Saints and Their Cults: Studies in Religious Sociology, Folklore and History*. Cambridge: Cambridge University Press, 1983.

Woodward, John, and George Burrett. *A Treatise in Heraldry, British and Foreign: With English and French Glossaries*. Vol. 2. Edinburgh: W. and A. K. Johnston, 1892.

Latin Dictionaries Used for This Translation

Cassell's Latin Dictionary. Revised by J. R. V. Marchant and Joseph F. Charles. New York: Funk and Wagnalls, 1959.

Latham, R. E. *Revised Medieval Word List from British and Irish Sources*. London: Oxford University Press, 1999.

Lewis, Charlton T., and Charles Short. *A Latin Dictionary*. Oxford: Clarendon Press, 1966.

Martin, Charles Tice. *The Record Interpreter: A Collection of Abbreviations, Latin Words and Names Used In English Historical Manuscripts and Records*. London: Stevens and Sons, 1949.

Muller, Richard A. *Dictionary of Latin and Greek Theological Terms: Drawn Principally from Protestant Scholastic Theology*. Grand Rapids, Mich.: Baker Academic, 1995.

Niermeyer, J. F., and C. Van de Kieft. *Mediae Latinitatis Lexicon Minus*. 2 vols. Leiden: Brill, 2002.

Smith, William, and John Lockwood. *Chambers and Murray Latin-English Dictionary*. Edinburgh: Chambers, 2001.

Souter, Andrew. *A Glossary of Later Latin to 600 A.D.* Oxford: Clarendon Press, 1996.

Stelten, Leo F. *Dictionary of Ecclesiastical Latin*. Peabody, Mass.: Hendrickson, 1997.

Index

Aachen, 129
Ableiges: manor of, 93
Abraham, 106
Adalbert (archbishop of Mainz, r. *1111–37*), 128–29
Adam (abbot of Saint-Denis, r. *1099–1122*), 3, 5–6, 81–82
Adam of Pithiviers, 83
Adela of Champagne (ca. *1140–1206*; pseud. Adelaide), 23–24; third wife of Louis VII, 147–48; birth of Philip II Augustus, 156–57; daughter of Theobald IV of Blois, 147
Adelaide of Maurienne (*1092–1154*; mother of Louis VII), 12, 16, 21, 54; lives with Louis VII, 130; returns to dower lands, 130–31
Adelaide (pseud. Alix; daughter of Louis VII and Constance), 146
Adrian IV (Nicholas Breakspear; pope, r. *1154–59*), 148
Agapitus, Saint: altar of, 58; oratory of, 44
Agnes of Champagne (d. *1207*; daughter of Theobald IV of Blois), 147. See also Bar
Aimery (bishop of Clermont, Auvergne, r. *1111–50*), 7
Aimery of Limoges (Latin patriarch of Antioch, r. *1140–96*), 202
Alain (bishop of Auxerre, r. *1152–67*), 155
Alain (bishop of Rennes, r. *1141–56*), 109
Alberic I (count of Dammartin, r. ca. *1100–81/83*), 71

Alberic of Reims (archbishop of Bourges, r. *1136–41*), 11
Albert (cantor of Paris), 148
Aldebert (bishop of Mende, r. *1151–87*), 180nlxix
Alexander III (Orlando of Sienna; pope, r. *1159–81*), 23–24; arrival at Montpellier, 149; elected pope, 148; Louis VII recognizes as pope, 150; peace with Frederick Barbarossa, 180
Alfonso II (king of Aragon, r. *1164–96*; "king of Spain" in text), 150
Alfonso VII (king of Castile, r. *1126–57*; "king of Spain" in text), 145
Algare (bishop of Coutances, r. *1132–50/51*), 54, 58
Alice (daughter of Louis VII and Eleanor), 143; marries Theobald V of Blois, 145
Alice (pseud. Petronilla; sister of Eleanor of Aquitaine): marries Ralph of Vermandois, 137
Alphonse (*1103–48*; count of St. Egidius, i.e., St. Giles): takes up cross on Second Crusade, 140
Alps, 151
Alvise (bishop of Arras, r. *1131–48*), 54, 58
Amadeus III (*1095–1148*; count of Savoy and Moraine): takes up cross on Second Crusade, 140
Amalric III (count of Evreux and Montfort, r. ca. *1101–37*), 42, 77
Anacletus II: (Pietro Pierleone; pseud. Peter Leo; antipope, r. *1130–38*), 8

283

INDEX

Andelle River, 143
Andrew, St. (apostle), 102
Angevins, 143, 191
Anselm II (lord of Traînel, r. *1152–85*; brother-in-law of Geoffrey III of Donzy), 146nliv; takes up cross on Second Crusade, 140
Ansold of Cornillon, 91–92
Antioch, 5, 170nxl, 202
Apulia, 6, 129. *See also* Isabelle of Champagne
Aquitaine, 10, 20, 92, 115, 127, 132, 134, 137, 145, 189
Argenteuil: abbey of, 72–73
Ark of the Covenant, 113
Arlange: manor of, 92
Arnulf (bishop of Lisieux, r. *1141–84*): takes up cross on Second Crusade, 140
Atlantic Ocean, 11, 22, 134–35
Autun, 131
Auvergne, 7, 24
Auxerre, 41, 131, 155

Baldwin II (bishop of Noyon, r. *1148–67*), 29, 210
Baldwin III (king of Jerusalem, r. *1143–63*), 150, 202
Baldwin of Corbeil, 78
Barnabas, St. (apostle), 52; altar of, 58
Barthélemy of Jur (bishop of Laon, r. *1113–51*), 107n129
Bartholomew, St. (apostle): oratory of, 43
Bar, countess of. *See* Agnes of Champagne
Bari, 129
Barville: manor of, 86
Basilie. *See* Heddiva
Baudemont: castle of, 143
Beauce, 5, 17, 46, 78–79
Beaugency, 23; assembly of, 144–45
Beaune: manor of, 85–86
Benedict, St.: altar of, 58
Benevento, 129
Berard of Ensonville, 84
Bernard (abbot of Clairvaux, r. *1115–53*), 9, 12, 27, 196; preaches Second Crusade at Vézelay, 138
Berneval: manor of, 93–94; Suger becomes provost of, 3, 5
Berry, 100

Bitonto, 6
Blidestroff: Kleinblidestroff, 70f; manor of, 92
Bohemond of Antioch, 5
Bondy: manor of, 73
Bordeaux, 9, 20
Boso (abbot of Saint-Benoît-sur-Loire, r. *1108–30*), 82
Bourdonné: manor of, 73
Bourges, 12
Brabantines, 152
Bray-et-Lû: castle of, 143
Brice, St., 147
Brunoy: manor of, 90–91
Burgundy, 21, 51, 131. *See also* Hugh III; Marie of Champagne

Cadurc (chancellor to Louis VI), 11
Caesar, Julius, 14, 193, 196, 212
Calixtus II (pope, r. *1119–24*), 6–7, 104. *See also* Guy of Vienne
Capua, 129
Carrières: village of, 94
Catulliacum, 35
Cato the Elder, 188, 212
Cergy: church of, 73; manor of, 75, 93
Chalon-sur-Saône, 153
Châlons-sur-Marne (Châlons-en-Champagne), 6
Champagne, 11
Champs: chapel of, 87–88
Charlemagne (emperor of the Romans, r. *800–814*; king of the Franks, r. *768–814*), 72, 96; gradual of, 90
Charles II the Bald (emperor of the Romans, r. *875–77*; king of West Francia, r. *843–77*), 104–5, 110; candlesticks of, 114
Charles III "the Simple" (king of Lotharingia, r. *911–19/23*; king of West Francia, r. *898–922*), 110, 135
Charles Martel (duke and mayor of the palace, r. *714–41*), 96
Château-sur-Epte: castle of, 143; village of, 94
Chaumont: abbey and castle of, 93
Chavenay: manor of, 73
Chenneviéres-les-Louvres: village of, 4
Chérisy: manor of, 73
Chevreuse: castle of, 76; manor of, 42; valley of, 42
Chrism, 43, 58

INDEX

Christopher the Martyr, St.: altar of, 58
Christians, 12, 138, 140, 203
Cicero, Marcus Tullius, 14, 193, 212
Cîteaux: abbey of, 103
Clermont, Auvergne, 149
Clothar II (king of Neustria, r. *584–629*; king of the Franks, r. *613–29*), 35, 221
Cluny, 6, 8, 24, 87, 152–53; abbey of, 22; Louis VII avenges monks of, 152–54, 156. *See also* Peter the Venerable
Cochelingen: Kochlingen, 70f; manor of, 92
Cologne, 150
Compiègne, 21
Conrad III (Roman emperor, r. *1138–52*), 129, 193; death of son, Frederick IV of Swabia, 150; goes on Second Crusade, 140
Constance of Arles (queen and wife of Robert II), 5
Constance of Castile, 23: death of, 146; marriage to Louis VII, 145
Constance (ca. *1124–56*; sister of Louis VII), 157
Constantinople, 150; treasures of, 95, 106
Corbeil, 17, 87, 91; castle of, 87
Corbie: abbey of, 111; town of, 154
Cormeilles: manor of, 74
Crusade, Second, 3, 12–13, 19–20, 22, 27–28, 138–43, 198, 202
Cucuphas, St.: altar of, 58

Dagobert I (king of the Franks, r. *629–39*), 1, 9, 15, 35, 50, 56, 78, 94, 103, 110; throne of, 112
Daimbert (archbishop of Sens, r. *1098–1122*), 82
Dammartin, 71. *See also* Alberic I
Dampierre: manor of, 76
Dangu: castle of, 143
David (king of Israel), 197
David I (king of Scotland, r. *1124–53*), 26, 190
Denis, St., 1, 35, 41, 50, 56–57, 67, 73, 97, 100–101, 103–4, 110–11, 114; feast of, 46, 91, 95, 133; legends and myths, 217–21; octave of, 68, 71
Desiderius (abbot of Monte Cassino, r. *1058–86*; Pope Victor III, r. *1086–87*), 16, 19
Dieppe, 5

Diocletian: palace of, 38
Divine Office, 187
Divine Scripture, 90, 188, 195
Donald (bishop of Alet, i.e., Saint-Malo, r. *1120–44*), 109
Donzy, 146n46. *See also* Geoffrey III; Herveus III
Dreux II (lord of Mouchy-le-Châtel): takes up cross on Second Crusade, 140
Dreux IV (*1138–1218*; lord of Mello), 148
Dreux IV (*1120–62*; lord of Mouchy-le-Châtel), 148
Dropsy: woman with, 89

Eastern Church, 202
Ebersing: manor of, 92
Ebles (count of Mauléon; castellan of Talmont-by-the-Sea), 164nxxiv
Edessa, 138
Edmund, St. (king of East Anglia, r. *855–69*): altar of, 58
Élancourt, 73
Eleanor of Aquitaine (*1122–1204*), 9, 12–13, 16, 115; attends consecration of Saint-Denis, 54; attends council of Beaugency, 144; attends council of Vézelay, 12, 22, 140; birth of Alice, 143; birth of Marie, 137; divorces Louis VII, 23, 144–45; marries Henry of Normandy, 145; marries Louis VII, 20, 22, 137; takes up cross on Second Crusade, 140
Eleutherius, St., 16, 35, 67
Elias (bishop of Orléans, r. *1137–46*), 54, 58
Eligius, St.: cloisonné work, 115; cross of, 106
England, 20, 143
English Sea, 38
Enguerrand II (*1110–48/49*; count of Coucy): takes up cross on Second Crusade, 140
Enguerrand II "Aiguillon" of Trie (ca. *1110–66*), 148
Epte River, 73, 143
Erchenbald VII (pseud. Archibald; count of Bourbon; d. *1171*): takes up cross on Second Crusade, 140
Essonnes, 17: burg of (now Corbeil), 87; church of, 87; district of, 17
Essonnes River, 87

INDEX

Étampes, 12, 80: council of *1130*, 8; council of *1147*, 27–28, 197–98. *See also* Guy I of Méréville
Ethiopia: people of, 81
Étrépagny: castle of, 143
Eugenius III (Bernard of Pisa; pope, r. *1145–53*), 4, 12, 27–28, 104, 196, 198–202, 208–9
Eugenius, St.: altar of 58
Europe, 2, 17
Eustace, St.: altar of, 57; door of, 96; oratory of, 43
Evrard III (count of Breteuil, *1095–48*), 19; son of Galeran II of Breteuil, 84, 121; takes up cross on Second Crusade, 140
Evrard III (lord of Le Puiset, r. *1067–99*; viscount of Chartres, r. *1073–99*), 121nxxv
Evrard of Barres (Master of the Sacred Temple, r. *1147–51*), 13, 29, 211
Evrard of Villepreux (lord of La Ferté, d. *1169*; knight and friend of Suger), 77

Fains: manor of, 84
Fathers of the Church, 194
Faucon of Bothéon (archbishop of Lyon, r. *1139–42*), 109
Felicissimus, St.: altar of, 58; oratory of, 44
Fleury: village of, 94
Fontevraud: abbey of, 103
France, 1–3, 5–7, 12–15, 20, 22–23, 25–26, 28–30, 92, 131, 133, 145, 147, 150, 191
Franconville: manor of, 75
Franks, 35, 107, 112, 114, 127, 135
Frederick I (archbishop of Cologne, r. *1100–31*), 128–29
Frederick I Barbarossa (duke of Swabia, r. *1147–52*; Roman emperor, r. *1155–90*; king of Burgundy, r. *1152–90*; king of Germany, r. *1152–90*; king of Italy, r. *1155–90*), 24; besieges Rome, 150–51; flees Italy, 151; supports antipope Victor IV, 150; takes up cross on Second Crusade, 140
Frederick II "the One-Eyed" (duke of Swabia, r. *1105–47*): denied throne at Diet of Mainz, 128; war with Lothar III, 129

Frederick IV (duke of Swabia, r. *1145–67*), 150; son of Conrad III, 150
Frenchmen, 136, 153, 156

Galeran II (*1070–1130*; viscount of Breteuil), 84. *See also* Evrard III; Judith
Gamaches: castle of, 143
Galo (bishop of Beauvais, r. ca. *1099–1104*; bishop of Paris, r. *1104–16*), 5
Garin (brother of Anselm of Traînel): takes up cross on Second Crusade, 140
Gascony, 199
Gâtinais: district of, 17, 85
Gaucher II of Montjay (*1112–48*): castle stormed by Louis VII, 138; takes up cross on Second Crusade, 140
Gaul(s), 54, 56, 104, 109, 149, 212
Gelasius II (Giovanni Caetani; pope, r. *1118–19*), 6
Geoffrey (brother of priest Roger of Berneval), 94
Geoffrey (monk of Saint-Denis), 25, 29, 104, 184, 204–5
Geoffrey II of Lèves (bishop of Chartres, r. *1116–49*), 50, 54, 57–58
Geoffrey III (*1100/5–53*; lord of Donzy and Gien), 146
Geoffrey III of Loroux (archbishop of Bordeaux, r. *1135–58*), 54, 58, 144
Geoffrey V "the Handsome" (*1113–51*; count of Anjou; son-in-law of Henry I of England), 23, 26, 143, 191
Geoffrey of La Roche (bishop of Langres, r. *1139–63*), 154; takes up cross on Second Crusade, 140
Geoffrey of Ronçon (ca. *1125–90*s; lord of Taillebourg): takes up cross on Second Crusade, 140
Geoffrey the Red, 84
George the Martyr, St.: altar of, 58
Germany, 2, 7, 151
Géza II (king of Hungary, r. *1141–62*), 150
Gien: castle captured by Louis VII, 23, 146. *See also* Geoffrey III
Gilduin (abbot of Saint-Victor of Paris, r. *1113–55*), 8
Girard (nephew of Suger), 68
Gisors: castle of, 143
Glaucinus: prison of, 111

Gournay: church of, 87
Greeks, 107, 200
Guemines: Sarreguemines, 70f; burg of, 92
Guido of Cremona, 150. *See* Paschal III
Guillerval: manor of, 78–79
Guy (archbishop of Vienne, r. *1088–1119*). *See* Calixtus II
Guy I of Méréville (viscount of Étampes), 81n48
Guy II (ca. *1120–47*; count of Ponthieu): takes up cross on Second Crusade, 140
Guy II of Montaigu (bishop of Châlons-sur-Marne, r. *1144–47*), 54, 57
Guy of Sens. *See* Hugh of Toucy

Hacqueville: castle of, 143
Hagia Sophia: church of, 106–7
Hamelin (bishop of Rennes, r. *1127–41*), 109
Heddiva (Basilie; wife of Nevelon of Pierrefonds, then of Enguerrand of Trie), 148
Helinand (father of Suger), 4
Henry I (king of England, r. *1100–35*), 5–7, 26, 94, 103, 129–30, 190
Henry I of Troyes (*1127–81*; count of Champagne, r. *1152–81*): brother of Theobald V of Blois, 145; marries Marie, daughter of Louis VII and Eleanor, 145; son of Theobald IV of Blois, 147; takes up cross on Second Crusade, 140
Henry II (count of Anjou, r. *1151–89*; duke of Aquitaine, r. *1152–89*; duke of Normandy, r. *1150–89*; king of England, r. *1154–89*), 23, 150; gives Norman Vexin to Louis VII, 143, 145; Louis VII returns Normandy, 143; Louis VII returns castles of Vernon and Neuf-Marché, 144; Louis VII takes castles of Vernon and Neuf-Marché, 143–44; marries Eleanor of Aquitaine, 145; performs and violates liege homage to Louis VII, 143; second pledge of fealty to Louis VII, 144; son of Count Geoffrey V of Anjou, 143
Henry V (German emperor, r. *1111–25*), 5–7, 128
Henry of Blois (bishop of Winchester, r. *1129–71*; abbot of Glastonbury, r. *1126–71*), 19
Henry Sanglier (bishop of Sens, r. *1122–42*), 57
Henry "the Young" (*1155–83*; son of Henry II and Eleanor of Aquitaine): marries Margaret, daughter of Louis VII and Constance, 145
Herbert II (count of Vermandois, d. *943*), 135
Herbert of Sens (abbot of Saint-Pierre-le-Vif, r. *1124–47*), 23; death of, 141; takes up cross on Second Crusade, 140
Hermenricus: creates foundation charter of Argenteuil, 72
Herveus (prior of Saint-Denis), 9, 88, 192
Herveus (pseud. Ernisius; abbot of Saint-Victor, r. *1162–72*), 156–57
Herveus III of Donzy (d. *1187*; son of Geoffrey III of Gien and Donzy): meets Louis VII, 146
Hilary, St.: altar of, 58
Hippolytus of Rome, St. (*170–235*): chapel of, 96; oratory of, 43–44
Holy Angels, 57, 96
Holy Cross, 140–41, 202–3
Holy Gospel, 111
Holy Land, 12, 138
Holy Martyrs (Sts. Denis, Rusticus, and Eleutherius), 12, 16, 18, 27, 35, 37–38, 40–42, 48–52, 54–57, 67, 74, 78, 81–82, 87, 95, 98, 101–2, 109, 115–16, 195–96
Holy of Holies (in church of Saint-Denis), 44
Holy Sepulcher, 5, 141
Holy Spirit, 34, 46, 48, 50, 104, 138, 152
Honorius II (Lamberto Scannabecchi; pope, r. *1124–30*), 72
Horace, 188
Hubert of Saint-Gaury, 84
Hugh (lord of Méréville, d. ca. *1186*), 79–80. *See also* Méréville, castle of
Hugh I (bishop of Laon, r. *1112–13*), 107
Hugh III (*1142–92*; duke of Burgundy), 153
Hugh III (lord of Le Puiset; son of Evrard III of Le Puiset), 2, 5–6, 80–81
Hugh IV of Amiens (archbishop of Rouen, r. *1130–64*), 43, 54, 57, 93, 96, 109, 144

Hugh VII (*1065–1151;* count of Lusignan), 164nxxiv; takes up cross on Second Crusade, 140
Hugh of La Ferté (r. *1133–47*), 109
Hugh of Maçon (bishop of Auxerre, r. *1137–51*), 54, 57
Hugh of Monceaux (abbot of Saint-Germain-des-Près, r. *1162–82*), 149, 156
Hugh of Toucy (archbishop of Sens, r. *1142–68*), 23, 54, 57–58, 144–45, 147

Innocent, St.: altar of, 57
Innocent II (Gregorio Papareschi dei Guidoni; pope, r. *1130–43*), 8–9, 104, 129
Investiture Controversy, 5–6. *See also* Wörms, concordat of
Isabelle of Champagne (duchess of Apulia; daughter of Theobald IV of Blois), 147
Isembard (pseud. Pagan; son of John of Étampes), 78
Île-de-France, 17
Italy, 2, 6, 17, 28, 92, 129, 151
Itier (pseud. Iterius) III of Toucy (*1100–1147/49*): takes up cross on Second Crusade, 140
Ives (pseud. Evenus; bishop of Vannes, r. *1137–43*), 109
Ivo, Saint (bishop of Chartres, r. *1090–1116*), 82
Ivo II of Nesle (pseud. Yves; count of Soissons, r. *1146–78*): takes up cross on Second Crusade, 140

James, St. (apostle): arm of, 108; tomb at Compostela, 9, 137
Jerusalem, 13, 84, 91, 106, 138, 141, 150, 197, 200, 202–4, 208. *See also* Baldwin III
Jesse, Tree of, 112
Job, 186, 189
Jocelin of Verzy (bishop of Soissons, r. *1126–52*), 11, 22, 29, 54, 58, 109, 135, 210
John II (bishop of Orléans, r. *1096–1135*), 82
John of Étampes, 78. *See also* Isembard
John the Baptist, St.: altar of, 58
John the Evangelist, St.: altar of, 58

Judas (apostle), 105
Judith (wife of Galeran II of Breteuil), 84

La Bucaille: castle of, 143
La Celle: priory of, 87–88, 92
La-Charité-sur-Loire: Suger attends dedication of church, 5
La Ferté-Baudouin, 83
Lagny: manor of, 69
Langres, 131. *See also* Geoffrey of La Roche
Lateran: council of, 7; synod of, 6
Latin language, 26, 188
Latins, 107
Lawrence, St., 44
Le Mesnil-Saint-Denis: manor of, 76
Lendit fair, 12, 17, 46, 68, 95
Leo of Ostia (*1046–ca. 1115/17;* monk of Monte Cassino), 16
Le Puiset: castle of, 5–6, 80–83. *See also* Hugh III
Lilly: village of, 94
Limousin, 199
Loire River, 28
Lombardy, 150
Lothar III of Supplinburg (duke of Saxony 1106; German king 1125; Roman emperor as Lothar II, r. *1133–37*): campaigns against Frederick II, 7, 129; election as emperor and coronation, 128–29
Lotharingia, 92, 104, 131, 135
Louis VI (king of France, r. *1108–37*), 1–9, 12, 15, 20, 22, 26, 68, 72–74, 80, 82–86, 93, 104, 115, 190; boyhood at Saint-Denis, 108; death of, 127; William's mention of Suger's *The Deeds*, 188
Louis VII (king of France, r. *1137–80*), 1, 3, 8–13, 15–16, 20–24, 26–29, 45–46, 52, 54–57, 68, 73, 115, 186, 188, 190, 193, 201–3; arranges marriages for daughters, 145; attacks count of Clermont in Auvergne and allies, 24, 151–52; attends council of Vézelay, 12, 22, 138; avenges monks of Cluny, 152–53; avenges murder of Abbot Herbert of Sens, 141; death of father, 127; death of Constance, 23, 146; death of Suger, 211; divorces Eleanor, 23, 144–45; Henry of Anjou pledges and violates

liege homage, 143–44; journey to Jerusalem, 141–43; leaves Suger in charge of kingdom, 208; marries Adela, 23, 147–48; marries Constance of Castile, 145; marries Eleanor of Aquitaine, 20, 22, 137; mother lives with him, 130–31; produces a male heir, 24, 156–57; receives fealty of Autun, 132; returns castles of Vernon and Neuf-Marché to Henry of Anjou, 144; sends envoy to Pope Alexander III, 149; storms castle of Gien, 146; storms castle of Montjay, 138; storms castle of Mouchy, 23, 148; storms castle of Talmont-by-the-Sea, 135–37; Suger warns of trickery of William of Lezay, 135–36; supports Pope Alexander III, 150; suppresses commune of Orléans, 127; suppresses commune of Poitiers, 133; suppresses commune of Vézelay, 154–55; takes up cross on Second Crusade, 138–41, 197–98; Theobald IV of Blois pledges and violates fealty, 131–32; William's mention of Suger's biography, 188

Louis XVIII (king of France, r. *1814–24*), 1

Louis the German (king of Bavaria, r. *817–43*; king of East Francia, r. *843–76*), 92

Louis the Pious (king of the Franks in *813*; Roman emperor, r. *814–40*), 72, 219

Louveciennes: manor of, 75–76

Luke the Evangelist, St.: altar of, 5

Maguelonne: island of, 6

Mainz, diet of, 7, 128–29. *See also* Adalbert

Manasses II (bishop of Meaux, r. *1134–58*), 54, 58, 91, 96, 109

Manasses of Bulles (count of Dammartin, d. *1148*): takes up cross on Second Crusade, 140

Manuel I Comnenus (Eastern Roman emperor, r. *1143–80*), 105

Mareuil: manor of, 91

Margaret (*1157–97*; daughter of Louis VII and Constance), 23; marries Henry the Young, 145

Marie (daughter of Louis VII and Eleanor), 137, 145

Marie of Champagne (duchess of Burgundy; daughter of Theobald IV of Blois), 147

Martin, St., 204

Mary (Mother of God), 43, 57–58, 87–89, 105, 147, 149, 156

Mary Magdalene: church of (formerly abbey of) at Vézelay, 149, 154–55

Master of the Sacred Temple. *See* Evrard of Barres

Matilda (countess of Perche; daughter of Theobald IV of Blois), 147; crown of, 115

Matilda (daughter of Henry I of England; wife of Geoffrey V of Anjou), 130

Matins, Office of, 41, 55, 156, 194

Matthew (precentor of Sens), 148

Matthew I (*1100–1160*; lord of Montmorency), 67

Maurice of Sully (bishop of Paris, r. *1160–96*), 156

Meaux, 91. *See also* Manasses II; Stephen of La Chapelle

Mediterranean Sea, 3

Melchizedek, 106

Melun, 73; meeting of prelates with Louis VI, 6

Méréville: castle of, 79. *See also* Guy I; Hugh

Michael the Archangel, St., 43–44

Milo II (ca. *1055–1118*; lord of Montlhéry): castellan of Chevreuse, 42

Milo III (ca. *1075–1147*; lord of Chevreuse), 77

Milon I (pseud. Milo; bishop of Thérouanne, r. *1131–58*), 54, 58

Miracle of the mute person, 88–89

Mitadolus (grandfather of Eleanor of Aquitaine), 115

Monnerville: manor of, 79–80

Monte Cassino: abbey of, 16

Montereau: manor of, 73

Montigny: manor of, 75

Montjay: castle of, 138

Montlhéry: castle of, 1

Montlignon: manor of, 67

Montmélian: manor of, 73

Montmorency, 67

Montpellier, 6, 149

Moret-sur-Loing: castle of, 155

Morgny: village of, 94

Mosaic Law, 112

Moses, 112–14
Mouchy: castle of, 23; castle and fief of, 148. *See also* Dreux II; Dreux IV
Mount St. Vincent, 153

Nanthilde (queen and wife of King Dagobert I), 110
Néaufles: castle of, 143
Neauphle: castle of, 76, 144. *See also* Simon III
Neuf-Marché: castle of, 144
Nevelon II of Pierrefonds (*1060–ca. 1147*), 148
Nicholas, St.: chapel of, 96
Nicholas I of Chièvres (bishop of Cambrai, r. ca. *1137/38–67*), 58, 64n19
Normandy, 17, 23, 93, 143
Normans, 144, 191
Notre-Dame: cathedral chapter of at Chartres, 82
Notre-Dame: cathedral of in Paris, 147, 192
Noyon-sur-Andelle: castle of, 143. *See also* Baldwin II
Numma (wife of Hermenricus), 72

Octavian of Monticelli. *See* Victor IV
Odo II (bishop of Beauvais, r. *1133–44*), 43, 54, 58, 109
Odo of Deuil (*1110–62*; historian and monk of Saint-Denis), 15, 25
Odo of Sully (abbot of Sainte-Geneviève, r. *1148–ca. 54*), 157
Odo of Torcy (monk at Saint-Denis), 88
Oise River, 73
Oriflamme, 12, 223–25
Orléans, 1, 7, 17, 20, 51, 83, 86, 127, 145; commune of, 127–28. *See also* Elias; John II
Osny: manor of, 74

Pagan (pseud. Isembard; father of John of Étampes), 78
Pagan of Gisors (*1075–1125*), 75
Pantera, 43, 68
Papal schism, 8, 23–24, 148–51
Papareschi, Gregorio. *See* Innocent II
Paris, 1, 6, 8–9, 17, 19, 21–22, 30, 41, 69, 74, 127, 132, 141, 155
Parthians, 138

Paschal II (Raniero of Bieda of Galeata; pope, r. *1099–1118*), 5–6
Paschal III (antipope, r. *1162–68*), 150. *See also* Guido of Cremona
Paul, St. (apostle), 68, 112
Pepin III (king of the Franks, r. *751–68*), 72, 96
Perche, countess of. *See* Matilda
Peregrine (pseud. Peregrinus), St.: altar of, 57
Peter, St. (apostle), 68, 104
Peter (brother of Suger), 4
Peter I (bishop of Senlis, r. *1134–51*), 29, 43, 54, 57, 96, 109, 210
Peter Leo, 8. *See also* Anacletus II
Peter of La Châtre, 11
Peter the Venerable (abbot of Cluny, r. *1122–56*), 27, 196–97
Pharaoh, 113
Philip (son of Philip I), 8–9
Philip I (king of France, r. *1060–1108*), 1, 9, 14, 68, 72–73, 104, 108, 115
Philip II "Augustus" (king of France, r. *1180–1223*; son of Louis VII and Adela), 24, 156–57
Pierre III of Solignac (bishop of Le Puy, r. *1159–90*), 151
Pithiviers: knight of, 78
Plato, 187
Poinville: manor of, 84
Poitiers, 3, 5, 10, 21; commune of, 10, 21, 132–34; council of, 5
Poitou, 11, 25, 132–34, 136, 199
Pons of Montboissier (abbot of Vézelay, r. *1138–61*), 140, 154–55
Pons III (viscount of Polignac, r. *1142–73*), 151
Pontoise, 40
Pseudo-Dionysus, 15

Rainald (*1096–ca. 1161*; lord of Courtenay and Montargis): takes up cross on Second Crusade, 140
Rainald II (count of Tonnerre, r. *1147–48*): takes up cross on Second Crusade, 140
Ralph (brother of *Suger*), 4
Ralph I (*1085–1152*; count of Vermandois), 12–13, 21, 131; marries Alice, sister of Eleanor of Aquitaine, 137
Raymond V (pseud. Raymond of Saint-Gilles; count of Toulouse, r. *1148–94*), 157

Raymond of Poitiers (prince of Antioch, r. *1136–49*), 202
Reginald of Dassel (archbishop of Cologne, r. *1159–67*): death of, 150
Reims, 7, 9
Rennes: bishop of, 109
Rigord, 15
Robert (abbot of Corbie; r. *1127–42*), 88, 111
Robert I (count of Dreux, r. *1137–88*; brother of Louis VII), 13, 28, 200; revolt of, 200; takes up cross on Second Crusade, 140
Robert II (king of the Franks, r. *996–1031*), 5
Roger (priest of Berneval), 94
Roger II (king of Sicily, r. *1130–54*), 26, 129, 190
Roman Curia, 196
Roman Empire, 20, 128–29
Roman pontiff, 201
Romans, 129, 150, 193
Romanus, St., 43: oratory of, 44, 96
Rome, 6–8, 16, 28, 38, 72, 129, 150–51, 200–201, 212
Rotrou of Beaumont-le-Roger (bishop of Evreux, r. *1139–65*), 54, 58
Rouvray: manor of, 80–81
Rueil: manor of, 110
Rusticus, St., 16, 35, 67

Saclas: manor of, 78
Saint-Aignan: church of at Orléans, 82
Saint-Benoît-sur-Loire: Suger studied at abbey of, 4, 9, 82
Saint-Denis, abbey of: church of, 1–9, 11–12, 14–17, 24–25, 27, 29; 53; consecration, July *1140*, 45–46, 52–56, 96–97; consecration, June *1140*, 43–45; consecration of new altars and chapels of the saints, 57–58; construction of new tombs of Holy Martyrs, 48–49; "Cross of Charlemagne," 110–111; Dagobert dedicates new basilica, 35–36; estates and revenues, 66–94; gilded cast-bronze doors, 97–98; golden altar, 49–50, 101, 104–6; golden crucifix, 18, 102–4; "holy altar" and relics, 18, 108–110; obtains revenues of Lendit Fair, 68; problems caused by small size, 36–37, 95; reconstruction of upper part of the church (crypt, nave, and apse), 45–48, 98–99, 100; reconstruction of the western end (narthex), 37–42, 48, 95–96; regains jurisdiction over convent of Argenteuil, 72–73; renovation of choir, 111; renovation of throne of Dagobert, 112; repair of walls, 95; stained-glass windows, 112–14; storm nearly collapses the roof, 50–51; transferal of the Holy Martyrs to new tombs, 56–57, 101–2; treasures and ornaments, 106–11, 114–16
Saint-Denis-de-L'Estrée: Suger and Louis VI attend school at priory of, 4
Saint-Denis-en-Vaux: priory of, 25
Sainte-Geneviève: abbey of, 157
Saint-Germain-des-Prés, 22, 137, 149, 156
Saint-Jean-en-Vallée: church of at Chartres, 82
Saint-Loup: manor of, 86
Saint-Lucien: manor of, 69
Saint-Martin-des-Champs: priory of, 87
Saint-Merri: manor of, 69
Saint-Michel-de-Platea: church of, 44, 156
Saint-Père-en-Vallée: abbey of, 82. *See also* William I
Saint-Pierre: church of, 93
Saint-Spire: church of, 91
Saint-Victor: abbey of, 16, 157
Salonnes: manor of, 92
Samson of Mauvoisin (archbishop of Reims, r. *1140–61*), 57, 109, 144
Sannois: manor of, 74
Saracens, 38, 79, 202–3
Saxony, 129
Schism in the Church (*1159*), 23–24, 148–51
Scipio Africanus, 212
Second Crusade, 1, 3, 12–13, 19–20, 22, 27–28, 138–41, 193, 198, 202–3; magnates and prelates who took up cross, 140
Seine River, 17, 38
Seneca, 187n9, 193n5, 194
Senlis: bishop of. *See* Peter I
Sens, commune of, 141. *See also* Herbert of Sens; Hugh (Guy) of Toucy; William of Sens
Simeon, St.: arm of, 15, 45, 51
Simon III (lord of Chevreuse; count of Neauphle; d. ca. *1150*), 77

Simon of Vermandois (bishop of Noyon, r. *1123–48*), 54, 57–58; takes up cross on Second Crusade, 140
Simon of Vilatin, 76
Sixtus, St. (pope, r. *257–58*): altar of, 58; oratory of, 44
Solomon, 38, 189
Spain, 9
Stephen I (*1133–91*; count of Sancerre; son of Theobald IV of Blois), 146–47
Stephen VI of Mercoeur (bishop of Clermont, Auvergne, r. *1151–69*), 151
Stephen of Blois (count of Boulogne, r. *1125–47*; duke of Normandy, r. *1135–47*; king of England, r. *1135–54*), 103, 130, 143
Stephen of Garland (chancellor), 8
Stephen of La Chapelle (canon of Sens; bishop of Meaux, r. *1162–71*), 147–48
Stephen of Senlis (bishop of Paris, r. *1123–41*), 7
Stephen the Protomartyr, St.: altar of, 58; arm of, 108
Suger (abbot of Saint-Denis, r. 1122–51): administrator and adviser to Louis VI and VII, 2–3, 5–8, 10–11, 131, 134–35, 186–89, 192–93, 197–99, 208; attends school with Louis VI, 108; attends wedding of Louis VII and Eleanor of Aquitaine, 9; concern for Christians in Holy Land, 203–4; co-regency during Second Crusade, 12–13, 197–201; discouraged by crusade's lack of success, 202; education, 4; elected abbot of Saint-Denis, 6–7; ends revolts and lawlessness, 198–99, 200–201; fairness and respect for others, 189–90, 191–92, 199–200, 209; first visit to Rome, 6; funeral, 210–11; generosity, 192, 195; illness and death, 4, 204–5, 207, 209–10, 211–12; intellect, 185, 187–88, 208; jealousy and intrigue of rivals, 187, 189, 191, 201, 205–6; meets with and writes to kings, popes, magnates, and prelates, 190–91, 196–97, 200–202; management of estates of Saint-Denis, 66–94; oblate at Saint-Denis, 1, 4; oratory skills, 188, 193, 208; performs religious duties, 192–95, 204, 208; personal habits and lifestyle, 194, 197; piety, 209–10; plans crusade to the East, 203–5; pleads with Louis VII for mercy on citizens of Poitiers, 133–34; renovation and management of church of Saint-Denis, 9–10, 33–60, 94–116, 196, 208; small stature, 4, 185, 187, 194, 204; studies at Saint-Denis, 95; warns Louis VII about treachery of William of Lezay, 135–36; writes histories of Louis VI and Louis VII, 188
Suger (cousin of Abbot Suger; oblate at Saint-Denis), 4
Susa, 150

Talmont-by-the-Sea, 3, 11, 21; castle captured by Louis VII, 135–37
Templars (knights of the Holy Temple), 13, 29, 203, 211
Terce, Office of, 109
Theobald (abbot of Saint-Colombe at Sens, d. *1146/47*): takes up cross on Second Crusade, 140
Theobald (abbot of Saint-Germain-des-Prés, d. *1162*): sent by Louis VII to meet Pope Alexander III at Montpellier, 149
Theobald IV (count of Blois and Chartres, r. *1102–52*; count of Champagne, r. *1125–52*), 10–11, 21, 26, 50, 91, 103, 116, 130–32, 140, 147, 190
Theobald V (count of Blois, r. *1151–91*): marriage to Alice, daughter of Louis VII and Eleanor, 145
Theobald of Bec (archbishop of Canterbury, r. *1139–61*), 54, 57
Theobald of Puiseux, 75
Thierry of Alsace (*1099–1168*; count of Flanders): takes up cross on Second Crusade, 140
Toury: manor of, 2, 81, 83; castle of, 84, 143; Suger as provost of, 3, 5–6, 82
Tours: Suger visits tomb of St. Martin, 204
Trappes: manor of, 73–74
Tremblay: manor of, 71
Tuscany, 150

Ursellus (Jew of Montmorency), 67

Val-de-Marne, 17
Vaucresson: manor of, 76
Vergonville: manor of, 84–85

Vernon: castle of, 143
Vernouillet: manor of, 76
Vespers, Office of, 55, 195
Vexillum, 12, 223–25
Vexin, 7, 12, 23, 26, 73, 93, 145; castles of, 142f, 143
Vézelay, 12, 22, 24, 154–56; abbey of, 22, 154–56; commune of, 154–55; council of (*1146*), 12, 22, 138, 140–41. *See also* Hugh of Monceaux; Mary Magdalene, church of; Pons of Montboissier
Victor IV (pseud. Octavian; antipope, r. *1159–64*), 23, 148–50
Villaine: manor of, 46, 81
Vincent the Levite, St.: arm of, 108
Vitry, 11–12

Walburga the Virgin, St.: altar of, 58
William (monk of Saint-Denis), 3–4, 13, 24–30, 184, 191, 195, 204–6
William I (abbot of Saint-Père-en-Vallée, r. *1102–29*), 82
William I (king of Sicily, r. *1154–66*), 150
William I (count of Chalon, d. *1174*), 22, 24, 152–53
William II (count of Nevers, r. *1098–1148*), 12
William III (count of Nevers, r. *1148–1161*), 146, 154, 181: takes up cross on Second Crusade, 140
William III (count of Warenne, r. *1138–48*): takes up cross on Second Crusade, 140
William IV (count of Nevers, r. *1161–68*), 152n1xxi, 153–55
William VI (*1096–1136*; count of Auvergne), 7

William VII of Le Puy "the Young" (count of Auvergne, r. *1145–55*), 24, 151–52
William VIII of Lezay (lord and castellan of Talmont-by-the-Sea), 3, 11, 21–22, 135–36
William VIII "the Old" (count of Auvergne, r. 1155–82; uncle of William VII), 24, 151–52
William X (*1099–1137*; duke of Aquitaine), 7, 9, 135–36; death of 137
William Aguillon II of Trie-Château (d. *1147*): takes up cross on Second Crusade, 140
William de la Tour of Senlis (masterbutler of Louis VII, *1137–42*): takes up cross on Second Crusade, 140
William Gouet (d. *1170*), 147
William of Cornillon, 44, 68
William of Courtenay: takes up cross on Second Crusade, 140, 204n51
William of Mello (abbot of Vézelay, r. *1161–71*), 22, 155
William of Sens (bishop of Auxerre, r. 1167–81), 148
William the Breton, 15
William the Butler. *See* William de la Tour of Senlis
William "White-Hands" (son of Theobald IV of Blois; bishop of Chartres, r. *1165–69*; archbishop of Sens, r. *1169–75*; archbishop of Reims, r. *1175–1202*), 147
Wörms: concordat of, 7. *See also* Investiture Controversy

Yvelines: forest of, 17, 42, 77

Selected Works of Abbot Suger of Saint-Denis was designed in Meridien,
and composed by Kachergis Book Design of Pittsboro, North Carolina.
It was printed on 60-pound Sebago IV B18 Cream and bound by
Maple Press of York, Pennsylvania.

www.ingramcontent.com/pod-product-compliance
Lightning Source LLC
Chambersburg PA
CBHW020316010526
44107CB00054B/1861